Getting the Expert Edge from SAP

Whether you are just beginning to work in R/3 System management, or you would like to improve your grasp of the subject, you will benefit from the first-hand, practical experience and information in these books.

Gerhard Oswald
Member of the Executive Board, SAP AG

Dr. Uwe Hommel
Executive Vice-President, SAP AG
R/3 Technical Core Competence

SAP™ R/3® Performance Optimization:

The Official SAP™ Guide

SAP™ R/3® Performance Optimization:

The Official SAP™ Guide

Thomas Schneider

SYBEX®

San Francisco • Paris • Düsseldorf • Soest • London

Associate Publisher: Amy Romanoff
Contracts and Licensing Manager: Kristine O'Callaghan
Acquisitions & Developmental Editor: Melanie Spiller
Editor: Ronn Jost
Project Editor: Raquel Baker
Book Designer: Kris Warrenburg
Graphic Illustrators: Tony Jonick, Jerry Williams
Electronic Publising Specialist: Adrian Woolhouse
Project Team Leader: Lisa Reardon
Proofreader: Nancy Riddiough
Indexer: Lynnzee Elze
Companion CD: Ginger Warner
Cover Designer: Calyx Design
Cover Photographer: Courtesy of West Stock

SYBEX is a registered trademark of SYBEX Inc.

SAP is a trademark of SAP Aktiengesellschaft, Systems Applications and Products in Data Processing, Neurottstrasse 16, 69190 Walldorf, Germany.

TRADEMARKS: SYBEX has attempted throughout this book to distinguish proprietary trademarks from descriptive terms by following the capitalization style used by the manufacturer.

The author and publisher have made their best efforts to prepare this book, and the content is based upon final release software whenever possible. Portions of the manuscript may be based upon pre-release versions supplied by software manufacturer(s). The author and the publisher make no representation or warranties of any kind with regard to the completeness or accuracy of the contents herein and accept no liability of any kind including but not limited to performance, merchantability, fitness for any particular purpose, or any losses or damages of any kind caused or alleged to be caused directly or indirectly from this book.

Library of Congress Card Number: 99-63828
ISBN: 0-7821-2563-8

Manufactured in the United States of America

10 9 8 7 6 5 4 3 2 1

Software License Agreement: Terms and Conditions

*To my wife, Carola, and to the person
I am curious to get to know*

FOREWORD TO THE SAP EXPERT KNOWLEDGE BOOK SERIES

Enabling you to operate your R/3 System at a minimum cost is of the utmost importance to SAP. You can attain this *lowest cost of ownership* both by implementing R/3 efficiently and quickly with *AcceleratedSAP* and through optimized and secure production operation. *TeamSAP* exists to provide you with active and close support. TeamSAP brings together the most important resources: *people, processes,* and *products.* SAP acts as the central contact in this team and shares its knowledge with partners and customers.

To keep your knowledge up-to-date, TeamSAP conceived this book series, which offers you a detailed overview of the technical issues and concepts of R/3 System management. The books cover subjects ranging from the technical implementation project to R/3 System and database operation.

Whether you are just beginning to work in R/3 System management or you would like to improve your grasp of the subject, you will benefit from the firsthand, practical experience and information in these books. This book series also supports you in your efforts to prepare for a Certified Technical Consultant exam for R/3 Release 4.0. However, this book series cannot, and makes no claim to, be a substitute for your own experience in working with the R/3 System. The authors provide recommendations for your daily work with R/3.

With the increase in R/3 installations, there is an increased need for qualified technical consultants. Through certification, SAP has been setting high standards for many years now. Certification not only confirms whether you are familiar with R/3 System administration for a particular R/3 release, it also establishes whether you can administer one of the database systems and the extent to which you are familiar with one of the supported operating system platforms.

Upgrades to the R/3 System regularly introduce new challenges and solutions for R/3 System management. A certification can therefore only be valid for specific R/3 releases and must be renewed with every major revision.

Gerhard Oswald
Member of the Executive Board, SAP AG

Dr. Uwe Hommel
Executive Vice-President, SAP AG
R/3 Technical Core Competence

Walldorf, July 1998

ACKNOWLEDGMENTS

When I was invited to write a book about performance optimization around a year ago, I gladly accepted, knowing that this book would fulfill a critical need.

"Everything should be made as simple as possible, but not simpler." These words of Albert Einstein were the guideline for the selection and arrangement of the material in this book. This process was strongly influenced by the experience of my colleagues and myself as part of SAP's Technical Core Competence Center (or TCC), working with numerous customer R/3 Systems in production operation. This experience was gained delivering TCC's customer-support services EarlyWatch and GoingLive Check, holding training courses on performance analysis, and delivering on-site support to customer R/3 Systems with critical performance problems. I am therefore confident that this book addresses a comprehensive range of important performance issues.

This book could not have been written without the help of many competent colleagues, including—to name but a few—Hartwig Brand, Bernhard Braun (from SAP Client/Server Technology Development), Matthias Buchmann, Guido Derwand, Susanne Glänzer, Jochen Hartmann (from SAP Integration and Platforms), Uwe Hommel, Anja Kerber, Frank Lackermeier, John Landis, Ulrich Marquard (from the SAP Performance and Benchmark Group), René Muth, Jens Pursche, Rüdiger Stöcker, Mark Thier, Fabian Tröndle, Gerold Völker, Liane Will, and Augustinus Wohlfart. Unless otherwise stated, these are TCC colleagues.

I wish to thank TCC's Melanie Freemann and André von Rekowski for their work as technical editors and translators.

—Dr. Thomas Schneider

—Walldorf, January–June 1999

CONTENTS AT A GLANCE

TABLE OF CONTENTS

INTRODUCTION

Systematic, proactive performance optimization increases the benefits of your R/3 System and reduces the cost of ownership. The consequences of poor performance tuning may be additional work, production delays, and financial loss.

Performance

Users are motivated to work, and can work efficiently, if the R/3 System has good response times. A slow system is not unlike downtime, and it causes frustration. If the situation deteriorates far enough to almost bring the R/3 System to a standstill, you no longer have the throughput you need to run business processes.

The performance of a data processing system is defined as the system's ability to meet the demands on the system as to response time and data throughput. For example, your system may be required to achieve a throughput of 10,000 printed invoices in 1 hour or a response time of under 1 second when creating a customer order. There are no absolute standards for what defines good performance; rather, performance is relative to the expected load on the system.

Performance Optimization

A medical joke states that there are no healthy people—only patients that have not yet been thoroughly diagnosed! As the irony of this remark implies, doctors can diagnose a health problem in anyone if they look hard enough. Common sense tells us that we should go to the doctor regularly for preventative check-ups. However, the doctor should reach for a prescription pad or recommend surgery only if our well-being is noticeably impaired, or if there is credible evidence that severe problems will emerge over the course of time.

The same thing goes for your data processing system: Analysis must be performed at regular intervals, but when you make any changes, you should thoroughly investigate the effects of the changes on the system. For this reason, performance optimization requires three steps:

- Identifying and analyzing problems systematically
- Implementing tuning measures
- Verifying the success of these measures

Be particularly careful to avoid arbitrarily changing configuration parameters or taking impulsive tuning measures. The goal of this book is to enable you to identify and analyze performance problems so that your response strategy effectively combats the real problem without indirectly creating new problems.

Technical Optimization

The R/3 System consists of numerous components such as R/3 work processes, R/3 buffers, database processes and buffers, hardware, hard disks, and networks. These components affect throughput and response time. If they do not interact smoothly, or if a component has reached its performance limit, wait situations can occur that reduce throughput and response time. In this book, technical optimization refers to the identification, analysis, and solution of performance problems by tuning these components and distributing the workload that occurs within the system.

Application Optimization

The second important task in performance optimization is removing the causes of unnecessary workload. Inefficient programs or the inefficient use of programs can also reduce performance. In this book, application optimization refers to the optimization of individual programs.

In summary, the goal of technical and application optimization is to improve the system settings and the application to achieve the desired performance with the available hardware. If this hardware is not sufficient, it must be extended in accordance with the knowledge gained from the performance analysis.

How Much Work Is Involved?

The amount of effort involved in analyzing and tuning R/3 System performance depends very much on the size of the system. For a small- or medium-sized installation containing no modifications to standard R/3 software objects, performance optimization is normally required only as follows:

- Shortly before and after the start of production

- After large-scale changes (such as upgrades, the start of production for new R/3 modules, an increase in the number of users, large data transfers, or client transports)

Of course, analysis and tuning are also required if acute performance problems occur. Tuning potential, and the effort involved in tuning, increases as the size of the system increases.

Experience shows that many performance bottlenecks are caused by the customers' own software developments and by customer modifications to the standard R/3 software objects. This is mainly due to insufficient testing, although it can also be caused by time constraints or software developers' inexperience.

An extreme example of this is a large installation for several hundred users and complex process chains, where continuous development work is being done at different times and in different locations by a dozen or more ABAP developers from different consulting firms, and where system management is outsourced. This type of system environment makes it absolutely necessary for a core group of system administrators and developers to constantly have an overview of the entire system and keep an eye on performance.

Help with Tuning

SAP's remote services offer help with performance analysis and tuning. These services include the GoingLive™ Check Service, which enables your system to make a smooth transition to production operation, and the EarlyWatch Service®, which monitors the early life of your production system and suggests additional optimizations.

If you look in SAP's Online Service System (OSS) for R/3 Notes related to Performance for R/3 Release 4.0B, you will receive a list of approximately 500 R/3 Notes. There is apparently no shortage of good advice on R/3 System performance, when you also consider the numerous entries on this topic in the R/3 Online Documentation and on SAP's Internet site, SAPNet. Instead, the question regarding R/3 Notes is as follows: How do I decide which R/3 Note is the right one for my system and for my problem? This book will help you answer this question.

Guidelines for Tuning

In addition to analysis strategies and background information, this book provides rules of thumb and guideline values to help you get started if you do not have much experience in the area of performance optimization. When applying these guideline values, observe the following general rules:

Analyze carefully: Before you change anything, analyze your system carefully. Determine the areas of your R/3 System in which performance problems occur. Changes should be performed only in these areas. Keep a record of your analysis data. Follow this principle: Change as little as possible, but as much as necessary.

Make no changes without analysis: You should never change parameters or take other tuning measures without first performing an analysis. Change suggestions should be implemented only in conjunction with analysis and verification. Blindly applying suggestions from any source can amount to professional negligence.

Verify: Once you have made the changes, perform another analysis. Verify whether the changes have provided the desired results. Keep a record of the data from the verification analysis.

Take small steps: As the term *tune* implies, the success of an optimization depends on the right amount. Therefore, you must not make too many changes at once. Only in this way can you maintain an overview of the tuning measures and verify which of them were successful.

Every guideline has exceptions: In some situations, you require a different approach than the guideline values or rules of thumb provided in this book. Despite taking every precaution, a recommendation may have negative results. Therefore, it is crucial that you perform a verification of every tuning measure taken. This will help you determine why a rule does not suit a particular situation.

The Structure of This Book

The methods for performance analysis presented in this book correspond to the methods used by the EarlyWatch Service and the GoingLive Service and are taught in the R/3 Basis training course BC315—Workload Analysis.

Chapter 1 is directed at R/3 System administrators, R/3 consultants, ABAP software developers, and SAP project managers. On a nontechnical level, the following fundamental questions about performance analysis are covered:

- What preventative measures do you have to take to ensure the optimum performance of an R/3 System?
- Which performance tuning measures should you consider?
- Who is involved in the tuning process?

Chapters 2–4 present the performance analysis. After you have read these chapters, you will be able to perform a systematic performance analysis.

Experienced performance tuners use the Workload Monitor (Transaction code *ST03*) to get an initial overview of the workload distribution in the R/3 System. This tells them in which Basis components or in which application components to look for the problem. Then they can begin investigating the affected components—for example, the database or a specific program. This is referred to as a top-down or bottleneck analysis. The advantage of this analysis is that it normally enables you to find the source of a performance problem quickly. However, to perform a top-down analysis, you require a considerable amount of experience because interpreting the data from the Workload Monitor can be difficult.

On the other hand, a bottom-up analysis is a systematic check of each component, such as the operating system, database, R/3

Basis, and so on. With proper instruction, a bottom-up analysis can even be performed by a consultant or system administrator who has little experience in performance analysis.

In this book, we will initially follow the bottom-up analysis starting in Chapter 2 with the analysis of the operating system, database, R/3 memory management, and R/3 work processes. Recommendations are provided to help the system administrator or consultant solve the most important performance problems. This level of tuning is often sufficient for small- and medium-sized installations.

Chapter 3 discusses the complex workload analysis that is part of top-down analysis. In Chapter 4, you will find out how to analyze the individual programs—for example, using the tools SQL trace and ABAP debugger tools.

The next chapters, 5–9, explain in-depth performance optimization. These chapters are directed at people who are responsible for the efficient functioning of large systems and who seek to take full advantage of their system's tuning potential. For the most part, Chapters 5–9 are independent units that can be read in any order once you have read Chapters 1–4.

The chapters cover the following topics:

- Chapter 5, R/3 Memory Management: The configuration of the memory areas allocated by the R/3 System has a substantial influence on performance.

- Chapter 6, Workload Distribution: The optimal workload distribution of dialog, update, and background requests contributes significantly to the performance of the R/3 System.

- Chapter 7, R/3 Table Buffering: Buffering database tables on R/3 application servers speeds up access to frequently read data and helps reduce the load placed on the database.

- Chapter 8, Locks and Enqueues: Database locks and R/3 enqueues ensure data consistency. Using the ATP server or number range buffering, for example, you can optimize the lock and enqueue processes and avoid throughput bottlenecks.

- Chapter 9, SQL Statement Optimization: SQL statements sometimes cause an excessively large database load and thus become a problem for the performance of the entire R/3 System. For this reason, a complete chapter has been dedicated to optimizing SQL statements.

- In the appendices at the end of this book, you'll find information that will further your knowledge of R/3 performance optimization. Appendix A lists the most important procedures for performance analysis. Appendix B explains database monitors, buffers, and SQL execution plans. Appendix C lists the R/3 profile parameters that are relevant to performance. Appendix D lists the most important transaction codes for R/3 performance optimization. Appendix E lists the review questions and answers. Appendix F is a glossary of common R/3 abbreviations and terms. Appendix G provides information on R/3 online help, training courses and workshops, and related Internet links. It also includes a bibliography of topics related to R/3 performance. The final appendix, Appendix H, is a compilation of R/3 Notes and references to help to keep you up to date with current developments and recommendations.

Chapters and Target Groups

The difference between technical optimization and application optimization has been defined in the above sections. Chapters 2, 5, and 6 cover technical optimization and are of interest primarily to people responsible for system administration (system administrators and technical consultants). Chapters 4, 7, 8, and 9 deal with the analysis and tuning of individual programs or applications, and therefore belong to application optimization. This portion of the analysis is also of interest to people responsible for R/3 applications (user departments, application consultants, and ABAP developers).

Prerequisites

This book assumes that you have some theoretical knowledge and practical experience in administering R/3 Systems. You should be able to use the Computer Center Management System (CCMS). For background information, see *SAP R/3 System Administration* (also part of the "Official SAP Guide" book series). Parts of the present book assume familiarity with relational database systems (RDBMS) and with SQL.

Limitations of This Book

This book does not cover the following topics:

- Hardware and Network Tuning: Although this book helps you to identify a bottleneck in the CPU, in main memory, in the I/O of the hard disks, or in the network, a detailed analysis requires the tools of the hardware or network manufacturer. In view of the large number of products on the market, this topic (especially tuning hard disks) cannot be included.

- Databases: The tools provided by SAP in the Computer Center Management System (CCMS) standardize most administrative and analysis tasks for the various database systems. However, to perform more in-depth database tuning, you need to know about the different database system architectures. This book does not cover the seven database systems that can be used in conjunction with R/3, as there is tuning literature available for all these database systems. The main focus of this book is the R/3-specific context of database tuning, and its concepts are valid for all database systems. The concrete examples used in this book always concern specific database systems. Appendix B contains an overview of the most important monitors for analyzing database systems.

- Application Tuning: Many performance problems can be solved only with detailed knowledge of the individual R/3 application modules. Often, a change to the Customizing settings can solve the problem. This book does not specifically cover each R/3 application module. It does, however, provide you with analysis strategies so that you can identify application-specific performance problems and consult the responsible developer or consultant.

Release Dependency

A much debated question prior to the printing of this book concerns the extent to which release-dependent and time-dependent information should be included. This affects, for example, menu paths, recommendations for configuration parameter settings, and guide values for performance counters. A new R/3 Release, a patch (for R/3, the database, or the operating system), a new generation of computers—these and other factors can render any previous information useless overnight. Obsolete recommendations can even have counterproductive effects on performance.

The author is aware of this risk. However, we have decided to include time-dependent information and rules in this book. This is the only way that the books in this series can serve as a reference for your daily work with R/3 administration. But this is not a book of inviolable tuning laws. Avoid blindly implementing its recommendations without reflecting on their appropriateness for the specific system. This book cannot replace analyzing the respective R/3 System, using R/3 Online Documentation, or checking current R/3 Notes in SAP's Online Service System (OSS).

All the information about menu paths, references to the screens of performance monitors, and the guide values for performance counters apply to R/3 Release 4.0B.

About the CD-ROM

The CD-ROM is a timed test engine containing practice questions and answers from each chapter of the book. The questions are designed to review the concepts presented in each chapter. The test engine simulates the SAP exam and allows you to determine which chapters you may need to review in more detail.

For details on how to install the test engine, see the `readme` file included on the CD-ROM.

CHAPTER
ONE

1

Performance Management

Good system performance is a prerequisite for the effectiveness of the R/3 System and its acceptance by users. Therefore, you should regularly monitor and perform quality assurance for your R/3 System.

In many R/3 implementation projects, the responsibility for the performance of the R/3 System is given to the system administrator alone. This chapter will explain that those responsible for good performance include the system and database administrators, the ABAP developers, the departments using the system, and the project managers.

This chapter will show which measures are necessary to ensure good performance, which tuning measures must be considered, and which people have to be involved in the tuning process and where their responsibilities lie. The main focus is on organizational questions about performance optimization. This chapter avoids the technical details that interest system administrators or software developers—these details are explained in later chapters.

When Should You Read This Chapter?

You should read this chapter before you read the other chapters in this book.

R/3 System Architecture and Tuning

Performance tuning can be divided into two categories:

Technical tuning   Configuring all the components of the R/3 System so that the load placed on the system by users can be optimally processed and does not cause performance bottlenecks. The components for technical tuning are the operating system, the database, the R/3 work processes, R/3 buffers, memory management, and the network.

Application tuning   Deals with the programs of R/3 application modules. The main focus is on verifying the necessity and efficiency of processes in applications and minimizing the use of resources, such as main memory, CPU, network transfers, and hard-disk accesses. Application tuning typically results in a more effective use of R/3 Transactions or improved performance of customer-developed ABAP programs.

Technical tuning is necessary for every R/3 System. In application tuning, the amount of work required increases with the size of the installation, as reflected in the data volume, the number of users, and the number of customer-developed programs and customer modifications to SAP objects.

Technical Tuning Architecture

The R/3 System has a three-layer client/server architecture. The presentation layer consists of the front ends and is where the users perform data input and output. The actual data processing occurs on the application servers. The database server is used for saving and accessing data (see Figure 1.1).

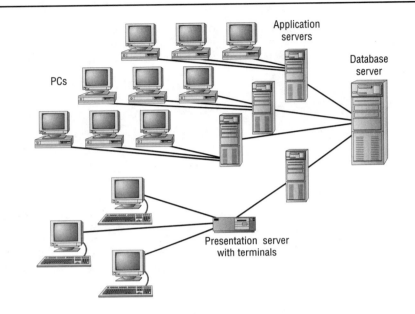

Presentation Server

A presentation server is normally set up as a personal computer (PC). If the PC's hardware conforms to the recommendations current for the respective R/3 Release, no further tuning is required on this layer. This is due to the fact that PCs are single-user machines—contrary to application servers and database servers, which process multiple processes at one time.

Application Server

After a user has entered data and pressed Enter, the presentation server sends this data to an application server as a user request. User requests are processed by R/3 work processes on the application server. One important tuning task is setting up (or configuring) the type and number of work processes on each application server.

Typically, the R/3 work processes are configured so that, on average, 5 to 10 active users share one R/3 dialog work process. This assumes that the users need around 10 times as long to enter data in the screen and interpret the results as the R/3 System needs to process the user requests. Therefore, the average number of free work processes available in the system should be sufficiently large to ensure that users' queries are processed without delay. If users start programs, such as reports with very long response times (or several such programs simultaneously), the affected work processes may be occupied for several minutes. This may mean that the number of remaining work processes is not sufficient to process the queries of other users, which could cause wait times. The R/3 System does not have any way of prioritizing users. If a bottleneck occurs, all users, regardless of their corporate role or the urgency of their request, must get in the queue and wait their turn.

In addition to the dialog requests for online or dialog transactions, an R/3 System also processes background requests, update requests, and print requests. Each of these request types is processed by a distinct type of R/3 work process. Appropriate tuning enables the workload to be distributed to optimally accommodate the demand across the system.

The main memory of each application server contains R/3 buffers for the temporary storage of data, such as programs, table and field definitions, and the contents of Customizing tables. This data is known as *global* data since it is available to all work processes on the R/3 instance. Tuning the settings for buffer sizes ensures that less data has to be read from the database server. Reading data from the R/3 buffer is approximately 10 to 100 times faster than reading data from the database server.

Database Server

If data is required to process a user request and this data is not yet in the application server's main memory, the data is read from the database server.

Database tuning is divided into three tasks:

- Optimizing database parameter settings, such as those for the size of database buffers.

- Optimizing the hard-disk layout of the database to distribute the workload as evenly as possible across the hard disks. This distribution of the workload avoids wait situations when writing to or reading from the hard disk.

- Optimizing excessively long-running SQL statements known as *expensive* SQL statements.

The R/3 System's client/server architecture allows the number of application servers and presentation servers to be increased almost indefinitely to meet the growing requirements of a rising number of users. However, the database layer is made up of a single database server (the exceptions, Oracle Parallel Server and DB2/390, are not discussed here). Certain processes in the database server, such as lock administration, cannot be distributed; that is, they cannot be located on multiple processes or database servers.

Experience shows that performance problems in large R/3 installations with more than 10 application servers are most often caused by bottlenecks in the database server. Therefore, tuning the database becomes increasingly important as the size of the system increases. When a system has been running in production operation for some time, most tuning settings will have been satisfactorily optimized and require no further change. These settings include buffer settings, load distribution, and so on. By contrast, the tuning of expensive SQL statements becomes increasingly important as the database data volume grows, and is an ongoing tuning process.

Hardware

For the database server and the application servers, you must verify whether the hardware capacity (CPU and main memory) is sufficiently large to accommodate the expected workload. In addition, you must optimize the settings of the operating system and the network parameters to achieve good hardware performance. To assist you here, the hardware manufacturer provides tools and documentation.

Network

The speed of transmission and the throughput between the application servers and the database server across the network are very important because they influence the performance of the entire R/3 System. The R/3 System is designed so that the volume of data flowing between the presentation server and the application server remains as low as possible. Typically, this data volume is only a fraction of the data volume flowing between the application server and the database server.

Application Tuning Architecture

Technical tuning concerns distributing the system load created by the applications, whereas application tuning aims to minimize this load by optimizing the use of system resources, such as CPU, main memory, and I/O.

Application tuning usually begins with a workload analysis—finding out which transactions and programs place a heavy load on the system and should, if possible, be optimized. When performing workload analysis, you should ask the following questions:

- Which programs or transactions consume the most system resources?

- Which SQL statements cause unnecessary database load through too many accesses, accesses that take too long, or accesses that consume too much memory or CPU? From which programs do the statements originate?

Optimizing R/3 Standard Functions

The first task in application tuning is to ensure that R/3 standard functions work efficiently. Normally, there are many ways of realizing business processes in the R/3 System. While these ways are equal from a business perspective, they differ in their technical implementation, and some are dramatically less efficient than others. The less efficient realizations ultimately result in a high response time for the user. As these implementations are configured during the Customizing phase, it is here that you can influence the subsequent performance of the R/3 System.

Since mid-1998, SAP has offered Empowering Workshops to optimize the technical implementation and Customizing of important standard functions that often cause performance problems. Sample workshops are as follows:

- *Technical Optimization of Pricing (R/3 application module SD)*
- *Technical Optimization of Due List Processing Including Scheduling (SD)*
- *Technical Optimization of the Availability Check (SD/PP)*
- *Technical Optimization of MRP Run and Long Term Planning (PP)*
- *Technical Optimization of Backflushing of Production Order (PP)*
- *Technical Optimization of Profitability Analysis (CO-PA)*

Space does not permit the optimization methods for these areas to be covered in this book. However, this book does provide techniques of analysis that enable you to identify performance problems in these areas.

Optimizing ABAP Code

Another area of application tuning is optimizing the ABAP code. This type of optimization is particularly useful for customer-developed programs, customer modifications to R/3 standard software objects, and the customer's use of user exits.

Unfortunately, in SAP implementation projects, the performance of customer-developed programs is almost never subjected to proper quality-assurance procedures. These programs are often written by developers who are inexperienced or working under time constraints. The programs are then tested with completely unrepresentative data. During production operation, as the volume of data in the system grows rapidly, these programs increasingly impair performance, and ultimately become a problem for the entire system. At this time, the original developer is often no longer available, and performance optimization requires considerable effort.

Therefore, performance optimization must be considered as early as the R/3 implementation phase; that is, when Customizing customer-developed programs, and before customer modifications of SAP software objects are implemented. If these implementation tasks are outsourced, the consultant performing them must be accountable not only for the resulting functionality, but also for its effects on performance.

Keep up to date with R/3 Notes in the Online Service System (OSS) to see whether there are any error corrections or recommended modifications that apply to your most important transactions. You may find R/3 Notes that enable you to correct ABAP code in standard R/3 programs to improve the performance of these programs. To locate these R/3 Notes in OSS, perform a search using the key word *performance* and the affected transaction code, program name, or table name.

Table Buffering and Indexing

Another area of application tuning is optimizing R/3 table buffering and defining suitable database indexes (secondary indexes) to considerably reduce the load on the database during read operations. Table buffering and indexes are set up during the installation of the R/3 System, but may need to be changed later to optimize the runtime of individual programs. For customer tables, these values must be set by the customer's developer.

Assigning Tuning Responsibility

Table 1.1 shows an overview of the most important tuning measures. The column *Person* lists the person responsible for each activity: *M* denotes the IT management; *S* denotes the people responsible for the system (R/3 System administrators, R/3 technical consultants); *A* denotes the application consultants (employees in the user departments, R/3 application consultants, ABAP software developers); and *U* denotes the R/3 users.

TABLE 1.1: Overview of Tuning Measures

Technical Tuning	Person
Set the system parameters for the operating system, database, and R/3 Basis System (database buffers, R/3 buffers, number of work processes, and so on).	S
Optimize the layout of the database (I/O balancing).	S
Define a daily, weekly, and monthly workload distribution (for example, background processing, logon).	A, S, U, M
Install additional, more powerful hardware.	S, M
Find and apply R/3 Notes in SAP's Online Service System (OSS) concerning patches, error corrections, or recommended modifications.	A, S
Optimize the Customizing of standard R/3 Transactions to improve performance.	A

Continued on next page

TABLE 1.1: Overview of Tuning Measures *(Continued)*

Application Tuning	Person
Optimize the ABAP code of customer-developed programs and customer modifications of SAP software objects.	A
Define table buffering.	A, S
Create, change, or delete secondary indexes.	A, S

Quality Assurance for Performance Optimization

To implement quality-assurance procedures for performance optimization, you should set up a standardized analysis and tuning framework. An optimization cycle within this framework should consist of four steps:

1. Monitor performance and identify performance problems.
2. Perform a detailed problem analysis and create an action list.
3. Perform tuning measures.
4. Verify the tuning results.

Step 1: Monitoring Performance and Identifying Performance Problems

To optimize performance systematically, you should perform a performance analysis at regular, predetermined intervals and document the results in a performance report. A good example of this type of report is the one offered by SAP's EarlyWatch™ service.

To help you analyze performance, the R/3 System contains several powerful monitoring programs, which are continuously being developed by SAP's performance experts. You can access the monitors from the *Performance menu* (Transaction code *STUN*):

Tools ➤ *Administration* ➤ *Monitor* ➤ *Performance*

or

Tools ➤ *CCMS* ➤ *Control/Monitoring* ➤ *Performance menu*

Table 1.2 lists the performance monitors that you can use for technical analysis and application analysis.

TABLE 1.2: R/3 Performance Monitors

Monitors for Technical Analysis

Name	Purpose
Operating System Monitor (ST06)	To monitor load on the CPU and the physical main memory.
Database Monitor (ST04)	To monitor load on the database buffers, database locks, wait situations, read and write access to hard disks, and SQL statements.
R/3 Memory Configuration Monitor (also called the Setups/Tune Buffers Monitor—ST02)	To monitor load on the R/3 buffer and other memory areas.
Work Process Overview (SM50)	To monitor load on R/3 work processes.
Workload Monitor (ST03)	To monitor workload distribution in the R/3 System. A technical analysis uses this monitor to identify and analyze problems in the database, R/3 memory management, or R/3 buffers.
Workload Monitor (ST03)	To monitor workload distribution in the R/3 System. An application analysis uses this monitor to identify and analyze transactions, programs, and users that place a heavy load on the system.

Continued on next page

TABLE 1.2: R/3 Performance Monitors *(Continued)*

Monitors for Application Analysis

Name	Purpose
Application Monitor (ST07)	To monitor the use of resources according to R/3 application module.
SQL Trace (ST05), ABAP Trace (SE30)	To trace ABAP programs for detailed analysis.

Step 2: Performing a Detailed Problem Analysis and Creating an Action List

After you identify performance problems, a detailed problem analysis helps you create an action list for performance optimization. This list helps you avoid getting lost in detailed questions during the tuning process. When prioritizing and scheduling the optimization measures on your list, consider the following questions:

- What dependencies exist between the problems? Will solving one problem wholly or partly solve other problems?

- Are there sufficient hardware resources (CPU, main memory, hard disks, and so on) in the areas affected by the performance problem, or can these resources be acquired within a given schedule?

- What type of downtime (if any) is required, and when can it be scheduled? Downtime may mean restarting the R/3 application servers, the database server, or the operating systems (for example, after changes to parameters), or an even longer downtime may be necessary.

- Is further analysis required?

- Is the required amount of personnel available? Examples of tuning measures that are personnel-intensive include tuning SQL statements and tuning application programs.

- Will the performance measures on the action list guarantee success? Can you implement them on your own? Do you require the help of a consulting partner, a hardware partner, or an SAP service, such as SAP Support or EarlyWatch?

There are often several solutions to a performance problem. When deciding which measures to take and in which order, remember that it is better to avoid workload than to distribute it. This principle also has exceptions, though. In some cases (or as a temporary solution), it may be more cost-effective to compensate for inefficient Customizing and nonoptimal customer programs by, for example, creating indexes, increasing the size of the buffer, or introducing faster hardware. You may need to modify the action list for regular performance tuning to reflect the results of a performance analysis or to reflect current circumstances.

Step 3: Performing Tuning Measures

This step involves executing the tuning measures developed in the previous two steps. Without providing a specific list here it is recommended that the careful planning of this process be matched by careful adherence to the plan. The documentation of the measures taken is important for the verification process described in the next step.

Step 4: Verifying the Tuning Results

After executing the action list, you should reanalyze the R/3 System to verify the success or failure of performance optimization. If the desired improvements are not achieved or only partially achieved, another optimization cycle is required. After large-scale performance tuning, new problems sometimes occur that also need to be solved. When in doubt about how to proceed, you may require the help of a consulting partner, your hardware partner, or SAP Support.

Example: Cooperation between Technical Tuning and Application Tuning

The following tuning example demonstrates how technical optimizers and application optimizers are often required to cooperate —they must decide between a number of alternative performance optimization measures. The specific technical details of the analysis have been largely omitted.

In a given R/3 System, users are complaining of substantial performance problems in Production Planning (R/3 application module PP)—specifically, when they create requirement lists and stock lists.

Performance analysis leads to the following results:

- The R/3 Work Process Overview shows that several programs are repeatedly reading from the table RESB for long periods of time.

- The analysis of the database shows that all the tables with transaction data reside on one hard disk. The total amount of all transaction data is 8GB, of which table RESB occupies 2GB.

- The Operating System Monitor shows that this same hard disk is completely overloaded, with 80% to 100% of maximum load, and response times are more than 100 milliseconds per access.

System administrators and application consultants are called on to solve the problem. From the viewpoint of the system administrators, the following technical solutions are worth considering:

- The data buffer on the database server could be increased to hold a large part of table RESB in the main memory of the database server.

- Table RESB could be moved to a separate hard disk. The hard-disk layout of the database could also be changed to distribute table RESB over multiple hard disks.

- As of Release 4, the R/3 System provides a new functionality, called the ATP server, to improve the availability check based on Available-to-Promise (ATP) logic. Using an ATP server would enable partial results from table RESB to be buffered in the main memory on the application server and reduce the database accesses to this table.

- As a last resort, faster hard disks could be installed.

From the viewpoint of the application consultants, the following measures can be considered:

- Table RESB contains reservation data and dependent requirement data concerning materials, components, and assemblies that are used in production planning. RESB is mainly read during the availability check. It may be that skillfully Customizing the availability check will reduce RESB's size and read frequency. The following questions should be investigated:

  - Can the availability check be simplified for some materials, such as screws and other small parts that are required for all products? If the availability check for these materials can be deactivated, this would slow the growth of table RESB and reduce the number of accesses to it, thus improving performance.

  - How often are the contents of table RESB archived and deleted? Does RESB contain data linked to specific dates and times that lie in the distant past, therefore making this data obsolete and capable of being deleted or archived?

  - Is table growth due to planning data that extends unnecessarily far into the future? Table RESB may also contain planning data linked to dates and times that lie in a too distant future.

Cooperation is required between the system administrator and the application consultants to find a solution from among these numerous possibilities. Often, the most effective method for performance tuning is to turn off unnecessary functionalities. After the system administrator has communicated the type of problem to the application consultant, the application consultant will know what to deactivate, or what to simplify in Customizing. A combined effort is required to find a solution.

Roles and Responsibilities

As shown in the previous section, performance optimization of an R/3 System requires various people to combine their efforts and expertise. Technical tuning requires knowledge of the operating system, the database system, and the R/3 Basis. Tuning is normally performed by an R/3 System administrator or an R/3 technical consultant.

Application tuning requires a wide-ranging knowledge of the R/3 System:

- Knowledge about the database system will help you decide when to create additional database indexes, or how to formulate SQL statements effectively.

- Knowledge about R/3 Basis will help you to buffer tables optimally.

- Knowledge of the ABAP programming language will help you optimize ABAP code.

- Knowledge of the R/3 application modules will help ensure that R/3 programs and functions are used effectively.

- Knowledge of business processes within the company will help you recognize time-critical processes and implement them to suit the users.

Because it is almost impossible for a single person to have all this R/3 knowledge, it is important to form teams.

Table 1.3 shows an overview of the performance optimization tasks and which people are responsible for these tasks. The third column of the table indicates to these respective people which chapters of this book are especially relevant.

NOTE   Compare also the roles and responsibilities in an R/3 implementation project, as further described in *SAP R/3 Implementation with ASAP* by Hartwig Brand, Sybex Inc., 1998.

The present book provides concrete information and instruction to technical team leads, R/3 System administrators, database administrators, ABAP software developers, and technical consultants. If, in the course of optimizing performance, these people require additional information or assistance in analyzing or solving performance problems, they should consult other people in the R/3 project: the project manager, the operating-system administrator, the network administrator, the quality manager, or the application consultant.

TABLE 1.3:   Who Does What?

Task	Role	See Chapters...
Verifying hardware sizing and planning the R/3 System configuration	Technical team lead and technical consultant	5 and 6
Optimizing technical performance after installation	R/3 System administrator, database administrator, and technical consultant	2, 5, and 6
Continuously monitoring the performance of system operation	R/3 System administrator and database administrator	2 and 3
Analyzing performance problems with bottleneck analysis	Technical team lead, R/3 System administrator, database administrator, ABAP software developer, and technical consultant	All

Continued on next page

TABLE 1.3: Who Does What? *(Continued)*

Task	Role	See Chapters...
Using quality-assurance procedures for the performance of customer-developed ABAP programs	R/3 System administrator, database administrator, ABAP software developer, and technical consultant	4, 7, 8, and 9

Hardware sizing is performed by the hardware partner because they are contractually bound to ensure that the delivered hardware meets the usage requirements. When considering the offers and proposals of hardware suppliers, you should previously have planned your R/3 System configuration so that you can double-check the proposed hardware sizing against your requirements. Chapters 5 and 6 provide more helpful hints on this topic.

For instructions on optimizing technical performance after installation, see Chapters 2, 5, and 6.

For instructions on continuously monitoring system operation, see the sections on workload analysis in Chapter 3; and the sections on hardware, the database, and the R/3 Basis in Chapter 2.

If acute performance problems occur, you should perform a bottleneck analysis. Refer to Appendix A for roadmaps showing bottleneck-analysis procedures and for tables summarizing the most important problems.

Unfortunately, customers do not often set up quality-assurance procedures for performance in relation to their own ABAP programs. For suggestions on setting up appropriate quality-assurance procedures, see "Monitoring Customer ABAP Developments" in Chapter 4.

Performance Forum

For large SAP implementation projects, it is necessary to set up a *performance forum* to enable regular meetings between people who represent the various aspects of performance optimization.

The long-term plan for performance optimization should include a regular performance analysis, based on workload analysis, to identify bottlenecks and their causes. This regular analysis is normally performed by people with experience in technical operation, who also know which functions in business processes are performance-critical. They should make a list of the transactions and programs that require special monitoring, and use this list to steer the analysis in the right direction.

If you do not attempt to steer the optimization process, you run the risk that your optimization team will improve the performance of "exotic" controlling programs (rather than time-critical business processes), because the employees in these areas complain louder than the rest. In practice, it is when bottlenecks occur, such as during order entry for sales, that business is disrupted. These types of bottlenecks should be analyzed as a top priority.

Technical and application-oriented considerations should lead to a defined and prioritized monitoring strategy. This is how you can ensure that the optimization measures you take are exactly the ones that will ultimately work.

Outlook: Performance 2000

SAP has announced a 64-bit kernel for the R/3 System for early 1999. The 64-bit kernel will make it easier to configure and more effective to use computers with large main memories.

64-Bit Architecture

At the time of publication, the prevailing 32-bit architecture is affected by administrative difficulties and limitations imposed by the operating system. As a result, you currently need extensive expert knowledge to effectively use computers with more than 2GB physical main memory (RAM). To benefit from the 64-bit architecture, you require a 64-bit operating system and a released 64-bit version of the R/3 kernel.

The new 64-bit architecture will also cause fundamental changes to the recommendations for R/3 memory management. Consequently, this book explains the terms and concepts of R/3 memory management separately from its concrete recommendations. These terms and concepts will remain current even after switching from 32-bit to 64-bit architecture, and will continue to form the requisite know-how with which to configure your system.

Recommendations regarding 64-bit architecture will be made available in SAP's Online Service System (OSS) or on SAP's Internet site, SAPNet. As a starting point in your search for these recommendations, see the relevant R/3 Notes listed in Appendix H.

Advanced Planner and Optimizer (APO)

Presently, companies implement multiple coupled R/3 Systems. In these complex system landscapes, SAP's Advanced Planner & Optimizer (APO) server will make it possible in the future to have systemwide materials management and inventory planning, and real-time decision support.

The APO server is an independent installation within the component-oriented Business Framework architecture. The impressive performance of the APO server is based on a series of new technologies and functions—for example, memory-based, liveCache processing for data objects, which enables data sharing between application servers and therefore the implementation of task-specific application servers. APO will be offered as an independent installation.

In the future, the APO server will provide many forms of R/3 cross-system support, such as the availability check function. The APO server works by providing quick, multistaged checks on product and resource availability, and considers customer or plant preferences as well as approved product substitutions. The server provides real-time results and availability simulations, the basis for a new performance dimension in the control and use of companywide resources.

As of R/3 Release 4, SAP enables customers to configure an application server within an R/3 System, which takes over the Available-to-Promise (ATP) check within the R/3 System centrally and keeps the interim results of the availability check in its global main memory. This book contains detailed information about the function and configuration of this ATP server in Chapter 8.

Business Information Warehouse (BW)

SAP's Business Information Warehouse (BW) is one of the new generation of SAP solutions for companywide data warehousing and is a component of the Business Framework. BW provides data warehousing that has all the advantages of the R/3 System: security, integration, scalability, high availability, interoperability, and leading information technology. Using the R/3 Transaction system to continuously adjust the metadata, BW ensures data integrity.

A companywide BW also has performance advantages. All data-warehouse applications are processed in BW by a specialized Online Analytical Processing (OLAP) processor. This frees the remaining R/3 Systems to be used primarily by Online Transaction Processing (OLTP) applications.

Summary

Two important prerequisites for good system performance are as follows:

- The long-term planning of performance optimization
- The cooperation of everyone who sets up or administers the R/3 System, performs Customizing, or develops ABAP programs

Only the cooperation of the various specialists can ensure adequate optimization in these dual areas:

- Technical optimization
  - Hardware capacity (long-term resource planning)
  - Database performance
  - R/3 Basis System (R/3 memory areas and R/3 work processes)
- Application optimization
  - Optimization of SAP standard functions through Customizing
  - Optimization of customer-developed ABAP programs

In a large SAP implementation project, cooperation can be ensured only through a performance forum that enables the specialists of each respective area to meet regularly.

CHAPTER
TWO

2

Monitoring Hardware, Database, and R/3 Basis

This chapter explains how to monitor and analyze the performance of your hardware, database, R/3 memory management, and R/3 work processes. Procedure roadmaps summarize the most important analysis paths and clarify when to use the various monitors.

Simple recommendations are provided to help you optimize each component, unless more in-depth explanations are required (these are given in subsequent chapters).

In this chapter, background information is intentionally kept to a minimum. This means that even application consultants or system administrators with limited experience in performance analysis can use this chapter to improve the performance of their R/3 System. For example, monitoring and customizing R/3 extended memory is described without explaining R/3 extended memory in detail. For more background information, see Chapters 5 to 9.

At SAP, our experience suggests that you can solve many performance problems in the operating system, database, and R/3 Basis using simple instructions, without referring to very many technical details.

The main tools for analyzing performance are the R/3 performance monitors. While these can be accessed in various ways, they are conveniently grouped together on the *Performance menu*. To access this menu, use Transaction *STUN*, or, from the R/3 initial screen, choose either of the following menu paths:

- *Tools* ➢ *Monitor* ➢ *Performance*
- *Tools* ➢ *CCMS* ➢ *Control/Monitoring* ➢ *Performance menu*

When Should You Read This Chapter?

You should read this chapter if you want to use R/3 to technically monitor and optimize the performance of your R/3 System, database, or operating system.

Basic Terms

This section explains the way some basic terms are used throughout this book: computer, R/3 instance, database, application server, database instance, database server, and server.

A *computer* is a physical machine with a CPU, a main memory, and an IP address.

An *R/3 instance* is a logical unit. It consists of a set of R/3 work processes that are administered by a dispatcher process. It also consists of a set of R/3 buffers located in the computer's shared memory and accessed by the R/3 work processes. On one computer, there can be multiple R/3 instances and therefore multiple dispatchers and multiple sets of buffers. An *application server* is a computer with one or more R/3 instances.

NOTE   The term *application server* is sometimes used in other literature where this book uses the term *R/3 instance*.

Every R/3 System has only one database. The term *database* refers to the set of data that is organized, for example, in files. The database may be thought of as the passive part of the database system, while the active part is the *database instance*, a logical unit that allows access to the database.

This database instance consists of database processes with a common set of database buffers in the shared memory of a computer. A *database server* is a computer with one or more database instances. A computer can be both a database server and an application server if a database instance and an R/3 instance run on it.

In the R/3 environment, there is normally only one database instance for each database. Examples of database systems where multiple database instances can access a database are DB2/390 and Oracle Parallel Server. The special features of these parallel database systems are not covered in this book.

Throughout R/3 literature, the term *server* is used in both a hardware sense and a software sense. Thus, *server* can refer to a physical computer as a hardware entity. This is often intended, for example, with the term *database server*. With reference to client/server software architecture, however, *server* can also be used to refer to a logical service. This is usually intended, for example, when using the terms *message server* or *ATP server*.

Monitoring Hardware

The Operating System Monitor is the tool for analyzing hardware bottlenecks and operating-system performance problems. To call the Operating System Monitor to monitor the R/3 application server you are currently logged on to, use Transaction *ST06*, or, from the R/3 initial screen, choose:

> *Tools ➤ Administration ➤ Monitor ➤ Performance ➤ Operating system ➤ Local ➤ Activity*

The screen *Local OS monitor* appears, which is the initial screen of the Operating System Monitor.

To start the Operating System Monitor for a database server or an application server other than the one you are logged on to, use Transaction *OS07*, or, from the R/3 initial screen, choose:

> *Tools ➤ Administration ➤ Monitor ➤ Performance ➤ Operating system ➤ Remote ➤ Activity*

After selecting the desired server, the screen *Local OS Monitor* for that server will appear.

Alternatively, to call the Operating System Monitor from the server overview, use Transaction *SM51*, or, from the R/3 initial screen, choose:

> *Tools ➤ Administration ➤ Monitor ➤ System Monitoring ➤ Servers*

Mark the desired application server and choose *OS collector*.

Analyzing CPU and Paging

The main screen of the Operating System Monitor (see Figure 2.1) lists the most important performance data for the operating system and the hardware. All the data is renewed every 10 seconds by the auxiliary program *saposcol*, but to update the data on the screen (after 10 seconds or longer), choose *Refresh display*.

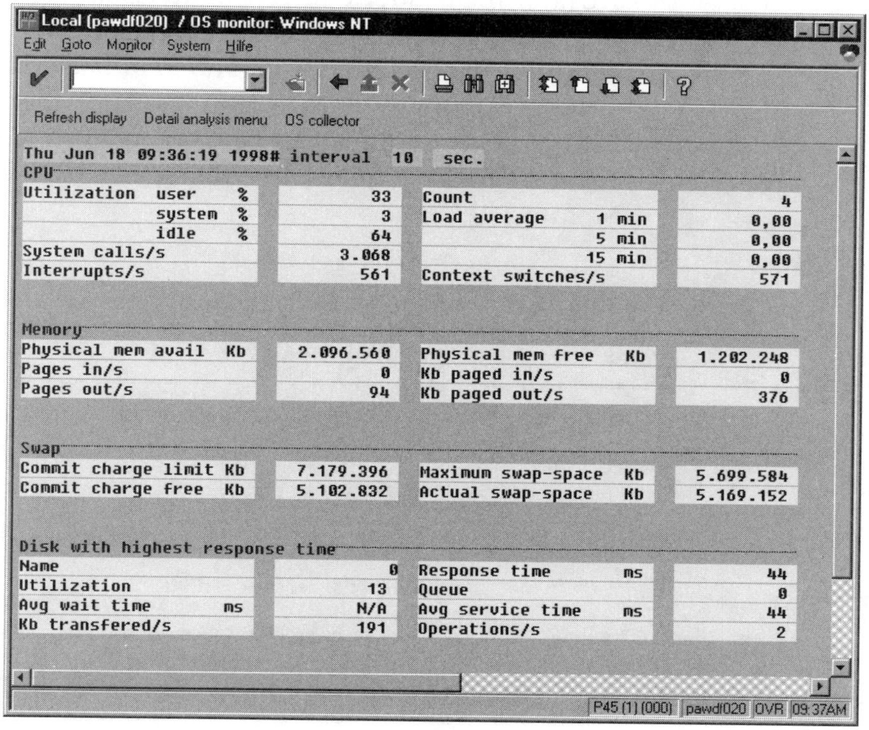

FIGURE 2.1:

Main screen of the Operating System Monitor (Transaction *ST06*)

CPU Workload

Under the header *CPU* in the Operating System Monitor initial screen, the percentage of *CPU Utilization* is indicated for *user, system*, and *idle*. These values indicate what percentage of the total CPU capacity is currently:

- Being consumed by processes such as R/3 work processes or database processes (*user*)

- Being consumed by the operating system (*system*)

- Not being consumed (*idle*)

Under the header *CPU*, the field *Count* indicates the number of processors. *Load average* is the average number of work processes waiting for a free processor, and is indicated for the previous minute, 5 minutes, and 15 minutes. The other values listed under *CPU* are less significant for analyzing system performance. See Table 2.1 for an explanation of values in the Operating System Monitor.

TABLE 2.1: An Explanation of Values in the Operating System Monitor (Transaction *ST06*)

Value	Explanation
Utilization user	CPU workload caused by user processes (R/3 System, database, and so on)
Utilization system	CPU workload caused by the operating system
Utilization idle	Free CPU capacity—this value should be at least 20%, optimally 35%
Count	Number of processors (CPUs)
Load average	Number of processes waiting for CPUs, averaged over 1, 5, or 15 minutes
Physical mem avail Kb	Available physical main memory (RAM) in kilobytes

Main Memory Workload

Under the header *Memory* in the Operating System Monitor initial screen, you will find the amount of available physical main memory and the operating-system paging rates and paged data quantities.

Swap Space

Under the header *Swap* in the Operating System Monitor initial screen, you will find the amount of currently allocated swap space (indicated by *Actual swap-space*). The swap space should be about three times as large as the physical main memory, and at least 2GB.

WARNING If the sum of the physical memory (indicated as *Physical mem avail Kb*) and swap space (indicated as *Actual swap-space*) is smaller than the total amount of memory required by the R/3 System, the database, and other programs, this may cause program terminations or even operating-system failure. Therefore, ensure that there is enough swap space.

History of CPU and Main Memory Usage

To display the CPU workload over the previous 24 hours, in the initial screen of the Operating System Monitor, choose *Detail analysis menu*. In the screen that appears, choose *CPU* (under the header *Previous hours*).

The screen *Local* (instance name)/*CPU last 24 hours* appears. The figures indicated in the table are hourly averages. The column headers are the same as in the fields under *CPU* in the Operating System Monitor initial screen. The rows identify to which hour in the last 24 hours the figures in the table correspond.

To display the main memory usage over the previous 24 hours, from the Operating System Monitor initial screen, choose *Detail analysis menu*. In the screen that appears, choose *Memory* (under the header *Previous hours*).

Guideline Values for CPU and Paging

The unused CPU (indicated in the Operating System Monitor as *CPU Utilization idle*) should normally be at least 20% on average per hour. This enables the system to accommodate temporary workload peaks. A reading of 35% idle CPU capacity is even better.

The paging rate should not become too large. As a rule of thumb, paging is not critical if, every hour, less than 20% of the physical main memory is paged. For operating systems that page asynchronously (for example, Windows NT), the value indicated in the Operating System Monitor as the *Kb paged in/s* rate is the key statistic on paging performance. For other operating systems that page only when necessary, such as most UNIX derivatives, the key statistic is the *Kb paged out/s* rate.

If the Operating System Monitor sometimes shows values that exceed these guideline values, this does not automatically mean that there is a hardware bottleneck. Use the Workload Monitor (Transaction *ST03*) to check whether the high CPU workload or the paging rate is associated with poor response times. (See Chapter 3, under "General Performance Problems.")

If you observe high paging rates on several computers, calculate the virtual main memory allocated by the R/3 instances and the database, and compare this with the available physical main memory. (To calculate the virtual memory, see "Displaying the Allocated Memory" and "Analyzing the Database Buffers" in the present chapter.) Experience shows that, as a rule of thumb, there should be around 50% more virtual memory than physical memory.

If you do detect a hardware bottleneck on one or more computers in the R/3 System, it may be due to one or more of the following causes.

Nonoptimal Workload Distribution

In a distributed system with multiple computers, if you discover a hardware bottleneck on at least one computer, while other computers have unused resources, the workload is probably not optimally distributed. To improve performance, redistribute the R/3 work processes and the user logons.

It is extremely important that the database server has enough resources. A CPU or main memory bottleneck on the database server means that the required data cannot be retrieved quickly from the database, which causes poor response times in the entire R/3 System.

Individual Processes That Consume Too Much CPU

To identify processes that place a heavy load on the CPU, use the Operating System Monitor (Transaction *ST06*) function *Top CPU Processes*. From the Operating System Monitor initial screen, choose:

Detail analysis menu ➤ *Top CPU processes*

R/3 work processes are indicated in the column *Command* by *disp+work* (Windows NT) or *dw_*instance (UNIX). Database processes are normally indicated by brand names such as Oracle or Informix that appear in the columns *Command* or *User name*.

To check whether individual processes are placing a heavy load on the CPU for long periods of time, refresh the monitor periodically and observe any changes in the value *CPU Util [%]*.

If R/3 work processes are causing high CPU load, open a new user session and call the Local Work Process Overview (Transaction *SM50*—see "Analyzing R/3 Work Processes" in the present chapter). Using the Operating System Monitor function *Top CPU Processes*, you can obtain the process ID (indicated as PID) to identify the R/3 work process causing the load. From the Work Process

Overview, note the name of the ABAP program and the user corresponding to the PID. If the user confirms that the program is functioning correctly, it may be necessary to consider an in-depth performance analysis for this program (see, for example, Chapter 9).

If a database process is causing high CPU consumption over a long time period, call the Database Process Monitor (within Transaction *ST04*—see "Identifying Expensive SQL Statements" in the present chapter). With this monitor, you can find out which SQL statements are currently running.

Thus, using the Operating System Monitor in conjunction with the Work Process Overview and the Database Process Monitor, you can fairly easily identify programs, transactions, and SQL statements that cause high CPU load.

External Processes That Consume Too Much CPU

External processes can also cause a CPU bottleneck. In the Operating System Monitor, if you find external processes (that is, processes that are neither R/3 work processes nor database processes) with a high CPU consumption that cause a CPU bottleneck, you should find out whether these processes are really necessary for your system, or whether they can be switched off or moved to another computer. Examples of external processes are administrative software, backups, external systems, screen savers, and so on.

TIP   In a sample situation, dramatically increased response times are observed during times of peak user activity. The Operating System Monitor function *TOP CPU Processes* reveals a single R/3 work process that is causing a CPU load of 30% over several minutes. At the same time, the R/3 Work Process Overview shows a long-running background program. It would appear that a CPU bottleneck is being caused or at least exacerbated by this background program. One suggestion for improving performance is to run the background program when the dialog load is lower.

Individual Programs That Use Too Much Memory

To search for programs with high memory requirements that may be causing a main memory bottleneck, use the Operating System Monitor and the Work Process Overview in a similar way as described above for identifying programs that use too much CPU. (See also Chapter 5, particularly under "Troubleshooting.")

The File System Cache Is Too Large

Operating systems normally administer their own file system cache. This cache is located in the main memory, where it competes for memory space with the R/3 System and the database. If the cache size is too large, this leaves insufficient memory space for R/3 and the database, thus causing high paging rates despite the fact that the physical main memory is more than large enough to accommodate both R/3 and the database. To minimize paging, you should keep the file system cache small. SAP recommends reducing this cache to between 7% and 10% of the physical memory.

The operating-system parameters for configuring the file system cache include *dbc_max_pct* (for HP-UX), *ubc-maxpercent* (for Digital UNIX), and *maxperm* (for AIX).

To reduce the size of the file system cache for Windows NT, from the NT screen, choose *Start* ➤ *Settings* ➤ *Control panel* ➤ *Network*. Choose the tab *Services*, the service *Server*, and *Properties*. In the following screen, under the screen area *Optimization*, select *Maximize Throughput for Network Applications*, and choose *OK*. To activate the file cache's new settings, you must restart the computer.

Excessive paging requires more CPU and can lead to a CPU bottleneck. Removing the cause of excessive paging usually causes the CPU bottleneck to disappear.

Analyzing I/O on the Hard Disks

The Hard Disk Monitor (see Figure 2.2), which is located within the Operating System Monitor, enables you to monitor not only the I/O or read/write load on the hard disk, but also—in as much as this can be correctly indicated in the operating system—the wait times and response times for the hard disk.

FIGURE 2.2:

The Hard Disk Monitor (part of the Operating System Monitor)

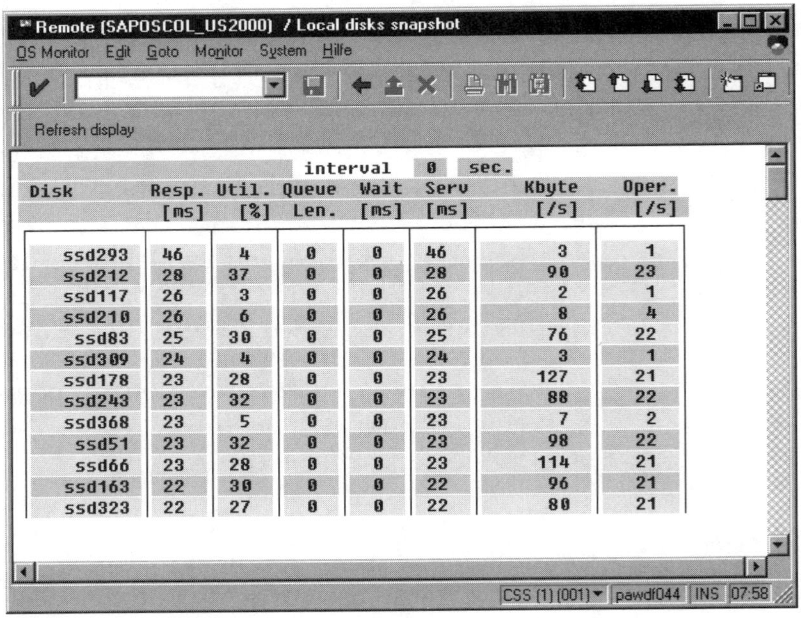

Disk	Resp. [ms]	Util. [%]	Queue Len.	Wait [ms]	Serv [ms]	Kbyte [/s]	Oper. [/s]
ssd293	46	4	0	0	46	3	1
ssd212	28	37	0	0	28	90	23
ssd117	26	3	0	0	26	2	1
ssd210	26	6	0	0	26	8	4
ssd83	25	30	0	0	25	76	22
ssd309	24	4	0	0	24	3	1
ssd178	23	28	0	0	23	127	21
ssd243	23	32	0	0	23	88	22
ssd368	23	5	0	0	23	7	2
ssd51	23	32	0	0	23	98	22
ssd66	23	28	0	0	23	114	21
ssd163	22	30	0	0	22	96	21
ssd323	22	27	0	0	22	80	21

To access the Hard Disk Monitor, use Transaction *ST06* and choose *Detail analysis menu*. In the screen that appears, choose *Disk* (under the header *Snapshot analysis*). The Hard Disk Monitor lists the relevant disks and, in subsequent columns, provides information on the disks as explained in Table 2.2.

TABLE 2.2: An Explanation of Columns in the Hard Disk Monitor (Part of the Operating System Monitor)

Column	Explanation
Disk	Operating-system name for the hard disk
Resp.	Average response times of the hard disk in milliseconds
Util.	Load on the hard disk (in %)
Queue Len.	Number of processes waiting for I/O operations
Wait	Wait time in milliseconds
Serv	Service time in milliseconds

By double-clicking a row in the Hard Disk Monitor, you can display an overview of the average response times over the previous 24 hours for the selected hard disk.

This 24-hour overview can also be accessed from the Operating System Monitor initial screen by choosing *Detail analysis menu* ➢ *Disk* (under the header *Previous hours*).

In the Hard Disk Monitor, a heavy load on an individual disk is signified by a value greater than 50% in the column *Util.* This may indicate an I/O bottleneck. However, to perform a more detailed analysis, you require the tools provided by the hardware manufacturer. An I/O bottleneck is particularly critical if it is on the hard disk where the operating system's paging file resides.

Monitoring is particularly recommended for the disks of the database server. To prevent bottlenecks during read or write operations to the database, use the Database Performance Monitor and the Hard Disk Monitor. (See "Identifying I/O Problems" in the present chapter.)

Other Checks through the Operating System Monitor

The Operating System Monitor also allows you to check other factors that may be contributing to hardware bottlenecks, such as operating-system parameter changes and LAN communication.

Parameter Changes Check

For UNIX operating systems, the R/3 System logs all operating-system parameter changes. This log, accessed from the Operating System Monitor, lets you determine whether the start of performance problems can be linked to the time when particular parameters were changed. Thus, you may discover parameter changes that contributed to the performance problem.

To display the log of operating-system parameter changes, from the Operating System Monitor, choose *Detail analysis menu* ➤ *Parameter changes*. Position the cursor on the name of a server and choose *History of file*.

LAN Check

A bottleneck in network communication may be the reason for poor system response times. To test LAN communication, from the Operating System Monitor, choose *Detail analysis menu* ➤ *LAN Check by Ping* (under the header *Additional functions*).

From the *LAN Check by Ping* screen, you can select any database server, application server, or presentation server and initiate one or more pings to that server. In the screen that follows after performing a ping, position the cursor on a server name and choose *Details*. This enables you to see the results of the ping—for example, the ping response times and whether there was any data loss.

To perform a more detailed analysis, use the tools from the hardware manufacturer.

Summary

Performance problems may be indicated if:

- The average idle CPU capacity is less than 20% every hour.
- More than 20% of the physical main memory is paged every hour.
- Utilization of individual hard disks is more than 50%.

Excessive utilization of the hard disks, particularly on the database server, can cause systemwide performance problems. To check whether the high CPU load or the high paging rate significantly damages response times in the R/3 System or the database, use the Workload Monitor (Transaction *ST03*—see Chapter 3).

Figures 2.3 and 2.4 show the procedure for analyzing a hardware bottleneck. A common solution for resolving a hardware bottleneck is to redistribute the workload (for example, by moving work processes).

FIGURE 2.3:

Procedure roadmap for analyzing a hardware bottleneck (CPU)

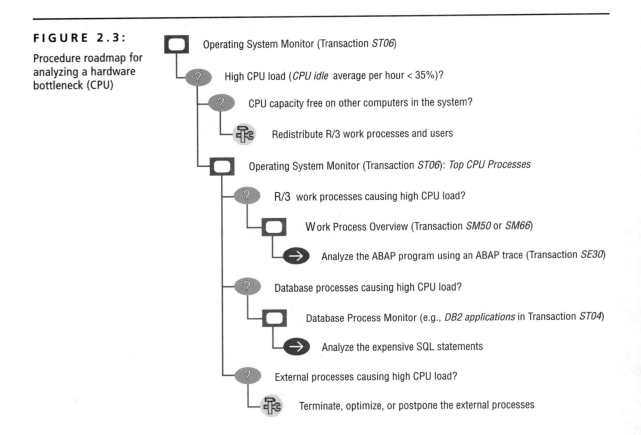

Possible causes of a CPU bottleneck include:

- Inefficient applications, which can usually be identified in the Database Process Monitor and the Work Process Overview

- External processes that do not belong to an R/3 instance or the database instance

You should always perform a complete performance analysis before deciding whether the existing hardware is sufficient for the demands on the R/3 System.

FIGURE 2.4:

Procedure roadmap for analyzing a hardware bottleneck (main memory)

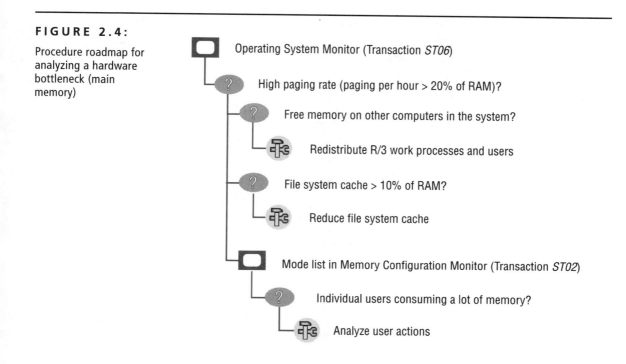

Operating System Monitor (Transaction *ST06*)

High paging rate (paging per hour > 20% of RAM)?

Free memory on other computers in the system?

Redistribute R/3 work processes and users

File system cache > 10% of RAM?

Reduce file system cache

Mode list in Memory Configuration Monitor (Transaction *ST02*)

Individual users consuming a lot of memory?

Analyze user actions

Throughout this book, you will find procedure roadmaps such as those in Figures 2.3 and 2.4 that guide you through the process of using the monitors and performing the analyses described.

Appendix A contains a collection of all the roadmaps and an explanation of the symbols used in them.

Monitoring the Database

The R/3 System currently supports seven different relational database systems that all have a different architecture. Many performance problems, however, occur independently of the type of database system implemented. To help R/3 customers analyze and tune their databases, the R/3 System has its own Database Performance Monitor (Transaction *ST04*) with basic functions that work independently of the respective database system. The Database Performance Monitor collects performance data from two sources:

- The database system: R/3 both displays performance data provided by analysis functions in the respective database system and is equipped with its own analysis functions, developed by SAP or partner companies.

- The R/3 System: A part of the performance data is entered and collected directly by the R/3 System—for example, in the database interface for the R/3 work processes.

NOTE   This book covers the basic functions of the R/3 Database Performance Monitor, which can be used with all database systems. Examples of analyses performed using this monitor for different database systems are included. Appendix B shows the relevant menu paths.

To start the Database Performance Monitor, use Transaction *ST04*, or, from the R/3 initial screen, choose:

Tools ➢ *Administration* ➢ *Monitor* ➢ *Performance* ➢ *Database* ➢ *Activity*

The screen *Database Performance Analysis: Database Overview* appears.

Analyzing the Database Buffer

Every database has various buffers that enable user data (data from tables) and administrative information from the database to be stored in main memory to reduce the number of accesses to the hard disk. Accesses to these buffers in main memory are normally 10 to 100 times faster than accesses to the hard disk. If the buffers are made too small, the data volume is too large for the buffer. Data is then forced out of the buffer and has to be reread (reloaded) from the hard disk. For this reason, monitoring buffer activity is an important element of performance analysis.

The most important buffer in a database is the data buffer or data cache, which stores parts of the most currently read database tables and their indexes. The data in the database tables is not read directly from the hard disk and sent to the user's R/3 work process. Rather, it is first stored temporarily in the data buffer. The data buffer is divided into blocks or pages, which can be 2KB, 4KB, or 8KB in size, depending on the database system and the operating system. Data is read from the hard disk in blocks or pages and then stored in the data buffer.

The following values characterize the quality of data buffer accesses:

- Physical read accesses: This value is the number of read accesses to the hard disk, and indicates how many blocks or pages must be loaded to satisfy the user queries being processed in an R/3 work process.

- Logical read accesses: This value is the total number of read accesses, and indicates how many blocks or pages are read from the buffer and the hard disk.

- Buffer quality or hit ratio: This value is given by the following relation:

  buffer quality=[(logical accesses–physical accesses)÷logical accesses]×100%

The smaller the number of physical accesses in relation to the number of logical accesses, the higher the buffer quality is. A buffer quality of 100% is ideal, and means that no database tables are read from disks. Instead, all required objects reside in the main memory of the database instance.

If the database instance has just been started, the buffer will just have been loaded, and the hit ratio is low. Therefore, when you evaluate the buffer quality, ensure that the database has already been in production operation for several hours.

In production systems, the size of the data buffer normally varies between 100MB and 500MB, depending on the size of the database. However, for large installations, the data buffer can be significantly larger.

Database Memory Areas

In an Informix database system, memory is divided into three areas whose respective sizes are shown under the header *Shared Memory* in the Database Performance Monitor (Transaction *ST04*). An example screen for the Informix Database Performance Monitor is shown in Figure 2.5.

NOTE The following section uses an Informix database to explain the various database memory areas. For information on other database systems, see Appendix B.

The following memory areas are shown for an Informix database:

- The *Resident Portion* of the shared memory contains, among other things, the data buffer and the buffer for the database log. When the database is started, the *Resident Portion* is allocated and is mainly taken up by the data buffer.

- The *Virtual Portion* of the shared memory covers, among other things, the memory for database processes called *session pools*. Their sizes are defined by the parameter SHMVIRTSIZE at database startup.

- The *Message Portion* is small and of no importance for tuning.

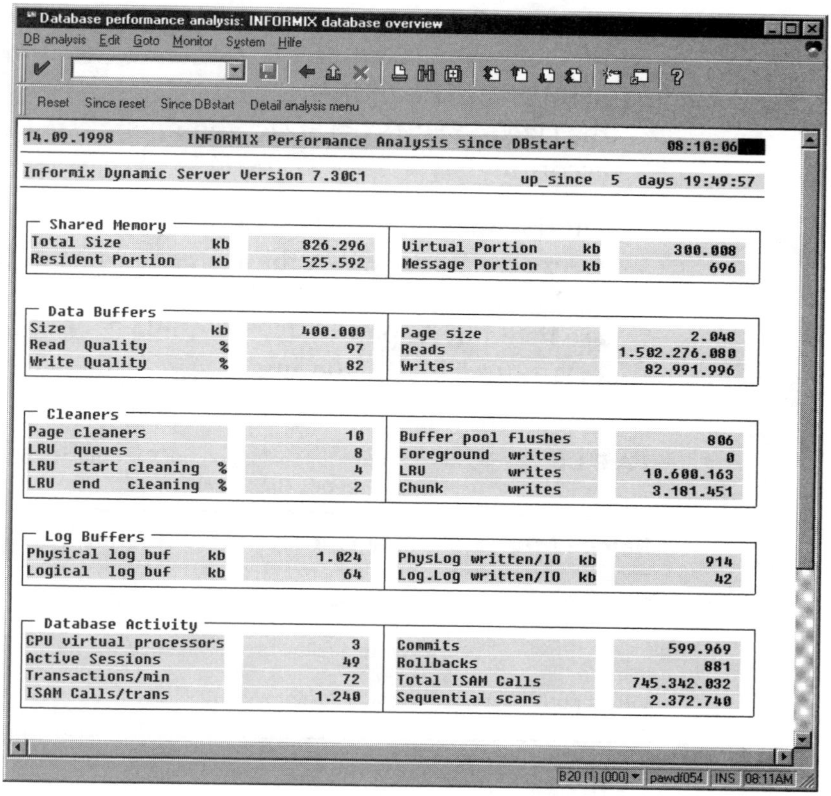

FIGURE 2.5:

Main screen of the
Database Performance
Monitor (for an
Informix database)

The *Virtual Portion* of the shared memory has the special feature
that it can enlarge itself while the database is running. However,
the enlargement process is resource-intensive. If you set the initial
size of the *Virtual Portion* parameter (SHMVIRTSIZE) too small,
you get continual enlargements during production operation,
which negatively impacts database performance. Therefore,
ensure that the database instance allocates sufficient memory to
the *Virtual Portion* at startup.

To verify the initial size of the *Virtual Portion*, before you stop the database, compare the current size of the *Virtual Portion* displayed in the Database Performance Monitor with the parameter SHMVIRTSIZE. If the current size of the *Virtual Portion* exceeds the size in SHMVIRTSIZE, you must increase the parameter accordingly.

If the operating system cannot provide sufficient memory, errors can occur when the *Virtual Portion* automatically enlarges. R/3 Notes containing explanations and solutions for the errors are listed in Appendix H. See Table 2.3 for an explanation of the key figures for evaluating the performance of database buffers.

TABLE 2.3: Key Figures for Evaluating the Performance of Database Buffers (for an Informix Database)

Name of Buffer	Key Figures (and Guideline Value)	Parameter
Data buffer	Read quality (greater than 95%)	BUFFERS
	Write quality (greater than 82%)	BUFFERS
Virtual portion	Virtual Portion=SHMVIRTSIZE	SHMVIRTSIZE

Data Buffer

In the initial screen of the R/3 Database Performance Monitor (Transaction *ST04*), under the header *Data Buffers*, you will find the most important information about the size and performance of the Informix data buffer. The size of the data buffer is defined with the parameter BUFFERS in the file ONCONFIG. To evaluate the *Read Quality* of the database buffer, you can use the general rule that the *Read Quality* should be higher than 95%, and the *Write Quality* should be higher than 82%.

The key figures to be considered when evaluating the database buffer with different database systems in the R/3 environment are listed in Appendix B, under "Monitoring Database." Poor buffering normally has two possible causes:

- Expensive SQL statements: These are the main cause for poor buffering in the data buffer and should be optimized with high priority. See "Identifying Expensive SQL Statements" in the present chapter.

- Data buffer is too small: If your database server still has sufficient main memory reserves, you can increase the respective buffer—for example, by 25%. Check whether the quality of buffering significantly improves as a result. If it does, you can try increasing the size of the buffer yet again. However, if this initial increase to the buffer has no effect, you need to look elsewhere for the cause of the poor buffer quality.

WARNING   These buffer quality values are only guideline values. In some cases, a database instance can still run well with a low buffer quality. Before investing time and energy in buffer optimization, perform a workload analysis to check the database response times (see Chapter 3).

Checkpoints and Savepoints

The data buffer of a database instance not only reduces the time required by database read accesses, it also speeds up database change operations. This is because a database change operation initially involves only changes to the respective data block in the data buffer. These changes are saved to the hard disk asynchronously—that is, at a later point in time—and this enables several change operations to be collected on a data block in the buffer before that block is saved to the hard disk. The database instance must write all the changed data blocks to the hard disks within a certain interval, defined by a *checkpoint* or a *savepoint*.

> **NOTE**   For all database systems, you can strategically define the frequency of checkpoints or savepoints by setting certain parameters. To find out which parameter defines the checkpoint for your specific database system, consult R/3 Online Documentation for the Database Performance Monitor. SAP's default parameter settings should be changed only after consulting SAP.

Number of Database Processors

For some database systems, you can specify the maximum number of processors that can be used by the database instance. For example, if you set the Informix parameter NUMCPUVPS to two, this tells the database instance to use only two processors, even if the database server has, for example, four processors.

To verify the setting of parameter NUMCPUVPS, call the Database Performance Monitor (Transaction *ST04*). The field *CPU virtual processors* (under the header *Database Activity*) indicates the maximum number of available processors for an Informix database (see Figure 2.5 earlier in this section).

Ensure that parameter NUMCPUVPS has the correct setting. If this parameter is set too small, there will not be enough CPU capacity available for the database instance, even if, in fact, CPU resources are still free.

Example: Configuring Logical Database Processors

A sample R/3 installation has a total of five computers. On the database server, there are four processors. Both the database instance and the central R/3 instance with enqueue and dialog work processes are located on the database server.

The Database Profile parameter, which limits the number of processors that the database instance can use, is set to one. Thus, the database instance can use only one processor. This assumes that the central R/3 instance also requires only one processor.

The Operating System Monitor (Transaction *ST06*) shows that there is an average CPU utilization of 50%, so there are no bottlenecks. However, you may see high database times with this configuration because one processor is normally too small to process database queries in a system with five computers.

If the Database Profile parameter that limits the number of processors used by the database instance is set too large, this can also limit performance. If the Database Profile parameter is set to four, the database instance has all of the processors to itself. The operating system and the R/3 instance with the enqueue work process would then suffer from a CPU bottleneck, causing the enqueue queries of all the R/3 instances to be processed very slowly.

NOTE   On computers with more than two processors, the maximum number of processors that can be used by the database instance is normally smaller than the number of the physically available processors. Chapter 6 provides guidelines on how many processors you should reserve for the database instance in an R/3 System.

Identifying Expensive SQL Statements

Expensive SQL statements are long-running statements and therefore one of the main causes for performance problems. In addition to causing long runtimes in the programs in which they are called, they also indirectly cause performance problems for other transactions or the entire system:

- They cause a high CPU utilization percentage and a high I/O load. This can lead to an acute hardware bottleneck on the database server, and reduces the performance of other programs.

- They block R/3 work processes for a long time. This means that user requests cannot be processed immediately and remain waiting in the R/3 dispatcher queue.

- They read many data blocks into the data buffer of the database server, which displaces data required by other SQL statements. This data must be read from the hard disk. The execution times of other SQL statements also increase.

It is not uncommon for a few expensive SQL statements to cause more than half of the entire load on the database server. Identifying these statements is therefore an important part of performance analysis.

Analyzing Currently Running SQL Statements

To help you identify any expensive SQL statements that are currently running, use the R/3 Database Process Monitor, which displays information from database monitors for SQL statements that are currently being executed.

NOTE This section uses a DB2 Universal Database (DB2 UDB) to explain how to identify expensive SQL statements that are currently running.

To call the Database Process Monitor, use Transaction *ST04* and choose *Detail analysis menu* ➤ *DB2 Applications*.

The screen *Database performance: Active Applications* appears. This monitor displays the currently active database processes, which, depending on the database system, may be called *agents*, *shadow processes*, or *threads*. To see the SQL statement being executed by one of the processes listed on the screen, double-click the process. The screen appears as shown in Figure 2.6.

FIGURE 2.6:

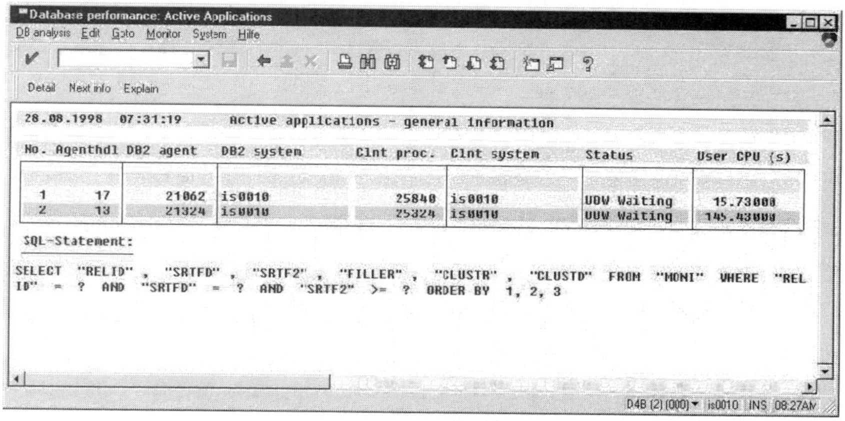

Database Process Monitor (for a DB2 Universal Database)

In the top section of the screen (after double-clicking a process), a selection of database processes is listed. For each process, the adjacent columns provide the following information:

- *DB2 agent:* This is the process ID (PID) of the database process.

- *DB2 system:* This is the name of the database server.

- *Clnt proc.* and *Clnt system:* These two columns indicate the process ID and application server of the allocated R/3 work process.

The bottom section of the same screen displays the SQL statement that is currently being executed by the database process currently selected.

Example: Reading the Database Process Monitor

In Figure 2.6, the database process with *2* in the column *No.* is currently executing the SQL statement SELECT "RELID", "SRTFD" ... FROM "MONI". The database process ID is 21324 on the database server is0010. The process ID of the related R/3 work process is 25324, and this process is also running on computer is0010. Clearly, this computer is both a database server and an application server.

Open a second user session and start the Systemwide Work Process Overview (Transaction *SM66*—see also "Analyzing R/3 Work Processes" in the present chapter).

To identify long-running SQL statements, you must continually refresh the monitors in both user sessions. Since both monitors display the application server and the PID of the related R/3 work process for the respective database processes, you can see which database process corresponds to which R/3 work process. From the two monitors, you can determine:

- Program names and R/3 transaction codes of the executed program (from the Work Process Overview)
- Table names (from the Work Process Overview and the Database Process Monitor)
- The user who started the program (from the Work Process Overview)
- WHERE conditions of the SQL statement (from the Database Process Monitor)
- Execution plan for the SQL statement (from the Database Process Monitor, using the *Explain* function—see Chapter 9)

This is all of the information that you require to perform a detailed analysis of an SQL statement.

Analyzing Previously Executed SQL Statements

For almost all the database systems, you can use R/3 to display various types of statistics on the previously executed SQL statements. These statistics cover, for example, the number of times an

SQL statement is executed, the number of logical and physical read accesses for each statement, and the number of lines read. For some database systems, these statistics are collected from the time the database was started; for other database systems, you must explicitly switch on these statistics. These are the statistics to use when analyzing expensive SQL statements.

NOTE   This section uses an Oracle database to explain how to view Shared SQL Area statistics in R/3 and then use them to identify expensive SQL statements.

For Oracle databases, monitoring statistics on previously executed SQL statements is commonly referred to as monitoring the Shared SQL Area (also referred to as the Shared Cursor Cache or the Shared SQL Cache). In this book, Shared SQL Area is also the collective term used for the previously executed SQL statements in database systems other than Oracle.

To monitor the Shared SQL Area in R/3, from the main screen in the Database Performance Monitor (Transaction *ST04*), choose *Detail analysis menu* and, under the header *Resource consumption by:*

- For Oracle, choose *SQL Request*.

- For Informix, choose *SQL Statement*.

In the dialog box that appears, change the automatically suggested selection values to zero and choose OK.

The screen *Database performance: Shared SQL* appears, listing all the SQL statements for which the database has statistics. Normally, these are all the statements that have been executed since database startup. The initial part of the SQL statement is located on the right side of the screen. To view the complete SQL statement, double-click the appropriate row. Figure 2.7 shows an example of this screen. For each SQL statement, the screen provides the data explained in Table 2.4.

TABLE 2.4: An Explanation of Columns in the R/3 Monitor for the Shared SQL Area
(for Oracle and Informix Databases)

Column	Explanation
Total Execution (Oracle and Informix)	Number of times the statement has been executed since the start of the database
Disk Reads (Oracle) or Page/Disk Reads (Informix)	Number of physical read accesses required for all the executions of the statement
Reads/Execution (Oracle) or Pg Reads/ Execution (Informix)	Number of physical read accesses required on average for one execution of the statement
Buffer Gets (Oracle) or Buffer Reads (Informix)	Number of logical read accesses required for all the executions of the statement
Gets/Execution (Oracle) or Buf.Read/Execution (Informix)	Number of logical read accesses required on average for one execution of the statement
Records processed (Oracle)	Number of rows read for all the executions of the statement

Continued on next page

TABLE 2.4: An Explanation of Columns in the R/3 Monitor for the Shared SQL Area (for Oracle and Informix Databases) *(Continued)*

Column	Explanation
Estimated Costs (Informix)	Estimated cost for the execution of the statement
Estimated Rows (Informix)	Estimated number of rows read for execution of the statement

Expensive SQL statements are indicated by a high number of logical read accesses and physical read accesses. Logical read accesses place a load on the CPU of the database server; physical read accesses place a load on the I/O system. To get the high numbers of accesses at the top of the list, sort the list according to the number of *Buffer Gets* (Oracle), *Buffer Reads* (Informix), *Disk Reads* (Oracle), or *Page/Disk Reads* (Informix). This organizes the expensive SQL statements in the order in which they require analysis and possible optimization.

Double-click a particular SQL statement in the Shared SQL Area monitor to find out:

- The table name

- WHERE conditions of the SQL statement

- Information provided by additional functions in the toolbar—for example, the Data Dictionary information and the execution plan for the SQL statement

Analyzing the Shared SQL Area using the Database Performance Monitor is an effective technique of performance analysis. However, considerable experience is required when it comes to deciding which of the expensive SQL statements can be optimized.

Identifying Expensive SQL Statements in the Shared SQL Area

To identify the most expensive SQL statements in the R/3 Database Performance Monitor for the Shared SQL Area, compare the indicated number of read accesses of a particular SQL statement with the number of read accesses for the entire database. To do this, in the screen *Database performance: Shared SQL*, proceed as follows:

1. Sort the Shared SQL Area by the column *Buffer Gets* (for an Oracle database).

2. Open a second user session and start the main screen of the Database Performance Monitor. Compare the data in the two sessions. The *Buffer Gets* in the Shared SQL Area correspond to the *Reads* in the main screen of the Database Performance Monitor; similarly, the *Disk Reads* in the Shared SQL Area correspond to the *Physical Reads* in the main screen of the Database Performance Monitor.

3. To calculate the percentage of all logical accesses made by a specific SQL statement, divide the number of *Buffer Gets* in the Shared SQL Area by the *Reads* in the main screen of the Database Performance Monitor.

4. Similarly, to calculate the percentage of all physical accesses made by an SQL statement, divide the *Disk Reads* in the Shared SQL Area by the *Physical Reads* in the main screen of the Database Performance Monitor.

5. If there are SQL statements that are causing more than 5% of the total logical or physical accesses on the entire database, tuning these statements normally improves database performance.

NOTE   For the detailed analysis and optimization of SQL statements, see Chapter 9. Before entering into a detailed analysis, however, you should look for R/3 Notes on the particular expensive SQL statements you have identified. Search for the R/3 Notes in SAP's Online Service System (OSS) using the search terms "performance" and the respective table name.

R/3 also has monitors for the Shared SQL Area of database systems other than Oracle and Informix (see Appendix B).

A further way of identifying expensive SQL statements is the SQL trace, which is discussed in Chapter 4.

Checking I/O Distribution

To achieve optimal database performance, I/O activity (read accesses and write accesses) should be evenly distributed on the hard disks of the database. For the database systems Oracle and Informix, there are R/3 monitors that display the I/O workload distribution at the file system level. From the main screen of the Database Performance Monitor (Transaction *ST04*), choose *Detail analysis menu* and start the relevant monitor as follows:

- For Oracle, choose *Filesystem requests*.
- For Informix, choose *Chunk I/O activity*.

For each file, the number of write and read operations is displayed. For Oracle, the write and read times are also listed, provided you have switched on the time statistics in the database.

Using this monitor, you can identify frequently used data files and ensure that they are located on different data mediums. This prevents the I/O requests for these objects from directly competing with each other.

For Oracle, to display statistics about wait situations on the file system level, choose *Goto* ➤ *Statistics* ➤ *File system waiting*.

Identifying I/O Bottlenecks

To identify whether there is an I/O bottleneck, use the Operating System Monitor (Transaction *ST06*) on the database server and choose *Detail analysis menu*. Then, choose *Disk* (under the header *Snapshot analysis*). The screen *Local* instance name/*OS Monitor* operating-system name appears, listing information about the load on the hard disks as well as wait times and response times for I/O operations on these disks.

There is a risk of an I/O bottleneck if:

- Individual disks have such a heavy load placed on them that the value in column *Util.%* is greater than 50%.

- Frequently accessed data files reside on these disks.

- Wait situations occur when you access these files.

You can resolve an I/O bottleneck by improving the table distribution on the file system (see previous section). In particular, ensure that the disks with a high load contain no additional frequently accessed files that could be relocated. The components listed in Table 2.5 are some of the most frequently accessed database objects. As a general rule, these objects should not reside on the same hard disk as the data files of the database, nor should they reside on a hard-disk array such as a RAID-5 system.

T A B L E 2 . 5 : Examples of Files and Database Objects with Large Amounts of Read/Write Activity

Database System	File or Database Object (and Priority of Optimizing Distribution for This File or Object)
Independent	Operating-system swap space (high priority)

Continued on next page

TABLE 2.5: Examples of Files and Database Objects with Large Amounts of Read/Write Activity *(Continued)*

Database System	File or Database Object (and Priority of Optimizing Distribution for This File or Object)
ADABAS D	Log area; system devspace
DB2 Universal Database	Online log directory (high priority); offline log directory (medium priority)
Informix	Dbspaces: ROOTDBS, PHSYDBS, and LOGDBS
Oracle	Redo log files (high priority); tablespace PSAPROLL (medium priority); directory for the offline redo log files (SAPARCH) (medium priority)
SQL Server	Transaction log (high priority); tempdb (medium priority)

To perform a detailed I/O analysis, you require the tools of the hardware manufacturer.

Additional R/3 Monitors for the Database

In addition to offering the above-mentioned monitors, the R/3 Database Performance Monitor also lets you monitor the following aspects of the database.

Exclusive Lock Waits

An *exclusive database lock* occurs when a user locks a row in a table—for example, with the SQL statement UPDATE or SELECT FOR UPDATE. If another user also tries to lock this row, that user has to wait until the first user releases the row. This wait situation is called an *exclusive lock wait*.

R/3's Exclusive Lockwaits Monitor (Transaction *DB01*) enables you to display exclusive lock waits for all database systems.

Alternatively, from the R/3 initial screen, choose either of the following menu paths:

- *Tools* ➤ *Administration* ➤ *Monitor* ➤ *Performance* ➤ *Database* ➤ *Exclusive lockwaits*

- *Tools* ➤ *Administration* ➤ *Monitor* ➤ *Performance* ➤ *Database* ➤ *Activity* ➤ *Detail analysis menu* ➤ *Exclusive lockwaits*

The Exclusive Lockwaits Monitor shows the following information for both the process holding the lock and the process waiting for the lock:

- ID of the database process.

- Client host (the name of the application server) and client PID (the process ID of the related R/3 work processes). This helps you find the related R/3 work processes in the R/3 Work Process Overview (Transaction *SM50* or *SM66*) and thus identify the program and the user holding the lock.

- Database-specific information such as the time since a lock was held, and information about the locked row.

Refresh this monitor several times to monitor the progress of wait situations caused by database locks.

To eliminate exclusive database locks, proceed as follows:

- If the Work Process Overview shows that the lock is being held by a database process that is not related to an R/3 work process, you can use operating-system tools to terminate the database process. This applies if, for example, an external program that is not related to the R/3 System is holding a lock, or if an error caused an R/3 work process to terminate and the related database process is not properly closed.

- If a program holds a lock for several minutes, you can contact the user who started the program. Together with the user, check whether the program is still working properly. If not, end the program after consulting the user.

- Determine whether the lock wait is due to users using programs in parallel in a way that ultimately causes the programs to lock the resources from each other. In this case, the user should study the documentation of the affected program and modify the way they are using the program, so they can avoid causing lock waits in the future.

- If none of the previous points apply, check whether there are other database performance problems that prevent SQL statements from being processed quickly and cause relatively long holds on database locks. After resolving these other database performance problems, check whether the database locks are released more quickly.

NOTE   Database locks are absolutely necessary to safeguard data consistency on the database. For this reason, short wait situations due to database locks should not be regarded as a performance problem. The situation becomes critical if locks are held for a long time and the wait situation cannot be resolved. This leads to a chain reaction where more and more users have to wait for locks. For more detailed information on database locks, see Chapter 8.

Database Alert Log File

Each database system writes messages in a file known as the database error log, database alert log, or database message log. This file is located in the database and contains important information about errors and the general condition of the database. You should regularly check this file. To view this file from R/3, choose:

Tools ➤ Administration ➤ Monitor ➤ Performance ➤ Database ➤ Activity ➤ Detail analysis menu ➤ Database message log (or *Database alert log)*

For more detailed information about the error messages, refer to the database manuals for your specific database.

Parameter Changes

The R/3 System logs all changes to database parameters. To view the change log, choose:

> *Tools* ➤ *Administration* ➤ *Monitor* ➤ *Performance* ➤ *Database* ➤ *Activity* ➤ *Detail analysis menu* ➤ *Parameter changes*

In the screen *Parameter changes of database*, choose *History of file*. From the dates of parameter changes indicated, you may be able to detect correlations between parameter changes and subsequent performance problems.

Update Statistics for the Cost-Based Optimizer

All the database systems that can be used in conjunction with the R/3 System use a cost-based optimizer, for which the relevant update-statistics program (a program gathering table statistics) must be scheduled to run regularly.

NOTE   The only database for which update statistics may not be required is the Oracle database, whose default setting is the rule-based optimizer prior to R/3 Release 4.0. To change the default setting for Oracle, use the Oracle profile parameter *OPTIMIZER_MODE*. To display the setting of this parameter, use Transaction *ST04* and choose *Detail analysis menu* ➤ *Parameter changes* ➤ *Active Parameters*. In the resulting list of active parameters, if the entry *OPTIMIZER_MODE* = CHOOSE is displayed, the cost-based optimizer is activated; if the parameter is set to RULE, the database uses the rule-based optimizer. For R/3 Releases prior to 4.0, this Oracle parameter must be set to RULE. As of R/3 Release 4.0, it must be set to CHOOSE. You should not use other settings unless explicitly advised to do so by SAP.

If your database uses a cost-based optimizer, update statistics on the sizes of tables and indexes must be generated regularly. The optimizer needs these statistics to create the correct execution plans for SQL statements. The administrator should regularly schedule the relevant update-statistics program. If these statistics are missing or obsolete, the optimizer creates ineffective access paths, which can lead to massive performance problems. Update statistics do not need to be generated for a rule-based optimizer.

To check whether the relevant update-statistics program has been scheduled, open the DBA Planning Calendar. To do this, from the R/3 initial screen, choose:

Tools ➤ *CCMS* ➤ *DB administration* ➤ *DBA scheduling*

The DBA Planning Calendar appears. If the update-statistics program is scheduled, you will regularly see the entry *AnalyzeTab* (for Oracle), *Update sta0* (for Informix), or *Update Statistics* (for SQL Server). View the logs regularly to check that the runs of the update-statistics program were successful.

NOTE   To generate update statistics, it is essential that you use the R/3 tools, such as the DBA Planning Calendar or, alternatively, the program SAPDBA. The statistics generated through these tools are specifically adapted to the SQL statements that are used by the R/3 System.

For more information about update statistics, see Chapter 9 and the relevant R/3 Notes listed in Appendix H. You can find additional information about the DBA Planning Calendar in the R/3 Online Documentation.

Missing Database Indexes

Missing database indexes can lead to significant reduction in system performance. To check the consistency of the indexes between the ABAP Dictionary and the database, use Transaction *DB02* or, from the initial screen of the R/3 System, choose:

> *Tools* ➢ *Administration* ➢ *Monitor* ➢ *Performance* ➢ *Database* ➢ *Tables/Indexes*

Then, choose *Missing indexes*. The screen *Database Performance: Tables and Indexes* appears, showing the number of problematic indexes, if any. The display of the missing indexes is divided into primary and secondary indexes. For instructions on creating indexes, see Chapter 9 under "Administering Indexes and Table Statistics."

WARNING   If a primary index is missing, the consistency of the data is no longer ensured. There is a danger that duplicate keys can be written. Furthermore, a missing primary index causes ineffective database accesses; in cases of large tables, this can then lead to massive performance problems. This status is critical for the system and requires immediate intervention by the database administrator.

Database Not Responding

If the database instance no longer responds, this soon causes the R/3 System to stop responding. The database instance stops responding particularly when critical memory areas of the database are full, such as the file system, or log areas such as the redo log files (for Oracle) or the transaction log (for SQL Server). Database errors that can cause the database to stop responding are especially likely to occur when a large volume of data is updated on the database—for example, when data transfers or client copies are performed. Consider the following examples of how an error situation on the database can cause the R/3 System to stop responding.

Example 1: Oracle Archiver Stuck

Because of fully used-up log areas, the database and the R/3 System are no longer responding, with the following results:

1. Because of an administration error or incorrect capacity planning, the redo log files for Oracle are full. As of this moment, no further database operations are possible. In the Oracle environment, this situation is called Archiver Stuck. The database instance writes an error message in the database error log file such as *All online log files need archiving*.

2. Every R/3 work process that tries to execute a database change operation will be unable to complete. You can view this process in the Work Process Overview (Transaction *SM50* or *SM66*).

3. Soon, there are no more R/3 work processes available, and the R/3 System stops responding. All users who send a request to the R/3 System must wait.

4. Normally, the error situation can be resolved without having to stop the R/3 System or the database. The data in the log area must be archived.

5. After archiving, the database instance can resume work and process the accumulated requests.

Example 2: Database File Overflow

R/3 is no longer responding because the database files have become full:

1. While attempting to fill data into a database table through an INSERT operation, an error occurs in the database because a database file is full or the hard disk is full. The database instance then returns an error message to the R/3 work process that called it, and the error message is written to the database error log file.

2. If the error occurs during an R/3 update, the work process deactivates the entire R/3 update service. As of this moment, R/3 update requests receive no response. To determine whether the update service has been deactivated, display update records. To do this, use Transaction *SM13*, or, from the R/3 initial screen, choose:

    Tools ➢ *Administration* ➢ *Monitor* ➢ *Update*

3. In the screen *Update Records: Main Menu*, determine whether the field *Status* displays the message *Updating by system deactivated*. If so, to find the associated error message and user, look at the R/3 system log (Transaction *SM21*).

4. Once updates are no longer being completed, dialog work processes, which are waiting for the updates to finish, will gradually stop responding. You can view this process in the Work Process Overview (Transaction *SM50* or *SM66*).

5. The error situation can normally be resolved without stopping the R/3 System or the database. First resolve the database error—for example, by expanding the file system. Then, activate the R/3 update service manually. To do this, from the R/3 initial screen, choose:

    Tools ➢ *Administration* ➢ *Monitor* ➢ *Update* ➢ *Update records* ➢ *Update* ➢ *Activate*

6. Now the R/3 update service can resume processing update requests.

The update service was stopped to enable the database administrator to correct a database error without terminating the updates. If the update service were not stopped, other update work processes would also be affected by the same database error. If the database error is not found quickly enough, many hundreds of terminated updates may result, all of which must then be individually updated by the users.

Ensuring that the database remains operational is a database administration task rather than a matter for performance optimization, and is therefore not covered in this book. See the literature on database administration and set up a contingency plan tailored to your company that provides procedures to:

- Ensure that the filling up of the log area or file system is detected well in advance.

- Determine which database error has occurred if the R/3 System is not responding.

- Explain how to locate the database error log file and which error messages are critical.

- Determine what must be done if an error occurs and whether the R/3 System or the database must be restarted.

- Simulate error situations and response procedures in a test system.

Summary

Performance problems in the database instance affect the performance of the entire R/3 System. Performance monitoring for this instance therefore has a high priority, and consists of the following tasks (listed in order of priority):

- Keep your database engine running. Database failure quickly brings R/3 to a standstill. Regularly monitor the fill level of the file system and the database log area—for example, the redo log files (for Oracle) or the transaction log (for SQL Server).

- Ensure that the database server has sufficient CPU and storage capacity. More than 20% CPU should be idle, and the paging rate should be low.

- If your database system has a profile parameter that limits the maximum number of processes that the database instance can occupy, check that this parameter's setting is neither too small nor too large.

- Ensure that individual hard disks are not showing more than 50% utilization in the Operating System Monitor.

- Check whether the configuration and performance of the database buffers are adequate, as outlined above.

- Identify and optimize any SQL statements that contribute more than 5% of the entire database load.

- Remove the causes of long lock waits.

- Ensure that table statistics for the cost-based optimizer are updated frequently, and regularly check the consistency of the database and look for missing indexes.

Monitoring R/3 Memory Configuration

To start the R/3 Memory Configuration Monitor for the R/3 instance you are currently logged on to, use Transaction *ST02*, or, from the R/3 initial screen, choose:

Tools ➤ *Administration* ➤ *Monitor* ➤ *Performance* ➤ *Setup/Buffers* ➤ *Buffers*

The screen *Tune Summary* instance name appears (see Figure 2.8.), displaying information on the configuration and the utilization of R/3 memory areas for the instance. The data shown corresponds to the time since R/3 instance startup.

FIGURE 2.8: R/3 Memory Configuration Monitor (Transaction *ST02*)

```
Tune Summary [pswdf727_TCD_00]
Tune  Edit  Goto  Environment  Monitor  System  Help

Current parameters    Detail analysis menu
```

System	: pswdf727_TCD_00	Tune summary	
Date & time of snapshot: 27.10.1998 11:29:46		Startup: 27.10.1998 10:46:38	

Buffer	Hitratio [%]	Allocated [kB]	Free space [kB]	Free space [%]	Dir. size Entries	Free directory Entries	Free directory [%]	Swaps	Database accesses
Nametab (NTAB)									
Table definition	98,89	5.043	3.822	93,17	30.000	27.952	93,17	0	4.406
Field description	95,75	5.348	614	20,47	60.001	59.607	99,34	10.387	11.055
Short NTAB	99,72	4.848	2.381	95,24	60.001	59.328	98,88	0	673
Initial records	99,55	6.348	3.532	88,30	60.001	58.388	97,31	0	1.613
Program	82,90	121.785	21.980	18,32	15.000	14.162	94,41	4.034	14.616
CUA	99,99	5.000	3.680	78,21	2.500	2.340	93,60	0	184
Screen	99,98	9.766	8.495	89,90	4.500	4.368	97,07	0	144
Calendar	83,85	488	403	84,31	200	99	49,50	0	101
Tables									
Generic key	99,93	48.828	39.398	83,17	10.000	9.358	93,58	0	1.020
Single record	99,66	30.000	29.260	97,73	500	449	89,80	0	0
Export/import	47,31	4.096	3.691	98,03	2.000	1.901	95,05	0	0
Message	100,00	9.766	9.432	100,00	4.500	4.500	100,00	0	0

SAP memory	Current use [%]	Current use [kB]	Max. use [kB]	In memory [kB]	On disk [kB]	SAP cursor cache	Hitratio [%]	Free Entries	Free [%]
Roll area	23,12	18.680	37.248	8.000	72.800	IDs	97,92	7.076	74,48
Paging area	0,15	384	912	40.320	221.824	Statements	58,00	1.867	39,31
Extended Memory	99,20	252.928	254.976	254.976					
Heap Memory		784	8.259						

```
TCD (1) (900)   pswdf727  INS  11:25AM
```

Analyzing R/3 Buffers

In the upper half of the R/3 Memory Configuration Monitor (Transaction *ST02*), the rows grouped under the header *Buffer* list the various R/3 buffers. Table 2.6 explains the columns corresponding to these buffers.

TABLE 2.6: An Explanation of Columns in the R/3 Memory Configuration Monitor Referring to R/3 Buffers

Column	Explanation
Hitratio	The percentage of data accesses that are satisfied by the buffer and do not require database accesses
Allocated	Maximum amount of memory area that can be occupied by the respective buffer, as defined by the parameter limiting the buffer size
Free space	Currently unoccupied memory space in the respective buffer
Dir. size Entries	Maximum number of objects that can be stored in the buffer
Free directory Entries	Difference between the current number of objects stored in the buffer and the maximum possible number of objects
Swaps	Number of buffer objects displaced from the buffer
Database accesses	Number of database accesses (which is also the number of data transfers from the database into the buffer)

As with the database buffer, the R/3 buffer also has to achieve a minimum hit ratio (also known as buffer quality) to ensure smooth operation of the R/3 System. If the buffers are too small, data is displaced, and the database has to be unnecessarily accessed to reload the buffer. When an object is loaded into the buffer and the free space in the buffer is too small to completely store the object, other objects have to be displaced from the buffer to make space available. The number of displacements is referred to in the Memory Configuration Monitor as the number of *swaps* (indicated in the column *Swaps*). For example, the number of swaps for the *Program* buffer and the *Field description* buffer are highlighted in Figure 2.8 (earlier in this section).

When monitoring the R/3 buffers, consider the following guidelines:

- The hit ratio for the R/3 buffers should generally be 98% or better. Hit ratios less than 98% can be regarded as acceptable only for the *Program* buffer, the *Single record* buffer, and the *Export/import* buffer.

- There should be no swaps (displacements) in the buffers of a production system. If there are swaps, however, the buffer size or the maximum number of entries should be increased. Here again, the exception is the *Program* buffer, for which approximately 10,000 swaps per day represents an acceptable number of buffer displacements.

- To help avoid subsequent displacements, ensure that each buffer has sufficient memory (indicated as *Free space*) and free entries (indicated as *Free directory Entries*).

Buffer Settings

If, in the Memory Configuration Monitor, you see that there have been displacements in an R/3 buffer (indicated as *Swaps*), proceed as follows:

1. Check whether the buffer is too small (indicated by there being no free space in the buffer) or whether the maximum number of possible buffer entries is too small (indicated by there being no free directory entries for the buffer).

2. Either increase the buffer size or the maximum number of allowed entries by 10% to 50%. To find out the relevant R/3 profile parameters, choose *Current parameters* from the main screen of the Memory Configuration Monitor. Before increasing the buffer size, ensure that the computer still has sufficient main memory reserves (see below, under "Displaying the Allocated Memory"); otherwise, you run the risk of a memory bottleneck.

Displacements and Invalidations

Do not confuse displacements with invalidations, which are not indicated in the column *Swaps* in the Memory Configuration Monitor.

Invalidation is when a buffered object such as a program or table is declared invalid because it has been changed. For example, invalidations occur when programs or Customizing settings have been transported into a production system or have been changed in production operation.

The effect of invalidations is to lower the hit ratio and cause objects to be reloaded from the database. Therefore, it is recommended that transports be scheduled one or two times per week when the system load is low.

Appendix C lists all R/3 buffers and the related R/3 profile parameters. To find out your current settings, call the R/3 Memory Configuration Monitor (Transaction *ST02*) and choose *Current parameters*.

NOTE Problems with table buffers may also be due to tables that are too large for buffering (see Chapter 7).

Analyzing R/3 Memory Areas

In the lower half of the R/3 Memory Configuration Monitor (Transaction *ST02*), the rows grouped under the header *SAP memory* contain some basic performance data for the various R/3 memory areas: R/3 *Roll area*, R/3 *Paging area*, R/3 *Extended Memory*, and R/3 *Heap Memory*. (For a more thorough investigation of R/3 memory areas, see Chapter 5.) The memory areas in the Memory Configuration Monitor are indicated in Figure 2.8 (earlier in this section) and explained in Table 2.7.

TABLE 2.7: An Explanation of Columns in the R/3 Memory Configuration Monitor (*ST02*) Referring to R/3 Memory Areas

Column	Explanation
Current use	Amount of memory currently in use in the respective memory area.
Max. use	Maximum amount of this memory area that has been used since the R/3 instance was started (also known as the high-water mark).
In memory	The amount of main memory allocated to this area at system startup. (For the R/3 *Roll area* and the R/3 *Paging area*, this space corresponds to the R/3 roll buffer and the R/3 paging buffer.)
On disk	The size of files (if any) that are part of this area and are located on the hard disk of the application server. Only the R/3 *Roll area* and the R/3 *Paging area* partly exist in such files (the R/3 roll file and the R/3 paging file).

When monitoring the R/3 memory areas in the Memory Configuration Monitor, consider the following guidelines:

- For the R/3 *Roll area*, the value in the column *Max. use* should not exceed the corresponding amount in the column *In memory*. In other words, the roll file should not be used.

- For the R/3 *Extended Memory*, the value in the column *Max. use* should be a minimum of 20% smaller than the corresponding amount in the column *In memory*. This ensures that there will continue to be sufficient free extended memory.

In the example in Figure 2.8 (earlier in this section), almost 100% of R/3 extended memory is in use. In addition, more roll memory is being used than is available in the roll buffer (*Max. use* is larger than *In memory*).

If you detect the problem that the roll memory or the extended memory requires all of the memory allocated to these areas at R/3 instance startup, increase the values in the R/3 profile parameters `rdisp/ROLL_SHM` and `em/initial_size_MB` (provided there is sufficient physical memory). Check whether this solves the problem. If the problem persists, see Chapter 5.

TIP   Experience shows that performance is dramatically reduced when R/3 extended memory is full, making it impossible to work productively in the R/3 instances. Therefore, monitoring the R/3 extended memory should have high priority. You can afford to allocate R/3 extended memory generously. Since unused R/3 extended memory is swapped out by the operating system, an overly large extended memory does not negatively affect performance.

Depending on the R/3 Release and the R/3 application module, use the following allocation guidelines when configuring R/3 extended memory:

- Allocate 6MB to 10MB of extended memory for each user.

- Allocate 70% to 120% of the computer's physical main memory as extended memory.

Ensure that the swap space on the operating-system level is large enough. Ensure also that the operating system can administer the desired memory size. (For a discussion of operating-system limits, see Chapter 5.)

Parameters for Memory Area Configuration

To display the current system settings, choose *Current parameters* in the Memory Configuration Monitor (Transaction *ST02*). Appendix C lists all the relevant R/3 profile parameters for the R/3 memory areas.

Zero Administration Memory Management

In R/3 Release 4.0, SAP introduces *Zero Administration Memory Management*, which, when implemented, makes manual settings unnecessary. Zero Administration dynamically allocates memory based on the hardware available to the R/3 instance, and adapts memory management settings automatically.

> **NOTE** For R/3 Release 4.0, Zero Administration Memory Management is available for Windows NT (see R/3 Note 88416). Other operating systems will follow.

Zero Administration Memory Management requires only one R/3 profile parameter: *PHYS_MEMSIZE*. This parameter defines how much of the computer's main memory should be used for the R/3 instance. If no value is entered in the instance profile for *PHYS_ MEMSIZE*, the full amount of physical main memory is automatically set for this parameter. All other memory management settings are automatically calculated on the basis of *PHYS_MEMSIZE*.

> **NOTE** After an upgrade to R/3 Release 4.0, all the R/3 profile parameters for memory management should be deleted from the instance profiles. For instances on the same computer as the database, set the parameter PHYS_MEMSIZE to limit the memory of the R/3 instance appropriately. In R/3 Release 4.0, Zero Administration Memory Management covers only R/3 extended memory, R/3 heap memory, R/3 roll memory, and R/3 paging memory. The R/3 buffers still have to be set manually.

Displaying the Allocated Memory

To find out the current memory allocations of the R/3 instance you are logged on to, use Transaction *ST02*, or, from the R/3 initial screen, choose:

Tools ➢ *Administration* ➢ *Monitor* ➢ *Performance* ➢ *Setup/ Buffers* ➢ *Buffers* ➢ *Detail analysis menu* ➢ *Storage* (the option *Storage* is located at the bottom of the screen under the header *Additional functions*)

The screen *Storage usage and requirements* appears. Figure 2.9 shows an example of this screen, and Table 2.8 describes the meanings of key figures in this screen.

FIGURE 2.9:

Display of allocated memory in the *Storage usage and requirements* screen of the Memory Configuration Monitor

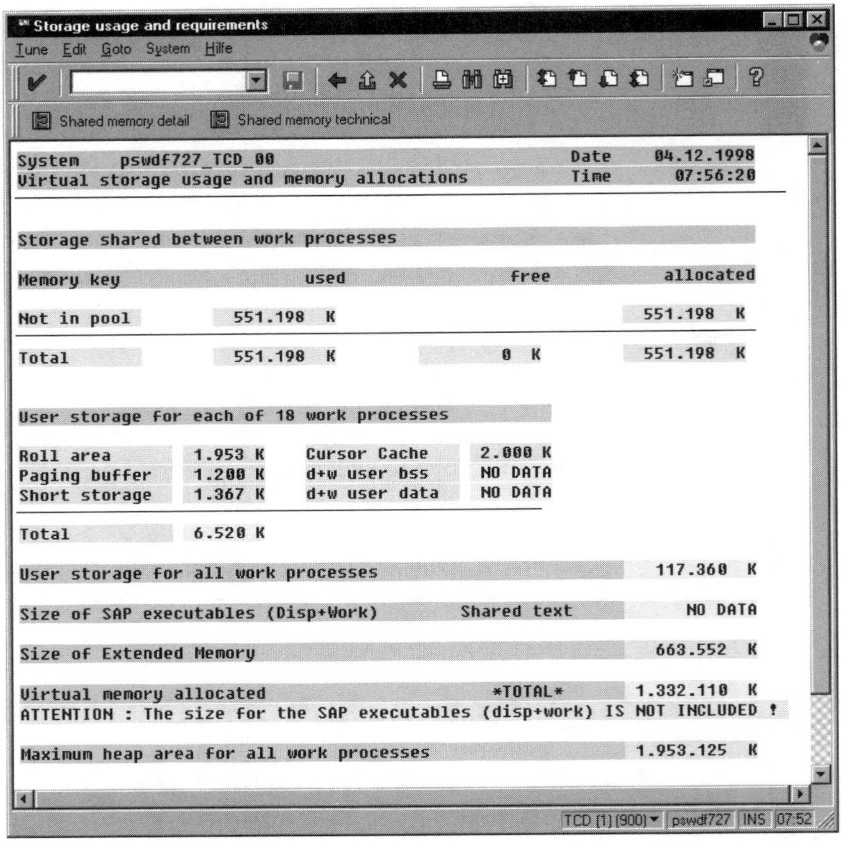

TABLE 2.8: Key Figures in the *Storage usage and requirements* Screen of the Memory Configuration Monitor (*ST02*)

Section of Screen	Key Figures
Storage shared between work processes	The value in the row *Total* for the column *allocated* is the total memory allocated to the R/3 buffers. (For UNIX operating systems, this section also displays the values for the allocated, used, and free memory space for each Shared Memory Pool.)
User storage for all work processes	This value is the size of the memory allocated for the R/3 work processes.
Size of Extended Memory	This value is the size of the memory allocated to the R/3 extended memory.
Virtual memory allocated	This value is the size of the total memory allocated at instance startup to the R/3 buffer, R/3 work processes, and R/3 extended memory. This is the critical value for assessing whether main memory bottlenecks are likely to occur.
Maximum heap area for all work processes	This value is the size of the R/3 heap memory that can be allocated as local memory by the R/3 work processes, if required. This value corresponds to the parameter *abap/heap_ area_total*.

To ensure that the total memory allocated by R/3 is not significantly disproportionate to the physically available main memory, compare allocated and physical memory. Begin by calculating the allocated memory as follows:

1. Obtain the amount of memory allocated by an R/3 instance since startup. This value is indicated as *Virtual memory allocated* (see Figure 2.9). If there are multiple instances on the computer, the values for all the R/3 instances should be added.

2. If the instance is on the same computer as the database, add the memory requirement of the database. (Rather than adding this value here, you can subtract it from the amount of physical

memory for the sake of the comparison.) To find out the database memory requirement, see the Database Performance Monitor (Transaction *ST04*).

3. Add around 50MB to 100MB for the main memory requirements of the operating system. (Again, rather than adding this value here, you can subtract it from the amount of physical memory for the sake of the comparison.)

To find out the amount of physically available memory on the computer, see the Operating System Monitor (Transaction *ST06*).

Normally, the amount of allocated memory is significantly larger than the amount of physically available memory. However, as a general rule of thumb, we assume that no critical paging should occur when the allocated memory is less than 50% larger than the physically available memory. If this limit is exceeded, use the Operating System Monitor to check the paging rates and the Workload Monitor to analyze the response times to determine whether there is a memory bottleneck.

You can use the *Storage usage and requirements* screen of the Memory Configuration Monitor to determine whether there is sufficient swap space at the operating-system level. First, calculate the maximum memory that can be allocated by the R/3 System—add the values of *Virtual memory allocated* and *Maximum heap area for all work processes*. When added to the memory requirements of any other systems on the same computer (such as a database, the operating system, and possibly other systems), the maximum allocable memory area should be smaller than the sum of the physically available main memory and the swap space. Otherwise, system failure may occur.

Other Monitors in the Memory Configuration Monitor

To access two additional R/3 monitors for R/3 buffer usage, from the Memory Configuration Monitor (Transaction *ST02*), choose:

Detail analysis menu ➢ *Call statistics*

and

Detail analysis menu ➢ *Buffer synchron*

Both of these monitors are explained in Chapter 7.

To access a monitor that shows a log of all changes to the R/3 parameters, from the Memory Configuration Monitor (Transaction *ST02*), choose:

Detail analysis menu ➢ *Parameters*

Alternatively, from the R/3 initial screen, choose:

Tools ➢ *Administration* ➢ *Monitor* ➢ *Performance* ➢ *Setup/Buffers* ➢ *Parameter changes*

Mark an application server and choose *History of file*. Note that very recent changes may not yet appear in the log. This monitor enables you to check for parameter changes that are linked to performance problems.

Summary

When you set the profile parameters for R/3 memory management, you define how much virtual memory can be allocated by an R/3 instance. You can allocate more memory virtually than is physically available, but if the combined memory allocations of all instances, systems, and programs on a computer are more than around 1.5 times the amount of physical memory, monitor the paging rates and response times more closely.

The R/3 Memory Configuration Monitor enables you to monitor the size and usage of the R/3 memory areas. Displacements should not occur in the R/3 buffers—with the exception of the program buffer, which may have up to 10,000 displacements each day. Ensure that neither the extended memory nor the roll buffer become full.

Make it a top priority to monitor the R/3 extended memory. If this memory is fully used up, productive work ceases, and immediate action is required to solve the problem. One solution is to increase the size of the extended memory; you should also check whether there are programs with excessive memory consumption that can be terminated or improved (see Chapter 5, under "Planning or Reviewing Your Memory Configuration" and "Troubleshooting").

If you detect displacements in the following R/3 buffers, adapt the corresponding parameters with medium priority (that is, within several days):

- The buffers TTAB, FTAB, SNTAB, and IRDB
- Roll buffers, program buffers, and table buffers

The settings of the following buffers have a somewhat lower priority:

- CUA buffer and screen buffer
- R/3 paging buffer

Note that the size of allocable memory is affected by operating system–specific limitations such as the maximum size of allocable shared memory and the maximum address space (see Chapter 5). If you change the memory configuration, check whether the new parameters allow the R/3 instance to start without error. See Figure 2.10 for a review of how to analyze R/3 memory configuration.

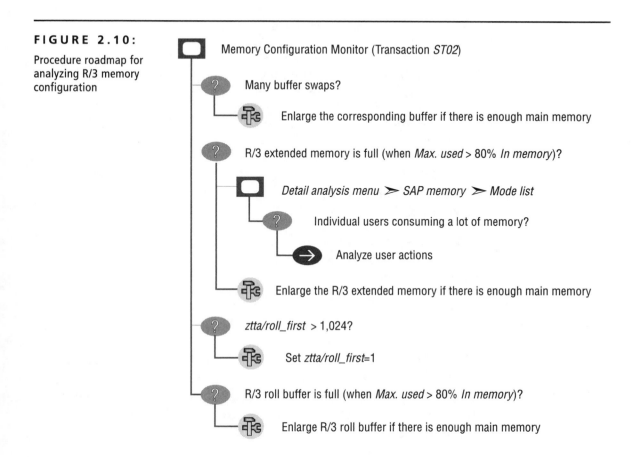

FIGURE 2.10:

Procedure roadmap for analyzing R/3 memory configuration

Memory Configuration Monitor (Transaction *ST02*)

Many buffer swaps?

Enlarge the corresponding buffer if there is enough main memory

R/3 extended memory is full (when *Max. used* > 80% *In memory*)?

Detail analysis menu ➤ *SAP memory* ➤ *Mode list*

Individual users consuming a lot of memory?

Analyze user actions

Enlarge the R/3 extended memory if there is enough main memory

ztta/roll_first > 1,024?

Set *ztta/roll_first*=1

R/3 roll buffer is full (when *Max. used* > 80% *In memory*)?

Enlarge R/3 roll buffer if there is enough main memory

Monitoring R/3 Work Processes

To display data on the R/3 work processes active on a particular application server, log on to that server and call the R/3 monitor known as the Local Work Process Overview. Use Transaction *SM50*, or, from the R/3 initial screen, choose:

Tools ➤ *Administration* ➤ *Monitor* ➤ *System monitoring* ➤ *Process Overview*

The screen *Process Overview* appears.

To see which R/3 work processes are configured on each server in your R/3 System, call the List of Servers with Transaction *SM51*, or, from the R/3 initial screen, choose:

Tools ➤ *Administration* ➤ *Monitor* ➤ *System monitoring* ➤ *Servers*

From *SM51*, to access the Local Work Process Overview for any of the listed servers, place the cursor on the desired application server and choose *Processes*.

To see a systemwide overview of all the work processes in the R/3 System, start the Systemwide Work Process Overview with Transaction *SM66*, or, from the R/3 initial screen, choose:

Tools ➤ *Administration* ➤ *Monitor* ➤ *Performance* ➤ *Exceptions/Users* ➤ *Active users* ➤ *All processes*

If a given performance problem has escalated so far that the Work Process Overview can no longer be called for that R/3 System, you can alternatively start the auxiliary program *dpmon* on the operating-system level. To view the Work Process Overview, in the menu that appears, choose *l*.

Interpreting the Work Process Overview

Table 2.9 describes the various columns that provide data on the R/3 work processes listed in the Local Work Process Overview (Transaction *SM50*—see Figure 2.11).

FIGURE 2.11:

The Local Work Process Overview (Transaction *SM50*). Notice that all the dialog work processes are occupied, which suggests a performance problem.

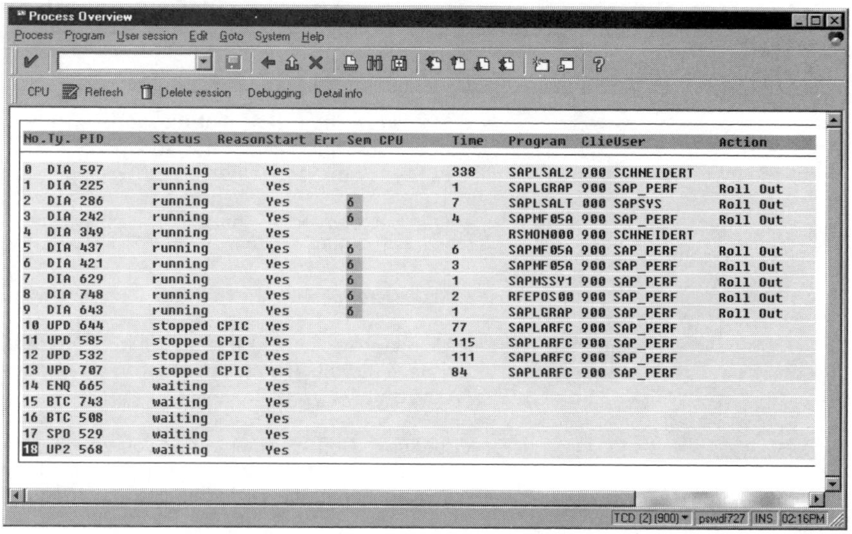

TABLE 2.9: An Explanation of the Columns Referring to Work Processes in the Local Work Process Overview (*SM50*)

Column	Explanation
No.	Each work process is numbered serially, and this number is unique for each R/3 instance. This number and the R/3 instance name (or the computer name and the process ID) uniquely identify an R/3 work process in an R/3 System.
Ty.	Type of work process—for example, DIA (dialog), BTC (background), UPD (update), ENQ (enqueue), or SPO (spool).
PID	Process ID for the operating system (unique for each computer).
Status	The status of each work process. For example: • Status *waiting* shows that the process is available for a user request. Normally there should always be sufficient work processes with status *waiting*; otherwise, users will experience poor response times.

Continued on next page

TABLE 2.9: An Explanation of the Columns Referring to Work Processes in the Local Work Process Overview (*SM50*) *(Continued)*

Column	Explanation
	• Status *running* means that the work process is processing a user request. To determine which action the work process is executing at the moment, look in the column *Action/Reason for waiting*.
	• Status *ended* means that the process was terminated because of an error in the R/3 kernel.
	• Status *stopped* means that the process is waiting.
Reason	For work processes with the status *stopped*, this column explains the reason for the wait time. (For information on the various reasons, see below, under "Analyzing R/3 Work Processes.")
Start	With Yes or No, this column tells you whether, for a given work process, the dispatcher is set to restart the work process if the work process terminates. (You can change the setting in this column by using the menu.)
Err	Number of times the work process has been terminated.
Sem	Number of the current semaphore indicating the type of semaphore. A number with a green background shows that this work process is holding a semaphore. A number with a red background shows that the work process is waiting for the semaphore.
CPU	The CPU time used by the work process so far (in minutes and seconds).
Time	The elapsed processing time for the current request (in seconds).
Program	Name of the program currently being executed.
Clie	Client.
User	Name of the user whose request is currently being executed.
Action /Reason for waiting	For work processes with the status *running*, this field displays the current action.
Table	The database table that was last accessed by the work process.

More about Process IDs

The combination of computer and process ID enables you to clearly identify an R/3 work process in an R/3 System. The process ID is also used in the following monitors:

- Process Overview in the Operating System Monitor: To access this monitor, use Transaction *ST06,* and then choose *Detail analysis menu* ➢ *Top CPU Processes.* This monitor enables you to determine how much CPU load a specific work process is creating.

- Database Process Monitor (for the DB2 Universal Database): To access this monitor, use Transaction *ST04,* and then choose *Detail analysis menu* ➢ *DB2 Applications.* This monitor enables you to determine which SQL statement is currently being processed by a work process.

- Database Lock Monitor: To access this monitor, use Transaction *ST04,* then choose *Detail analysis menu* ➢ *Exclusive lock-waits.* This monitor enables you to determine whether a work process is currently holding a database lock or waiting for a lock to be released.

In summary, these four monitors—the Work Process Overview, the Process Overview in the Operating System Monitor, the Database Process Monitor, and the Database Lock Monitor—provide you with an extensive overview of the current situation with regard to work processes in your R/3 System.

More about Semaphores

Every application server has resources that can be used by only one work process at a time. If an R/3 work process wants to use these resources, it sets a *semaphore.* If other processes also require this resource, they have to wait until the process that is holding the process has completed its action. If, for example, an entry in an R/3 buffer needs to be changed, a semaphore is set because only one process can perform changes in the buffer.

Each type of semaphore has its own number. For example, if a work process changes the program buffer, it must request sema- phore 1. If several processes are waiting for a semaphore, this is called *serialization*. The semaphore number 6 is set during roll in or roll out, so only one process at a time can perform a roll in or roll out.

Problems That Can Be Detected Using the Local Work Process Overview

If you watch the Work Process Overview for several minutes and repeatedly choose the *Refresh* button to update the display, you can usually determine whether there is a current performance problem related to work processes on the R/3 instance, and you can roughly estimate its cause. The key indication suggesting a performance problem for work processes is when all the work processes of a particular type (such as dialog or update) are occupied.

Under the following headings, each referring to a particular performance problem, you will learn how to recognize the prob- lem in the Work Process Overview. You will also learn which other tools can help you find out more about the problem.

Long Database Response Times

There is a problem in the database area if the Work Process Overview in the column *Action* shows numerous database-related actions such as Sequential Read, Direct Read, Update, Commit, or Waiting for DB Lock.

You can proceed by looking for expensive SQL statements or database locks. To do this, start two additional user sessions and call the Database Process Monitor (*ST04* ➤ *Detail analysis menu* ➤ *DB2 Applications* or *Oracle Session* [for example]) and the Database Lock Monitor (Transaction *DB01*).

Deactivated Update Service

A deactivated update service is indicated if you find that all the update work processes (UPD) in the Work Process Overview are occupied, and the column *Action/Reason for waiting* indicates a database activity such as Sequential Read, Direct Read, Update, or Commit.

Check whether the update service has been deactivated using the monitor Display Update Records (Transaction *SM13*). If the update has been deactivated, there will be a message in the column *Status* that reads *Update by system deactivated*.

To find out who deactivated the update service, when, and for what reason, look in the R/3 system log (Transaction *SM21*). As soon as the underlying problem is resolved—for example, a database error—you can reactivate the update work process in Transaction *SM13*.

Problems with R/3 Memory Configuration

Problems with R/3 memory configuration are often indicated in the Work Process Overview as follows:

- The entries Roll In or Roll Out in the column *Action/Reason for waiting*. This is accompanied by a semaphore of type 6.

- Numerous occurrences of *stopped* (in the column *Status*) with the corresponding entry PRIV (in the column *Reason*). This indicates that there are numerous work processes in Private mode.

NOTE	Figure 2.8 (the Memory Configuration Monitor—earlier in this chapter) and Figure 2.11 (the Local Work Process Overview—earlier in this section) are screenshots that were taken at the same time, and indicate a performance problem. The problem is more evident in the Local Work Process Overview (Figure 2.11), in which you can see that almost all the work processes are in the roll-out phase. Furthermore, the Memory Configuration Monitor (Figure 2.8) shows that the cause for the wait situation is that both the R/3 extended memory and the roll buffer are completely full. Increasing the size of the extended memory (parameter *em/initial_size_MB*) is likely to solve the problem.

Stopped Work Processes

If a work process listed in the Local Work Process Overview has the status *stopped*, the cause is indicated in the column *Reason*. To obtain a list of the different possible reasons, place the cursor in the column *Reason* and press F1.

Normally, it is not a problem if some work processes have the status *stopped* for short periods of time. However, if the number of work processes that are stopped for the same reason exceeds 20%, or if these work processes continue to have the status *stopped* for a long time, you should analyze the situation in detail. A single ineffective or defective work process often starts a chain reaction that stops other work processes. You can often assume that the work process with the longest runtime (indicated in the column *Time*) caused the problem. If the problem is acute, consider manually terminating the defective work process.

The example of the Local Work Process Overview in Figure 2.11 shows that all the update work processes have the status *stopped* with CPIC as the reason. The cause for this wait situation is that the update work processes are trying to start an RFC call. Since a dialog work process is required to process an RFC call, and (as indicated in the column *Status*) all dialog work processes are occupied, the update work processes are prevented from continuing their work.

Work Processes in Status *Complete*

In the Local Work Process Overview, if you detect numerous terminated work processes (indicated as *complete* in the column *Status*), and find that you cannot restart them, it is likely that there is a problem with the R/3 kernel or with logging on to the database.

Examine the relevant trace file by marking the appropriate work process and choosing *Process* ➤ *Trace* ➤ *Display file*. As the trace file will be overwritten when the work process is restarted, to enable subsequent troubleshooting, save the trace file to a local file by choosing *System* ➤ *List* ➤ *Save* ➤ *Local file*.

Look for R/3 Notes relevant to the problem in the Online Service System (OSS), or consult SAP.

Nonoptimal Load Distribution

In a distributed system with several computers, you may find that all work processes on one or more computers are busy and keeping users waiting, while other computers have idle work processes.

Check how many users are logged on to each R/3 instance (see the note below). If you discover a very unevenly distributed load, your logon distribution should be optimized. To do this, use the Transaction Maintain Logon Group (Transaction *SMLG*). Here, you can check whether all the servers are available for logon distribution, or whether there are any relevant error messages. Proceed to reorganize the logon distribution.

NOTE   For an overview of the current user distribution, look at the screen *CCMS: Load Distribution* in the Transaction *Maintain Logon Group*. To do this, use Transaction *SMLG* or, from the R/3 initial screen, choose *Tools* ➤ *CCMS* ➤ *Configuration* ➤ *Logon groups*. The screen *CCMS: Maintain Logon Groups* appears. Choose *Goto* ➤ *Load distribution*. To see the numbers of users distributed across the available instances for the current logon group, look in the column *User*.

Too Few Work Processes

As you can see from the variety of work-process problems described above, there are many reasons why all work processes of a given type may be occupied. If, for a particular R/3 System you are examining, you can rule out all the problems discussed so far, and yet still have a work-processes bottleneck, it may be that you have not configured enough work processes. In this case, you should increase the number of work processes. However, before doing so, you should check whether the computer has sufficient CPU and main memory (using the Operating System Monitor, Transaction *ST06*). If the CPU is already being utilized to 80%, an increase in the number of work processes will probably not increase, but more likely decrease, performance.

Table 2.10 summarizes the parts of this book that explain how to deal with the problems that can be identified through the Local Work Process Overview (Transaction *SM50*).

TABLE 2.10:   References in This Book to Problems That Can Be Detected Using the Work Process Overview (*SM50*)

Problem	Chapter	Title of Chapter or Section
Long database response times	2	Identifying Expensive SQL Statements
	2	Exclusive Lock Waits

Continued on next page

TABLE 2.10: References in This Book to Problems That Can Be Detected Using the Work Process Overview (*SM50*) *(Continued)*

Problem	Chapter	Title of Chapter or Section
	8	Locks and Enqueue
	9	Optimizing SQL Statements
R/3 memory configuration	2	Monitoring R/3 Memory Configuration
	5	Configuring R/3 Memory Areas
Nonoptimal load distribution, too few work processes	6	Workload Distribution

Systemwide Work Process Overview

To monitor a system with multiple R/3 instances, use the Systemwide Work Process Overview (Transaction *SM66*). The kinds of information you will see are as follows (to see all the columns on the screen, you may need to use the arrow button in the toolbar).

For a dialog work process, the initial screen of the Systemwide Work Process Overview provides data in the following columns:

- *Tcod:* Code for the transaction currently running
- *CUA rep.:* Name of the program, from which the currently running transaction was started by the user (also known as the main program)
- *Scre:* Name of the screen last processed
- *Fcod:* Code for the last function called in the current program

For a background work process, the initial screen of the Systemwide Work Process Overview provides data in the following column:

- *Job:* Name of the executed background job

For both dialog and background work processes, the following fields are displayed:

- *Ext. Mem:* Current extended memory utilization
- *Priv. Mem:* Current heap memory utilization

By choosing *Settings* in the Systemwide Work Process Overview, you can select or deselect the following four display options:

- *Display connections and status in the status line:* Selecting this option displays the server connection or other status issues in the status line at the bottom of the screen. This is helpful if, for example, the connection is problematic or takes a long time. By default, this option is not selected.

- *Hide own work processes used for analysis:* Selecting this option hides data on the work process used by Transaction *SM66* itself to set up an RFC connection to every server (which it will do if the next option is deselected). By default, this option is selected.

- *Display only abbreviated information, avoid RFC:* Selecting this option means *SM66* gets its information from the message server rather than from each application server (through RFC). As the application servers report the status of their work processes to the message server only after a delay, the message server is not always up to date. By deselecting this option, an RFC connection is established to each application server so that the information is up to date; however, this takes more time. By default, this option is selected. For a complete analysis, deselect this option and frequently refresh the display.

- *Do not search for exclusive database locks:* Selecting this option stops *SM66* from searching for exclusive locks in the database and, if it finds any, displaying the message *Stopped DB Lock* or *Waiting for DB Lock* (in the column *Action/Reason for waiting*). By default, this option is not selected, which means that *SM66* does try to provide information on database locks.

To display only a specific group of work processes in the Systemwide Work Process Overview (Transaction *SM66*), choose *Select process*. In the screen that appears, you will see, for example, that, by default, *SM66* does not display waiting work processes. The *Select process* function lets you simplify troubleshooting for large installations with many work processes.

Monitoring the Dispatcher Queue

Occasionally, it may be useful to monitor the dispatcher queue to see how many user requests are waiting to be assigned to a work process. Statistics on dispatcher activities are provided in the Server Overview screen *Display Request Queue*. To call the Server Overview, use Transaction *SM51*, or, from the R/3 initial screen, choose:

> *Tools* ➤ *Administration* ➤ *Monitor* ➤ *System monitoring* ➤ *Servers*

Then mark an R/3 instance with the cursor and choose *Goto* ➤ *Queue information*. The screen *Display Request Queue* appears, which provides data on dispatcher activity according to request type, using the columns explained in Table 2.11.

TABLE 2.11: An Explanation of Columns in the Server Overview (*SM51*) Screen *Display Request Queue*

Column	Explanation
Request type	Type of work process
Req. waiting	Currently waiting user requests
Max. req. wait	Maximum number of user requests waiting at any one time since the R/3 instance was started
Max. req	Maximum possible number of user requests for each queue
Req. written	Number of user requests received by the dispatcher
Req. read	Number of user requests dispatched to a work process

The information about the dispatcher queue is especially important when the system is not responding because the number of requests in the queue is much larger than the number of work processes. Since, in this situation, the R/3 System does not have any more work processes available to perform an analysis, to obtain the above dispatcher-queue data, use the program *dpmon*.

Summary

To monitor the actions of the R/3 work processes, use the Local Work Process Overview (Transaction *SM50*), referring in particular to the columns *Time*, *Status*, *Reason*, *Action/Reason for waiting*, and *Table*. Use this monitor to:

- Ensure that there are sufficient numbers of free work processes (indicated as *waiting* in the column *Status*) for each work-process type on each R/3 instance.

- Ensure that there are no programs that occupy work processes for excessive lengths of time (look in the column *Time*). If you do find such programs, contact the relevant user and determine whether the program is functioning correctly. It may be necessary to perform a detailed analysis of this program.

- Check the fields *Status*, *Reason*, *Action/Reason for waiting*, and *Table* to see whether more than 20% of the work processes are performing the same action. For example:

  - If more than 20% of the work processes are in PRIV mode, or in the roll-in or roll-out phase, this indicates a problem with R/3 memory management.

  - If more than 40% of the work processes are performing a database action, such as sequential read or commit, this indicates a database problem.

  - If more than 20% of the work processes are reading the same table at the same time, this means there may be a problem with an expensive SQL statement or exclusive lock waits in the database.

If R/3 is not responding, you can call the Local Work Process Overview on the operating-system level with the program *dpmon*.

Figures 2.12 and 2.13 show the analysis procedure for the R/3 work processes.

FIGURE 2.12:

Procedure roadmap for analyzing R/3 work processes (I)

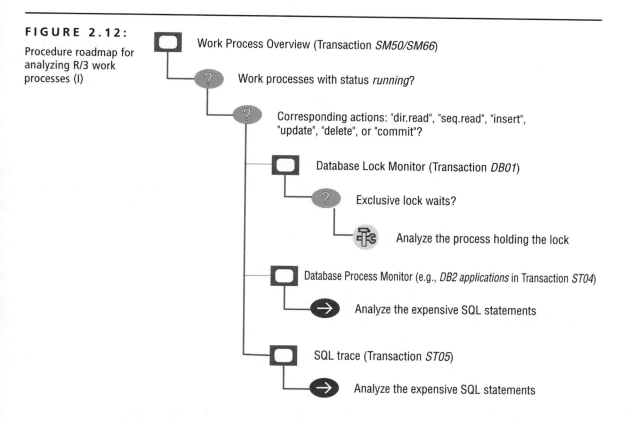

Work Process Overview (Transaction *SM50/SM66*)

? Work processes with status *running*?

? Corresponding actions: "dir.read", "seq.read", "insert", "update", "delete", or "commit"?

Database Lock Monitor (Transaction *DB01*)

? Exclusive lock waits?

Analyze the process holding the lock

Database Process Monitor (e.g., *DB2 applications* in Transaction *ST04*)

→ Analyze the expensive SQL statements

SQL trace (Transaction *ST05*)

→ Analyze the expensive SQL statements

FIGURE 2.13:

Procedure roadmap for analyzing R/3 work processes (II)

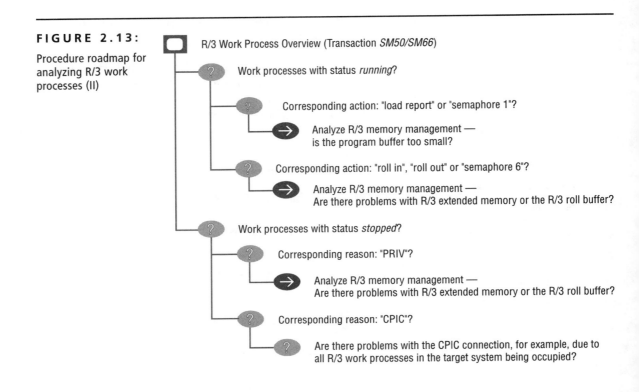

R/3 Work Process Overview (Transaction *SM50/SM66*)

? Work processes with status *running*?

? Corresponding action: "load report" or "semaphore 1"?

→ Analyze R/3 memory management — is the program buffer too small?

? Corresponding action: "roll in", "roll out" or "semaphore 6"?

→ Analyze R/3 memory management — Are there problems with R/3 extended memory or the R/3 roll buffer?

? Work processes with status *stopped*?

? Corresponding reason: "PRIV"?

→ Analyze R/3 memory management — Are there problems with R/3 extended memory or the R/3 roll buffer?

? Corresponding reason: "CPIC"?

? Are there problems with the CPIC connection, for example, due to all R/3 work processes in the target system being occupied?

Summary

The summaries in this chapter are located at the end of each section.

Important Concepts in This Chapter

After reading this chapter, you should be familiar with the following concepts:

- Hardware bottleneck

- Logical database read access to buffers, as contrasted with physical database read access to disks
- Expensive SQL statement
- Exclusive database lock
- Allocated and physical memory
- R/3 work-process bottleneck
- Semaphore

Review Questions

1. Which of the following can cause a CPU bottleneck on the database server?

   A. External processes that do not belong to the database or an R/3 instance are running on the database server.

   B. The R/3 extended memory is configured too small.

   C. Work processes that belong to an R/3 instance running on the database (for example, background or update work processes) require CPU capacity.

   D. There are expensive SQL statements—for example, those that contribute 5% or more of the entire database load in the Shared SQL Area.

   E. The database buffers are set too small, so that data must be continuously reloaded from the hard disks.

2. Which of the following are necessary to achieve optimal database performance?

   A. Table analyses (through a program such as Update Statistics) must be regularly scheduled.

   B. The number of R/3 work processes must be sufficiently large, so that there are enough database processes to process the database load.

    C. The database buffers must be sufficiently large.

    D. You should regularly check whether expensive SQL statements are unnecessarily occupying CPU and main memory resources.

    E. The database instance should be run only on a separate computer without R/3 instances.

3. Which points should you take into consideration when monitoring R/3 memory management?

    A. The total memory allocated by the R/3 and database instances should not be larger than the physical main memory of the computer.

    B. The extended memory must be sufficiently large.

    C. If possible, no displacements should occur in the R/3 buffers.

4. In the Local Work Process Overview, the information displayed for a particular work process over a considerable time period is as follows: Running, Sequential Read, and a specific table name. What does this tell you?

    A. There may be an expensive SQL statement that accesses the table that can be analyzed more closely in the Database Process Monitor.

    B. There may be a wait situation in the dispatcher, preventing a connection to the database. The dispatcher queue should be analyzed more closely.

    C. There may be an exclusive lock wait that you can detect in the monitor for exclusive lock waits.

    D. There may be a network problem between the application server and the database server.

CHAPTER
THREE

Workload Analysis

Performing a workload analysis gives you reliable data on throughput, load, and response times for the R/3 System and its components. As described in the Introduction, an experienced performance analyst begins by using a workload analysis to reveal areas of R/3 that have noticeable performance problems, and then proceeds with a more detailed top-down analysis.

When to Use Workload Analysis

Assuming that you have systematically performed the analyses explained in Chapter 2 and have discovered several problems both in the database area and in R/3 memory configuration, you can determine which problem is the most serious and requires the most urgent attention by performing a workload analysis.

Workload analysis examines the various response times measured by the system. The kinds of performance problems identified by workload analysis are those that negatively affect throughput and response time, and are termed *bottlenecks*. Bottlenecks can critically affect production operation and therefore require speedy removal. Workload analysis can also be used to prioritize performance problems.

In addition, workload analysis reveals the load distribution for each application's programs or transactions and indicates which of these are placing the greatest load on the R/3 System. Workload analysis should be the starting point for a detailed application analysis.

The first section of this chapter ("Basic Concepts of Workload Analysis") explains the basic concepts of workload analysis, introduces the Workload Monitor, and covers which statistics are measured in units of time by the R/3 System and how you can use these measurements to identify performance problems. The second section of the chapter ("Performing Workload Analysis") provides recommendations on how to monitor your system performance regularly. The third section of the chapter ("Application Monitor") introduces the Application Monitor, which is used to analyze the workload from the perspective of the application.

When Should You Read This Chapter?

Read this chapter when you want to monitor, analyze, and interpret the response time of the R/3 System, including database and hardware, or of individual programs and transactions.

If you want to technically monitor and optimize the performance of the R/3 System, you can read Chapter 3 either before or after Chapter 2.

If you want to monitor and optimize the performance of programs and transactions, you should read this chapter and then read Chapter 4.

Understanding workload analysis is a precondition of successful performance optimization.

Basic Concepts of Workload Analysis

This section explains how to use the Workload Monitor and understand its statistics. Guideline values are provided to enable you to distinguish good from poor system performance.

The Workload Monitor

In the R/3 System, statistics such as response times, memory use, and database accesses are collected and stored for all transaction steps. These statistics are organized in load profiles that can be displayed in the Workload Monitor. The Workload Monitor enables you to obtain a comprehensive overview of load distribution within an R/3 System.

1. To access the initial screen of the Workload Monitor, use Transaction code *ST03*, or, from the main R/3 menu, choose *Tools* ➤ *Administration* ➤ *Monitor* ➤ *Performance* ➤ *Workload* ➤ *Analysis*.

    *   The initial screen of the Workload Monitor appears: *Workload: Analysis of SAP System* SID.

2. From this initial screen, you can access the main screen. First, choose the button *Performance database*.

    *   In the dialog boxes that appear, you must specify a server or the entire R/3 System (server *TOTAL*) and then specify a period to be analyzed. After this, the main screen of the Workload Monitor appears: *Performance: Workload summary of server* selected server.

3. If you are interested in the current statistics for the server you are connected to, from the initial screen of the Workload Monitor, choose *This application server* ➤ *last minute load*.

    *   In the dialog box that appears, specify a time period. After this, the main screen of the Workload Monitor appears: *Performance: Recent Workload for server* selected server.

The main screen of the Workload Monitor (see Figure 3.1) is divided into three sections: *Instance*, *Workload*, and *Task types*. The section *Instance* contains administration information. For example, the fields *SAP System*, *Server*, and *Instance no.* indicate the R/3 System name and the name of the selected servers (or *TOTAL* if you are analyzing the entire R/3 System). The times beside *First record* and *Last record* more precisely identify the time period in which the statistics were gathered.

The lower section, *Task types*, tells you which task type you have chosen (beside the field *Current*), and provides buttons that enable you to choose other task types. These task types correspond to the work-process types *dialog*, *update*, *background*, and *spool*. The work-process type *dialog* is divided into the task types *dialog* and *RFC*.

Transaction Step

In the main Workload Monitor screen, the central section, *Workload*, contains the statistical data that helps you to evaluate the performance of the R/3 System and to discover the causes of performance problems. The first values to look at are the number of transaction steps (indicated as *Dialog steps*) and the average response time (indicated as *Av. response time*).

In a dialog task, a transaction step corresponds to a screen change—that is, to a request that is executed for a user by the R/3 System. But a background-processing step also produces "dialog steps" in the sense used in the Workload Monitor. Thus, the term *dialog step* may be somewhat misleading, as dialog steps used in the Workload Monitor are performed not only in dialog tasks (immediate responses to input from online users), but also in background tasks, update tasks, and spool tasks. Processing an update request or a spool request is counted by the Workload Monitor as one dialog step. Similarly, a background program may involve one or more dialog steps.

To avoid ambiguity, this book will use the term *transaction step* for the processing steps referred to in the Workload Monitor as dialog steps to differentiate them from background dialog steps. The number of transaction steps per unit of time will be referred to as *system activity* or *throughput*.

Response Time

The average response time for a transaction step in a dialog task (indicated as *Av. response time* in the Workload Monitor) is seen by many R/3 users as the criterion for the acceptable performance in an R/3 System. Another generally accepted rule of thumb is that good performance is indicated by an average response time of 1 second or less. However, a broad generalization of this kind is not always accurate when you consider the variety of R/3 Systems and the different requirements placed on these systems.

In addition to the average response time, there are many other statistics, such as database time, CPU time, and so on, that enable you to understand performance problems and their possible causes. These statistics are explained in the next section.

Load profiles enable you to perform a detailed analysis of load distribution and response times. To access one of the various load profiles from the main screen of the Workload Monitor, choose *Goto* ➤ *Profiles*.

The available profiles include technical-analysis profiles such as Task Type Profile, Time Profile, and Memory Profile, as well as application-analysis profiles such as the Transaction Profile, User Profile, Client Profile, and Accounting Profile.

Processing within a Transaction Step

This section details the various kinds of processing within a single transaction step and explains the related Workload Monitor statistics, with reference to Figures 3.2 and 3.3.

When an R/3 user finishes making an entry, the presentation server sends the request to the dispatcher of the application server. The response time (indicated as *Av. response time* in the Workload Monitor) is measured from the moment when the request of the presentation server reaches the dispatcher in the application server (see *1* in Figure 3.2). The response time is regarded as ended when the request is processed and data is returned on its way to the presentation server. The time taken by the network transfer between the presentation server and the application server is not included in the Workload Monitor response-time statistic.

FIGURE 3.2:

Processing a single transaction step

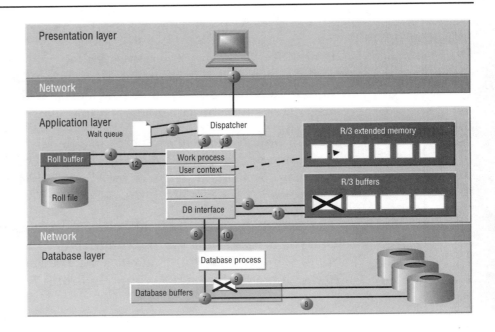

Dispatcher Wait Time

When the R/3 dispatcher receives a processing request, it looks for an R/3 work process of the required type (dialog, update, and so on). If the work process is not already busy processing another request, the dispatcher sends the request to this work process, which begins the processing work. If all R/3 work processes of the required type are busy when the request initially reaches the dispatcher, the request is placed in the dispatcher queue (see 2 in Figure 3.2).

In the dispatcher queue, the request waits until a work process of the required type is free. As soon as a work process is free, the dispatcher sends the request to it (see 3 in Figure 3.2). The time the request spends in the dispatcher queue is indicated as *Av. wait time* in the Workload Monitor. Note that there are many other kinds of wait time in the R/3 System—for example, waiting for RFC calls, locks, CPU access, database access, and so on. However, the wait time indicated as *Av. wait time* in the Workload Monitor is the dispatcher wait time.

Roll In and Roll Out

Roll in and roll out are concepts related to the user context, which can be explained as follows: An R/3 transaction normally extends over several transaction steps or screen changes. During these steps, data such as variables, internal tables, and report lists is set up and stored in the main memory of the application server. This data is known as the *user context*. Different transaction steps are frequently processed by different dialog work processes. For example, the first transaction step may be processed by work process number 3, the second transaction step by work process number 4, and so on.

At the beginning of a transaction step, the user context is made available to the appropriate work process by the process known as a *roll in* (see *4* in Figure 3.2). The technical processes comprising a roll in, such as copying data into the local memory of the work process, are described in Chapter 5.

The analogous process of *roll out* saves the current user-context data to the virtual memory at the conclusion of a transaction step (*12* in Figure 3.2). The duration of the roll in is referred to as *roll in time,* and the duration of the roll out is referred to as *roll out time*. The average roll times are indicated as *Time per roll in* and *Time per roll out* in the Workload Monitor for R/3 Release 3.*x*. To obtain the average roll times in R/3 Release 4.*x*, divide the values *Roll in time* and *Roll out time* by the values indicated as *Roll ins* and *Roll outs* respectively.

Note that the roll out time is not part of the response time of a transaction step. At roll out, when the user context is copied from the local memory of the work process to the roll memory, the processed data has already been returned to the presentation server.

Load Time

All ABAP programs and R/3 screens that are required and are not yet available in the buffers of the application server must be loaded and possibly generated. This time taken by loading and generating is indicated as *Av. load+gen time* (or *Load time*, depending on the R/3 Release) in the Workload Monitor. Loading a program also entails accesses to database tables storing the programs—for example, the tables D010S and D010L.

Database Time

When data is read or changed in the database, the time required is known as *database time* and is indicated as *Av. DB request time* in the Workload Monitor. Database time is measured from the moment of sending the database request to the database server and continues until the moment at which data is returned to the application server (see *6* to *10* in Figure 3.2). Because database time is measured by the application server, database time includes not only the time required by the database to produce the requested data, but also the time required for the network transfer of that data. Thus, a network problem between the database and the application server results in a greater database time.

Before accessing the database, the database interface of the work process checks whether the required data is already in the R/3 buffers. If the data is already in the buffers, the buffers are accessed because using buffers is up to 100 times faster than a database access (see *5* and *11* in Figure 3.2). Buffer accesses do not contribute to database time.

Enqueue Time

Enqueue time, indicated as *Av. enqueue time* in the Workload Monitor, is the time during which a work process sets an enqueue request.

Roll Wait Time

Roll wait time occurs in connection with an RFC call. For an explanation of roll wait time, see "Monitoring RFC Connections" later in this chapter. This statistic is visible as of R/3 Release 4.0, where the sum of roll in time and roll wait time is indicated as *Av. roll time*.

Processing Time

Processing time is the total response time minus the sum of the following: dispatcher wait time, roll times, load time, enqueue time, and database request time.

CPU Time

All the statistics discussed above concern actions that are part of an R/3 work process. That is, whenever the respective action runs, the work process times it by finding out the start and finish times for the activity from the operating system.

CPU time, indicated as *Av. CPU time* in the Workload Monitor, is measured by the operating system whenever a work process is occupying the CPU. The R/3 work process asks the operating system at the end of a transaction step how much CPU time expired during the transaction step. CPU time is not an additive component of transaction response time, but is consumed during load time, roll time, and processing time (see Figure 3.3).

FIGURE 3.3:

Response time and its components: dispatcher wait time, roll in time, roll wait time, load time, database time, processing time, and CPU time

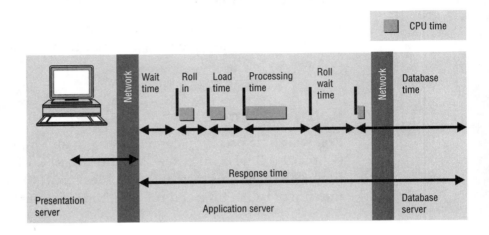

Interpreting Response Times

To analyze response times for dialog processing, use the guideline values in Table 3.1. For the task type Update, these values may be 50% higher than the values for the dialog tasks. The right-hand column tells you the kind of problem that may be indicated if the observed value lies significantly outside the guideline range of values.

TABLE 3.1: Guideline Values for Analyzing the Response Time Averages for Task Type *Dialog*

Statistic	Guideline Values	Problem Indicated
Dispatcher wait time (Wait time)	< 10% of response time; < 50 milliseconds	General performance problem with many possible causes
Load time (Load+gen time)	< 50 milliseconds	Program buffer too small or CPU bottleneck

Continued on next page

TABLE 3.1: Guideline Values for Analyzing the Response Time Averages for Task Type *Dialog (Continued)*

Statistic	Guideline Values	Problem Indicated
Roll in time, Roll out time (Roll in time in R/3 Release 4.0=Roll in time÷Roll ins; in R/3 Release 3.0/3.1: Time per Roll In [the calculation is similar for roll out time])	< 20 milliseconds	R/3 roll buffer or R/3 extended memory too small or CPU bottleneck
Enqueue time	< 5 milliseconds	Enqueue service or network unavailability
Processing time, CPU time	Processing time < 2×CPU time	CPU bottleneck or problem with communication between systems
Database time (DB request time)	< 40% of (response time minus dispatcher wait time); 200 to 600 milliseconds	Database problem, network problem, or CPU bottleneck
Time per DB request	< 5 milliseconds	Database problem
Direct reads	< 2 milliseconds	Database problem
Sequential reads	< 10 milliseconds	Database problem
Changes and commits	< 25 milliseconds	Database problem

NOTE If the values you observe in the Workload Monitor are significantly outside the guideline range indicated here, there may be a performance problem in the relevant area. Note that these values are based on standard situations and may differ in some R/3 Systems.

Lost-Time Analysis

In addition to comparing your statistics with the guideline values, you should perform an analysis that looks for a discrepancy (lost time) between two time measurements that should be roughly equivalent. As mentioned above, there are two different sources of time statistics. All times other than CPU time are measured from the perspective of the R/3 work process, whereas CPU time is measured from the perspective of the operating system. The lost-time analysis aims to calculate a value for CPU time from work process–related response times and compares this figure with the actual CPU time. If the difference between the two figures is too large, the performance analyst will want to try to explain the cause of the lost time.

To generate a figure for CPU time from work process–related response times, proceed as follows: From the total average response time, subtract all times in which the R/3 work process requires no CPU time—namely, dispatcher wait time, database time, enqueue time, and roll wait time. (As of R/3 Release 4, to find the average roll wait time from the Workload Monitor, divide the *Roll wait time* by the *Dialog steps*.) To use the example values from Figure 3.1 (earlier in this section), we get the following result:

1041ms–136ms–6ms–320ms–63ms=516ms

This result roughly corresponds to the processing time, if we assume that the roll in time and the load time are negligible. During processing time, mainly programs that are processed are measured and consume CPU capacity. Therefore, processing time should be a good measure for CPU time, and the CPU time and the processing time should be similar. In the present example, with a processing time of 516ms and a CPU time of 358ms, the difference between these times is around 30%. As a guideline value, this difference between processing time and CPU time should not be greater than 100%. Greater discrepancies (lost times) indicate performance problems.

Possible causes of a large discrepancy between processing time and CPU time may be as follows:

- A CPU bottleneck: This would mean there is not enough CPU capacity available to the R/3 work processes, which must therefore wait until CPU becomes available. Thus, processing time is being measured in the work process while no CPU time is used, and this processing time is considerably larger than CPU time.

- Wait times in the R/3 work process: Whenever the R/3 work process has a status *stopped*, processing time is being measured without CPU time being used. This type of wait situation can be identified in the Work Process Overview (Transaction code *SM50*; see Chapter 2 for more details).

Monitoring RFC Connections

This section explains special considerations applying to the workload analysis of programs that use Remote Function Calls (RFCs).

Roll Wait Time

While the program issuing an RFC from within a transaction step waits for a response, the user context is rolled out of the work process to make the work process available to other users. After completing the RFC, the user context is rolled back into a work process, and the transaction step is resumed. The time in which the user context was not in a work process is indicated as *Roll wait time* in the Workload Monitor.

While the RFC is in progress, the response time for the calling program continues increasing, even though no CPU time is used. When performing a lost-time analysis, subtract the roll wait time (which reflects waiting on the RFC) from the total response time when calculating the estimate of CPU time.

RFC Time

In the Workload Monitor, the field *Av. RFC+CPIC Time* indicates the average time for establishing an RFC connection. This time should be very small, less than 10ms.

Task Type RFC

RFCs increase response time in both the calling R/3 System and the called R/3 System. The average response times for RFCs are indicated in the Workload Monitor as of R/3 Release 4.0 under the task type RFC.

Release 3.1

In the Workload Monitor for Release 3.1, no statistics are indicated for RFC time and roll wait time. You can, however, find the average response times for RFCs in the called R/3 System in the transaction profile as follows: In the Workload Monitor, choose *Transaction Profile* and look at the statistics for the program CPIC/RFC.

Activity, Throughput, and Load

The concepts of system activity, throughput, and load can best be explained by using the task type profile. This profile is a summary of the most important performance statistics for all task types, and can be accessed from the Workload Monitor main screen by choosing *Goto* ➢ *Profiles* ➢ *Task type profile*.

An example of this profile is shown in Table 3.2.

TABLE 3.2: Excerpt from a Task Type Profile in the Workload Monitor

Task Type	Dialog Steps	Response Time Total(s)	Response Time Average (ms)	Database Time Total(s)	Database Time Average (ms)
TOTAL	719,372	1,933,546	2,688	410,348	570
BCKGRD	29,829	265,154	8,889	115,163	3,861
DIALOG	525,830	547,393	1,041	168,146	320
RFC	37,619	832,928	22,141	70,932	1,886
SPOOL	1,083	1,169	1,079	6,362	5,875
UPDATE	55,938	234,087	4,230	8,692	715

In the task type profile, the column *Dialog steps* indicates the number of transaction steps.

Activity or throughput is defined as the number of transaction steps per unit of time. In the example shown in Table 3.2, users have performed 525,830 screen changes in dialog processing mode in the time period selected. Thus, around 75% of system activity (525,830 out of 719,372 transaction steps) consisted of dialog processing.

Load can be thought of as proportional to the time during which a task occupies the R/3 System, and thus, as proportional to response time. So, if two users each execute 100 transaction steps in a given time period, they are creating equal system activity, but not necessarily equal load. If the first user creates *invoices* and performs 100 transaction steps with an average response time of 500ms, this user has occupied the R/3 System for 50 seconds. If the second user creates *auditing reports* and performs 100 transaction steps with an average response time of 5 seconds, this user occupies the R/3 System for 500 seconds.

In summary, we may say that the second user has created a system load that is 10 times larger with the same amount of system activity as the first user. In this way, total response time provides an indication of load.

TIP   To be more exact, subtract dispatcher wait time from the total response time, because a request is not creating system load while it waits in the dispatcher queue.

Analogously, database load created by the different task types can be measured by the total database time, indicated as *DB time total* in the task type profile. Similarly, CPU load on the application server is measured by *CPU time total* in the task type profile (not indicated in Table 3.2).

The task type profile example in Table 3.2 indicates that 75% of system activity is in dialog mode, and only 4% is in background mode (see the column *Dialog steps*). Looking at the database load in the column *DB time total* shows quite a different situation: Around 40% of the database time (16.46 seconds out of 41.48 seconds) is consumed by dialog mode, 28% by background mode. Background processing is more than 10 times as expensive per transaction step as dialog processing. This can also be seen by comparing the average response times (indicated as *Response time avg* in the task type profile). We can conclude that the distribution of response times (database time, CPU time, and so on) reflects the load distribution for the R/3 System better than the number of transaction steps, which is the measure of activity for a given process.

Active Users

The simplest and most graphic measure for the size of an R/3 System is the number of users. Unfortunately, *the number of users* is also an imprecise expression, and its meaning varies according to context. It can mean, for example, the number of licenses or the number of user master records, to mention just two possible meanings. To avoid confusion, this book distinguishes three types of users, as follows:

- Occasional user: On average, a user of this type performs fewer than 400 transaction steps (screen changes) per week. For a 40-hour work week, this corresponds to an average of one transaction step every 6 minutes. This is typically a user seeking information occasionally.

- Regular user: On average, a user of this type, typically a clerk or accountant, performs up to 4,800 transaction steps per week. This corresponds to less than one transaction step every 30 seconds. These are users who use the R/3 System regularly and continuously.

- High data volume user: Typical examples of this kind of user are people working in data entry or telephone sales. These users perform more than 4,800 transaction steps per week, or more than one transaction step every 30 seconds. They use R/3 constantly for high-volume processing.

For the purposes of this book, *active users* are users who correspond to either the *regular user* or the *high data volume user* categories.

To display statistics on system activities according to user, call the user profile as follows: From the main screen of the Workload Monitor, choose *Goto* ➤ *Profiles* ➤ *User profile*.

The user profile indicates the type and frequency of activities of users who are logged on in the time period selected in the Workload Monitor.

Technical Settings for the Workload Monitor

To ensure that the individual statistical records created and saved for each transaction step are regularly collated in profiles, the data collector program RSCOLL00 must be scheduled as an hourly background job (generally under the name SAP_COLLECTOR_ FOR_PERFORMANCE).

To display or modify the parameters affecting the creation of profiles, in the Workload Monitor initial screen, choose *Goto* ➤ *Parameters* ➤ *Performance database*. Here, beside *Standard statistics*, you can enter the retention periods for profiles—that is, the time before they are automatically deleted. Beside *Time comparison data*, you can enter the retention period for the data displayed under the Workload Monitor menu option *Compare time periods*.

To specify systemwide statistics, select the option *Cumulate server statistics to a system-wide total statistics*. It is recommended that you select this option. To specify when the individual statistical records are deleted, and also the maximum number of records that are to be collated in each run of the program RSCOLL00, enter the appropriate parameters beside *Delete seq. statfile after cumulation if size >* and *Max. number of records cumulated per call*.

For troubleshooting the data collector program RSCOLL00, you can access a log kept for each run as follows: In the Workload Monitor, choose *Environment* ➤ *Data collector* ➤ *Display protocol*.

Explanations of the functions and settings of the data collector may be found in R/3 Online Documentation and in the R/3 Notes in the Online Service System (OSS). Some relevant R/3 Notes are listed in Appendix H.

Performing Workload Analysis

This section provides a step-by-step description for performing workload analysis.

In general, the first input for performance analysis is the observations of users. The Workload Monitor helps you to verify the subjective comments of users and narrow down the causes of performance problems. Before performing workload analysis, you should distinguish between:

- General performance problems: These are performance problems that result in poor response times and unsatisfactory throughput in all transactions. Problems of this type can negatively impact business processes and cause financial loss.

- Specific performance problems: These are performance problems that affect single transactions. Specific performance problems can negatively impact business processes if the transactions involved belong to the company's core business processes (for example, goods issued in the SD application module).

Specific and general performance problems are treated separately in the following sections, each with their own set of troubleshooting questions. To help you to apply these questions to your situation, use the guideline values and examples provided. Note that it may not always be possible to answer the questions with a simple yes or no.

General Performance Problems

Use the questions in the following subheadings to assist you in troubleshooting general performance problems.

Is There a General Performance Problem?

The regular and high data volume users will know if there is a general performance problem. However, you should use the Workload Monitor to quantify the users' observations and check whether longer-than-optimal response times affect all transactions. The following criteria, which apply to dialog tasks, may help you to decide which response times are too large:

- Dispatcher wait time much greater than 50ms: A significantly large dispatcher wait time always affects all transactions. It implies that programs are too slow and blocking work processes for lengthy periods over a long time—or that too few work processes have been configured.

- Database time much greater than 40% of (response time minus dispatcher wait time); database time > 400ms: A large database time slows performance for all transactions.

- Processing time > (2×CPU time): A large processing time slows performance for all transactions, and may be caused by a CPU bottleneck or a communication problem between systems.

- Average response time > system-specific guideline value: The average response time for a dialog task is seen by many IT specialists as the decisive R/3 performance criterion. A guideline value must be defined for each individual R/3 System. As a rule of thumb, an average dialog response time of less than 1 second indicates a good performance. A broad generalization of this kind is not always valid for all R/3 Systems in all contexts.

Is the Performance Problem Temporary or Permanent?

After verifying that there is a general performance problem, try to find out how frequently the problem occurs:

- Is the problem permanent or temporary?

- Does the problem occur at regular intervals—for example, at particular times of day?

- Is it a nonrecurring problem?

- Which response times are large when the problem occurs: database time, CPU time, or processing time?
- Does the problem occur following only specific system activities—for example, when background programs run on the R/3 System?

To examine these questions more closely, compare the workload statistics of recent days with each other as follows: From the initial screen of the Workload Monitor, choose *Performance database*. Then select *TOTAL*, *Previous days*, and a recent day. Repeat this procedure for several days and see whether the performance problem is restricted to particular days.

Next, create a time profile for each day (see Figure 3.4). To do this, from the main screen of the Workload Monitor, choose *Goto* ➢ *Profiles* ➢ *Time profile*. The time profile shows the transaction steps and response times according to the hour (or other time period, depending on what you selected on entering the Workload Monitor).

FIGURE 3.4:

Time profile for dialog processing

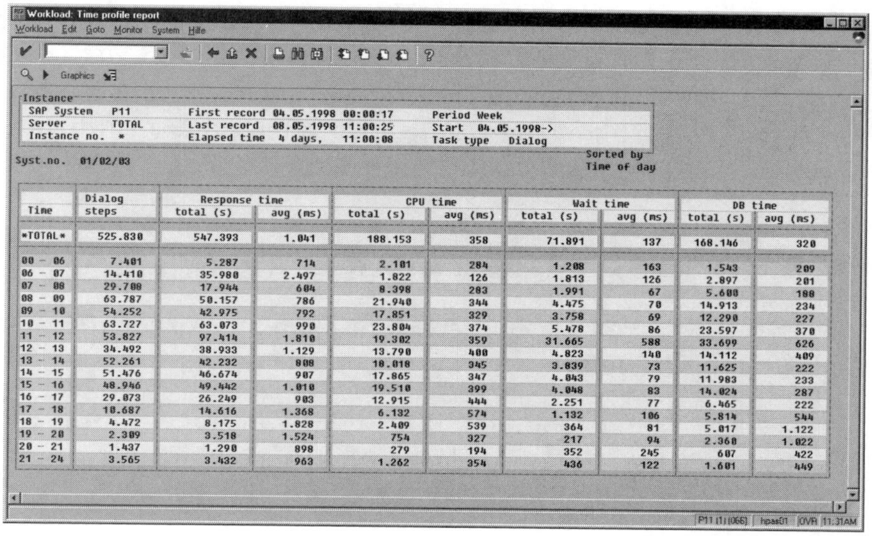

Workload: Time profile report

Workload Edit Goto Monitor System Hilfe

Graphics

Instance

SAP System P11	First record 04.05.1998 00:00:17	Period Week
Server TOTAL	Last record 08.05.1998 11:00:25	Start 04.05.1998->
Instance no. *	Elapsed time 4 days, 11:00:08	Task type Dialog

Syst.no. 01/02/03

Sorted by Time of day

Time	Dialog steps	Response time total (s)	Response time avg (ms)	CPU time total (s)	CPU time avg (ms)	Wait time total (s)	Wait time avg (ms)	DB time total (s)	DB time avg (ms)
TOTAL	525.830	547.393	1.041	188.153	358	71.891	137	168.146	320
00 - 06	7.401	5.287	714	2.101	284	1.208	163	1.543	209
06 - 07	14.410	35.980	2.497	1.822	126	1.813	126	2.897	201
07 - 08	29.700	17.944	604	8.398	283	1.991	67	5.600	188
08 - 09	63.787	50.157	786	21.940	344	4.475	70	14.913	234
09 - 10	54.252	42.975	792	17.851	329	3.758	69	12.290	227
10 - 11	63.727	63.073	990	23.804	374	5.478	86	23.597	370
11 - 12	53.827	97.414	1.810	19.302	359	31.665	588	33.699	626
12 - 13	34.492	38.933	1.129	13.790	400	4.823	140	14.112	409
13 - 14	52.261	42.232	808	18.018	345	3.839	73	11.625	222
14 - 15	51.476	46.674	907	17.865	347	4.043	79	11.983	233
15 - 16	48.946	49.442	1.010	19.510	399	4.048	83	14.024	287
16 - 17	29.073	26.249	903	12.915	444	2.251	77	6.465	222
17 - 18	10.687	14.616	1.368	6.132	574	1.132	106	5.814	544
18 - 19	4.472	8.175	1.828	2.409	539	364	81	5.017	1.122
19 - 20	2.309	3.518	1.524	754	327	217	94	2.360	1.022
20 - 21	1.437	1.290	898	279	194	352	245	607	422
21 - 24	3.565	3.432	963	1.262	354	436	122	1.601	449

P11 (1) (066) hpas01 OVR 11:31AM

Using the time profile, you can analyze the daily loads on the R/3 System. If you find that the average response time increases dramatically only at particular periods of high load, you can infer that the system is overloaded at these times. If the average response times are also unsatisfactory at times of low system load, the performance problem is load-independent.

The time profiles enable you to determine whether excessive use of background processing during periods of peak system load has a negative impact on dialog processing. To create time profiles for dialog processing and background processing, from the main screen of the Workload Monitor, choose the button *Dialog* or *Background* respectively, and then choose *Time profile*. Find out at what time of day the dialog or background load occurs by looking at the fields *Response time total*, *CPU time total*, and *DB time total*.

During peak periods of dialog processing, particularly if there are performance problems, ensure that the background processing load remains low in the same period.

You may also find it helpful to compare the time profile per day in the Workload Monitor with the time profile per day for CPU load and for paging (both indicated in the Operating System Monitor). This comparison enables you to determine whether a worsening of response times correlates with a large CPU load or high paging rate. If so, a temporary hardware bottleneck is indicated (see the following question).

Is There a Hardware Bottleneck?

A CPU bottleneck or main memory bottleneck can be detected as follows.

1. Find out if the hourly averages for the CPU load or paging rate are large. As a rule of thumb, the risk of a hardware bottleneck is regarded as high when either:

   - The hourly average of free CPU capacity (indicated as *CPU idle* in the Operating System Monitor) is less than 20%

or

- The paging rate per hour exceeds 20% of the physical main memory (indicated as *Physical mem available*)

See Chapter 2, in the section "Analysis of a Hardware Bottleneck," for more details on this subject.

2. Check whether the large CPU load or high paging rate really does negatively affect R/3 response times and cause a hardware bottleneck on either the application server or the database server:

   - To check whether there is a hardware bottleneck on an application server, look at the processing time. If the processing time is much greater than double the CPU time, this indicates that the work processes are waiting for CPU. (However, an increased processing time may have other causes. See "Interpreting Response Times," earlier in this chapter.) A further indication of a hardware bottleneck on the application server is given by increased load times, roll in times, and dispatcher wait times.

   - To check whether there is a hardware bottleneck on the database server, see whether the database time is too large. Compare, for example, the average database times in the daily time profile at times of high and low load.

3. To check whether there is a main memory bottleneck, compare whether the virtually allocated memory is significantly greater than the physically available main memory. As long as the virtually allocated memory is smaller than 1.5 times the physical main memory, there is normally no risk of a main memory bottleneck. (See Chapter 2, in the section "Displaying the Allocated Memory," for more on this subject.)

It is only if all three of these checks (the first two apply for CPU and memory, the final one only for memory) indicate a hardware bottleneck that you can be fairly certain that there is, in fact, a hardware bottleneck.

The three possible causes of a hardware bottleneck are as follows:

- Poor load distribution: The load is not optimally distributed across the servers. There may be servers with free CPU or main memory capacity. Alternatively, load distribution may become nonoptimal at certain times of the day—for example, when several background processes are run in parallel during periods of peak system load. You should be able to reschedule these programs to run at times of low system load.

- Individual processes causing a high CPU load: Individual processes with a high CPU load may be running at times of high system load. Such processes may include database processes (with expensive SQL statements), R/3 work processes (with programs running as background jobs), or processes external to R/3. To improve performance, you may be able to tune, reschedule, or (in the case of external processes) cancel these processes.

- Insufficient hardware capacity: If the two previously mentioned causes of a hardware bottleneck do not apply, the hardware capacity may be too small for your R/3 System load.

If you have correctly identified a hardware bottleneck, proceed as described in Chapter 2, in the section "Analyzing a Hardware Bottleneck."

Is There a General Database Performance Problem?

A general database performance problem is indicated by increased database times. The following guideline values for dialog tasks in the Workload Monitor indicate a general database performance problem:

- Database time much greater than 40% of (response time minus dispatcher wait time); database time greater than 400ms

- Direct reads much greater than 2ms

- Sequential reads much greater than 10ms

- Changes and commits much greater than 25ms

A database performance problem has many possible causes. If you have correctly identified a database performance problem, proceed as described in Chapter 2, in the section "Analyzing the Database."

Is Load Distribution Nonoptimal?

A performance problem caused by nonoptimal load distribution can be detected by comparing the CPU load and the paging rates for the various servers (in the Operating System Monitor). You should also compare the response times for the various application servers in the Workload Monitor.

To display the server profile, from the initial screen of the Workload Monitor, choose *Goto ➤ Performance database ➤ Analyze all servers ➤ Compare all servers*.

Select the appropriate time period by choosing *Edit ➤ Choose period type*, and then using the buttons *Prev. period* and *Next period*.

The server profile shows the transaction steps and related response times for each server. If there are several R/3 instances on one application server, the statistics indicated for the server are the totals for all instances on that server. To obtain details of the task types on individual servers, double-click a row in the list of servers.

In the server profile, check the load distribution across your servers. For example, if the dispatcher wait time occurs only on one server or on a small number of your servers, this implies either that too many users are working on these servers or that too few work processes are configured on these servers.

Total CPU time (indicated as *CPU time total*) on all application servers should be roughly equal if all servers have the same CPU capacity. If you have servers with different CPU capacities, CPU time should differ proportionately.

One cause of a poor load distribution may be a nonoptimal configuration of logon groups or work processes. To optimize load distribution, see Chapter 6, "Workload Distribution."

If the average database times (indicated as *DB time average*) for the various servers differ greatly, this may indicate a network problem. You can assume that application servers are configured with the same work processes and that users on the various application servers are, on average, using the same transactions. Thus, there is no obvious reason apart from a network problem as to why the database should serve one application server more slowly than another application server. This argument applies only to servers that are configured with the same work processes. For background servers or update servers, the average database time will be greater than that for dialog servers.

Is There a Performance Problem Caused by R/3 Memory Configuration?

Performance problems caused by R/3 memory configuration may be the result of R/3 buffers or R/3 extended memory being too small (see also "Memory Configuration" in Chapter 2). Check the Workload Monitor for:

- An increase in the average load time to much greater than 50ms: This indicates a too small R/3 program buffer, CUA buffer, or screen buffer.

- An increase in the average roll in or roll out times to much greater than 20ms: This indicates that the R/3 extended memory or the R/3 roll buffer is full.

These guideline times apply to dialog tasks.

If you notice unusually large roll times or load times, proceed as described in Chapter 2, in the section "Analyzing R/3 Memory Configuration."

R/3 memory configuration should also be monitored in the main memory profile as follows: From the Workload Monitor main screen, choose *Goto* ➤ *Profiles* ➤ *Memory profile*.

The memory profile shows memory usage per program, indicating R/3 extended memory and R/3 heap memory (in the column *Priv. mem.*). The memory profile also shows how often work processes entered PRIV mode (in the column *Workproc. reservations*) and how often a work process was restarted after its use of R/3 heap memory exceeded the value of the parameter *abap/heaplimit* (indicated in the column *Workproc. restarts*).

Specific Performance Problems

The previous section explained troubleshooting for general performance problems. This section helps you troubleshoot specific performance problems—that is, performance problems affecting only specific transactions.

Is There a Performance Problem with a Specific Transaction?

The Workload Monitor is an analysis tool used for both technical analysis and application analysis. For application analysis, the most important part of the Workload Monitor is the transaction profile:

1. To display the transaction profile, start the Workload Monitor (Transaction code *ST03*), and choose *Performance database*. Then select *TOTAL* or a specific server, and a time period.

2. The main screen of the Workload Monitor is displayed. You can toggle between displayed task types using the buttons *Total*, *Dialog*, and so on, located in the lower part of the screen.

3. Finally, to display the transaction profile, choose *Transaction profile* (see Figure 3.5).

FIGURE 3.5:

Transaction profile

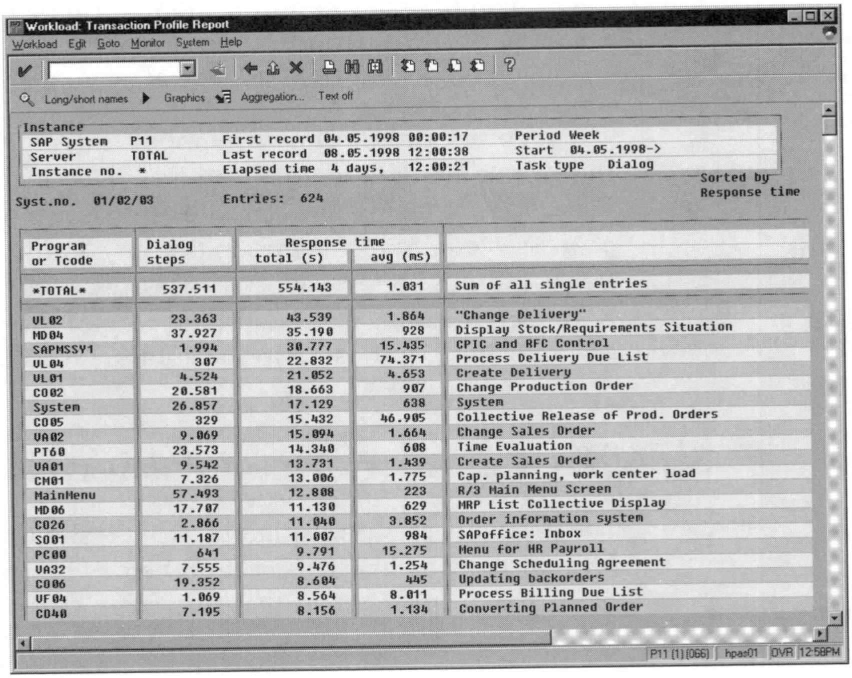

The transaction profile shows a list of all transactions (or programs) started in the selected period. In the column *Dialog steps*, the number of transaction steps for each transaction is recorded, a measure of the activity of a transaction. Other columns in the transaction profile show the total response times and the average response times, including the proportion of CPU time, dispatcher wait time, and database time. To access other columns with more information, use the arrow button. To see a column containing short texts describing the program or transaction named in the left-hand column, use the *Text* button (Figure 3.5 shows these short texts).

From the number of transaction steps (in the column *Dialog steps*), you can estimate how frequently the transaction was executed if you know how many transaction steps (screen changes) each regular user requires on average per procedure. For example, if a regular user requires around 5 transaction steps to create a sales order (Transaction code *VA01*) and the transaction profile shows 100,000 transaction steps for the selected time period, you can calculate that around 20,000 sales orders were created. If you wish to see which transactions had the most activity, sort by the column *Dialog steps*.

The column *Response time total* provides a measure for the entire load on the system. (See the section "Activity, Throughput, and Load," earlier in the chapter.) To find out which transactions produced the most load on the system, successively sort the list by the columns *Response time total*, *CPU time total*, or *DB time total*. After each sort, the programs at the top of the list are the likely candidates for performance optimization.

How to Read the Transaction Profile

In the example of the transaction profile in Figure 3.5, the R/3 main menu (transaction indicated as MainMenu) is the most frequently executed transaction and is responsible for 11% of the total number of dialog steps. However, the main menu represents only 2% of the total system load (see the column *Response time total*). Transaction *VL02*, with 4% of all transaction steps, produces 8% of the load. Thus, when the list has been sorted according to *Response time total*, Transaction *VL02* is at the top of the list.

An important index of performance for the users is the average response time of the transactions they are using. Monitor and create guideline values for the average response times of core transactions—that is, transactions whose performance is central to business operations.

In general, when analyzing the transaction profile, consider the following questions:

- Which transactions cause the greatest database load? (Sort by the column *DB time total*.)

- Which transactions cause the greatest CPU load? (Sort by the column *CPU time total*.)

- Are there transactions for which the proportion of database time or CPU time is higher than 60% of the total response time? Analyze these transactions using an SQL trace or ABAP trace as described in Chapter 4, "Performance Analysis for ABAP Programs."

- Are there any customer-developed programs (or transactions) that produce a large load?

Monitor and keep a copy of the transaction profile at regular intervals. This enables you to determine whether the response times of individual transactions grow continuously over time, or whether there is a sudden worsening of response times following a program modification. By recognizing trends in the transaction profile early, you can initiate a detailed program analysis before a program causes a bottleneck for an entire process chain, or worse, reduces the performance of the entire R/3 System through large CPU or database loads.

Table 3.3 provides guideline response times for common R/3 System programs.

TABLE 3.3: Common R/3 Programs in the Transaction Profile

Transaction/ Program	Description	Acceptable Response Time
MainMenu	The main R/3 menu. MainMenu frequently appears near the top of the transaction profile if sorted according to the column *Dialog steps*.	< 100ms

Continued on next page

TABLE 3.3: Common R/3 Programs in the Transaction Profile (*Continued*)

Transaction/ Program	Description	Acceptable Response Time
Login_Pw/ Logoff	Logon or logoff screen.	
AutoABAP	The AutoABAP runs periodically in the background and executes actions such as those required by the Alert Monitor.	< 1,000ms
Buf.Sync	Buffer synchronization.	< 1,000ms
Rep_Edit	Actions in the ABAP Editor.	
(B)SCHDL	The batch scheduler runs periodically and checks whether background programs are due to be started.	
RSCOLL00	The performance collector runs periodically and collects data on performance. If you sort the transaction profile according to *Response time total*, this program is often near the top of the list. However, the columns *CPU time total* and *DB time total* indicate that this program produces little CPU or database time. Most of the response time for this program occurs when this program is waiting in work processes to receive performance data.	
RSM13000	The update program is used to summarize all update module statistics that cannot be ascribed to a transaction.	< 3,000ms

Application Monitor

Another important instrument for workload analysis is the Application Monitor (Transaction code *ST07*), which you can use to create a load profile for each R/3 application module. To call the Application Monitor, use Transaction code *ST07*, or, from the R/3 initial screen, choose *Tools* ➤ *Administration* ➤ *Monitor* ➤ *Performance* ➤ *Workload* ➤ *Application monitor*.

All screens of the Application Monitor show performance-relevant data according to R/3 application module. By successively double-clicking the appropriate names in the *Application* column, you can narrow the focus of statistics in the monitor until you reach particular programs, transactions, or tables. This is because the Application Monitor organizes its statistics according to the R/3 application component hierarchy, with the application modules situated at the top of the hierarchy. For example, to see statistics on the transaction Create Customer Order (Transaction code *VA01*), double-click *Sales* and choose *Distribution* ➤ *Sales* ➤ *Create Sales Order*. (To see an outline of the full R/3 component hierarchy structure, use Transaction *HIER*.)

Many screens in the Application Monitor show data that is also displayed in other monitors, such as the Workload Monitor, the R/3 Storage Configuration Monitor (Transaction code *ST02*), the Table Call Statistics (Transaction code *ST10*), and so on. The advantage of using the Application Monitor is that the data is grouped according to the R/3 application component hierarchy; from an initial overview, you can drill down to an increasingly detailed view of the particular R/3 application modules, sub-modules, and transactions that are consuming the most system resources.

User Profile

The initial screen of the Application Monitor shows the current user profiles for the different R/3 application modules (see Figure 3.6). The user profile for each listed application consists of the numbers of *logged on* users, *active* users, and the users currently waiting for a request to be processed (users *in WP*). To drill down to a lower level of the R/3 application component hierarchy and thus see the user profile for a more specific area within an R/3 application module, successively double-click the appropriate rows in the *Application* column. At the lowest level of the hierarchy, you can see user activity in the individual transactions.

FIGURE 3.6:

The user profile in the Application Monitor

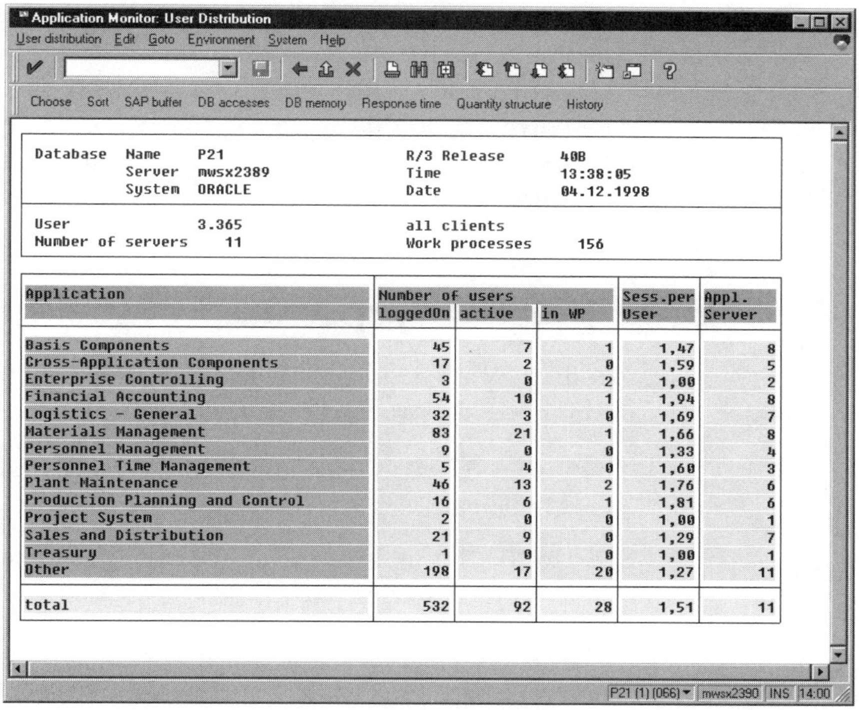

```
Application Monitor: User Distribution                                              _ □ ×
User distribution  Edit  Goto  Environment  System  Help

✔ [                    ▼] 🖫  ← 🗘 ✗ | 🖴 🏭 🏭 | 🏭 🏭 🏭 🏭 | 🏭 🖸 | ?

Choose  Sort  SAP buffer  DB accesses  DB memory  Response time  Quantity structure  History

┌──────────────────────────────────────────────────────────────────────────────┐
│ Database  Name     P21              R/3 Release      40B                        │
│           Server   mwsx2389         Time             13:38:05                   │
│           System   ORACLE           Date             04.12.1998                 │
│                                                                                 │
│ User                3.365           all clients                                 │
│ Number of servers   11              Work processes      156                     │
└──────────────────────────────────────────────────────────────────────────────┘
```

Application	Number of users			Sess.per	Appl.
	loggedOn	active	in WP	User	Server
Basis Components	45	7	1	1,47	8
Cross-Application Components	17	2	0	1,59	5
Enterprise Controlling	3	0	2	1,00	2
Financial Accounting	54	10	1	1,94	8
Logistics - General	32	3	0	1,69	7
Materials Management	83	21	1	1,66	8
Personnel Management	9	0	0	1,33	4
Personnel Time Management	5	4	0	1,60	3
Plant Maintenance	46	13	2	1,76	6
Production Planning and Control	16	6	1	1,81	6
Project System	2	0	0	1,00	1
Sales and Distribution	21	9	0	1,29	7
Treasury	1	0	0	1,00	1
Other	198	17	20	1,27	11
total	532	92	28	1,51	11

```
                                                    P21 (1) (066) ▼  mwsx2390  INS  14:00
```

How to Read the Application Monitor

In the Application Monitor's user profile, double-clicking the R/3 application module Sales and Distribution shows the user profile for sub-modules such as Sales, Shipping, Billing, and Basic Functions. A subsequent double-click of Sales shows the user profile for transactions belonging to Sales, such as *VA01* and *VA02*.

Looking at the user profile in the Application Monitor is a convenient way of finding out the number of logged on and active users. An *active* user is a user who has performed a transaction step in the last 30 seconds. To redefine this time period, from the menu, choose *User distribution* ➤ *Change active time.*

To analyze the user distribution on the application servers, from the menu, choose *User distribution* ➤ *Choose app. server*. The user profile in the Application Monitor is especially useful when you wish to check whether logging on with logon groups is functioning correctly, so that users are logged on to application servers independently of one another, according to the R/3 application module.

Load per R/3 Application Module

To display the load profile for each of the different R/3 application modules, proceed as follows:

1. From the Application Monitor initial screen, choose *Response time.*

2. In the dialog boxes that appear, specify the relevant server and time period.

The screen *Application Monitor: Response times* is displayed. The data on this screen matches that in the transaction profile in the Workload Monitor and includes transaction steps, response times per transaction step, CPU times, wait times, and database times. To toggle between average and total values, use the button *Total ⇔ Average*. The entries in the *Application* column are linked to the R/3 application component hierarchy. Thus, by successively double-clicking the appropriate names in that column, you can drill down to statistics on more specific component areas.

You can use the Application Monitor in the same way as you used the transaction profile in the Workload Monitor. The advantage of using the Application Monitor is that the data is displayed according to the R/3 application component hierarchy; from an initial overview, you can drill down to an increasingly detailed view of the particular R/3 application modules, sub-modules, and transactions that are consuming the most system resources.

In the Application Monitor, you can create graphs and diagrams illustrating load distribution. Use the button *Total* ⇔ *Average* to show total values, and choose *Graphic*. Depending on the R/3 application module, the graphics screen shows, for example, the distribution of the transaction steps (indicated as *Dialog steps*) and the response times (*Response time*). Each pie chart indicates the distribution of particular features across the available R/3 application modules.

Here's what the various pie charts show:

- *Dialog steps* shows the activity distribution.
- *Response time* shows the load distribution.
- *DB time* shows the load distribution on the database server.
- *CPU time* shows the load distribution on the application servers.
- *Requested bytes* shows the distribution of network traffic between the database server and application servers.

These pie charts are useful for administrators and managers who want to know where the most load is and which area has the greatest optimization potential.

R/3 Buffers

To monitor the R/3 buffers, from the initial screen of the Application Monitor, choose *SAP buffer*.

The figures displayed show the usage in KB of the R/3 buffers according to R/3 application module. The R/3 buffers include the program buffer (in the *program* column), the table buffers for generic buffering (in the *generic* column), and single record buffering (in the *single* column), as well as the CUA buffer (in the *CUA* column). To access statistics for more specific areas within an R/3 application module (following the R/3 component hierarchy), successively double-click the appropriate rows in the *Application* column, drilling down to individual programs and tables.

Summary

The Workload Monitor enables you to make detailed statements about the distribution of response times not only across different system components, such as the database, hardware, and R/3 Basis components, but also across different transactions and programs.

By performing a workload analysis, you can determine the system areas in which you require further analysis and tuning. Always remember to compare the results of your workload analysis with the observations of R/3 System users. This helps you avoid jumping to the wrong conclusion when a superficial analysis of the Workload Monitor indicates a performance problem where, in fact, there is no real problem. It also avoids the opposite situation of not noticing that the Workload Monitor is indicating a performance problem that is readily apparent to users.

Figure 3.7 summarizes performing a workload analysis for a general performance problem. You can find the corresponding detailed analyses for hardware, database, and R/3 memory configuration in Chapter 2.

Important Terms in This Chapter

After reading this chapter, you should be familiar with the following terms:

- Dispatcher wait time, load time, and database time
- Roll in time and roll out time
- Processing time and CPU time
- Activity, throughput, and load

FIGURE 3.7: Summary of the most important steps of a workload analysis

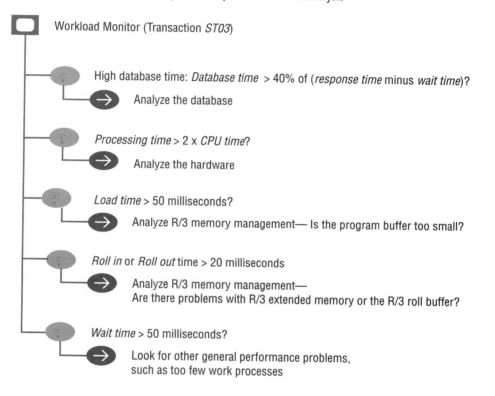

Workload Monitor (Transaction *ST03*)

High database time: *Database time* > 40% of (*response time* minus *wait time*)?

→ Analyze the database

Processing time > 2 x *CPU time*?

→ Analyze the hardware

Load time > 50 milliseconds?

→ Analyze R/3 memory management— Is the program buffer too small?

Roll in or *Roll out* time > 20 milliseconds

→ Analyze R/3 memory management—
Are there problems with R/3 extended memory or the R/3 roll buffer?

Wait time > 50 milliseconds?

→ Look for other general performance problems,
such as too few work processes

Review Questions

1. Which of the following statements are correct?

    A. The CPU time is measured by the operating system of the application server.

    B. The database time is measured by the database system.

    C. High network times for data transfers between the presentation server and the application server are reflected in an increased response time in the Workload Monitor.

    D. High network times for data transfers between the application server and the database server are reflected in an increased response time in the Workload Monitor.

    E. The roll out time is not part of the response time because the roll out of a user occurs only after the answer has been sent to the presentation server. Nevertheless, it is important for the performance of the R/3 System to keep the roll out time to a minimum, as during the roll outs, the R/3 work process remains occupied.

2. How is the term *load* defined in the R/3 environment?

    A. The *load* generated by a particular process is defined as the percentage of time that that process occupies the CPU of a computer, and can be monitored in the Operating System Monitor as *CPU utilization*.

    B. *Load* is the sum of response times. Thus, *total load* refers to the total response time, *CPU load* refers to the total CPU time, and *database load* refers to the total database time.

    C. *Load* means the number of transaction steps for each unit of time.

3. The Workload Monitor displays increased wait times for the dispatcher, such that *Av. wait time* is much greater than 50ms. What does this tell you?

   A. There is a communication problem between the presentation servers and the dispatcher of the application server—for example, a network problem.

   B. There is a general performance problem—for example, a database problem, a hardware bottleneck, or insufficient R/3 extended memory; or there are too few R/3 work processes. This statement does not provide enough information to pinpoint the exact problem.

   C. An increased dispatcher wait time is normal for an R/3 System. It protects the operating system from being overloaded, and can be ignored.

CHAPTER
FOUR

4

Performance Analysis for ABAP Programs

This chapter explains how to perform a detailed performance analysis for programs and transactions you have already identified as expensive. That is, you have performed a workload analysis and consulted users, and discovered that these programs consume too many system resources and have a negative effect on system performance. The next step is the analysis process.

To begin the analysis, analyze the single statistics records of the R/3 System to decide whether the performance of the program in question has expensive database accesses or high CPU and memory consumption. For expensive database accesses, perform an SQL trace. For high CPU and memory consumption, apply an ABAP trace or the ABAP debugger.

When Should You Read This Chapter?

You should read this chapter if you have identified a program or a transaction as critical for performance and now wish to make a detailed analysis of it. Before reading this chapter, you should read Chapters 1 and 3. Depending on the problems you analyze in this chapter, you can continue your reading with Chapters 7, 8, or 9.

Single Statistics Records

A *single statistics record* is a statistical record specific to each transaction step in the R/3 System. It is recorded in files on the application servers and includes response times, memory requirements, database accesses, and so on. These records are collected hourly by the collector program RSCOLL00, and the results can be viewed as described in this section. Single statistics records are deleted after approximately one day (see also Chapter 3, in the section "Technical Settings for the Workload Monitor").

1. Provided they have not been deleted yet, the single statistical records may be displayed as follows: Call the Workload Monitor (Transaction code *ST03*) and choose *This application server ➢ Single stat records* from the menu. Alternatively, use Transaction code *STAT*.

2. A dialog box appears in which you should specify a transaction or program name and a particular time period.

3. The screen *Workload: Display Statistical Records* appears, showing records that match your selection criteria. Figure 4.1 shows an example of single statistics records relating to Transaction *VF01* and user SAP_PERF.

FIGURE 4.1: Single statistics records (in this example, for Transaction *VF01*).

Workload: Display Statistical Records

Workload Edit Goto Monitor System Help

Long/short names ▲ Records ▼ Records ▲ 1 hour ▼ 1 hour Expansion

Server : pswdf727
Statistic file: E:\usr\sap\TCD\DVEBMGS00\data\stat.DAT
Analyzed time : 31.08.1998/10:00:00 − 31.08.1998/10:56:43

End time	Tcod	Program	T	Scr.	Wp	User	Response time(ms)	Memory used(kB)	Wait time(ms)	CPU time(ms)	DB req. time(ms)	Load/Gen time(ms)	kBytes transfer
10:00:00	VF01	*		*	*	*							
10:54:23	VF01	SAPMV60A	D	0011	4	SAP_PERF	24	3.958	0	16	0	2	0,0
10:54:29	VF01	RSM13000	U	3000	10	SAP_PERF	19.949	1.339	16	641	19.632	15	2.610,3
10:54:30	VF01	SAPMV60A	D	0011	1	SAP_PERF	27	3.638	0	0	4	2	0,1
10:54:33	VF01	SAPMV60A	D	0011	4	SAP_PERF	32	3.638	0	0	3	2	0,1
10:54:35	VF01	SAPMV60A	D	0102	0	SAP_PERF	59	1.301	0	47	0	23	0,0
10:54:46	VF01	SAPMV60A	D	0102	0	SAP_PERF	913	3.872	0	797	106	63	24,3
10:54:48	VF01	SAPMV60A	D	0102	1	SAP_PERF	64	1.301	0	63	0	25	0,0
10:54:56	VF01	SAPMV60A	D	0102	7	SAP_PERF	65	1.301	0	47	0	25	0,0
10:54:56	VF01	SAPMV60A	D	0011	0	SAP_PERF	23	3.958	0	16	0	2	0,0
10:54:59	VF01	SAPMV60A	D	0102	1	SAP_PERF	910	3.872	0	797	153	64	24,3
10:55:00	VF01	RSM13000	U	3000	11	SAP_PERF	508	1.339	0	188	351	15	306,9
10:55:03	VF01	RSM13000	U	3000	10	SAP_PERF	17.257	1.339	0	766	16.963	15	2.610,3
10:55:06	VF01	SAPMV60A	D	0011	0	SAP_PERF	39	3.638	0	0	3	2	0,1
10:55:07	VF01	SAPMV60A	D	0102	7	SAP_PERF	891	3.872	0	797	154	63	24,3
10:55:09	VF01	SAPMV60A	D	0011	1	SAP_PERF	19	3.958	0	16	0	2	0,0
10:55:13	VF01	SAPMV60A	D	0102	2	SAP_PERF	64	1.301	0	63	0	25	0,0
10:55:17	VF01	SAPMV60A	D	0011	7	SAP_PERF	18	3.958	0	16	0	2	0,0
10:55:19	VF01	SAPMV60A	D	0102	6	SAP_PERF	94	1.301	0	63	0	25	0,0
10:55:19	VF01	SAPMV60A	D	0011	1	SAP_PERF	130	3.638	0	0	4	2	0,1
10:55:24	VF01	SAPMV60A	D	0102	2	SAP_PERF	1.013	3.872	0	875	171	70	24,3
10:55:25	VF01	RSM13000	U	3000	11	SAP_PERF	437	1.339	0	141	275	15	306,9
10:55:27	VF01	SAPMV60A	D	0011	7	SAP_PERF	40	3.638	0	0	4	2	0,1
10:55:28	VF01	RSM13000	U	3000	10	SAP_PERF	20.845	1.339	0	2.969	19.959	15	11527,9
10:55:30	VF01	SAPMV60A	D	0102	6	SAP_PERF	1.144	3.872	0	859	172	80	24,3
10:55:34	VF01	SAPMV60A	D	0011	2	SAP_PERF	22	3.958	0	16	0	2	0,0
10:55:40	VF01	SAPMV60A	D	0011	6	SAP_PERF	17	3.958	0	16	0	2	0,0

TCD (1) (900) ▼ pswdf727 INS 11:10AM

- Single statistics records can help you get a clearer picture than that provided by the averaged values of the transaction profile. For example, single statistics records enable you to determine whether the response times for all transaction steps are equally large, or whether they are generally small and occasionally extremely large (in which case, the averages would be deceptively large). On the *Workload: Display Statistical Records* screen, you can use the screen ID numbers in the *Scr.* (screen) column to determine whether observed large response times are always associated with a particular transaction screen.

- In the example in Figure 4.1, the response times for the transaction are generally less than 1 second. Some response times, however, are larger than 10 seconds— and these occur during updates (indicated as *U* in the *T* column). This is an indication that the records relating to updates should be analyzed in more detail.

4. To display more details on an individual record, double-click it and choose *All details*. The resulting display should resemble Figure 4.2.

The following list provides you with an overview of typical problems that you can recognize with the help of single statistics records:

- Large database times:

  - These usually indicate a database problem that can be analyzed using an SQL trace. Two situations can be distinguished using the values for *kBytes transfer* (in Figure 4.1) or *Database rows* (in Figure 4.2).

  - The database time is large because the quantity of transferred data is large. This is true in the example in Figure 4.2. For 18,530 transferred records (in the column *Database rows*), 19,959ms (indicated as *Request time*) are required. This corresponds to an average time of around

FIGURE 4.2:

Single statistical record with a large database time due to a large amount of transferred data

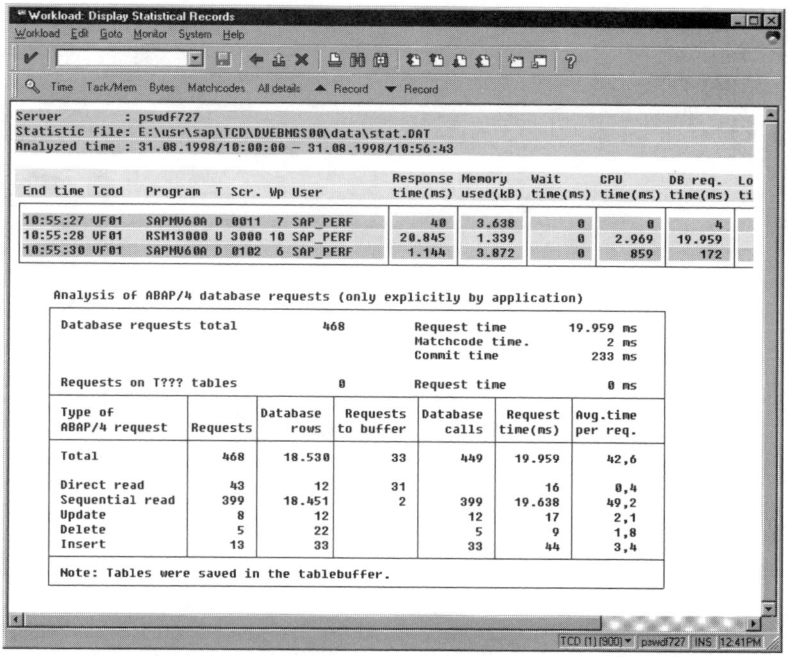

```
Workload: Display Statistical Records
Workload  Edit  Goto  Monitor  System  Help

Q  Time  Task/Mem  Bytes  Matchcodes  All details  ▲ Record  ▼ Record

Server       : psudf727
Statistic file: E:\usr\sap\TCD\DVEBMGS00\data\stat.DAT
Analyzed time : 31.08.1998/10:00:00 - 31.08.1998/10:56:43

                                          Response Memory   Wait    CPU     DB req.  Lo
End time Tcod  Program  T Scr. Wp User    time(ms) used(kB) time(ms) time(ms) time(ms) ti

10:55:27 VF01  SAPMV60A D 0011  7 SAP_PERF      40    3.638       0       0       4
10:55:28 VF01  RSM13000 U 3000 10 SAP_PERF  20.845    1.339       0   2.969  19.959
10:55:30 VF01  SAPMV60A D 0102  6 SAP_PERF   1.144    3.872       0     859     172
```

Analysis of ABAP/4 database requests (only explicitly by application)					
Database requests total		468	Request time		19.959 ms
			Matchcode time.		2 ms
			Commit time		233 ms
Requests on T??? tables		0	Request time		0 ms

Type of ABAP/4 request	Requests	Database rows	Requests to buffer	Database calls	Request time(ms)	Avg.time per req.
Total	468	18.530	33	449	19.959	42,6
Direct read	43	12	31	16		0,4
Sequential read	399	18.451	2	399	19.638	49,2
Update	8	12		12	17	2,1
Delete	5	22		5	9	1,8
Insert	13	33		33	44	3,4

Note: Tables were saved in the tablebuffer.

```
                                          TCD (1) (900) ▼  pswdf727  INS  12:41PM
```

1ms per record. This is an optimal rate of transfer. (According to the classification proposed in Chapter 9 for SQL statements, this indicates an expensive SQL statement of type 1.)

- The database time is large despite the fact that relatively little data is transferred. Figure 4.3 shows a single statistics record in which 33,567ms (indicated as *Request time*) are required for 265 selected records (in the column *Database rows*), making the average time 110ms per record. (According to the classification proposed in Chapter 9 for SQL statements, this indicates an expensive SQL statement of type 2.)

FIGURE 4.3:

Single statistics record with a high database time and a small volume of transferred data

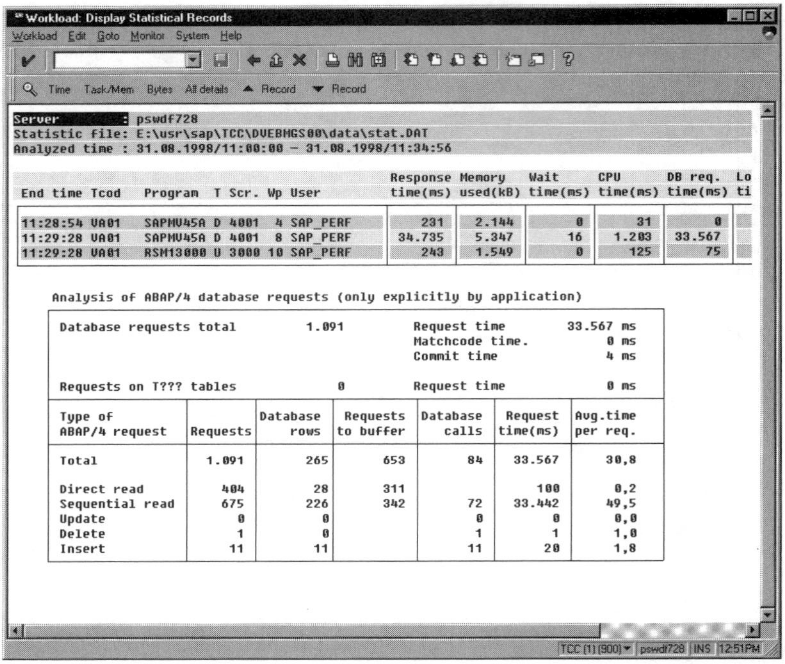

| | Workload: Display Statistical Records |
| Workload Edit Goto Monitor System Help |

```
Server         : pswdf728
Statistic file: E:\usr\sap\TCC\DUEBMGS00\data\stat.DAT
Analyzed time : 31.08.1998/11:00:00 - 31.08.1998/11:34:56
```

| | | | | | | Response time(ms) | Memory used(kB) | Wait time(ms) | CPU time(ms) | DB req. time(ms) | Lo ti |
End time	Tcod	Program	T	Scr.	Wp	User						
11:28:54	VA01	SAPMV45A	D	4001	4	SAP_PERF	231	2.144	0	31	0	
11:29:28	VA01	SAPMV45A	D	4001	8	SAP_PERF	34.735	5.347	16	1.203	33.567	
11:29:28	VA01	RSM13000	U	3000	10	SAP_PERF	243	1.549	0	125	75	

Analysis of ABAP/4 database requests (only explicitly by application)

Database requests total	1.091	Request time	33.567 ms
		Matchcode time.	0 ms
		Commit time	4 ms
Requests on T??? tables	0	Request time	0 ms

Type of ABAP/4 request	Requests	Database rows	Requests to buffer	Database calls	Request time(ms)	Avg.time per req.
Total	1.091	265	653	84	33.567	30,8
Direct read	404	28	311		100	0,2
Sequential read	675	226	342	72	33.442	49,5
Update	0	0		0	0	0,0
Delete	1	0		1	1	1,0
Insert	11	11		11	20	1,8

`TCC [1] (900) ▼ pswdf728 INS 12:51PM`

NOTE

For more information on the interpretation and analysis of database times, see Chapter 9.

- Large database times occurring only sporadically:
  - To analyze this problem, look in the single statistics record for the entry *Note: Tables were saved in the table buffer* (as in Figure 4.2 earlier in this section). This entry indicates that tables read from the database are being stored in the table buffer. If the R/3 System has been running for some time in production operation, all required tables should be in the table buffer and no longer need to be loaded there. If you find the above entry frequently in

production operation, the large database times are due to tables being displaced or invalidated in the table buffer. In that case, proceed with the analysis in Chapter 7, "R/3 Table Buffering."

- Large CPU times:
  - These indicate either excessively complex calculations in the ABAP code or frequent accessing of the table buffer. You should analyze programs with a CPU time of more than 50% with an ABAP trace or the ABAP debugger.

- Other problems:
  - These include problems with the loading processes for the program buffer, R/3 lock administration (enqueues), or RFC calls.

The analysis with the SQL trace, which is useful only for investigating programs that cause large database times, is significantly simpler than an analysis using the more comprehensive ABAP trace or the ABAP debugger (which is normally used by ABAP developers). In practice, considerably more than 50% of all performance problems in ABAP programs are due to inefficient database accesses. Therefore, this book focuses mainly on analyzing expensive SQL statements.

SQL Trace

The SQL trace is the most important tool for analyzing programs with database accesses that cause performance problems. The SQL trace is a record of all database accesses of programs concurrently run by a user. It was developed for the R/3 System and works in almost the same way regardless of the database system used.

To access the initial screen of the SQL trace, use Transaction code *ST05* or, from any R/3 screen, choose *System* ➢ *Utilities* ➢ *SQL trace*.

The *Trace requests* screen is displayed, showing the buttons for starting, stopping, and displaying the results of the SQL trace. This screen also lets you select the trace modes SQL trace, enqueue trace, and RFC trace. By default, the SQL trace is the mode selected. The following section concerns only the SQL trace.

Activating an SQL Trace

To start or stop the SQL trace from the *Trace requests* screen, use the buttons *Trace on* and *Trace off*. On a given application server, you can run only one SQL trace at a time. The field *State of traces* tells you whether a trace is already switched on and who the user is who activated it. When you start a trace, a dialog box appears in which you can enter the users for whom the trace will be activated. The username you logged in with appears by default. Enter a different username if you wish to perform a trace for another user. The user who activates the trace may be different from the user whose activity in the system is being traced.

When activating a trace, bear in mind the following:

- Ensure that the user whose actions are traced executes only one program during the trace—otherwise, the trace results are confusing. Ensure also that no background jobs or update requests are running for this user.

- An SQL trace is performed through the database interface of the application server. For each database operation, data is written to a trace file on the application server. Therefore, ensure that you are logged on to the same application server as the user being traced. To trace an update request or a background job in an R/3 System with a distributed update or background services, start the trace on all application servers that have update or background work processes. You have to trace this broadly because you do not know on which application server the update request or background job will be started.

- The SQL trace monitors only accesses to the database. SQL statements that can be satisfied from the data in the R/3 buffer do not appear in the trace. However, the buffer load process shows up in the trace.

- Since you are normally not interested in recording the buffer load process in the SQL trace, you should first execute a program once without activating the trace to allow the buffers to be loaded (that is, the R/3 buffers and database buffers). Then run the program again with the SQL trace activated and use the results of this trace for evaluation.

- During the trace, look at the following monitors:

- Work Process Overview (for general monitoring)

- Operating System Monitor of the database server (for monitoring possible CPU bottlenecks on the database server)

- Database Process Monitor (for direct monitoring of the executed SQL statements)

NOTE   It makes no sense to look at these monitors during the trace if you are logged on as the user being traced. The SQL statements of your activity in the monitors would appear in the trace.

- The default trace filename is set with the R/3 profile parameter *rstr/file*. In the *Trace requests* screen, you can assign another name to the trace file. Writing to the trace file is cyclical in that, when it is full, the oldest entries are deleted to make room for newer entries. The size of the trace file in bytes is specified through the R/3 profile parameter *rstr/max_diskspace*, for which the default value is 16,384,000 bytes (16MB).

Evaluating an SQL Trace

To evaluate a trace, in the *Trace requests* screen, choose *List trace*. A dialog box is displayed enabling you to specify the trace you wish to list, using the fields listed in Table 4.1.

TABLE 4.1: Fields in the Dialog Box for Specifying Which Trace You Wish to Evaluate

Field	Meaning
Trace filename	Name of the trace file. Normally, this name should not be changed.
Trace mode	The default setting for trace mode is SQL trace. Hence, to perform an SQL trace, you do not need to change the mode.
Trace period	Period in which the trace runs.
User name	The user whose system actions were traced.
Object name	The names of specific tables to which the display of trace results is to be restricted. Note that by default, the tables D010*, D020*, and DDLOG are not shown in the trace results, as these tables contain the ABAP code of the program being traced and the buffer synchronization data.
Duration	This field is used to restrict the display to SQL statements having an execution time longer than the value specified in this field.
Operation	This field is used to restrict the trace data to particular database operations.

After making the appropriate selections in the dialog box, choose *Execute*. The screen *Basic SQL Trace List* is displayed. Figure 4.4 shows an example of the data for a DB2/390 database; Table 4.2 explains the columns displayed in the list.

NOTE   To view the last three columns listed in Table 4.2, use the button *More Info*.

FIGURE 4.4: Example of a Basic SQL Trace List for database system DB2/390

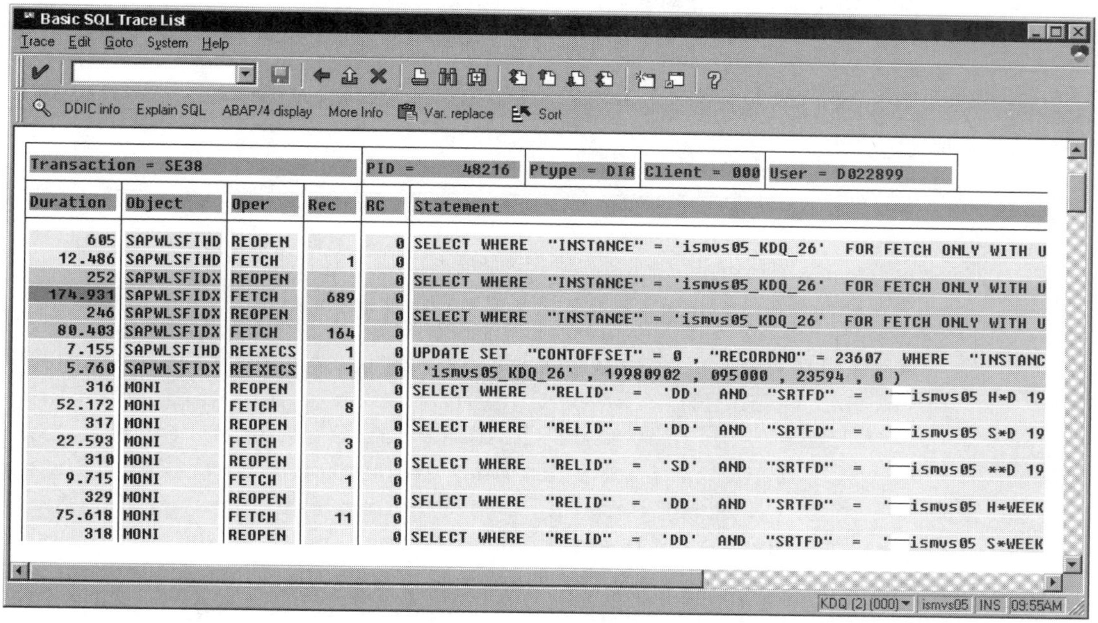

TABLE 4.2: Columns in the Results Display of an SQL Trace

Column	Meaning
Duration	Runtime of an SQL statement in microseconds (millionths of a second). If the runtime is more than 150,000 microseconds, the corresponding row is colored red to signify that the SQL statement has a long runtime. The value 150,000 microseconds is a somewhat arbitrary boundary.
Object	The name of the database table or database view.
Oper	The operation executed on the database.
Rec	The number of records read from the database.
RC	Database-specific return code.
Statement	Short form of the executed SQL statement. The complete statement can be displayed by double-clicking the corresponding row.

Continued on next page

TABLE 4.2: Columns in the Results Display of an SQL Trace *(Continued)*

Column	Meaning
hh:mm:ss:ms	Time stamp in the form hour:minute:second:millisecond.
Program	Name of the ABAP program from which the SQL statement originates.
Curs	Database cursor number.

Direct Reads

The first SQL statement listed in Figure 4.4 accesses the table SAPWLSFIHD. The field INSTANCE specified in the WHERE clause is the only key field in the table. Therefore, the result of the SQL request can only be either exactly one record (Rec=1) or no record (Rec=0), depending on whether a table entry exists for the specified key SQL statements that use the equals sign (=) to specify all key fields of the respective table are called *fully qualified accesses* or *direct reads*. A fully qualified database access should normally not last longer than from 2–10ms. However, in individual cases, they may last up to 10 times longer. For example, when blocks cannot be found in the database buffer and must be retrieved from the hard disk, the wait might be noticeable.

In Figure 4.4, the database access consists of two database operations: REOPEN and FETCH. The operation REOPEN transfers the concrete values in the WHERE clause to the database. In Figure 4.4, for example, this data is INSTANCE = 'ismvs05_ KDQ_26'. The operation FETCH locates the database data and transfers it to the application server. In Figure 4.4, REOPEN and FETCH are two separate operations. In some database systems, REOPEN and FETCH form a single operation during a direct read.

Sequential Reads

In Figure 4.4, the second object accessed is table SAPWLSFIDX (indicated in the column *Object*). The table key, as defined in the ABAP dictionary, consists of the fields INSTANCE, REC_DATE, and REC_TIME. However, in Figure 4.4, only the field INSTANCE is specified in the WHERE clause. This access can transfer multiple records. Thus, in Figure 4.4, there are 689 transferred records (indicated in the column *Rec*). This type of fetch is known as an *array fetch*. The data records are transferred in packets to the application server in one or more FETCHES. An array fetch offers better performance than transferring individual records in a client/server environment.

The maximum number of records that can be transferred in a FETCH is determined by the R/3 database interface as follows: Each R/3 work process has an input/output buffer for transferring data to or from the database. The size of this buffer is specified in the R/3 profile parameter *dbs/io_buf_size*. The number of records transferred from the database by a FETCH is calculated as follows:

Number of records=value of *dbs/io_buf_size*÷bytes of one record

The number of records per FETCH depends on the SELECT clause of the SQL statement. If the number of fields to be transferred from the database is restricted through a SELECT clause, more records fit into a single FETCH than when a SELECT * is used. The default value for the R/3 profile parameter *dbs/io_buf_size* is 33,792 bytes and should not be changed unless this is recommended by SAP.

Guideline values for the optimal response times of array fetches are under 10ms per selected record. The actual runtime strongly depends on the WHERE clause, the index used, and how conveniently the data is stored.

Changes

In Figure 4.4, the next two operations (indicated in the *Oper* column) are REEXECS operations, which show changes to the tables SAPWLSFIHD and SAPWLSFIDX.

DECLARE, PREPARE, and OPEN

Other database operations that may be listed in the SQL trace are DECLARE, PREPARE, and OPEN. The DECLARE operation defines a *cursor* to manage the data transfer between ABAP programs and a database, and assigns a cursor ID used for subsequent communication between an R/3 work process and the database system.

Next, in the PREPARE operation, the database process determines the access strategy for the statement. In the *Statement* column, instead of the concrete values of the WHERE clause, a *binding variable* is indicated (for example, "INSTANCE" =:A0).

PREPARE operations can be time consuming. To reduce the need for PREPARE operations, each work process of an application server retains a certain number of cursors for already parsed SQL statements in a buffer known as the *R/3 cursor cache* (or *SAP cursor cache*). Each R/3 work process buffers the operations DECLARE, PREPARE, OPEN, and EXEC in its own R/3 cursor cache. Once the work process has defined a cursor for a DECLARE operation, the same cursor can be used repeatedly until, after a certain time, it is displaced from the cursor cache due to the latter's limited size.

The database does not receive the concrete values of the WHERE clause (for example, "INSTANCE" = 'ismvs05_KDQ_26' in Figure 4.4) until the OPEN operation is used. A PREPARE and an OPEN operation are necessary only for the first execution of a statement, as long as that statement has not yet been displaced from the R/3 cursor cache. Subsequently, the statement, which has already been prepared (parsed), can always be reaccessed with a REOPEN.

Figure 4.4 shows the SQL trace for the second run of the same report. As the DECLARE, PREPARE, and OPEN operations are executed only in the first run of a report, in the second run, performance analysis focuses only on the REOPEN and FETCH operations.

Network Problems

If, through an SQL trace, you identify an SQL statement with a long runtime, you should perform a second and third SQL trace to deepen your analysis. It is useful to perform the trace at a time of high system load and again at a time of low system load. If you find that the response times for database accesses are large only at particular times, this indicates throughput problems in the network or in database access (for example, an I/O bottleneck on the hard drive). If, on the other hand, the response times for database access are poor in general (not only at particular times), the cause is probably an inefficient SQL statement, which should be optimized.

When evaluating database response times, remember that the processing times of SQL statements are measured on the application server. The runtime shown in the trace comprises not only the time required by the database to furnish the requested data, but also the time required to transfer data between the database and the application server. If there is a performance problem in network communication, the runtimes of SQL statements increase.

Network problems between the database and the application server may best be recognized by comparing traces as follows:

Execute the same SQL trace at least twice:

- Once on the R/3 instance on the same computer as the database and directly connected to the database (through Inter-Process Communication, or IPC)

- Once on an application server connecting to the database through the TCP/IP network

Compare both SQL traces. If there are significantly larger response times (larger by 50% or more) on the application server connected through the network, you have a network problem. Perform this test at a time of low system load, and repeat it several times to rule out runtime differences due to the buffer load process on the database and the application servers. This test functions only when your R/3 instance on the database server is connected to the database through IPC.

Other Tools

To further your analysis of SQL statements, SAP provides a number of other tools including compressed data, identical selects, and other functions.

Compressed Data

The *compressed data* for SQL traces is an overview of the most expensive SQL accesses. To display the compressed data, choose *Goto* ➢ *Summary* ➢ *Compress* from the *Basic SQL Trace List* screen.

A list is displayed whose columns are explained in Table 4.3. Sort the list according to the runtime of the SQL statements (for example, by placing your cursor on a figure in the column *Time* and using the *Sort* icon or F5). The SQL statements with the longest runtimes should be optimized first.

TABLE 4.3: An Explanation of the Fields in the *Compressed Data* Overview of SQL Traces

Field	Meaning
SQL op	Database operation: select, update, insert, or delete
Accesses	Number of accesses per table
Records	Number of records read per table
Time	Runtime per table in microseconds
Percent	Runtime per table as a percentage of the sum of all runtimes

Identical Selects

Programs that reduce performance often read identical data from the database several times in succession. To identify these identical SQL statements, use the *identical selects* function as follows: From the *Basic SQL Trace List* screen, choose *Goto* ➤ *Identical selects.*

A list of identical selects is displayed that tells you how often each identical select was executed. By using this function in conjunction with the *compressed data,* you can see roughly how much of an improvement in performance you stand to gain by optimizing the programming for identical SQL statements.

Other Functions

You can access the information and functions needed for a detailed analysis from the *Basic SQL Trace List* screen. For example:

- Program name and Transaction code of the executed program: To jump directly to the code location that executes the SQL statement, use the button *ABAP display.*

- Table name: The button *DDIC info.* provides important ABAP Dictionary information for the table accessed by the SQL statement, including the table name.

- Detailed analysis of the SQL statement—for example, using the *explain* function through the *Explain SQL* button.

For more information on the functions in the *Basic SQL Trace List* screen, see Chapter 9.

Monitoring Customer ABAP Developments

For customer-developed ABAP programs, perform at least the following checks as a form of program quality control:

1. For each customer-developed ABAP program, perform an SQL trace either on the production system or on an R/3 System with a representative volume of test data.

2. Display the compressed data to find the SQL statements with the largest runtimes as follows: From the *Basic SQL Trace List* screen, choose *Goto* ➢ *Summary* ➢ *Compress*.

3. Display a list of identical accesses to find SQL statements that are executed several times in succession. From the *Basic SQL Trace List* screen, choose *Goto* ➢ *Identical selects*.

4. Using the *compressed data* overview and identical access lists, decide whether the program should be approved, or whether the program can be improved by the responsible ABAP developer.

5. Save a copy of the lists where you keep the program documentation. If program performance later decreases (whether due to a modification or due to the growing data volume), perform a further SQL trace and compare it to the earlier one. Monitor performance in this way after each significant program modification.

NOTE   An SQL trace can be used not only to monitor customer-developed programs, but also to regularly monitor frequently used standard R/3 transactions that are critical for performance. If the runtime of particular SQL statements grows over time, you may need to archive the corresponding table.

ABAP Trace or Runtime Analysis

You should use an ABAP trace when the runtime of the programs to be analyzed comprises mainly CPU time. An ABAP trace measures not only the runtime of database accesses (by SELECT and EXEC SQL, for example), but also the time required by:

- Individual modularization units (such as MODULE, PERFORM, CALL FUNCTION, and SUBMIT)

- Internal table operations (such as APPEND, COLLECT, SORT, and READ TABLE)

- Other ABAP statements

Activating an ABAP Trace

To activate an ABAP trace, proceed as follows:

1. From any R/3 screen, choose *System ➢ Utilities ➢ Runtime analysis ➢ Execute*.

2. The *ABAP Runtime Analysis: Initial Screen* is displayed. Enter an R/3 transaction code, an ABAP program name, or an R/3 function module, and from the menu, choose *Runtime analysis ➢ Execute*. The ABAP trace is switched on.

3. The R/3 System starts measuring the runtime of the program you specified and creates a file to store the resulting measurements.

4. When you wish to return to the initial runtime analysis screen, simply exit the program, function module, or transaction in the normal way, or use the R/3 menu to navigate to the runtime analysis screen as above. The initial screen for runtime analysis shows the newly created measurement data file in the lower part of the screen. To display the results of the ABAP trace, choose *Analyze*.

When activating an ABAP trace, you can use filter functions. These enable you to restrict the trace to a particular function module or a particular group of ABAP statements.

Bear in mind the following points, which are similar to those applying to an SQL trace:

- As you are normally not interested in tracing the buffer load process, you should first execute the program once without a trace to load the R/3 buffers and the database buffers. Then, activate and evaluate the ABAP trace for the second run of the program.

- Repeat the ABAP trace at various times of both high and low system loads. Ensure that the measured times are not influenced by a temporary system overload (for example, a CPU overload).

To enable you to perform runtime analysis, the R/3 System requires the R/3 profile parameters *abap/atrapath* and *abap/atrasizequota*. These parameters are set when the R/3 System is installed. For more information on these parameters, see the parameter documentation in Transaction *RZ11*.

Evaluating an ABAP Trace

To display the results of a completed ABAP trace, on the screen *ABAP Runtime Analysis: Initial Screen,* choose *Analyze.* The screen *Runtime Analysis Evaluation: Overview* is displayed showing different views of the ABAP trace results and providing the following functions:

- The button *Hit list* displays the execution time in microseconds for each statement executed by the program or transaction. This list is sorted in decreasing order of the gross times.

- The button *Tables hit list* lists the database tables that were accessed by the transaction or program.

- The button *Group hit list* displays the ABAP trace results in groups according to modularization unit.

- The button *Call hierarchy* displays all the statements in chronological order of execution.

The screen *Runtime Analysis Evaluation: Overview* shows the gross and net execution times of a program call in microseconds. The *gross* time is the total time required for the call. This includes the times of all modularization units and ABAP statements in this call. The *net* time is the gross time minus the time required for the called modularization units (MODULE, PERFORM, CALL FUNCTION, CALL SCREEN, CALL TRANSACTION, CALL DIALOG, SUBMIT) and for separately specified ABAP statements. For statements such as APPEND, the gross time equals the net time. If the gross time differs from the net times for such statements, the call contains other calls or modularization units. The hit list enables you to see each individual component of each call.

ABAP Debugger

Apart from expensive SQL statements, the most important causes of performance problems are internal tables that have many entries. These tables with many entries lead to large requirements for memory and CPU during copy, sort, or search operations on internal tables.

The ABAP debugger enables you to display a list of all internal tables built by a particular program. The ABAP debugger is actually a tool for performing functional troubleshooting of programs. Detailed descriptions of the debugger may be found in SAP literature on ABAP programming. Performance analysis using the ABAP debugger is not a standard procedure and is best performed by an ABAP developer.

WARNING   When working with the ABAP debugger, the ABAP program being debugged may terminate and display the error message *Invalid interruption of a database selection,* or the R/3 System may automatically trigger a database commit. In both cases, an SAP logical unit of work (LUW) has been interrupted, which may lead to inconsistencies in the application tables. Therefore, you should debug only on a test system or in the presence of someone who is very familiar with the program being analyzed and who can manually correct the inconsistencies in the database tables if necessary. See "Debugging Programs in the Production Client" in R/3 Online Documentation for the ABAP debugger.

---

1. Begin performance analysis with the debugger by starting the program to be analyzed. Then open a second session where you can monitor the program to be analyzed in the Work Process Overview (Transaction code *SM50*). Enter the debugger from the Work Process Overview by choosing *Debugging*.

    *   By using the debugger several times in succession, you can identify the parts of the program that cause a large CPU consumption. Often, these sections consist of LOOP … ENDLOOP statements affecting large internal tables.

2. In the debugger, to display the current memory requirements, from the menu, choose *Goto* ➤ *Other screens* ➤ *Memory use*.

   - Check for cases of unnecessary memory consumption that may have been caused by a nonoptimal program or nonoptimal use of a program. As a guideline value, bear in mind that a program being used by several users in dialog mode should not allocate more than 100MB. Background programs (for example, billing runs at night on a dedicated application server) should not require more than 1GB. With the current 32-bit architecture, program termination typically results when from 1GB–3GB of memory are required.

3. In the debugger, to display a list of the internal tables of the program, first choose *Goto* ➤ *System* ➤ *System areas*. Then, in the *Area* field, enter **ITAB**. In the resulting display, the *FILL* column shows the number of rows in the respective table. To calculate the memory requirements for the listed tables, multiply the number of rows (indicated in the *FILL* column) by the width of the header line (indicated in the *LENG* column).

Experience shows that there are two common programming errors that cause large memory or CPU requirements for programs:

- Missing REFRESH or FREE statements: The ABAP statements REFRESH and FREE delete internal tables and release the memory that was allocated to them. If these statements are not used, memory resources may be unnecessarily tied up.

- Reading in internal tables: The ABAP statement READ TABLE...WITH KEY... allows searching in internal tables. If you use this statement by itself for a standard table, the search is sequential, which is a time-consuming process for large tables. You can significantly improve search performance by adding the statements ...BINARY SEARCH (thus specifying a binary search) and SORT TABLE (to sort the table). (See also the F1 Help for ABAP on the statement READ TABLE.)

> **NOTE** As of R/3 Release 4.0, you can optimize the performance of operations on large tables by using sorted tables (through the SORTED TABLE statement) or hash tables (through the HASHED TABLE statement).

See also R/3 Online Documentation on the ABAP programming environment.

Summary

R/3 provides numerous tools for a detailed performance analysis of individual ABAP programs.

Analyzing single statistics records lets you narrow down the causes of the performance problems of individual programs to one of the following problem areas:

- Inefficient table buffering
- Expensive SQL statements
- High CPU consumption

The SQL trace is the tool to use for analyzing expensive SQL statements in ABAP programs. Evaluating the trace enables you to identify throughput bottlenecks in the database or due to network problems.

For problems of high CPU consumption, use the ABAP trace. In contrast to the SQL trace, this enables time measurements for operations on internal tables such as LOOP, READ, and SORT. Alternatively, CPU-consuming programs can be monitored through the ABAP debugger from the Work Process Overview. This form of analysis should be performed only by ABAP developers.

Figure 4.5 summarizes the procedure for analyzing a single program or transaction.

FIGURE 4.5: Performance analysis procedure for an ABAP program

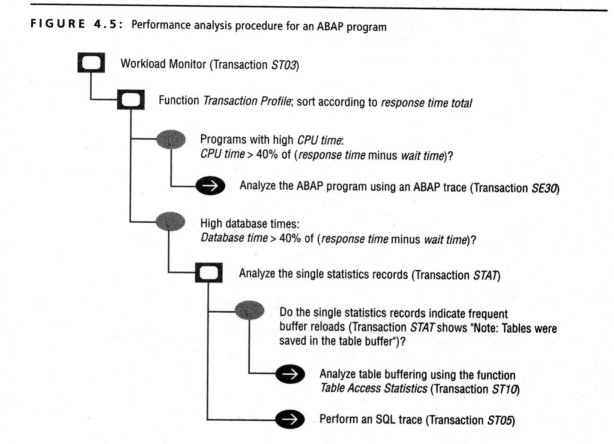

Workload Monitor (Transaction *ST03*)

Function *Transaction Profile*; sort according to *response time total*

Programs with high *CPU time*:
CPU time > 40% of (*response time* minus *wait time*)?

Analyze the ABAP program using an ABAP trace (Transaction *SE30*)

High database times:
Database time > 40% of (*response time* minus *wait time*)?

Analyze the single statistics records (Transaction *STAT*)

Do the single statistics records indicate frequent buffer reloads (Transaction *STAT* shows "Note: Tables were saved in the table buffer")?

Analyze table buffering using the function *Table Access Statistics* (Transaction *ST10*)

Perform an SQL trace (Transaction *ST05*)

Review Questions

1. What do you have to consider when you perform an SQL trace?

   A. There is only one trace file in each R/3 System. Therefore, only one SQL trace can be performed at a time.

   B. The user whose actions are being traced should not run multiple programs concurrently.

   C. You should perform the SQL trace on a second execution of a program because the relevant buffers are then already loaded.

   D. SQL traces are useful on the database server, but not on application servers, which yield inexact results due to network times.

2. When should you perform an ABAP trace?

   A. If a problem occurs with the table buffer

   B. For programs with high CPU requirements

   C. For I/O problems with hard disks

CHAPTER
FIVE

5

Configuring R/3
Memory Areas

This chapter helps you optimize the configuration of the R/3 memory areas for each R/3 instance: R/3 buffers, R/3 roll memory, R/3 extended memory, R/3 paging memory, R/3 heap memory (variable local memory for R/3 work processes), and fixed local memory for R/3 work processes.

The first part of the chapter explains the function of each memory area and its effect on R/3 System performance. The second part explains how to optimally configure these memory areas for different operating systems and provides concrete configuration recommendations.

The decisive factors affecting memory configuration are as follows:

- Physical memory (RAM): The amount of physically available main memory should be proportionate to the amount of virtually allocated memory. Ask yourself which memory areas within physical memory are the most urgently required at times of high system load.

- Limits of the operating system: Is the desired size of particular memory areas too large for a given type of operating system?

When Should You Read This Chapter?

Read this chapter if you wish to configure R/3 memory areas in a new installation; after an upgrade or extension to your R/3 System; or if you have detected performance problems related to memory area configuration.

R/3 Memory Areas

This section introduces the basic terms and concepts of R/3 memory areas.

Basic Terms

The basic terms associated with R/3 memory configuration include *physical memory, virtual memory, local memory,* and *shared memory.*

Physical and Virtual Memory

In all operating systems, you can allocate more memory than is physically available. The term *memory* usually means the *virtual memory* allocated by the operating system either as physical memory or as swap space. The maximum amount of virtually allocable memory is limited as follows:

- All operating-system processes combined cannot allocate more memory than the sum of physical memory plus the available swap space. This limit reflects physical hardware limits.

- Each individual operating-system process cannot allocate more memory than the maximum addressable memory area (address space) allowed by the operating system. This logical limit reflects the operating-system architecture. For the 32-bit architecture currently in general use, the size of the address space is between 1.8GB and 3.8GB (that is, no more than 2^{32} bytes).

Local and Shared Memory

The operating system allocates two types of memory: *local memory* and *shared memory* (or *global memory*). Local memory is assigned to exactly one operating-system process—for example, an R/3 work process. Only this process can write to or read from this memory area. Shared memory, on the other hand, is available to multiple operating-system processes. Thus, all R/3 buffers, for example, lie in shared memory, because all the R/3 work processes of an R/3 instance need to be able to access the R/3 buffer.

Local memory is also created for each R/3 work process. The local memory of an R/3 work process includes, for example, the R/3 cursor cache and the I/O buffer for transferring the data to or from the database. (See Chapter 4, under "Evaluating an SQL Trace.")

The total amount of allocated virtual memory is equivalent to the sum of local memory and shared memory.

If, on a single server, there are several R/3 instances, or an R/3 instance and a database instance, the processes on an instance can always access only the shared memory of their instance; they cannot access the global objects of other instances.

Inexact use of terminology can create confusion when discussing R/3 memory management. The same terms on the operating-system level and the R/3 System level may refer to different things. You should differentiate, for example, between *operating-system paging* and *R/3 paging*, and between *context switch* on the operating-system level and *context switch* on the R/3 level. Similarly, the term *heap* is used on the operating-system level to mean the local memory allocated by an operating-system process. However, on the R/3 level, *heap* refers to one particular type of local memory, and thus constitutes only one part of the heap on the operating-system level.

NOTE   To minimize confusion, in this book, the prefix *R/3* explicitly differentiates, for example, the terms *R/3 heap memory* or *R/3 paging memory* from their counterparts on the operating-system level. When reading other literature or R/3 Notes in the Online Service System (OSS), you will need to judge from the context whether the author means to use a term in the R/3 sense or in the operating-system sense.

R/3 Roll Memory, R/3 Extended Memory, and R/3 Heap Memory

This section explains *R/3 roll memory*, *R/3 extended memory*, *R/3 heap memory*, and associated terms and parameters.

User Context

An R/3 transaction normally extends over several transaction steps or screen changes. During these steps, data such as variables, internal tables, and screen lists is created and stored in the application server memory. This data is called the *user context*.

User Sessions

Whenever you create a new session using the menu option *System ➤ Create session*, a new user context is created. The transaction data you use in one session is located in a separate memory area from the transaction data you use in another session. User-started sessions of this type are called *external sessions*. An ABAP program can also start a new session, called an *internal session*, which similarly creates a new user context. The ABAP commands that start user sessions are SUBMIT, CALL TRANSACTION, CALL DIALOG, CALL SCREEN, CALL FUNCTION IN UPDATE TASK, CALL FUNCTION IN BACKGROUND TASK, and CALL FUNCTION STARTING NEW TASK.

Depending on their size, user contexts are stored in one or more of the following areas: R/3 roll memory, R/3 extended memory, or R/3 heap memory. By changing the amounts specified in particular memory parameters, you can influence the extent to which a particular memory area is used.

R/3 Roll Memory

Roll memory can be local or global. The initial part of the user context is stored in the local roll area of the R/3 work process. This memory area is *local* to the work process, meaning that each R/3 work process can access only its own roll area. Figure 5.1 depicts the local roll areas of two R/3 work processes. At the completion of a transaction step, the work process that processed the transaction step is freed so that, if need be, another user can work in this work process. The user's data in the local roll area of the work process must be saved to enable the user to resume work through subsequent transactions. To save the data, the system copies it from the local roll area into the global roll area. This action is called the *roll out*. (See Chapter 3.)

FIGURE 5.1:

Roll memory areas

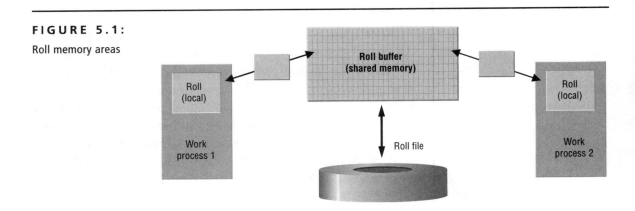

The global roll area is either part of the shared memory of the application server (known as the R/3 roll buffer) or a file on a hard disk of the application server (the R/3 roll file)—or a combination of both these areas. The global roll area is accessible to all work processes of an instance. If the first user continues and performs subsequent transaction steps, the system may assign a different work process to do the work. The user context is then copied from the global roll area to the local roll area of the new work process in a roll in, to enable the user to continue working with his or her data. Figure 5.1 shows the roll buffer and the roll file. The arrows in the diagram represent the copying processes of roll in and roll out.

Use the R/3 profile parameters below to configure the size of R/3 roll memory areas:

- *ztta/roll_area* specifies the size of the local roll area for all types of R/3 work processes.

- *rdisp/ROLL_SHM* specifies the size of the R/3 roll buffer.

- *rdisp/ROLL_MAXFS* specifies the size of the total global roll area (that is, the R/3 roll buffer plus the roll file).

R/3 Extended Memory

As of R/3 Release 3.0, a user context is mainly stored in R/3 extended memory, which is allocated as shared memory. All R/3 work processes of an R/3 instance can process the user context when it is stored in R/3 extended memory. During roll in, it is not the entire user context that is copied to the local memory of the work process, but only the addresses (also known as pointers), which are used to locate the user context in R/3 extended memory. Thus, the volume of data that is copied during roll in or roll out is considerably reduced through the use of R/3 extended memory. This dramatically speeds up the roll process.

The following R/3 profile parameters affect R/3 extended memory:

- *em/initial_size_MB* specifies the size of the R/3 extended memory allocated at R/3 instance startup.

- *em/blocksize_KB* specifies the size of blocks within the space allocated to R/3 extended memory. The default block size is 1,024KB and should not be changed unless recommended by SAP.

- *ztta/roll_extension* specifies the maximum size of a single user context in R/3 extended memory. Having a maximum size prevents users with transactions that consume lots of memory from occupying all of the R/3 extended memory and blocking other users.

R/3 Heap Memory

The third memory area in which the user context may be stored is R/3 heap memory. Whereas the size of the local roll area is permanently allocated for work processes at system startup, R/3 heap memory is allocated as variable local memory; that is, it is allocated as needed (when the user context exceeds a certain size). R/3 heap memory is released as soon as a transaction is completed.

The R/3 profile parameters affecting R/3 heap memory are as follows:

- *abap/heap_area_dia* and *abap/heap_area_nondia:* These specify the maximum amount of R/3 heap memory that can be allocated by a dialog work process or a nondialog work process respectively.

- *abap/heap_area_total:* This parameter specifies how much R/3 heap memory can be allocated in sum by all work processes.

The maximum possible value for parameters of type *abap/heap_area* is 2,000,000,000 bytes (2GB) or, more precisely, 2^{31} minus 1. This limit applies for R/3 Release 4.0B and the 32-bit kernel, but will no longer apply in Releases with a 64-bit kernel.

An R/3 work process that has allocated R/3 heap memory must release this memory after the transaction is completed. Technically, this is achieved by the work process being newly started when the allocated R/3 heap memory exceeds the value of the R/3 profile parameter *abap/heaplimit*. If the work process allocates less R/3 heap memory than is specified in this parameter, after transaction completion, the memory is released at the ABAP level (and can be used by the next transaction), but is not released on the operating-system level. Thus, to release this heap memory at the operating-system level, after transaction completion, the work process is restarted. The corresponding entry in the System Log (Transaction *SM21*) should therefore not be understood as an error message, but rather simply as information.

Figure 5.2 summarizes the R/3 memory areas and the corresponding R/3 profile parameters that affect the sizes of the memory areas.

FIGURE 5.2:

R/3 memory areas and the corresponding R/3 profile parameters

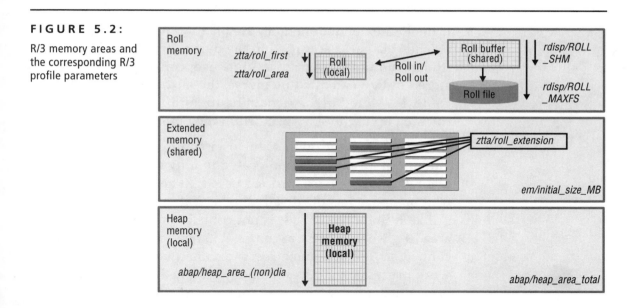

Usage Sequence of Memory Areas

Dialog work processes store user context data in the different memory areas in the following order.

1. At the start of a transaction, user context data up to the amount specified in the parameter *ztta/roll_first* is stored in the local roll area of the work process. The parameter *ztta/roll_first* should be set to 1 byte. This means that, initially, no user context data is stored in R/3 roll memory. However, the R/3 roll memory always contains a small amount of administrative data, which requires around 100KB in the local roll area of the work process, even if *ztta/roll_first* is set to 1. An example of this administrative data is the addresses or pointers used to locate the user contexts in R/3 extended memory.

2. If the user context is larger than the value of the parameter *ztta/roll_first*, the data is stored in R/3 extended memory.

3. If the R/3 extended memory area is full, or if the user context reaches the value specified in the parameter *ztta/roll_extension* (the maximum amount of a single user context that can be stored in R/3 extended memory), the next part of the user context is stored in the remaining (noninitial) part of the local roll area up to the size specified in the parameter *ztta/roll_area*.

4. If the continuing growth of the user context exceeds the amount of local roll area allocated to it by the parameter *ztta/roll_area*, the work process uses R/3 heap memory. R/3 heap memory has the disadvantage that it is local and—unlike R/3 roll memory—is not copied to a global memory area. If a work process allocates R/3 heap memory, the user context cannot be transferred to another work process. The work process remains exclusively assigned to a particular user in what is known as private mode (mode PRIV). In the Work Process Overview (Transaction *SM50* or *SM66*), private mode usage is indicated in the columns *Status* and *Reason* by the values *waiting* and *PRIV* respectively.

5. If the data volume for one work process reaches the value specified in the parameter *abap/heap_area_dia*, or the total data volume for all work processes reaches the value of *abap/heap_area_total*, the respective program terminates.

Figure 5.3 shows the memory areas accessed by a dialog work process. These include memory areas for user-independent objects (for example, the R/3 buffers), as well as user-dependent objects (the user contexts), which are stored by the work processes in R/3 roll memory, R/3 extended memory, or R/3 heap memory.

FIGURE 5.3:

Memory area usage sequence for R/3 work processes

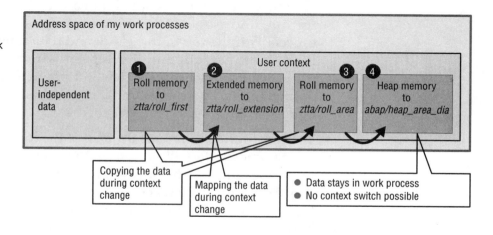

Performance and the Memory Usage Sequence

Performance is affected by issues related to the memory usage sequence such as the R/3 extended memory becoming full, certain default settings for R/3 Release 4.0B, and special considerations that apply to nondialog work processes.

The bulk of user context data should be stored in R/3 extended memory rather than in roll memory. In other words, for optimal performance, the data volume initially using R/3 roll memory in a context switch should be kept to a minimum. To implement this, for R/3 Release 4.0 for all operating systems, set parameter *ztta/roll_first* to 1.

When the R/3 extended memory becomes full, common performance problems are as follows:

- User context data is again deposited in the local roll area, this time to the amount specified in the parameter *ztta/roll_area* (see Figure 5.3 above and Table 5.1 below). This may mean several MB of data are copied for each context switch during the roll processes, which commonly causes wait situations, especially if the roll buffer is full and data must be written in the roll file. Large application servers with more than 100 users may experience a sudden and dramatic performance reduction. This type of example is analyzed in Chapter 2, under "Analyzing R/3 Work Processes."

- You may decide to reduce the size of the local roll area (with the parameter *ztta/roll_area*) to reduce the roll process waits mentioned above. This means only little roll memory is used, and the amount of data copied at context switch is reduced. However, now the user context data will be stored in R/3 heap memory—as a consequence, the work processes are no longer rolled in or out, but enter private mode and remain exclusively assigned to one user. If too many work processes are simultaneously in private mode, the dispatcher will not have enough free work processes at its disposal. This can cause large dispatcher wait times, which, in turn, may also create a dramatic performance problem.

For R/3 Release 4.0B, the SAP default values for the local roll area parameter *ztta/roll_area* are as follows:

- 6,500,000 bytes for UNIX operating systems
- 2,000,000 bytes for Windows NT

The default value should not be changed unless recommended by SAP.

Clearly, it is best if R/3 extended memory is made extremely large, and if the use of R/3 roll memory and R/3 heap memory is completely avoided. Up until now, however, operating-system restrictions have limited the size of the R/3 extended memory. Therefore, R/3 contains mechanisms to reduce the need for R/3 extended memory—such as those described as follows for nondialog work processes.

Memory Usage Sequence for Nondialog Work Processes

To reduce the need for R/3 extended memory, nondialog work processes have a different memory usage sequence from that of dialog work processes for certain R/3 Releases. This applies to all operating systems for R/3 Release 3.*x*. It also applies to UNIX operating systems for R/3 Release 4.0. The nondialog memory usage sequence is as follows:

1. Initially, user context data is stored in the local roll memory of the work process up to the amount specified by the parameter *ztta/roll_area*.

2. If more memory is required, the work process uses R/3 heap memory up to the amount specified in the parameter *abap/heap_area_nondia* or *abap/heap_area_total* (total heap memory).

3. If still more memory is required, the work process uses R/3 extended memory up to the amount specified in the parameter *ztta/roll_extension* or until the R/3 extended memory is full.

4. If still more memory is required, the respective program terminates.

Table 5.1 summarizes the different sequences of memory usage for dialog and nondialog work processes. Whereas dialog work processes mainly use global R/3 extended memory, nondialog work processes primarily use local R/3 heap memory. The reason for the different sequences is that nondialog work processes do not exchange user contexts and do not roll data in and out. Instead, background, update, and spool requests are always performed completely, without interruption, and by a single work process. Therefore, nondialog work processes use mainly local R/3 heap memory, which in turn reserves the global R/3 extended memory for dialog work processes.

Note that the use of a different memory usage sequence for nondialog work processes is being phased out in later R/3 Releases as operating-system platforms become more sophisticated and enable a larger R/3 extended memory.

NOTE   Newer versions of the various operating systems allow significantly more shared memory to be allocated. Therefore, to simplify administration, in R/3 Release 4.0 for some operating systems such as Windows NT, there is no longer a difference between the memory management for dialog and nondialog work processes. As soon as the respective operating-system version can provide sufficient shared memory for the R/3 extended memory, the sequence of memory usage for nondialog work processes will be made identical to that for dialog work processes.

T A B L E   5 . 1 :   Sequence of Memory Usage for Dialog Work Processes and Nondialog Work Processes

Dialog Work Process Memory Usage Sequence	Nondialog Work Process Memory Usage Sequence
1. Local R/3 roll memory is used up to the amount of *ztta/roll_first*.	Local R/3 roll memory is used up to the amount of *ztta/roll_area*.
2. R/3 extended memory is used up to the amount of *ztta/roll_extension* or until R/3 extended memory is full.	R/3 heap memory is used up to the amount of *abap/heap_area_nondia* or until R/3 heap memory is full.
3. Local R/3 roll memory is used up to the amount of *ztta/roll_area*.	—

Continued on next page

TABLE 5.1: Sequence of Memory Usage for Dialog Work Processes and Nondialog Work Processes *(Continued)*

Dialog Work Process Memory Usage Sequence	Nondialog Work Process Memory Usage Sequence
4. R/3 heap memory is used up to the amount of *abap/heap_area_ dia* or until R/3 heap memory is full.	R/3 extended memory is used up to the amount of *ztta/roll_extension* or until R/3 extended memory is full.
5. Program termination.	Program termination.

Zero Administration Memory Management

A new R/3 memory management strategy called *Zero Administration Memory Management* is used for Windows NT, as of R/3 Release 4.0A. The new strategy aims to reduce the number of R/3 profile parameters and thus simplify administration. Zero Administration Memory Management requires no manual settings and adapts itself dynamically to the memory requirements of users. Even hardware changes such as adding memory are recognized and the parameters set accordingly.

The R/3 profile parameter *PHYS_MEMSIZE* specifies how much of the total physical memory of a computer is to be used for the R/3 instance installed on it. By default, the parameter is set to the full size of the physical memory. Based on the parameter *PHYS_MEMSIZE*, all other parameters for memory configuration are automatically calculated.

The central feature of Zero Administration Memory Management is a dynamically extending R/3 extended memory, whose maximum size is determined either by the R/3 profile parameter *em/max_size_MB* or by the filling up of the address space in the NT paging file. Since the default value of the parameter *em/max_size_MB* is 20,000MB, in practice the only real limit on R/3 extended memory is the size of the NT paging files.

In R/3 Release 4.0, for Windows NT, the R/3 heap memory plays a far less significant role than it did in previous R/3 Releases—here, both dialog and nondialog work processes allocate mainly R/3 extended memory, which is limited only by the size of the NT paging files. The R/3 profile parameters of the type *abap/heap_area* are therefore practically obsolete and are set by default to 2,000,000,000 bytes.

The R/3 profile parameter *ztta/roll_extension* is also virtually obsolete and set by default to 2,000,000,000 bytes. The limit on the amount of R/3 extended memory that may be occupied by a single user context is set by the parameter *em/address_space_MB*, whose default value is 512MB.

NOTE   For the latest information on Zero Administration Memory Management, see R/3 Note 88416 in the Online Service System (OSS).

R/3 Paging Memory

A memory area not discussed so far is R/3 paging memory. R/3 paging should not be confused with operating-system paging. In R/3 Release 2.2 and previous R/3 Releases, R/3 paging memory was mainly used to store internal tables and screen lists. As of R/3 Release 3.0, this data is stored in R/3 roll memory, R/3 extended memory, or R/3 heap memory. R/3 paging memory has therefore lost much of its former significance.

The objects that continue to be stored in R/3 paging memory in R/3 Releases 3.x and 4.x can be divided into three groups:

- ABAP data clusters that are temporarily stored in R/3 paging memory with the ABAP statement IMPORT/EXPORT FROM/ TO MEMORY:

- The data in these clusters is not stored in a user context, but is imported to and exported from user contexts by the above ABAP statement. R/3 paging memory provides a temporary storage space to enable this process.

- Variables, lists, or internal tables transferred from one ABAP program to another program that is called by the former program:

  - If an ABAP program calls another program or transaction, a new user context is created. The variables, lists, or internal tables transferred to a second program from the program that called it, or returned to the first program when the second program is completed, are stored in R/3 paging memory.

- Data extracts created by the ABAP statement EXTRACT:

  - Note that as of R/3 Release 4.5, these data extracts are no longer stored in R/3 paging memory, but rather in a memory buffer (for a small number of extracts) or in local files (for a large number of extracts).

Table 5.2 summarizes the data objects that use R/3 paging memory and the corresponding ABAP statements.

TABLE 5.2: ABAP Objects and Statements That Use R/3 Paging Memory

ABAP Object	Corresponding ABAP Statement	R/3 Release
Data extracts	EXTRACT	4.0B and earlier
Data clusters	IMPORT/EXPORT FROM/TO MEMORY	Release-independent
Parameters for calling programs and transactions	SUBMIT REPORT, CALL TRANSACTION, CALL DIALOG, CALL SCREEN, CALL FUNCTION IN UPDATE TASK, CALL FUNCTION IN BACKGROUND TASK, CALL FUNCTION STARTING NEW TASK	Release-independent

Like global roll memory, R/3 paging memory consists of:

- A memory area in the application server's shared memory (known as the R/3 paging buffer)
- An R/3 paging file on the application server's hard disk
- A local paging memory area in each R/3 work process

The R/3 profile parameters *rdisp/PG_MAXFS* and *rdisp/PG_SHM* specify the size of the R/3 paging memory and the R/3 paging buffer respectively. R/3 paging memory is not normally critical to performance. However, the parameter *rdisp/PG_MAXFS* should be set large enough to avoid program terminations with the error messages *TSV_TNEW_PG_CREATE_FAILED* or *SYSTEM_NO_MORE_PAGING*.

The recommended value of 32,000 (corresponding to 256MB) for *rdisp/PG_MAXFS* should be adequate for all normal requirements. If the parameter is set to 32,000 and program terminations with the above error messages still occur, the cause is probably a programming error—see the relevant R/3 Notes in the Online Service System (OSS).

The R/3 paging memory will disappear entirely in the future, when there are 64-bit versions of all operating systems.

Optimizing R/3 Memory Configuration

Optimizing R/3 memory configuration has two goals:

- Performance: A large number of users should be able to work efficiently.

- Security: Programs should not terminate because of a memory bottleneck (especially background programs with large memory requirements).

These goals would be easy to realize if all areas of R/3 memory could be made as large as required to avoid program terminations and bottlenecks. Unfortunately, there are three factors that limit the size you can set for R/3 memory areas:

- Physical memory (RAM): The amount of virtual memory should not be disproportionate to the amount of physical memory available. This avoids memory bottlenecks and loss of performance that are caused by excessive operating-system paging.

- Swap space (operating-system paging file): The swap space must be sufficiently large to enable the creation of required memory areas. However, this presents no major problems, since swap space can be made as large as necessary without incurring extra monetary costs.

- Operating-system limits: The 32-bit architecture currently in widespread use limits the amount of memory that can be addressed by R/3 work processes. This is a serious limitation, especially for servers with 2GB or more of main memory, since it means that the required memory areas cannot be made sufficiently large to allow optimal performance.

For servers with a small main memory, the various R/3 memory areas compete for scarce main memory resources. On a central server, the database instance also competes for these resources. For servers with a large main memory, the chief performance consideration is how large a memory area can be configured without causing program terminations due to the address space limits of the operating system. For both servers with small memory capacity and servers with large memory capacity, fine-tuning the R/3 memory management is currently necessary if you want to make maximum use of your hardware capacity.

Zero Administration Memory Management, delivered with R/3 Release 4.0 for Windows NT (and subsequently to be available for other operating systems), is a first step toward simplifying memory configuration.

64-bit architecture, when it becomes widespread, will remove the problem of address space limits, as well as simplify memory configuration for servers with a large main memory.

Figure 5.4 and Table 5.3 show the different memory areas and their characteristics.

TABLE 5.3: R/3 Memory Areas

Memory Area	Realization	Typical Size (MB)	Description
R/3 roll memory	Shared memory (roll buffer), roll file	100 to 250	Stores the initial part of user contexts (temporary transaction-related data associated with a user session)
R/3 extended memory	Shared memory	200 to 2,000	Stores the main part of user contexts (temporary transaction-related data associated with a user session)
R/3 heap memory	Local memory	200 to 2,000	Stores the variable part of user contexts (temporary transaction-related data associated with a user session)
R/3 buffer	Shared memory	200 to 500	Stores global data that can be accessed by all users—for example, program code, tables, and field definitions
R/3 paging memory	Shared memory (paging buffer), R/3 paging file	100 to 250	Stores temporary data exchanged between user contexts, such as data extracts

Continued on next page

TABLE 5.3: R/3 Memory Areas (*Continued*)

Memory Area	Realization	Typical Size (MB)	Description
Local R/3 work process memory	Local memory	5 to 15 per work process	Stores executable programs, local data, local roll memory (parameter *ztta/roll_area*), local paging memory (parameter *rdisp/PG_local*), R/3 cursor cache, and so on
For Comparison...			
Database instance memory	Shared memory, local memory	200 to 2,000	Stores database buffers and processes

FIGURE 5.4:

Relationships between R/3 memory areas

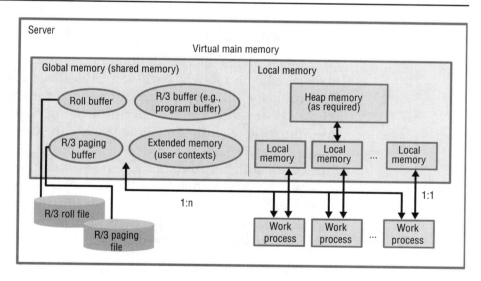

Physical Memory

To enable users to enjoy maximum system performance, the amounts of physical and virtually allocated memory should not be disproportionate to one another. To check that they are reasonably proportionate, compare the amount of virtual memory allocated at R/3 instance startup with the amount of physical memory. Experience shows that we can regard main memory sizing as optimal if the amount of virtual memory allocated is not more than 50% greater than the amount of physical memory.

When there are several R/3 instances or a database instance and an R/3 instance on the same server, the amounts of virtually allocated memory for each instance are summed.

Hardware Sizing

Hardware sizing is the calculation of how much hardware capacity is required by an R/3 System. It includes calculating the required CPU capacity, the required amount of main memory, and the required hard-disk sizes. To perform sizing, SAP's hardware partner companies require details regarding the demands users will place on the R/3 System. Based on the practical requirements of these users and benchmark values, hardware partners create a proposal specifying the required hardware dimensions. In an R/3 implementation project, the customer obtains proposals from several alternative hardware partners. See Figure 5.5 for an illustration of how hardware is sized.

Sizing is performed in accordance with detailed guideline values based on research into the memory requirements of users and transactions. These guidelines change continually and therefore cannot be included here.

To simplify and standardize sizing for small- and medium-sized R/3 Systems, SAP's Internet site SAPNet offers the Quick Sizer, a program that enables you to make a rough assessment of your

FIGURE 5.5:

The hardware sizing procedure

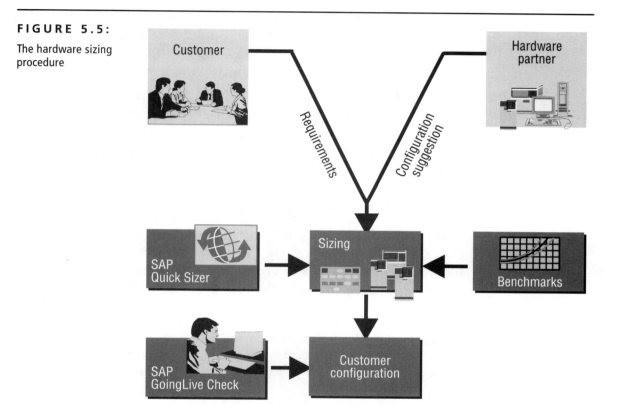

hardware needs (CPU, main memory, and disk capacity) based on published benchmarks created using Standard SAP Application Benchmarks. The Quick Sizer performs the following types of sizing, which differ according to the kinds of information you must supply to the program:

- User-based sizing: You supply the number of users in the various R/3 modules.

- Document-based sizing (quantity structure): You supply the quantity structure—that is, the number of business documents required to be processed in particular time frames. These documents can include customer orders, deliveries, manufacturing orders, or printed documents. This type of sizing has the advantage that it takes into account the data volume of background processes such as Batch Input or ALE, as well as the daytime distribution of document volumes.

Normally, the Quick Sizer uses a combination of both of the above types of sizing. However, either type of sizing is valid only when applied to standard R/3 System software, as it cannot take into account system load caused by customer-developed ABAP programs.

Using detailed guideline values based on research into memory and CPU usage in the different R/3 modules, the Quick Sizer program calculates the required amount of main memory, CPU capacity, and hard-disk sizes. The Quick Sizer program calculates a minimum value and an optimum value for the amount of main memory required for your database and R/3 instances.

NOTE   To access the Quick Sizer program at SAP's Internet site SAPNet, use the Internet address `http://sapnet.sap.com/quicksizing`. The Quick Sizer program can be used by SAP's customers, partner companies, and employees.

Swap Space

The recommendations in this book assume that your system has sufficient swap space. The amount of swap space should be equivalent to at least three times the amount of physical memory and at least 2GB in size.

To ensure that the swap space is large enough and that the R/3 profile parameter *abap/heap_area_total* is set correctly, perform the three steps of the following check.

Check Step 1: Calculating the Available Virtual Memory

The available memory is the sum of the amount of physical memory on the server and the amount of available swap space:

Available Memory=Physical Memory+Swap Space

You can find both values in the Operating System Monitor (Transaction *ST06*), in the fields *Physical memory avail* and *Configured swap*. For Windows NT, the available memory is also known as the *commit charge limit*.

Check Step 2: Calculating the Required Virtual Memory

To perform this step, call the R/3 Memory Configuration Monitor (Transaction *ST02*) and choose *Detail analysis menu* ➤ *Storage*.

The total virtual memory required for a particular server is the sum of the following amounts:

- The amount of virtual memory allocated at startup by the R/3 instance (indicated as *Virtual memory allocated*).

- The maximum heap area for all work processes of the instance (indicated as *Maximum heap area for all work processes*). This value is the memory that can be temporarily allocated as required by the R/3 instance, specified in the parameter *abap/heap_area_total*.

- The amount of memory needed for additional R/3 instances on the same server. To determine this value, perform the first two steps for each R/3 instance (by logging on separately for each instance and calling the R/3 Memory Configuration Monitor).

- An additional 100MB for the operating system and to act as a safety margin.

- The memory requirements of the database instance—if there is one on the server (see the section on database analysis in Chapter 2, or see Appendix B).

- The memory requirements of any other programs that run on the server.

Check Step 3: Comparing the Available Virtual Memory with the Required Virtual Memory

When comparing the available virtual memory with the required virtual memory, the following condition must apply:

Required Virtual Memory < Available Virtual Memory

If this condition does not apply, there are two things you can do:

- Reduce the amount of required virtual memory. You can do this by, for example, reducing the value of the parameter *abap/heap_area_total*. However, it is recommended that the value of this parameter should be greater than 600,000,000 (600MB).

- Increase the swap space.

If the required virtual memory is *much* smaller than the available virtual memory, you can increase the value of the virtual memory parameter *abap/heap_area_total* accordingly. The maximum value of this parameter is 2,000,000,000 (2GB).

WARNING Insufficient swap space can cause unpredictable errors and terminations. Memory bottlenecks due to insufficient swap space can cause an important operating-system or database process to terminate. As these bottlenecks affect all processes, the process that terminates first is purely a coincidence. See R/3 Note 38052 *System Panic, Terminations Due to Low Swap Space*.

Address Space

For various operating-system platforms, there are operating-system limits that restrict the address space—that is, the amount of memory that can be addressed from an operating-system process. For R/3, the address space is the sum of all memory addresses that are available to a work process.

It was explained above that the virtual memory must fulfill two conditions:

- It must not be disproportional to the physical memory.

- It must be less than the available virtual memory (the sum of physical memory and swap space).

A third condition on virtual memory is that it must be capable of being *addressed* from the work processes. If there is a limit on the amount of memory that can be addressed from a work process, this reduces the amount of virtual memory that can be used.

Address Space Limits

The size of the addressable memory for the 32-bit versions of the R/3 kernel current at the time of publication is between 1.8GB and 3.8GB (that is, no more than 2^{32} bytes). The addressable memory must be large enough to contain all memory areas that a work process must access. These memory areas include:

- Local memory of the work process

- R/3 buffers, including the R/3 roll buffer and the R/3 paging buffer (several hundred MB)

- R/3 extended memory (between several hundred MB and 1,000MB)

- R/3 heap memory (between several hundred MB and 1,000MB)

If one memory area occupies a very large portion of the available address space, there is less address space available for the other memory areas. Thus, the sizes of the addressable memory areas are interdependent. (See Figure 5.6 in the following subsection.)

We can sum up the difference between the available address space and the available memory (the sum of physical memory and swap space) as follows: The available address space must be large enough to contain the memory areas of a single work process (the shared memory of a single instance and the local memory of a single work process). However, the available virtual memory on a given server must be large enough to contain the memory areas of all work processes (that is, the shared memory of all instances and the local memory of all work processes).

For example, if a single server contains either several R/3 instances or an R/3 instance and a database instance, the address space contains only the memory areas of a single instance (since a work process addresses only the memory areas of its instance), whereas the available memory must be large enough to contain the shared memory areas of all instances.

UNIX Address Space

Figure 5.6 shows the standard implementation of R/3 extended memory for UNIX operating systems. A work process must be able to address the entire R/3 extended memory area. As we saw above, if the R/3 extended memory is too large, the work process cannot address, for example, R/3 heap memory. Therefore, it is recommended that the size of the R/3 extended memory (specified in the parameter *em/initial_size_MB*) is not greater than 2GB. This recommendation applies to operating systems with 32-bit architecture. For some operating systems, the maximum size of the R/3 extended memory may be even smaller.

FIGURE 5.6:

Memory areas addressed by a work process in a standard R/3 implementation for a UNIX operating system

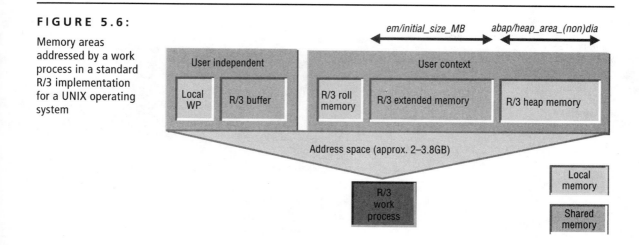

Therefore, on a UNIX operating system, the maximum address space limits the combined size of R/3 memory areas. This is of particular significance for the R/3 extended memory since this limits the number of users who can work in an R/3 instance. Particularly on servers with more than 2GB of physical memory, the problem may arise that the main memory of a server cannot be used effectively with only one R/3 instance configured on the server, since the main memory is too large to be addressed by the work processes of one instance. A common solution is to install more than one R/3 instance on a server.

Windows NT Address Space

To overcome the effects of the operating-system limit on the size of the addressable R/3 extended memory, for some operating systems, there is an alternative implementation of the R/3 extended memory. Figure 5.7 shows this implementation using the example of Windows NT.

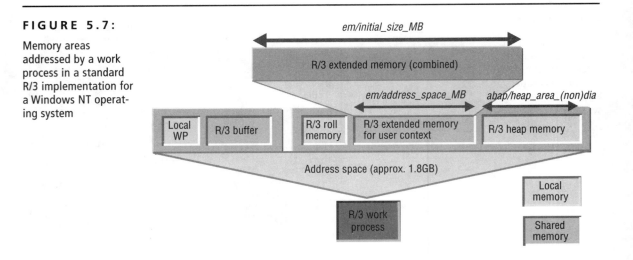

FIGURE 5.7:

Memory areas addressed by a work process in a standard R/3 implementation for a Windows NT operating system

In this implementation, the work process addresses only one part of the R/3 extended memory, as specified by the parameter *em/address_space_MB*. This has the advantage that the R/3 extended memory can be larger than the amount of R/3 extended memory that can be addressed by the work process. Thus, the R/3 extended memory is limited only by the size of the maximum available virtual memory (the sum of the physical memory and the paging file).

Note that each work process can access all objects stored in the R/3 extended memory. However, during a single transaction step, a work process can access only an R/3 extended memory area of the size specified in the parameter *em/address_space_MB*. This R/3 profile parameter thus specifies the maximum amount of R/3 extended memory that can be occupied by a user context. The default value for this parameter is 512MB.

In R/3 Release 4.0, the R/3 profile parameter *ztta/roll_extension* (the maximum amount of a single user context that can be stored in R/3 extended memory) should not be explicitly set in the R/3 instance profile. Rather, use the default value of 2,000,000,000 bytes.

NOTE A similar implementation of R/3 extended memory to that used for Windows NT is feasible for the AIX operating system. See R/3 Note 95454 in the Online Service System (OSS).

Address Space and R/3 Heap Memory

The maximum amount of R/3 heap memory that can be addressed from a single work process equals the size of the address space minus the size of the shared memory areas addressed by the work process, minus the size of the local work process memory.

If a work process tries to allocate more R/3 heap memory than the amount of address space available to it, the result is program termination and the error message *STORAGE_PARAMETERS_ WRONG_SET*. How to proceed after receiving this error is explained under "Troubleshooting" later in this chapter.

Other Operating-System Limits

In addition to the limits caused by the use of a 32-bit address space, there are other operating-system limits. At the time of publication, one or more of the following limits may be encountered with the various operating systems:

- A maximum amount of addressable local memory for a work process (known as *process local heap memory*)

- Limits caused by the fixed sizes and numbers of shared memory segments

- A limit on the size of the shared memory per server

- A limit on the size of the shared memory per R/3 instance

NOTE   For a list of R/3 Notes on the operating-system limits, associated errors, and solution options, see Appendix H. You should also consult your hardware partner or SAP AG on limits that may be current for your system environment.

WARNING   Operating-system limits signify that memory areas that are too large will cause the R/3 instance to fail to start or to start only with errors, or cause ABAP errors at runtime, such as *STORAGE_PARAMETERS_ WRONG_SET*. See the "Troubleshooting" section later in this chapter.

MEMLIMITS Program

MEMLIMITS is a program that enables you to test the limits of the amount of memory that can be addressed by your operating system. Start MEMLIMITS on the operating-system level. The terminology in the output of MEMLIMITS will be specific to the operating system.

On UNIX systems, using MEMLIMITS gives you results such as those shown in this sample extract:

```
Result (UNIX)
Maximum heap size per process........: 640 MB
Maximum protectable size (mprotect)..: 996 MB
   em/initial_size_MB > 996 MB will not work
Maximum address space per process....: 1252 MB
Total available swap space...........: 1300 MB
```

The main values named in this extract are as follows:

- *Maximum heap size per process:* This value tells you how much local memory can be addressed by an R/3 work process. Thus, the sum of fixed local memory and variable local memory (R/3 heap memory) for an R/3 work process must be less than the value of this parameter.

- *Maximum protectable size (mprotect):* This value limits the amount of R/3 extended memory that can be addressed.

NOTE

In this example, the warning provided by MEMLIMITS—that *em/ initial_size_MB > 996MB* will not work—should not be taken to imply that an operating-system process can address R/3 extended memory up to the amount of 996MB. However, for some operating systems, there are special solutions for large installations that enable more than 996MB of R/3 extended memory to be addressed. See the relevant R/3 Notes in Appendix H or consult your hardware partner.

- *Maximum address space per process:* This value tells you the maximum address space per R/3 work process. It limits the sum of all memory areas that a work process can address (such as the R/3 buffer, the R/3 extended memory specified in *em/initial_size_MB*, and R/3 heap memory).

On Windows NT, using MEMLIMITS gives you results such as those shown in this sample extract:

```
Result (Windows NT)
Maximum heap size per process........: 1988 MB
Total available swap space...........: 1988 MB
```

The main value named in this extract is as follows:

- *Maximum heap size per process:* On Windows NT, this is the maximum allocable memory per R/3 work process. Since on Windows NT 4.0, there are no other limits regarding shared memory or local memory, this value defines the upper limit of the sum of all memory areas that can be addressed by an R/3 work process (such as the R/3 buffer, the R/3 extended memory specified in *em/address_space_MB*, and R/3 heap memory).

NOTE   The Windows NT value *Maximum heap size per process* defines the upper limit of all allocable memory for a single R/3 work process. Since a part of the address space is always lost through fragmentation, the actual total of allocable memory is less than this figure.

TIP   To ensure that MEMLIMITS produces valid results, execute it when R/3 and the database are not running. To obtain documentation on MEMLIMITS and its options, use the command MEMLIMITS –h on the operating-system level.

Planning or Reviewing Your Memory Configuration

This section explains the main system features to be considered when planning or reviewing your memory configuration. Note that there may also be additional factors not mentioned here that are relevant to your particular R/3 System.

Step 1: Defining the Total Main Memory Required

Your hardware partner assesses the main memory requirements for your R/3 system based on the tasks you expect your R/3 system to perform. For small- and medium-sized installations, you can perform the sizing yourself using the Quick Sizer program (on SAP's Internet site, SAPNet).

Step 2: Defining the Number of Servers and Instances

You must determine the number of servers you wish to integrate into your R/3 System. You should do this in conjunction with your hardware partner, as the number of servers depends to a large extent on your choice of hardware platform. See also Chapter 6, "Load Distribution."

The decision as to whether you should install more than one R/3 instance per server is also one to make in consultation with your hardware partner. For UNIX servers with more than four processors and 2GB of main memory, there are three reasons why you should install more than one R/3 instance on each server:

- With only one R/3 instance, you cannot make effective use of the physical memory due to operating-system limits on address space, shared memory, and so on. These limits will, however, no longer apply after the introduction of 64-bit architecture.

- In R/3 Release 3.*x*, additional instances are often set up, because you can configure only one spool work process for each instance. This no longer applies as of R/3 Release 4.0.

- For servers with more than four processors and correspondingly many R/3 work processes, excessive wait times may occur in the dispatcher, or in the roll or buffer processes. These wait times can be reduced if several R/3 instances are configured.

As a rule, avoid installing an unnecessarily large amount of instances, since each instance adds administration and monitoring work. The first two reasons mentioned for setting up multiple R/3 instances per server may soon no longer apply. The third reason may no longer apply after the introduction of the 64-bit kernel—it remains to be seen whether the new kernel will in fact eliminate the source of the wait times.

Step 3: Defining the Size of the R/3 Memory Areas

The memory requirements for R/3 buffers depend on which R/3 modules are being run on the R/3 instance. The largest buffers are the R/3 program buffer with a typical size of 150MB to 400MB and the R/3 table buffer (for generic buffering and single record buffering) with a typical size of 50MB to 120MB. In total, you normally need from 250MB to 500MB for all R/3 buffers in R/3 Releases 3.1 and 4.0.

The memory area for the R/3 buffer is allocated per R/3 instance. If the R/3 System has many instances with few users, and few work processes on each instance, the amount of memory required for the entire R/3 System is greater than if the system has relatively few instances with many users and work processes per instance. How to monitor the R/3 buffers after going live is explained in Chapter 2, under "Analyzing the R/3 Memory Configuration."

The Zero Administration Memory Management system automatically configures the R/3 extended memory and roll buffer on the basis of the R/3 profile parameter *PHYS_MEMSIZE*. For R/3 Systems in which Zero Administration Memory Management is not yet activated, see the end of this section on how to configure and monitor the R/3 extended memory and R/3 roll buffer.

Step 4: Defining the Memory for R/3 Work Processes

The memory required for an R/3 work process is around 7.5MB. For more information on the number of required work processes and their distribution, see Chapter 6, "Load Distribution."

Step 5: Defining the Memory for the Database Instance

To obtain a recommendation as to how large the main memory should be, use the Quick Sizer program (on SAP's Internet site, SAPNet). As a guideline value, the database instance requires from 20% to 30% of the total memory, which is the sum of the main memories of all servers. For more information on the memory areas of the various database systems and on monitoring these areas during production operation, see also Chapter 2, under "Analyzing the Database Buffer," and Appendix B.

R/3 Extended Memory

The amount of R/3 extended memory you should specify in the parameter *em/initial_size_MB* depends on the number and activities of the users, and cannot easily be assessed before the start of production. When initially setting this R/3 profile parameter in a nonproduction R/3 System, simply go by the size of the physical memory. Specify a value for R/3 extended memory of around 70% to 100% of the physical memory available to the relevant R/3 instance.

NOTE   On a server with 1,500MB of physical memory, you want to configure a database instance and an R/3 instance. For the database instance, you are planning a main memory of 500MB. This leaves 1,000MB for the R/3 instance. Therefore, you can initially specify between 700MB and 1,000MB as R/3 extended memory.

For most operating systems, you cannot assign more than 1,000MB to 2,000MB to the R/3 extended memory. This limit is due to the operating system's 32-bit architecture (see above, under "Address Space Limits"). For some operating systems, the maximum size of the R/3 extended memory per R/3 instance is even considerably smaller.

In a production R/3 System, the size of the R/3 extended memory should match the real memory need. To monitor R/3 extended memory in the R/3 Memory Configuration Monitor (Transaction *ST02*), see Chapter 2. If the R/3 extended memory is frequently 100% full, you should first think of increasing the size of the R/3 extended memory. Bear in mind that the maximum size may be limited by your operating system, and that the size of the R/3 extended memory should not normally exceed the size of the physical memory significantly.

If it is not possible to increase the R/3 extended memory, check whether any users are occupying an above-average amount of space in the R/3 extended memory—if so, see if you can improve the programming of the programs they are using. To find users using too much R/3 extended memory, access the *Mode List* as follows.

1. From the R/3 Memory Configuration Monitor (Transaction *ST02*), choose *Detail analysis menu* ➢ *SAP memory* ➢ *Mode list*.

2. The screen *Tune: Detail Analysis <server>* appears, listing the currently logged-on users (in the column *Name*). Each occurrence of a particular username represents one session for that user. The columns *Ext mem* and *Heap* indicate in KB how much R/3 extended memory or R/3 heap memory a user is using. Beneath this list, another list indicates the users with the highest memory consumption since system startup.

3. Using the first of the two lists, find out if there are any users with above-average memory consumption. Then find out which programs these users are currently using (for example, with Transaction *SM04*) and see if these programs can be optimized.

If you cannot increase the size of the R/3 extended memory due to operating-system limits, and if the *Mode List* indicates that some users are consuming too much R/3 extended memory, you can reduce the maximum size of a user context in R/3 extended memory with the parameter *ztta/roll_extension*. This compels an earlier switch to R/3 heap memory and enables the individual user session to occupy less R/3 extended memory. Reducing this parameter has two disadvantages:

- Work processes are more likely to enter private mode (PRIV), which means that you may have to increase the number of dialog work processes.

- The total amount of memory a user can access is decreased, which may mean that programs with high memory consumption terminate unexpectedly.

Troubleshooting

Optimizing memory configuration should not only guarantee sound system performance, but also prevent program terminations due to memory bottlenecks.

Incorrect memory configuration can cause the following errors:

- R/3 instance startup failure: When the operating system cannot provide the requested memory areas.

- User session termination: An error message appears saying *roll out failed*, the session terminates, and the user is logged off.

- ABAP program termination: To see a log of this error (known as a *dump*), use Transaction *ST22*, or, from the R/3 initial screen, choose *Tools* ➤ *Administration* ➤ *Monitor* ➤ *Dump analysis*.

ABAP program terminations have four possible causes:

- A programming error (for example, an endless loop) or a user technique that results in unnecessary memory consumption

- Incorrectly set R/3 profile parameters

- Insufficient swap space

- Incorrectly set parameters for operating-system configuration, or operating-system limits such as the maximum addressable memory

ABAP Program Terminations

To see the log of ABAP program terminations, use Transaction *ST22*. In the log, you may see the following error messages:

- STORAGE_PARAMETERS_WRONG_SET, SYSTEM_ROLL_IN_ERROR, TSV_TNEW_BLOCKS_NO_ROLL_MEMORY, TSV_TNEW_PAGE_ALLOC_FAILED, TSV_TNEW_INDEX_NO_ROLL_MEMORY: Any of these messages means the memory for a user context is full.

- PXA_NO_SHARED_MEMORY—or, when you try to log on to the R/3 System, you get the message *System in trouble (PXA_NO_SHARED_MEMORY):* At startup, the program buffer is the last object created by the R/3 System in the shared memory. If at this time there is insufficient shared memory, the R/3 System cannot create the program buffer. As a result, the R/3 System is started only as an emergency system with a minimal program buffer. This normally occurs when the allocated areas in the shared memory (particularly R/3 extended memory and the program buffer) exceed the limits of the operating system.

- DBIF_RTAB_NO_MEMORY: The program encounters a memory bottleneck during an operation in the database interface. This error may occur as a result of the previous errors.

- RABAX_CALLING_RABAX: This error results if there is insufficient memory for writing an error message after a program terminated. This error may also occur as a result of the previous errors.

- SYSTEM_NO_MORE_PAGING, TSV_TNEW_PAGE_ALLOC_FAILED: The R/3 paging memory is full (in the present chapter, see "R/3 Paging Memory").

- SET_PARAMETER_MEMORY_OVERFLOW: The memory for the *SET/GET* parameter (SPA/GPA memory) is full. Terminations may result, particularly during a file transfer to the presentation server (during file download or upload), or while executing a program on the front end through the ABAP program SAPLGRAP. The solution to this error is to increase the memory area with the R/3 profile parameter *ztta/parameter_area*.

Performing Troubleshooting Checks

The error logs contain detailed information about how much memory was requested when a program terminated. In this example, the following two lines appear in an error log:

```
Extended memory (EM) 52431655
Assigned memory(HEAP) 80004928
```

These values are critical for the error analysis and may be understood as related to a user context as follows:

- *Extended memory (EM):* Amount of R/3 extended memory that was occupied by a user context at the time of termination.

- *Assigned memory (HEAP):* Amount of R/3 heap memory that was occupied by a user context at the time of termination.

The requested memory for the user context in this example is 52,431,655 bytes+80,004,928 bytes=132.5MB. To this, you must add the R/3 roll memory specified in the parameter *ztta/roll_area*, which is normally less than 10MB.

To continue analyzing the problem, check for the following types of errors.

Program Error

Check whether there was a program error or a user technique that required excessive amounts of memory. As a guideline value, we can assume that a program executed by several users in dialog processing mode will not allocate more than 100MB, and that background programs, such as billing runs performed at night on a dedicated application server, will not use more than 1GB. Depending on the operating system, in 32-bit architecture, a program will terminate after approximately 1GB to 3GB of memory have been consumed.

- If a program terminates with a memory consumption greater than this guideline value, ask the user whether there was a user technique that could have been avoided, or whether the work can possibly be divided into smaller portions to be performed separately, with each portion requiring less memory.

- If a program terminates with a memory consumption less than the guideline value, consult the responsible developer if it is a customer-developed program, or look for R/3 Notes in SAP's Online Service System (OSS) that provide optimization strategies for the program.

Parameter Limits Reached

Check whether the program's memory requirements exceed the limits set in the relevant R/3 profile parameters. The amount of memory available to a user context is the sum of the amounts specified in the parameters *ztta/roll_extension* (limit of R/3 extended memory) and *abap/heap_area_dia* or *abap/heap_area_nondia* (limits of R/3 heap memory). To this, you must add the R/3 roll memory, which is normally less than 10MB per user context (as specified in the parameter *ztta/roll_area*).

In the present example, the program terminates due to these limits being reached, since, from the original error log information, we know we can infer that *ztta/roll_extension* is set to 52,428,800 bytes and *abap/heap_area_dia* is set to 80,000,000 bytes.

Full Roll Area, R/3 Extended Memory, or R/3 Heap Memory

If the error is not caused by the limits set in the parameters *ztta/roll_extension*, *abap/heap_area_dia*, and *abap/heap_area_nondia*, use the R/3 Memory Configuration Monitor (Transaction *ST02*) to check whether, at the time of program termination, the roll area, the R/3 extended memory, or the R/3 heap memory were 100% full. If so, increase the sizes of these memory areas if possible, using the R/3 profile parameters *rdisp/ROLL_MAXFS*, *em/initial_size_MB*, and *abap/heap_area_total*.

Operating-System Limits Reached

A further possible cause of the error is that the R/3 kernel has requested memory from the operating system and this memory cannot be supplied. For example, for the error *STORAGE_PARAMETERS_WRONG_SET*, the error log displays the following entry:

> The program had already requested 532533792 bytes from the operating system with 'malloc' when the operating system reported after a further memory request that there was no more memory space available.

Please note that the amount of memory (532,533,792 bytes) referred to in this error message is the amount of memory allocated as R/3 heap memory for this work process, and does not include the amount of R/3 extended memory that the work process uses.

The error may be due to incorrectly set operating-system parameters, the limits of the operating system, or too little swap space. If there are incorrectly set R/3 profile parameters, the operating-system limits can also prevent the R/3 instance from starting.

Memory Errors Due to the R/3 Kernel

To avoid memory-related errors due to having the wrong R/3 kernel, ensure that you have the current R/3 kernel.

Developer Traces

Further data to help you analyze memory configuration errors can be found in the developer trace (also known as *dev_traces*), which is an ongoing log of system messages for each work process. To look at the developer trace or log for a particular work process, call the Work Process Overview (Transaction *SM50*), select a work process by placing the cursor on the appropriate row, and then, from the menu, choose:

Process ➤ Trace ➤ Display file

The *Trace Data* screen appears.

If the R/3 instance containing the trace you want to see will not start, you can find the trace file in the directory \usr\sap\<SID>\ <instance name><instance number>\work. When an error occurs, you should keep a copy of these developer trace files, since they are overwritten at work process startup, and it is difficult to analyze errors without them.

Checking R/3 Profile Parameters

You can use successive executions of the following ABAP report to find out how much memory can be allocated on your R/3 System with its current parameter settings:

```
report zusemem.
* Report for checking the memory limits
parameters mb type I.
data itab(1024) type c occurs 0.
data str(1024).
do mb times.
```

```
    do 1024 times. append str to itab. enddo.
enddo.
skip.
write: / 'Currently using', mb, 'MB.'.
```

The report allows you to specify the amount of memory that the report itself occupies. Create and execute the report in the ABAP Editor (Transaction *SE38*). A screen appears asking you to specify an amount of MB that will then be occupied by the report. To cause the report to allocate this memory, choose *Program ➤ Execute.*

In successive uses of the report ZUSEMEM, by degrees, increase the amounts of memory consumed by the report, until the program terminates. This enables you to discover the amount of memory that causes the report to terminate.

To use this report for background jobs, create a variant and schedule it to run as a background job.

To monitor the memory consumption of the report, open a second user session in the R/3 Memory Configuration Monitor or in the *Mode List* (as described above in the section "R/3 Extended Memory").

Parameter *abap/heap_area_dia*

If the report ZUSEMEM is run in dialog processing mode, it initially allocates R/3 extended memory up to the amount specified in the parameter *ztta/roll_extension* and thereafter allocates R/3 heap memory up to the amount specified in the parameter *abap/heap_area_dia*. If more memory is required than the sum of both these parameter values, the program terminates and creates the error message *TSV_TNEW_PAGE_ALLOC_FAILED.*

We are assuming that the value selected for *abap/heap_area_dia* is sufficiently small so that the sum of R/3 extended memory, R/3 heap memory, and all other memory areas to be addressed by the work process does not exceed the address space of the work process. However, if the value selected for *abap/heap_area_dia* is so large that the requested R/3 heap memory exceeds the address space, the report terminates with the error message *STORAGE_ PARAMETERS_WRONG_SET*. If this were depicted in a diagram like those in Figures 5.6 and 5.7 (earlier in the chapter), the box representing R/3 heap memory would extend outside the area corresponding to the address space.

Parameter *abap/heap_area_nondia*

If the report ZUSEMEM is run in background processing mode, whether the report first allocates R/3 extended memory or R/3 heap memory depends on your operating system and your R/3 Release of your kernel. If the report first allocates R/3 extended memory (as it does for R/3 Release 4.0B and Windows NT), the same parameter settings are recommended as for dialog processing: Set the R/3 profile parameter *abap/heap_area_nondia* to 2GB to enable the report to allocate the maximum amount of R/3 heap memory allowed by the operating system.

If the report allocates R/3 heap memory before R/3 extended memory, the amount of R/3 heap memory allocated grows to the amount specified in the parameter *abap/heap_area_nondia*. If the value set in the parameter *abap/heap_area_nondia* is too large—that is, larger than the maximum amount of R/3 heap memory allowed by the operating system—then, instead of switching to R/3 extended memory, the report terminates and produces the error message *STORAGE_PARAMETERS_WRONG_SET*. You should reduce the value of *abap/heap_area_nondia* until the error no longer occurs.

Summary

There are six memory areas to be configured for an R/3 instance:

- R/3 buffer

- R/3 roll memory

- R/3 extended memory

- R/3 heap memory

- R/3 paging memory

- Local memory of the R/3 work processes

When configuring R/3 memory, your goal should be a configuration that ensures *stability* (the absence of program terminations due to memory bottlenecks) and *performance* (fast access to data and quick context switches).

The following factors affect configuration:

- Physical memory (RAM): More memory can be virtually allocated than is physically available. An optimal main memory configuration is one in which the ratio of virtual main memory to physical memory is ≤ 150%. The Quick Sizer program in SAPNet is a tool for assessing the physical memory requirements for small- and medium- sized installations.

- Swap space or operating-system paging file: The recommendations in this chapter assume that there is sufficient swap space. The amount of swap space should be around three or four times the amount of RAM, and at least 2GB.

- Operating-system limits: Ensure that the operating-system limits allow the desired configuration. These limits may be due to 32-bit architecture and affect, for example, the maximum size of the address space.

Zero Administration Memory Management as initially released for R/3 Release 4.0A for Windows NT simplifies memory management considerably. The 64-bit architecture that will be available in the future will make it easier to configure servers with a large main memory and use them effectively.

The following R/3 profile parameters are especially relevant to security (absence of program terminations):

- *em/initial_size_MB*
- *em/address_space_MB*
- *ztta/roll_extension*
- *rdisp/roll_area*
- *rdisp/ROLL_MAXFS*
- *abap/heap_area_dia*
- *abap/heap_area_nondia*
- *abap/heap_area_total*
- *rdisp/PG_MAXFS*
- *abap/buffersize*

The following R/3 profile parameters are especially relevant to performance:

- *em/initital_size_MB*
- *ztta/roll_first*
- *rdisp/ROLL_SHM*
- *rdisp/PG_SHM*
- All parameters for the R/3 buffers

Important Terms in This Chapter

After reading this chapter, you should be familiar with the following terms:

- Physical memory, swap space (or operating-system paging file), and virtually allocated memory

- Local memory and shared memory

- User context

- R/3 roll memory, R/3 extended memory, R/3 heap memory, and R/3 paging memory

- Address space and 32-bit architecture limitations

- Sizing

Review Questions

1. Which R/3 profile parameters define the amounts of extended memory and heap memory that should be kept in the physical main memory or in the paging file?

   A. R/3 extended memory is always kept completely in the physical memory, and R/3 heap memory is created in the operating-system paging file.

   B. None. The memory areas in the physical main memory and the paging file (that is, the page-out or page-in process) are automatically distributed by the operating system. An application program (such as R/3 or a database program) cannot influence the distribution.

   C. The R/3 profile parameter *ztta/roll_extension* defines the amount of R/3 extended memory in the physical memory. The parameters *abap/heap_area_ dia* and *abap/heap_ area_nondia* define the amount of R/3 heap memory.

2. Which of the following can cause an R/3 instance to not start, or to start with an error message, after you change R/3 parameters for memory management?

   A. The program buffer size specified in the parameter *abap/buffer_size* exceeds the limit that exists due to address space restrictions.

   B. There is not enough physical memory to allow the new settings.

   C. The paging file is not large enough to allow the new settings.

   D. The amount of R/3 extended memory specified in the parameter *em/initial_size_MB* exceeds the limit that exists due to address space restrictions.

CHAPTER

SIX

6

Workload Distribution

To optimize R/3 System performance, you need to distribute the system load across the CPU resources of all available servers. This helps these CPU resources to cope with the demands on the system—for example, with the number of users and user activities, as well as with the number of background programs.

In addition to improving performance, optimizing workload distribution also protects performance-critical processes and gives these processes priority in accessing resources.

The techniques for optimizing workload distribution include:

- Distributing work processes across application servers
- Dynamic user distribution

When Should You Read This Chapter?

You should read this chapter if you want to find out how to optimize workload distribution within the R/3 System.

Fundamentals of Workload Distribution

This section explains the ideal numbers and locations of R/3 services; the optimal ratios between users, work processes, and CPU processors; and R/3 benchmarks for work process distribution.

R/3 Services

The R/3 services are available in the application layer of an R/3 System (in contrast to the presentation layer and the database layer). Each service is provided by one or more R/3 work processes.

Table 6.1 indicates the number of work processes of each type that can be located in your R/3 System as a whole and in each individual R/3 instance. For a description of the three-layer system, the function of the different services, and how these services are configured, see *SAP R/3 System Administration* (also part of the "Official SAP Guide" book series).

TABLE 6.1: Type and Number of R/3 Work Processes That Provide Particular Services in R/3

Service	Number of Work Processes per R/3 System	Number of Work Processes per R/3 Instance
Message Server	1	0 or 1
Enqueue	1	0 or 1
Dialog	≥ 2	≥ 2
Update (U and U2)	≥ 1	≥ 0
Batch	≥ 1	≥ 0
Spool	≥ 1	R/3 Release 3.1: 0 or 1; as of R/3 Release 4.0: ≥ 0
Gateway	≥ 1	1

Message Server

The message server (also called the message service) is a service that enables messages to be exchanged between the various R/3 instances. There is only one message server per R/3 System. The message server is a logical unit. An example of the communication between R/3 instances that is managed by the message server is the distribution of update requests between R/3 instances.

Enqueue Service

R/3-specific locks, which are called enqueues, are managed by the enqueue service. The enqueue service is provided by one R/3 work process. The R/3 instance containing the enqueue service is often called the enqueue server.

ATP Server

The ATP server is a service available as of R/3 Release 4.0, providing a materials availability check using Available-to-Promise (ATP) logic. There is only one ATP server for each R/3 System.

NOTE   For more on R/3 enqueues or the ATP server, see Chapter 8.

Since an R/3 instance can fulfill multiple functions, a single instance can simultaneously host the message server, the enqueue service, and the ATP server.

Dialog, Update, Background, and Spool Services

Dialog, update, background, and spool services are provided by one or more R/3 work processes. More than one R/3 instance in an R/3 System can host a dialog, update, background, or spool service.

For example, when the update or background services are offered on only one R/3 instance, this is referred to as *central* update or background processing. If these services are located on more than one R/3 instance, this is referred to as *distributed* update or background processing.

The dispatcher of the respective R/3 instance recognizes which service each work process provides. The dispatcher is itself an R/3 work process that coordinates the work of the other R/3 work processes and hence the services they offer. While the message server manages communication between R/3 instances, the dispatcher of each R/3 instance coordinates the work processes within the instance.

Users, Work Processes, and CPU Capacity

How many work processes should you configure in one R/3 System, and how should you distribute them among the application servers? Two ratios are relevant here:

- Number of users ÷ number of dialog work processes

- Number of work processes ÷ number of processors

To calculate the optimal value for the first ratio, use the following formula:

Number of users÷number of dialog work processes=(think time+response time)÷response time

The response time here is the average time that the R/3 System requires to process a user request. The think time is the time one user takes to enter his or her data at the presentation server and to interpret it, and includes any user pauses. It is difficult to provide a general rule for these values, since they depend on the type of user activities, the installed R/3 modules and components, the R/3 Release, and the CPU type; and these factors vary from one customer system to another.

NOTE   The ratio *(think time+response time) ÷ response time* concerns the response time measured from the GUI layer, not the response time indicated in the Workload Monitor, which is purely the response time of the application server. The difference between these response times is equivalent to the network time required for the data transfer between the application server and the presentation server. This network time should, however, be small (less than 10% of the response time of the application server).

The optimal value for the ratio *number of work processes ÷ number of processors* will also vary from one customer system to another. There is no guideline value that is valid for all R/3 Systems. To calculate the optimal value for this ratio, use the following formula:

Number of work processes÷number of processors=response time÷CPU time

If in a sample R/3 System, the CPU time is at least 20% of the response time, you should set up no more than five work processes for each CPU.

Does Adding More Work Processes Always Increase Performance?

If user requests must wait for work processes in the R/3 dispatcher queue, it is tempting to configure more work processes and thereby increase the number of user requests that can be dispatched simultaneously.

This strategy may appear to improve performance if work processes are being blocked through wait situations that are not consuming CPU, such as when work processes are blocked by private modes (mode PRIV) or by database locks. However, a better solution is to remove the real cause of the problem—that is, in this example, the database lock or the private modes.

If the number of work processes that are simultaneously occupied is significantly greater than the number of processors, this causes wait situations in the operating-system queue. Because work processes receive CPU time more or less simultaneously (or, to be more precise, in time slices), the number of context switches on the operating-system level increases with the number of work processes. Note that what is meant by context switches here is a processor switching back and forth between R/3 work processes, and not an R/3 context switch, which is an R/3 work process switching between user contexts through roll in and roll out.

If more work processes are waiting for free CPU, this triggers more operating-system context switches and increases the load on the available CPU resources. Waiting in the R/3 dispatcher queue, however, does not consume any CPU resources. Therefore, if all available CPU resources are continually in use, it is better *not* to increase the number of work processes and, instead, to tolerate the R/3 dispatcher wait times. This avoids increasing the load of context switches on the operating system. Benchmark measurements show that, if all available CPU resources are continually in use, reducing the number of work processes actually improves performance.

CPU wait time is not explicitly indicated in the Workload Monitor (Transaction *ST03*), but can be inferred from an increased processing time statistic. Thus, you can determine the CPU wait time by comparing the processing time and the CPU utilization as shown in Chapter 3, under "Lost Time Analysis."

Other situations that suggest reducing the ratio of work processes to CPU processors include:

- If the operating system is Windows NT: In contrast to UNIX, with Windows NT, the context switch on the operating-system level is particularly expensive. Therefore, particularly for Windows NT, a small number of work processes per CPU processor is recommended. (See also R/3 Note 68544 in the Online Service System.)

- If reducing the number of work processes reduces the need for main memory.

- If reducing the number of work processes reduces the number of database processes and their main memory needs: The advantage of reducing the number of work processes here is particularly significant for databases in which each R/3 work process has only one database process assigned to it.

NOTE You should increase the number of R/3 work processes only if neither the CPU nor the memory of the application server are being consumed to the maximum. Do not increase the number of work processes if either a CPU bottleneck or a main memory bottleneck exists in addition to a large processing time on an application server. You may even improve performance by reducing the number of work processes in this situation.

R/3 Benchmarks for Work Process Distribution

Figure 6.1 shows the CPU needs of dialog, update, and database services for the R/3 modules FI, WM, MM, SD, PS, and PP. The results shown are the findings of numerous R/3 benchmark tests (R/3 Standard Application Benchmarks). If you assume that for a certain number of FI users you need one processor, then around 9% of the CPU capacity is used for database requests, 13% is used for updates, and the remaining 78% is used for dialog activities. The number of FI users that can be served by one processor depends largely on the processor model and the R/3 Release, and varies as shown in the diagram. The scale for the height of the columns is relative to module FI, whose column is taken as having a height of 1.

The usefulness of the R/3 Standard Benchmarks expressed in Figure 6.1 can be explained as follows:

- R/3 Standard Benchmarks provide reference values for the CPU needs of various R/3 modules. The different heights of the columns show the dramatic difference in CPU needs. Thus, one user in module PP requires five times as much CPU capacity as one user in FI. Accordingly, the number of work processes to be configured depends very much on the applications installed in the respective R/3 instance.

CPU needs of dialog,
update, and database
services for various
R/3 modules

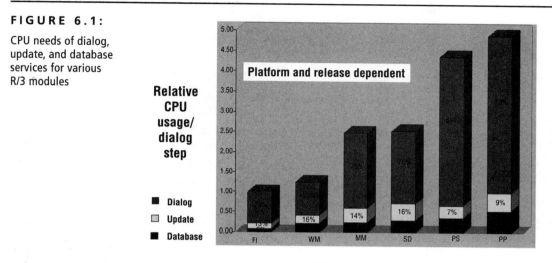

R/3 business component

- R/3 Standard Benchmarks also provide an indication of the CPU needs of individual services. The lower part of the columns in Figure 6.1 shows the CPU needs of the database instance. Depending on the R/3 module, the database consumes between 10% and 15% of the total CPU consumption for the R/3 System. The middle part of each column shows the CPU needs of the update service, which is around 10% to 15% of the total CPU requirement. The dialog services account for the remaining CPU need, which lies between 70% and 80% of the total CPU requirement. Using these relationships, you can estimate the ratios of dialog work processes to update work processes.

In summary, the simulations used to produce the R/3 Standard Benchmarks provide us with useful results that can help us to configure real R/3 Systems. These benchmarks cannot, however, reflect certain factors:

- An R/3 Standard Benchmark does not reflect whether in your system there is more online transaction processing (OLTP) or more reporting (online analytical processing—OLAP). The R/3 Standard Benchmark assumes that the majority of processing in your R/3 System is OLTP, since OLTP is normally more critical to performance. For customer orders, deliveries, and invoices, data entry (update processing) is more performance-critical than reporting. Reporting normally consumes more database resources; therefore, in a production R/3 System, the database load is proportionally greater than the dialog and the update load. Typically, the load on the database instance is between 10% and 30% of the system load. The ratio of the number of dialog work processes to the number of update work processes also depends on the concrete demands placed on the R/3 System.

- The benchmarks in Figure 6.1 do not reflect possible background loads. In a given R/3 System, the part of the columns that represents dialog processes consists of both dialog and background parts. The ratio of dialog to background load varies from one R/3 System to another.

In the R/3 Standard Benchmark for the applications module SD, customer orders, deliveries, and invoices are created in dialog processing mode. In a sample customer R/3 System, however, only customer orders are created in dialog processing mode. Deliveries and invoices are created in background processing mode, through collective processing. If you were to create a load profile for this sample system and compare it with the R/3 Standard Benchmarks in Figure 6.1, the ratio of database load to update load would be the same. The difference would affect only the ratio of the background and nonbackground subdivisions of the *dialog* part of the column.

Configuring and Monitoring Workload Distribution

The Workload Monitor (Transaction *ST03*) and the Local Work Process Overview (Transaction *SM50*) are the monitors for workload distribution. The analyses to be used for determining whether the workload distribution on the system is optimal are outlined in Chapter 2 (under "Analyzing R/3 Work Processes") and in Chapter 3 (under "General Performance Problems"). If you find a bottleneck caused by poor workload distribution, distributing the work processes is an effective optimization strategy. The present section offers detailed recommendations for optimally distributing work processes.

Message, Enqueue, and ATP Services

Message, enqueue, and ATP services work closely together and should be located on the same instance for better performance. The corresponding R/3 profile parameters are as follows:

- *rdisp/mshost: <server>*

- *rdisp/enqname: <server>_<instance>_<number>*

- *rdisp/atp_server: <server>_<instance>_<number>*

High availability is when the system is virtually always available to execute processing. The message, enqueue, and ATP services, as well as the database instance, are the critical points for high R/3 System availability. Such critical points are known as *single points of failure* (SPOFs). If a server with one of these services fails, general system failure results for the entire R/3 System.

It is mainly for reasons of high availability that the database instance and the central R/3 instance (with message, enqueue, and ATP services) should be located on a single server that is protected by means of, for example, the type of switchover solution offered by most hardware manufacturers. To achieve better performance for large installations, however, it is sometimes necessary to locate the database instance and the central R/3 instance on separate servers.

Dynamic User Distribution through Logon Groups

After a user has logged on to an R/3 System, he or she remains attached to a particular R/3 instance until he or she logs off. During a user session, there is no feature enabling a dynamic, load-related switch to another R/3 instance.

During logon, however, it is possible for users to be dynamically distributed across R/3 instances through logon groups. That is, prior to logging on, the user chooses a particular user group, for which particular R/3 instances have been reserved, and the system automatically selects an R/3 instance from that group for the user to log on to. To guide this automatic selection, the administrator will have defined a maximum response time and a maximum user number to ensure that the user logs on to an R/3 instance with optimal performance.

NOTE To set up logon groups, use Transaction *SMLG*, or, from the R/3 initial screen, choose *Tools* ➤ *CCMS* ➤ *Configuration* ➤ *Logon groups*. See also the R/3 Online Documentation and *SAP R/3 System Administration* (also part of the "Official SAP Guide" book series).

The simplest logon group arrangement features a single logon group containing all R/3 instances. This ensures that when users log on, they are connected to an R/3 instance with optimal performance. Alternative arrangements use multiple logon groups. In these arrangements, the groups are distinguished according to criteria such as the following:

1. R/3 modules: For example, you can set up the logon groups FI/CO, HR, and SD/MM. The advantage of setting up the logon groups according to R/3 modules in this way is that, for example, only the programs related to the assigned R/3 modules are loaded into the program buffer of each instance. This means less storage space is used in the buffer and frequent displacements are avoided.

2. Languages, countries, or company departments or divisions: If your R/3 System extends over several countries or languages, you can create logon groups such as *Australia*, *Japan*, and *Russia*. This ensures that only the data relevant for one country and language is kept in the buffers of the corresponding R/3 instances. Again, this means less storage space is used in the buffer and frequent displacements are avoided.

3. Special user groups: You can set up a special logon group for, for example, employees in Telephone Sales, because their activities are particularly performance-critical. The corresponding R/3 instances should operate with a particularly high level of performance. These instances should have, for example, no background or update work processes, few users per server, particularly fast processors, or a dedicated network.

- A further example of a user-specific logon group is a logon group for employees in Controlling who use time-consuming reports in dialog processing mode. This group should be assigned to R/3 instances with a particularly high value for the R/3 profile parameter *rdisp/max_wprun_time*, which limits the runtime of an ABAP program in dialog processing mode. In addition, by setting a low value for this parameter on other instances, you avoid lengthy reports of this type being run on those instances and creating performance problems. In this way, performance-critical applications such as order entry in Telephone Sales can be separated from less critical, resource-intensive applications such as those of Controlling.

When setting up logon groups, bear in mind the following restrictions:

- After assigning the instances to the logon groups, check whether this causes successful load balancing, or whether one of the logon groups has too few or too many R/3 instances (and resources) assigned to it.

- If there are temporary load peaks—for example, increased activity in the logon group FI/CO at the end of the business month or year—bottlenecks may result on the corresponding instances. This may, however, be desirable to preserve resources for critical users—for example, users in Telephone Sales.

- If one application server fails, or if you temporarily remove one application server, the user distribution must be newly configured with Transaction *SMLG*.

- Assign at least two R/3 instances to each logon group.

NOTE Avoid setting up unnecessarily large numbers of logon groups to cut down the amount of administration and monitoring required later.

Background Processing

In a distributed R/3 System, the services dialog, background, and spool are distributed across the application servers. In practice, while the dialog work processes are located away from the database server on a separate application server, one common error is to leave the background work processes on the database server. Some good reasons why the background work processes should not be located on the database server are as follows:

- The load created by background programs normally varies considerably over time (for example, due to background programs run on particular days or at the end of the business month). This variation can cause a temporary CPU bottleneck on the database server if several background programs are started simultaneously. By distributing the background work processes across nondatabase servers, these load peaks can be accommodated more easily.

- Dialog and background load are frequently complementary to each other. That is, if dialog load occurs during the day, background load should be scheduled for the night. While application servers that are configured only for dialog work processes will remain unused at times of no dialog load, the background programs running in parallel at night may cause a CPU bottleneck on the database server.

- System administrators sometimes claim that background programs run up to twice as quickly on the database server than on the application servers. This, however, is not a good argument for locating the background work processes on the database server. Rather, it implies that there is a network problem between the database server and the application servers that should be solved. For example, there may be problems in the TCP/IP connection between R/3 instances and an Oracle database, as described in R/3 Note 72638 and R/3 Note 31514.

Operation Modes

The demands placed on an R/3 System over a 24-hour period may fall into distinct operation phases, and on specific days may require an entirely different (*exception*) form of operation. During a normal business day, for example, there are usually many dialog users in the R/3 System, while at night, the demands of background programs are greater. To cause the number and type of R/3 work processes to adapt to changing demands, R/3 allows you to define different operation modes—that is, different time phases in which a specific arrangement of work processes is available. For example, you can define a day operation mode, a night operation mode, and an exception operation mode. After naming the operation mode, you assign the number and type of work processes to it. If desired, R/3 automatically switches between operation modes.

To define operation modes, from the R/3 initial screen, choose *Tools* ➤ *CCMS* ➤ *Configuration* ➤ *OP Modes/Servers*.

To schedule daily or one-off switches between operation modes, from the R/3 initial screen, choose *Tools* ➤ *CCMS* ➤ *Configuration* ➤ *OP modes timetable*.

For more information on operation modes, see *SAP R/3 System Administration* (also part of the "Official SAP Guide" book series) or the R/3 Online Documentation.

Update Processing

Figure 6.2 shows the processing stages for a sample update. *DIA* denotes a dialog work process, *UPD* denotes an update work process, and *MSG* is the message service.

FIGURE 6.2:

Steps in asynchronous
update processing

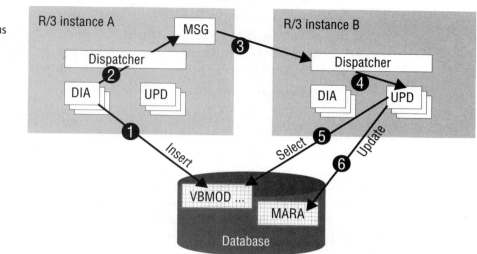

By executing a transaction in R/3, a user causes application
tables to be changed. In Figure 6.2, for example, when changing
the characteristics of a material recorded in the system, the change
is ultimately written to the application table MARA. However,
the dialog part of the transaction does not effect changes to the
database *synchronously* (that is, directly and immediately); instead,
the data to be changed is first temporarily stored in special database tables known as update tables.

Thus, step 1 in Figure 6.2 shows an insert operation (indicated
as *Insert*) that writes to the update table VBMOD (among others).

After completing the dialog part of the transaction, the dialog
work process sends a message to the message server (indicated in
step 2), which locates an application server (R/3 instance *B*) with
an update work process and transfers the update request to the
dispatcher of that application server (indicated in step 3).

The dispatcher sends the request to an update work process (indicated in step 4). The update work process reads the information from the update tables (indicated as *Select* in step 5) and subsequently changes the application table (here, MARA) through an update operation (indicated as *Update* in step 6). The entire process is known as an *asynchronous* update.

When update processing is completed, the temporary entries in the update tables are deleted. Thus, update tables are empty except for update data that is currently being processed.

If update processing is terminated, the relevant update request receives the status *Err* in the screen *Update Records* (accessed from Transaction *SM13*). This is also the screen where you must manually restart or delete updates with status *Err*.

The status *Init* in the same screen indicates that update processing could not be started—for example, because the update process was deactivated, or because no application server with update work processes was available. If the R/3 profile parameter *rdisp/vbstart* is set to 1 (the default setting), the update for update requests with status *Init* is automatically repeated at the next R/3 System startup. If *rdisp/vbstart* is set to a value other than 1, or if the repeat fails, you must manually restart or delete the update.

WARNING Updates that were terminated or not executed prevent the affected documents from being saved in the corresponding application tables. This means these documents effectively do not exist. R/3 System administrators should therefore monitor the update requests daily. If unsuccessful updates are not promptly attended to, by the time several days have passed, you are unlikely to be able to establish the cause of the error. Unsuccessful update requests that are not deleted can also cause performance problems.

As an alternative to using Transaction *SM13*, from the R/3 initial screen, choose *Tools* ➢ *Administration* ➢ *Monitor* ➢ *Update*.

For more information on update processing, see also *SAP R/3 System Administration* (also part of the "Official SAP Guide" book series).

Update Work Process Distribution

In small R/3 installations, the update work processes are located on the same server as the database instance, the message server, the enqueue service, and the ATP server. In medium-sized and large R/3 installations, the update work processes should not be located centrally on the database server.

When setting up the R/3 System, you need to decide whether to locate update work processes on a dedicated update server (an R/3 instance used mainly to host update processing) or distribute them symmetrically (in equal numbers) over all the application servers. Some good reasons why you should use a distributed arrangement are as follows:

- If you had a dedicated update server, the failure of this server would cause system activity to come to a standstill. With distributed update work processes, this problem does not occur.

- A symmetrical distribution of update work processes across all application servers enables you to add or remove application servers to or from the R/3 System without needing to readjust the workload distribution.

- Distributed update work processes can handle temporary load peaks better than a dedicated update server because they distribute the load over more than one server.

Thus, there are good arguments for distributing not only background work processes, but also update work processes, in equal numbers on all application servers.

Dispatching Update Requests

Dispatching for update requests is activated if the R/3 profile parameter *rdisp/vb_dispatching* is set to 1, which is the default value. The message server performs the initial dispatching, ensuring that all instances receive update requests proportional to the number of update work processes configured on them. Within an instance, the dispatcher distributes the update request to the appropriate work processes. This dual form of dispatching normally ensures a balanced workload distribution. However, the message server does not check the current workload distribution between the various servers. If a sample R/3 instance has only one update work process, which is occupied with a very long-running update request, the message server continues to send update requests to this instance even if update work processes on other instances are free (not occupied). Thus, you should never configure only one update work process on an instance—instead, configure at least two.

NOTE   Update dispatching as described here is the standard solution for all applications. Only in special cases and on the express recommendation of SAP should you use the methods *local updates* or *update multiplexing*. These methods are not explained in this book.

Update Tables VBMOD, VBHDR, and VBDATA

The update tables VBMOD, VBHDR, and VBDATA are among the most frequently changed tables in the R/3 System.

If bottlenecks arise when accessing these tables on the hard disk, it may be useful to perform *partitioning*—that is, to distribute these tables over several hard disks.

For some database systems, it may be useful to change the sequence of the key fields in these tables. However, this should be performed only by people with experience in tuning the database and R/3, or following the specific instructions of SAP.

See the R/3 Online Documentation and R/3 Notes relating to the R/3 profile parameter *rdisp/vb_key_comp*.

Multiple R/3 Instances per Server

For UNIX servers with more than four CPUs and 2GB of main memory, there are several good reasons why you should set up more than one R/3 instance on each server:

- Experience shows that performance bottlenecks may arise on servers with more than four processors, but only one R/3 instance with a large number of work processes. These bottlenecks particularly affect the dispatcher, roll in and roll out, and buffer management.

- The physical main memory cannot be used optimally due to operating-system limits affecting address space, global memory, and so on. For details, see Chapter 5, "Configuring R/3 Memory Areas."

- In R/3 Release 3.*x*, it was common to set up additional instances, because only one spool work process could be set up on each R/3 instance. This is no longer necessary with R/3 Release 4.*x*.

As a rule of thumb, however, you should avoid setting up more instances than are strictly necessary, since with each additional instance, you increase the amount of required administrative and monitoring work.

Summary

The most important means of optimizing workload distribution in an R/3 System is to properly set up R/3 work processes. The number of work processes to be set up depends on the demands placed on the R/3 System and on the available CPU resources. Is the system to be used mainly for OLTP (online transaction processing) applications or for OLAP (online analytical processing) applications? Will there be more dialog processing or more background processing?

When configuring the number and type of work processes, use the following guidelines:

- Around 10% to 30% of the CPU needs of the entire R/3 System are consumed by the database service. Ensure that any R/3 instances that reside on the database server do not consume too much CPU capacity. Too many R/3 work processes on the database server can cause a CPU bottleneck that in turn leads to increased database times, and thus inconveniences all users.

- Around 10% to 20% of the CPU needs and also 10% to 20% of the R/3 work processes of the entire R/3 System are typically consumed by the R/3 update service.

The following guidelines should be observed when distributing the work processes on the instances:

- The message, enqueue, and ATP services should be on one R/3 instance (known as the central R/3 instance), which should have at least five dialog work processes. For small- and medium-sized installations, this central R/3 instance is located on the database server. For large installations, the central instance may require a dedicated application server.

- The dialog, background, update, and spool work processes should be evenly distributed across the remaining application servers in a symmetrical manner (equal numbers and types of each work process on each R/3 instance). The work process configuration should be appropriate for the CPU capacity of each instance. If you configure an update service on one R/3 instance, at least two update work processes should be configured there.

Additional techniques for R/3 System load management include:

- Central update servers and dedicated background servers

- Logon groups for dynamic user distribution

- Local updates and update multiplexing (these are not discussed in this book)

Note that these additional techniques increase administration and monitoring effort. Aside from these techniques, the general rule is to configure the work processes in the R/3 System *as symmetrically as possible and as asymmetrically as necessary*. Symmetrical distribution in this context means having equal numbers of each type of work process on each R/3 instance.

There is no hard rule as to how many R/3 work processes should be configured per processor. A guideline value is around 5 to 10 work processes per processor. R/3 administrators and consultants sometimes make the error of automatically increasing the numbers of work processes, regardless of the type of performance problem. This rarely leads to a performance improvement—in some cases, it even reduces performance.

Important Terms in This Chapter

After reading this chapter, you should be familiar with the following terms:

- Workload distribution

- Logon groups

- Distributed update

Review Questions

1. Where should background work processes be configured?

   A. Background work processes should always be located on the database server. Otherwise, the runtime of background programs will be negatively affected by network problems between the database server and the application server.

   B. If background work processes are not located on the database server, they must all be set up on a dedicated application server known as the background server.

   C. Background work processes can be distributed evenly over all the application servers.

2. How should you configure and monitor the dynamic user distribution?

   A. By setting the appropriate R/3 profile parameter—for example, *rdisp/wp_no_dia*.

   B. By using Transaction *SM04*, User Overview.

   C. By using Transaction *SMLG*, Maintain Logon Groups.

CHAPTER
SEVEN

7

R/3 Table Buffering

Every R/3 instance has various buffers, including table buffers, in which data is stored that is needed by users at runtime. When the data is in the buffer, it does not have to be obtained from the database, because buffers enable direct reads from the main memory of the application server. There are two advantages in accessing a buffer for data rather than accessing the database:

- Buffer accesses are normally between 10 and 100 times faster than accesses to the database.

- Database load is reduced, a fact that becomes increasingly important as your system grows in size.

For each table defined in the ABAP Dictionary, you can decide whether and how the table will be buffered. To enable the buffering of these tables, each R/3 instance has two table buffers: the *single record table buffer* (TABLP) and the *generic table buffer* (TABL).

When your R/3 System is delivered, all tables already have default buffering settings. However, to optimize runtime performance, you may need to change some of these settings depending on the usage of your R/3 System. For customer-created tables, the responsible developer configures the buffering settings.

When Should You Read This Chapter?

You should read this chapter to help you:

- Learn about table buffering options in R/3.

- Monitor and optimize the efficiency of your buffering of R/3 tables at regular intervals.

- Decide whether to buffer customer-created database tables.

- Decide whether to buffer the condition tables created during Customizing for central SAP functions such as price determination or output determination.

To better understand this chapter, you should have some familiarity with ABAP programming and SQL programming.

Preliminary Remarks for Chapters 7, 8, and 9

The following remarks concern the tuning measures covered in the present and following two chapters of this book, particularly the measures involving the setting of table buffering or number range buffering, and the creation, changing, or deletion of database indexes.

When these measures are correctly implemented, they are important techniques of performance optimization. However, incorrectly implementing these measures can lead to massive performance problems and sometimes even to data inconsistencies. These measures involve changes to the R/3 System that can be made only by experienced developers or consultants.

The goal of these three chapters is to enable you to identify and locate the program or table that is related to a performance problem. Before making any concrete changes to solve the problem, however, you must perform a technical analysis and a logical analysis.

The technical analysis, which determines which changes are to be made, can be performed, for example, by the system administrator or database administrator. The procedure for this technical analysis is explained in these chapters.

In the logical analysis for determining which changes are to be made, the procedure depends on whether the objects related to the problem are customer-developed objects or objects delivered by SAP:

- For customer-developed objects, changes to buffering or to database indexes should be performed only after careful consideration by the responsible developer, acting in consultation with the system administrator to verify the soundness of the proposed change strategy.

- For SAP objects, the default buffering configuration and SAP-delivered database indexes may sometimes need to be changed. Before you perform a change, look in SAP's Online Service System (OSS) for R/3 Notes pertaining to the relevant program, table, or number range names, which tell you whether the object is allowed to be changed. These R/3 Notes are the SAP developer's input for this analysis. Changes performed without the proper expertise can cause unexpected performance problems and data inconsistencies. Note the warnings and recommendations provided in the respective sections of this book.

Finally, bear in mind that two vital steps are often overlooked during performance optimization:

- Verifying the success of the changes that were intended to effect optimization

- Fully documenting the analysis, optimization, and verification stages

Figure 7.1 depicts the distribution of the R/3 table buffers in the system landscape.

Fundamentals of R/3 Table Buffering

In this section, we discuss the fundamentals of R/3 table buffering: buffering types, activating R/3 table buffering, and buffering guidelines.

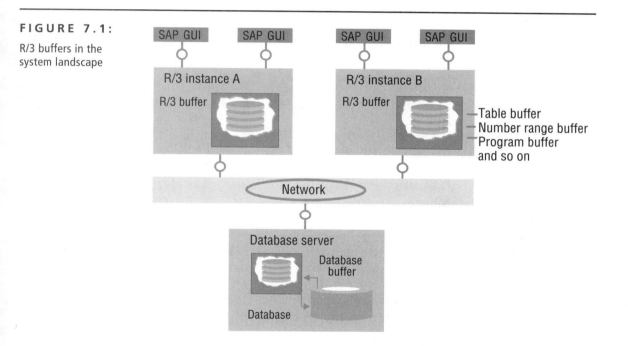

Buffering Types

There are three types of table buffering:

- Single record
- Full
- Generic

Single Record Buffering

Single record buffering is suitable for accesses that are executed using all table keys—in other words, all fields of the primary index. The first access reads the single record (that is, an entire row) from the database table and loads it into the buffer. Then, whenever the record needs to be read again, it can be read directly from the buffer.

The following SQL statement is an example of a statement that seeks to access a single record from the table *tab_sngl*, whose key fields are *key1*, *key2*, and *key3:*

```
SELECT SINGLE * FROM tab_sngl WHERE key1 = a1 AND key2 = a2 AND key3
= a3
```

If single record buffering is activated for the table *tab_sngl* and the single record has already been buffered, this SQL statement will access the data in the single record buffer instead of in the database.

NOTE   To enable access to the single record buffer, the SQL statement must contain the ABAP keyword SINGLE, and the WHERE clause must contain all the key fields of the table. If one of these conditions is not met, the statement will access the data through the database.

On the first attempt to access a table for which single record buffering is activated, if the required record is not in the database, information is stored in the buffer indicating that the record does not exist. On a second attempt to access this record, the buffer search recognizes that the record does not exist and thus makes no attempt to access the database. Therefore, the number of entries for a specific table in the single record buffer may be larger than the number of actual records in that table in the database.

Full Buffering

If full table buffering is activated for a specific table, the first reading of the table in the database loads the entire table into the buffer. This type of buffering is mainly used for small tables.

Figure 7.2 shows the three different ways of buffering, indicating the buffered records as darkened rows. The left-hand table shows full table buffering. The two center tables show generic buffering by one and two key fields respectively. The right-hand table shows three single records buffered at different times.

FIGURE 7.2:

Generic regions of a table

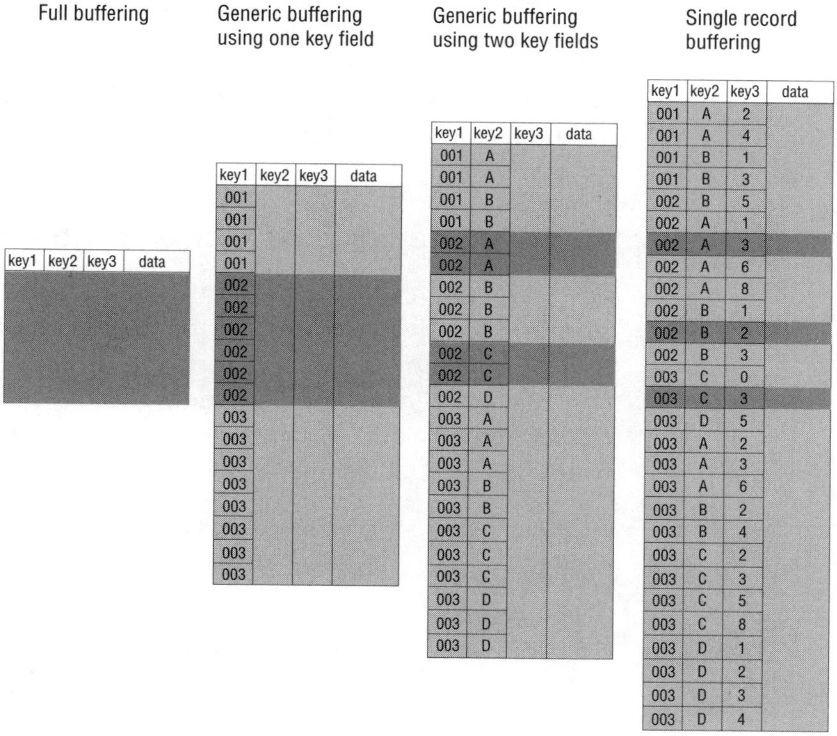

Full buffering

key1	key2	key3	data

Generic buffering using one key field

key1	key2	key3	data
001			
001			
001			
001			
002			
002			
002			
002			
002			
002			
003			
003			
003			
003			
003			
003			
003			
003			

Generic buffering using two key fields

key1	key2	key3	data
001	A		
001	A		
001	B		
001	B		
002	A		
002	A		
002	B		
002	B		
002	C		
002	C		
002	D		
003	A		
003	A		
003	A		
003	B		
003	B		
003	C		
003	C		
003	C		
003	D		
003	D		
003	D		

Single record buffering

key1	key2	key3	data
001	A	2	
001	A	4	
001	B	1	
001	B	3	
002	B	5	
002	A	1	
002	A	3	
002	A	6	
002	A	8	
002	B	1	
002	B	2	
002	B	3	
003	C	0	
003	C	3	
003	D	5	
003	A	2	
003	A	3	
003	A	6	
003	B	2	
003	B	4	
003	C	2	
003	C	3	
003	C	5	
003	C	8	
003	D	1	
003	D	2	
003	D	3	
003	D	4	

Generic Buffering

Generic buffering is buffering with <n> key fields, which not only buffers the particular data record that is required by an SQL statement, but also buffers all other data rows that have the same <n> key values as the targeted record. The value of <n> is specified when buffering is set for the table.

The center-left table in Figure 7.2 is a table for which generic buffering is activated and n = 1. Thus, this table has *generic 1* buffering. When an SQL statement first accesses a record with the value *002* for the first key field, all other records with the same key field value are loaded into the buffer. Considered as a group, these records are said to form a *generic region* of the table.

The center-right table in Figure 7.2 shows generic buffering with two key fields. Here, the generic region that is buffered consists of all the records whose first *two* key fields match.

Further Example of Generic 2 Buffering

For table *tab_gen2*, generic 2 buffering has been set. The first two primary key fields are the client (*mandt*) and the company code (*bukrs*). The table also contains the primary key fields *key3* and *key4*, as well as data corresponding to the company codes *Poland*, *Czech Republic*, and *Slovakia*. The table is now accessed with the following SQL statement:

```
SELECT * FROM tab_gen2 WHERE mandt = '100' AND bukrs = 'Poland' AND
key3 = a3
```

This statement causes the buffering of all the records of the table *tab_gen2* that correspond to client *100* and company code *Poland*. If your R/3 System has the users corresponding to the different company codes working on different application servers, only the data that is relevant to the company code used on a particular application server is loaded into the buffers of that server.

Buffer Accessing

Buffer management is performed by the database interface in the R/3 work process program. Single record buffered tables are stored in the R/3 single record buffer (TABLP); generic and full buffered tables are stored in the generic R/3 table buffer (TABL). Each table in the buffers is sorted according to the primary key.

Even after a table is stored in the buffer, the database interface does not automatically access the table buffers, but requires certain information from the WHERE clause of the SQL statement.

To enable access to a single buffered table, the EQUALS conditions in the WHERE clause must specify all the fields of the table's primary key.

To enable access to a table that has generic <n> buffering, the EQUALS conditions in the WHERE clause must specify the first <n> primary key fields.

Example of Generic 3 Buffering

Table *tab_gen3* has generic 3 buffering. The fields *key1*, *key2*, *key3*, and *key4* are the key fields in the table.

The following SELECT statements access R/3 buffers:

- SELECT * FROM tab_gen3 WHERE key1 = a1 AND key2 = a2 AND key3 = a3

- SELECT * FROM tab_gen3 WHERE key1 = a1 AND key2 = a2 AND key3 = a3 and key4 > a4

The following SQL statements do not access R/3 buffers, but require a database access:

- SELECT * FROM tab_gen3 WHERE key1 = a1

- SELECT * FROM tab_gen3 WHERE key3 = a3

Even though table *tab_gen3* has generic 3 buffering, these last two SQL statements do not access the buffer because they do not specify all of the fields *key1*, *key2*, and *key3*.

In contrast to generic buffering, full buffering always causes a buffer access, provided the respective table has already been loaded into the buffer.

Example of Full Buffering

Table *tab_ful* has full buffering. Its key fields are *key1*, *key2*, *key3*, and *key4*.

The following SQL statements access the table buffer:

- `SELECT * FROM tab_ful WHERE key1 = a1 AND key2 = a2 AND key3 = a3`

- `SELECT * FROM tab_ful WHERE key3 = a3`

Because the second of these two SQL statements does not specify the fields *key1* and *key2*, and the table in the buffers is sorted according to these key fields, all data in the buffered table will be read sequentially. Therefore, if the table is relatively large—for example, with more than 100 rows—it will be more effective to optimize table access by not buffering the table and instead creating a secondary index using field *key3*.

As this example shows, in some situations, it is paradoxically less optimal to access the buffers than to access the database. See "Buffering Guidelines" below.

Other SQL Statements That Do Not Access Buffers

The following SQL statements do not access the buffers:

- SQL statements with the clause BYPASSING BUFFER. This clause is used to deliberately avoid accessing the buffers.

- SELECT FOR UPDATE statements. These SQL statements access the database to set a database lock.

- SQL statements using the aggregate functions SUM, AVG, MIN, and MAXIMUM.

- SELECT DISTINCT statements.

- SQL statements with the operator IS NULL.

- SQL statements that trigger sorts (except sorts by primary key).

- SQL statements that access views (except projection views).

- Native SQL statements.

Buffer Synchronization

Buffer synchronization is the process whereby a change to an entry in a buffered table on one R/3 instance is updated in the table buffers of other R/3 instances.

The synchronization process varies depending on whether or not an ABAP statement has a WHERE clause.

NOTE   Synchronization as described here applies to the table buffer and all other R/3 buffers, such as the program buffer.

Buffer Synchronization for ABAP Statements without a WHERE Clause

If changes to tables are performed without a WHERE clause, they use the *work area mode* and change only one specific row in the table. Examples of this type of ABAP statement include:

- UPDATE <table>

- INSERT <table>

- MODIFY <table>

- DELETE <table>

Buffer synchronization occurs in the four steps shown in Figure 7.3, which concerns a change to the buffered table T001. The four steps are as follows:

1. On R/3 instance A, the ABAP statement UPDATE T001 changes table T001, both in the database and in the local buffer. Thus, the local buffer is updated synchronously. The buffers on all the other R/3 instances are not up to date concerning the change made to the table in R/3 instance A.

2. After table T001 is changed in the database, the database interface (DBIF) for R/3 instance A logs the change by writing an entry in the database table DDLOG.

3. Table DDLOG is periodically read by all R/3 instances. Because of the DDLOG entry, the buffered table T001 is invalidated in the other R/3 instances.

4. If table T001 is now read on R/3 instance B, the database interface recognizes that the data in the buffer is no longer valid. The data is then reloaded from the database into the buffers. Thus, the buffers of all the other R/3 instances except instance A are updated asynchronously in relation to the time of the original change.

Pending Period between Invalidation and Synchronization

After an invalidation, a *read* access to the invalidated table in the buffer does not immediately trigger the table contents to be reloaded into the buffer from the database. Instead, a specified period is maintained, during which attempts to access the table are satisfied through a direct database access. This period (called the *pending* state) protects the buffer from frequent successive invalidations and reloading operations. After the pending period has elapsed, the buffer is reloaded from the database.

FIGURE 7.3:

Buffer synchronization
in the system
landscape

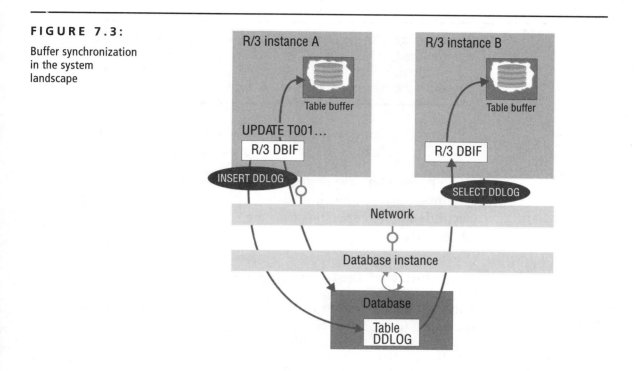

Synchronization Parameters *rdisp/bufrefmode* and *rdisp/bufreftime*

Buffer synchronization is controlled through the R/3 profile parameters *rdisp/bufrefmode* and *rdisp/bufreftime*.

For an R/3 System with only one R/3 instance, the parameter *rdisp/bufrefmode* should be set to *sendoff, exeauto*. The entry *sendoff* signifies that no DDLOG entries are written (because there are no other R/3 instances that require synchronization). The entry *exeauto* signifies that the DDLOG table is read periodically. This is necessary for buffer synchronization after an import through the transport program *tp* or *R3trans*. R/3's Change and Transport System (CTS) also writes entries in the DDLOG table to enable buffer synchronization after object imports affecting table contents and programs.

TIP Invalidations also occur when programs or Customizing settings are transported, so you should avoid imports to a production system during periods of high load. Instead, schedule imports once or twice per week in the evening at times of low system load.

In an R/3 System with multiple R/3 instances, the parameter *rdisp/bufrefmode* must be set to *sendon, exeauto*.

The parameter *rdisp/bufreftime* specifies the frequency of buffer synchronization; you should not change the default setting of 60 (seconds), which specifies that the DDLOG table is read every 60 seconds.

Granularity of Table Invalidation

Three granularities of invalidation can be distinguished corresponding to the three types of buffering:

- If a record is changed in a table with single record buffering, only this record is invalidated—all other buffered table entries remain valid.

- If a record is changed in a table with full buffering, all the table contents are invalidated.

- If a record is changed in a table with generic buffering, the generic area in which the record resides is invalidated.

Thus, table contents are invalidated in the same way as the buffers are filled.

Buffer Synchronization for ABAP Statements with a WHERE Clause

A somewhat different buffer synchronization procedure is used when a buffered table is changed through an ABAP statement that uses a WHERE clause. For example:

- UPDATE <table> WHERE...

- DELETE FROM <table> WHERE...

These ABAP statements usually change several records in a table. Subsequently, this causes the whole table to be invalidated in the respective buffers on all R/3 instances. Thus, change operations using a WHERE clause can decrease the buffer hit ratio and increase the system load due to buffer reloads, much more than change operations that do not use a WHERE clause.

Displacements (*Swaps*)

Be sure not to confuse invalidations with displacements, which are displayed in the R/3 Memory Configuration Monitor (*ST02*) in the column *Swaps*.

Displacements occur when the buffer is almost full, or when the access quality falls below a certain point. The data for which there are the fewest recent accesses is then displaced from the buffer to make space for new data.

Activating or Deactivating Buffering

To access the buffering options and set the buffering for a table, call the ABAP Dictionary Maintenance function. To do this:

1. Use Transaction code *SE13*. Enter the table name and choose *Change*.

- Alternatively, use Transaction code *SE11*, or, from the R/3 initial screen, choose *Tools* ➤ *ABAP Workbench* ➤ *Dictionary*. Enter the table name and choose *Change* ➤ *Technical settings*.

- The ABAP Dictionary maintenance screen appears (see Figure 7.4). (For some tables, a dialog box may first appear, requesting a change request.)

2. To activate buffering, select *Buffering switched on*. Then select the buffering type (*Single records*, *Generic*, or *Full*). For generic buffering, enter the number of key fields to be used.

3. Choose *Save*.

4. To activate the changes, choose *Activate*. The statuses *active* and *saved* will then be indicated beside the settings.

NOTE Since the technical settings affecting a table are linked to the R/3 Change and Transport System (CTS), to change the buffering for a table, you require a change request. Buffering can be activated or deactivated while the R/3 System is running.

The three options for setting buffering within ABAP Dictionary Maintenance (Transaction *SE13*) are as follows:

- *Buffering not allowed:* This setting deactivates the buffering for a table. It is set by the developer if the table is never to be buffered—for example, if a table contains transaction data that is frequently changed.

- *Buffering allowed but switched off:* This setting also deactivates the buffering for a table for which buffering remains possible. If you deactivate buffering with this option, you are usually trying to improve performance in a particular R/3 System— for example, with respect to a table that is too large. Whether a given type of table should in fact be buffered is explained in the section "Buffering Guidelines."

FIGURE 7.4:

Changing the buffering
settings for a table in
ABAP Dictionary
Maintenance
(Transaction *SE13*)

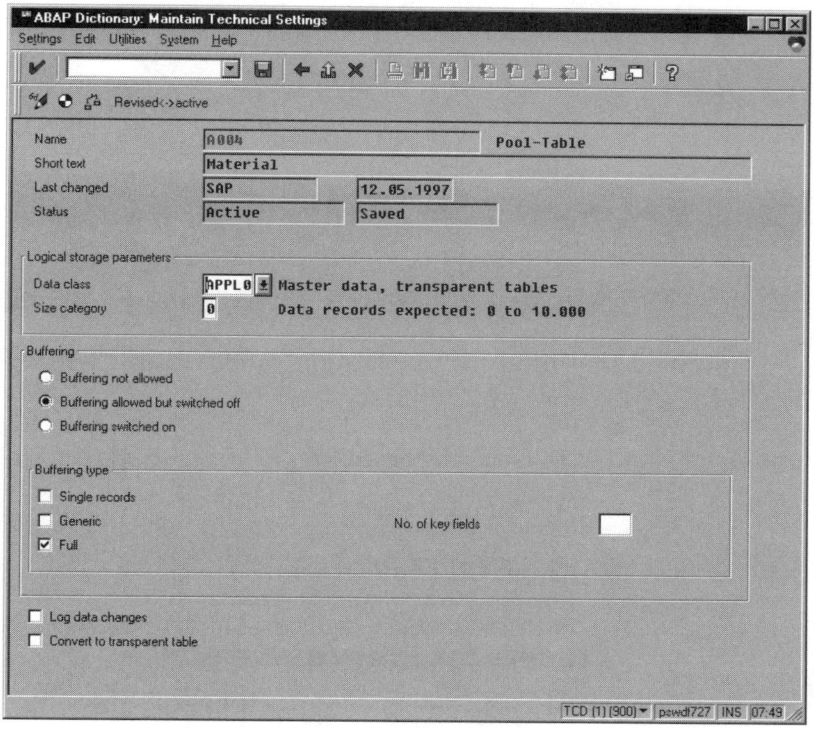

• *Buffering switched on:* This setting activates the buffering for the respective table.

WARNING If a table is delivered by SAP with the setting *Buffering not allowed* and you try to activate buffering for this table, this is considered a modification to the R/3 System and must be registered in SAP's Online Service System (OSS). Activate the buffering for such tables only after receiving an explicit recommendation from SAP.

> **NOTE**   If you set the buffering for a client-dependent table to *full*, the table will automatically receive generic 1 buffering.

Buffering Guidelines

For each table defined in the ABAP Dictionary, you can decide whether buffering is appropriate or inappropriate.

Different buffering guidelines apply to the following different types of R/3 data:

- Transaction data
- Master data
- Customizing data

Technical Prerequisites

Before deciding which guidelines apply to a given table, note that a table cannot be buffered unless it satisfies the following technical prerequisites:

- The tables must be small and frequently read. This is because buffering causes data to be stored redundantly on all R/3 instances.

- The tables must not incur frequent *write* accesses. This is because when buffered tables are changed through *write* accesses, the resulting buffer synchronization process causes a relatively large loss in performance.

- The tables must not be tables that are typically accessed using a secondary index. Since buffered tables are sorted by key fields, table buffering is optimal for those ABAP statements that access the table through the key fields (rather than through secondary indexes).

- The tables must be tables where short-term inconsistencies between buffers and the database do not matter, since buffer synchronization occurs only after a time delay.

Never Buffer Transaction Data

The amount of transaction data in an R/3 System tends to grow significantly over time and may reach several megabytes or even gigabytes. This volume of data is too large for any buffer.

Examples of transaction data include sales orders, delivery notes, goods movement, and goods reservations. This data is stored in tables such as VBAK, LIKP, MKPF, and RESB.

Master Data Is Normally Not Buffered

Tables with master data grow slowly over time and can reach sizes of several hundred MB. Therefore, as a rule, master data is not buffered.

A second argument against buffering tables that contain master data is that master data is normally accessed through many differing selections and not necessarily through the primary index key. To optimize these accesses collectively, you should use secondary indexes instead of buffering.

Examples of typical master data are materials, customers, and suppliers. This data is stored in tables such as MARA, KNA1, and LFA1.

Customizing Data Is Normally Buffered

Customizing data individualizes your company's business processes in the R/3 System.

Normally, Customizing tables are small and are rarely changed after the start of production. This, plus the fact that they are frequently read, makes them very suitable for table buffering.

Examples of Customizing data include definition of R/3 client systems, company codes, plants, and sales organizations. This data is stored in tables such as T000, T001, T001W, and TVKO.

Example of When Not to Buffer a Customizing Data Table

Table TCURR contains the exchange rates for foreign currencies. The key fields in this table are MANDT (client), KURST (type of exchange rate), FCURR (source currency), TCURR (target currency), and GDATU (start of validity period).

In most customer systems, this table is small and is seldom changed, so it meets the prerequisites for buffering. Consequently, this table is delivered by SAP with *full* buffering.

In some R/3 Systems, however, this table may grow very quickly because many exchange rates are required, each tied to their own validity period, and new exchange rates for new validity periods are constantly being added. Because the table is set to full buffering, even entries with validity periods far in the past are loaded into the buffer, despite the fact that they are rarely required. Thus, the table reaches a particular large size, and table buffering becomes ineffective. Additionally, if the table is changed during daily operation, invalidations and reloading processes significantly reduce performance.

For tables like this, you should deactivate buffering. To achieve a long-term, application-specific solution, you need to examine issues such as whether all of the table entries are really necessary, and whether old entries can be removed—for example, through archiving. (Further analysis for this example is given below in the section "Detailed Table Analysis.")

Condition Tables

Condition tables contain the Customizing data for the central logical functions that determine such information as price, output device, partner, account, and so on. These functions are part of the business process chain—for example, for incoming sales orders, goods issue, and billing.

Because these transactions are extremely critical for performance in many R/3 Systems, optimizing buffering for condition tables should receive special priority.

Most condition tables take the form A<nnn>, B<nnn>, C<nnn>, D<nnn>, KOTE<nnn>, KOTF<nnn>, KOTG<nnn>, or KOTH<nnn>, where <nnn> is a value in the range 000 to 999.

Tables where <nnn> lies in the range 000 to 499 are a part of the SAP standard and—with few exceptions—are delivered set to *buffering activated*.

Tables where <nnn> lies in the range 500 to 999 are generated by the customer as required during Customizing and are initially not buffered.

Example of When Not to Buffer a Condition Table

Table A005 contains price conditions corresponding to customer and material. A price condition is possible for every combination of customer and material in this table. Additionally, each price condition also has a validity period.

If customer-dependent prices are used intensively in an R/3 System and new prices are frequently added or existing prices are changed, this table may grow quickly. Thus, the table reaches a particular large size, and table buffering becomes ineffective. Again, if the table is changed during daily operation, invalidations and reloading processes reduce performance.

Therefore, you should also deactivate buffering on this table. Other examples of condition tables that tend to grow quickly are A017 and A018 (prices for suppliers and material numbers).

Monitoring R/3 Table Buffering

Monitoring for R/3 table buffering should focus on the following problems:

- Displacements occur: These are indicated as *swaps* in the R/3 Memory Configuration Monitor (Transaction *ST02*). These displacements are due to the table buffer being too small. Ensure that table buffering has at least 10% free space and at least 20% free directory entries. (See Chapter 2.)

- Tables are buffered that should not be buffered: The reason these tables should not be buffered is usually either because they are changed and invalidated too often or because they are too large.

- Tables are not buffered that should be buffered: These are normally tables that are created in the customer system—either explicitly created in the ABAP Dictionary or implicitly created through Customizing (for example, condition tables).

Monitoring table buffering is not something that needs to be done according to a rigid timetable, but only as required—for example, when:

- Users complain about occasional long response times in a transaction that normally runs quickly.

- Analyzing the Shared SQL Area or performing an SQL trace reveals expensive SQL statements related to buffered tables. These may indicate reloading processes caused by incorrect buffering.

- You frequently see the entry *Note: Tables were saved in the table buffer* when analyzing the single statistics records with Transaction *STAT* (see Chapter 4, under "Single Statistics Records").

Table Access Statistics Monitor (Transaction *ST10*)

To monitor table buffering, use the Table Access Statistics Monitor. The statistics shown in this monitor are also called *table call statistics*. Access the monitor as follows:

1. Use Transaction code *ST10*, or, from the R/3 initial screen, choose *Tools* ➢ *Administration* ➢ *Monitor* ➢ *Performance* ➢ *Setup/Buffers* ➢ *Calls*.

2. In the selection screen that appears, select the type of table to be used for the analysis, the time period, and the R/3 instance. For the present analysis, select *All tables, Since startup*, and *This server*.

3. The *Performance analysis: Table call statistics* screen is displayed, listing the tables and corresponding statistics on database accesses and buffer status (see Figure 7.5).

    - As of R/3 Release 4.0, you can view further columns by using the arrow button.

    - To display all the available information on an individual table, double-click the respective row.

FIGURE 7.5: The Table Access Statistics Monitor (Transaction *ST10*)

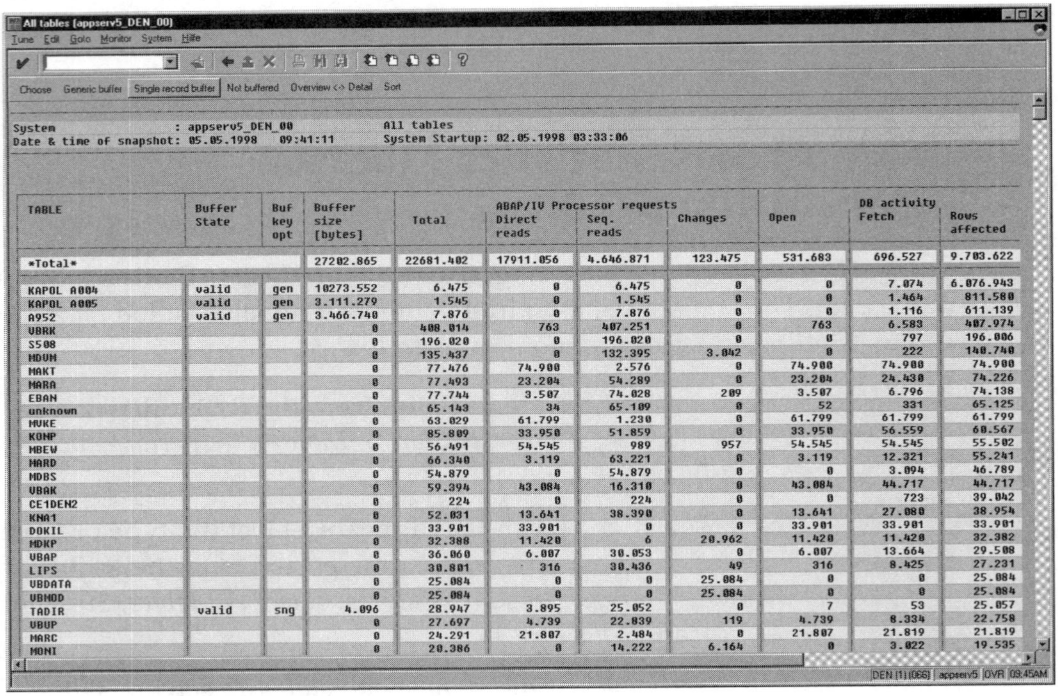

TABLE	Buffer State	Buf key opt	Buffer size [bytes]	Total	ABAP/IV Processor requests Direct reads	Seq. reads	Changes	Open	DB activity Fetch	Rows affected
Total			27202.865	22681.402	17911.056	4.646.871	123.475	531.683	696.527	9.703.622
KAPOL A004	valid	gen	10273.552	6.475	0	6.475	0	0	7.074	6.076.943
KAPOL A005	valid	gen	3.111.279	1.545	0	1.545	0	0	1.464	811.580
A952	valid	gen	3.466.740	7.876	0	7.876	0	0	1.116	611.139
VBRK			0	408.014	763	407.251	0	763	6.583	407.974
S508			0	196.020	0	196.020	0	0	797	196.006
MDVM			0	135.437	0	132.395	3.042	0	222	140.740
MAKT			0	77.476	74.900	2.576	0	74.900	74.900	74.900
MARA			0	77.493	23.204	54.289	0	23.204	24.430	74.226
EBAN			0	77.744	3.507	74.028	209	3.507	6.796	74.138
unknown			0	65.143	34	65.109	0	52	331	65.125
MVKE			0	63.029	61.799	1.230	0	61.799	61.799	61.799
KONP			0	85.809	33.950	51.859	0	33.950	56.559	60.567
MBEW			0	56.491	54.545	989	957	54.545	54.545	55.502
MARD			0	66.340	3.119	63.221	0	3.119	12.321	55.241
MDBS			0	54.879	0	54.879	0	0	3.094	46.789
VBAK			0	59.394	43.084	16.310	0	43.084	44.717	44.717
CE1DEN2			0	224	0	224	0	0	723	39.042
KNA1			0	52.031	13.641	38.390	0	13.641	27.080	38.954
DOKIL			0	33.901	33.901	0	0	33.901	33.901	33.901
MDKP			0	32.388	11.420	6	20.962	11.420	11.420	32.382
VBAP			0	36.060	6.007	30.053	0	6.007	13.664	29.508
LIPS			0	30.801	316	30.436	49	316	8.425	27.231
VBDATA			0	25.084	0	0	25.084	0	0	25.084
VBMOD			0	25.084	0	0	25.084	0	0	25.084
TADIR	valid	sng	4.096	28.947	3.895	25.052	0	7	53	25.057
VBUP			0	27.697	4.739	22.839	119	4.739	8.334	22.758
MARC			0	24.291	21.807	2.484	0	21.807	21.819	21.819
MONI			0	20.386	0	14.222	6.164	0	3.022	19.535

Table 7.1 describes the most important columns in the Table Access Statistics Monitor.

TABLE 7.1: Explanation of the Columns in the Table Access Statistics Monitor (Transaction *ST10*)

Column	Explanation
Table	Name of the table. If it is a pooled table, the name of the table pool is given first—for example, *KAPOL A004*.

Continued on next page

TABLE 7.1: Explanation of the Columns in the Table Access Statistics Monitor (Transaction *ST10*) *(Continued)*

Column	Explanation
Buffer State	For bufferable tables, the *Buffer State* tells you, for example, whether the table is currently accessible in the buffer (for a full list of possible buffer states, see Table 7.2 later in this chapter).
Buf key opt	Type of buffering: *ful* indicates full buffering, *gen* indicates generic buffering, and *sng* indicates single record buffering.
Buffer size [bytes]	Size of the table in the R/3 table buffer.
Size maximum [bytes]	Maximum size of the table in the R/3 table buffer since system startup. (This value occurs when you double-click a line in the screen for a specific table.)
Invalidations	Number of invalidations since system startup. (This value occurs when you double-click a line in the screen for a specific table.)
ABAP/IV Processor requests	Numbers of ABAP access requests that are received by the database interface. This column is divided into *Total, Direct reads, Seq. reads, Updates, Deletes, Inserts*, and *Fails*. (The last four values occur when you double-click a line in the screen for a specific table.) The values of *Updates, Deletes, Inserts*, and *Fails* are summarized as *Changes* in Figure 7.5.
DB activity	Number of database operations, such as PREPARE, OPEN, REOPEN, FETCH, or EXEC, that are requested in the database by the database interface. This column is divided into *All prepares, Direct fetches, Sequential reads (opens and fetches), Inserts, Deletes*, and *Updates*. (Some of these values occur only when you double-click a line in the screen for a specific table.)
DB activity: Rows affected	Number of table rows that are transferred between the database and the R/3 instance.

Requests, Opens, and Fetches in the Table Access Statistics Monitor

A table access in an ABAP program is called a *request,* and can be either a *read* or a *change* request.

Read requests can be either *direct reads* or *sequential reads*. Direct reads are SELECT SINGLE statements that have specified all the primary key fields in the WHERE clause with an EQUALS condition. All other SELECT statements are called sequential reads.

Change requests can be *inserts*, *updates*, or *deletes*.

In any request, the ABAP program calls the database interface of the R/3 work process. The database interface checks whether the table buffer for the R/3 instance can supply the data for the query. If not, the database interface passes on a corresponding SQL statement to the database.

An SQL statement performing a read consists of:

- An OPEN operation that transfers the SQL statement to the database

- One or more FETCHES that transfer the resulting data from the database to the R/3 work process

Similarly, an SQL statement performing a change consists of an OPEN operation and an EXEC operation.

NOTE   For more information on the operations PREPARE, OPEN, REOPEN, FETCH, and EXEC, see Chapter 4, under "Evaluating an SQL Trace."

For tables that cannot be buffered, the database interface of the R/3 work process automatically passes every request to the database. For direct reads, inserts, updates, and deletes, every request corresponds to exactly one OPEN and one FETCH. For sequential reads, the situation is more complex: For each request, there can be more than one OPEN and more than one FETCH.

For tables that can be buffered, the corresponding requests encounter one of three situations:

- The table contents are located in the buffer with the status *valid*. In this situation, the requested data can be read from the buffer, and no database activity is required.

- The buffered table has the status *valid*, but the SQL statement either does not specify the correct fields or contains the clause BYPASSING BUFFER to prevent reading from the R/3 buffer. In this situation, database activity is required to satisfy the request. Examples of SQL statements that do not access R/3 buffers are listed earlier in this chapter under "Buffer Accessing."

- The table contents are not yet located in the buffer or are not valid. In this situation, the requested data cannot be read from the buffer. If the table is not in the wait period between invalidation and synchronization, the database interface loads the buffer. If the wait period is running, the data is directly accessed from the database without loading the buffer.

Database Rows Affected in the Table Access Statistics Monitor

In the Table Access Statistics Monitor (Transaction *ST10*), the statistic in the column *Rows affected* (under *DB activity*) does not increase following the initial loading of the buffer. Thus, if a table has been loaded only once into the buffer and all subsequent requests are read from the buffer, the value in *Rows affected* remains zero. This value increases only according to the number of database table rows that are read either:

- When the buffered table is invalidated or displaced and then reloaded from the database into the buffer

- When a request bypasses the buffer

Figure 7.5 (earlier in this chapter) shows an example of the Table Access Statistics Monitor in an R/3 System with Release 3.1. The list is sorted by the column *Rows affected* (under *DB activity*), which indicates the number of rows read by the database after they are initially loaded into the buffer. The tables at the top of the list are buffered tables such as the condition tables A004, A005, and A952. The entry KAPOL preceding the table names in the column *Table* signifies that these tables are in the KAPOL table pool.

Buffer State in the Table Access Statistics Monitor

In the Table Access Statistics Monitor (Transaction *ST10*), the column *Buffer State* shows whether or not buffered data is accessible, and why. Table 7.2 lists the various statuses that may be listed in this column.

TABLE 7.2: Explanation of Values in the Column *Buffer State* in the Table Access Statistics Monitor (Transaction *ST10*)

Status	Explanation
Valid	The table data in the buffer is ready to be accessed to satisfy requests.
Invalid	The table was invalidated and cannot yet be reloaded into the buffer because the operation that changed the table has not yet been completed with a COMMIT.
Pending	The table was invalidated and cannot yet be reloaded because the wait period between invalidation and synchronization has not yet expired.
Loadable	The table was invalidated, the wait period before synchronization has expired, and the table will be reloaded with the next request for data from the table.
Loading	The table is currently being loaded.
Absent, displaced	The table is not in the buffer, either because it was displaced or because it was never loaded.
Multiple	For tables with generic buffering: Some generic areas are valid, others have been invalidated.
Error	An error occurred when the table was loaded into the buffer, so the table is effectively not buffered.

Identifying Buffered Tables That Should Not Be Buffered

To identify the buffered tables whose buffering reduces rather than increases system performance, call the Table Access Statistics

Monitor. To start this monitor, use Transaction code *ST10*, or, from the R/3 initial screen, choose *Tools* ➤ *Administration* ➤ *Monitor* ➤ *Performance* ➤ *Setup/Buffers* ➤ *Calls*.

In the dialog box that appears, select *All tables*, *Since startup*, and *This server*.

The screen that appears resembles the one in Figure 7.5 (earlier in this chapter).

Step 1: Analyzing Database Accesses

Sort the Table Access Statistics Monitor by the column *Rows affected* (under *DB activity*), which indicates the number of rows read from the database at any time after they were initially loaded into the buffer. This value is an indication of the database load caused by a table despite the fact that it is buffered.

After sorting, the top of the list will contain tables with high database activity. These should be nonbuffered tables such as transaction data tables or large master record tables. Examples of these in Figure 7.5 are the tables VBAK, S508, and MDVM. For many of these nonbuffered tables, the total number of requests (in the column *Total* under *ABAP/IV Processor requests*) will be of the same order of magnitude as the number of *Rows affected*.

The tables for which buffering has been activated can be recognized by an entry in the column *Buf key opt*. For these tables, the number of *Rows affected* should be small, because accesses to these tables should read data from the buffer and not from the database. Therefore, these tables should not be at the top of the list sorted by *Rows affected*.

If, however, you do find buffered tables with a high number of *Rows affected*, there are two possible causes for this:

- The table is relatively large and has been changed or displaced. The reloading process and database read accesses during the wait period before synchronization result in a high number of *Rows affected*. You need to decide whether to deactivate buffering for this table. (See steps 2 to 4 below.)

- The type of buffering does not match the WHERE clause in the read accesses, so the database interface cannot use the buffer.

NOTE   If buffered tables appear among the top entries in a Table Access Statistics Monitor sorted by database *Rows affected,* this indicates that buffering these tables reduces performance. These tables require further analysis using steps 2 to 4 below.

Step 2: Analyzing the Invalidation Rate

Sort the Table Access Statistics Monitor by the column *Invalidations*. Calculate the invalidation rate for the top-listed tables, which is the ratio of invalidations to total requests. Use the respective figures from the column *Invalidations* and the column *Total* (under *ABAP/IV Processor requests*).

For tables showing a high invalidation rate, use the guidelines relating to table size given in step 3 below to decide whether buffering should be deactivated.

Step 3: Analyzing Table Size

For tables with a large number of rows affected (see step 1) or a high invalidation rate (see step 2), you can use the following guidelines, which are based on the evidence available at the time of publication:

- It is OK to buffer tables that are smaller than 1MB and have an invalidation rate lower than 1%.

- It is OK to buffer tables between 1MB and 5MB if the invalidation rate is lower than 0.1%.

- For tables larger than 5MB, the developer must decide individually for each table whether buffering is worthwhile.

The table size can be found in the column *Buffer size*.

Step 4: Logical Analysis

Before deactivating buffering for a table, consider the following recommendations:

- For customer-created tables: Changes to table buffering should be made only after careful, joint consideration by the responsible developer and the system administrator.

- For SAP-created tables: In some R/3 installations, it may become necessary to deactivate buffering for an SAP table such as TCURR or the condition tables. However, you should never deactivate buffering unless you have analyzed it closely and checked for related R/3 Notes in the Online Service System (OSS). This applies in particular to the tables in the R/3 Basis area, such as the tables DDFTX and USR*.

Verifying the Effects of Changes to Buffering

After you have made any changes to table buffering, you should verify whether these changes have had a positive effect on the system performance associated with accessing the respective tables.

Using your knowledge of the programs and transactions that access the tables whose buffering you changed, you can investigate the effect of the changes during the programs' runtime.

The purpose of the table buffer is to reduce the number of database accesses for a given table. Whether the changes you made to buffering have achieved this should be apparent in the Table

Access Statistics Monitor (Transaction *ST10*). Look at the ratio of the value in the column *Total* (under *ABAP/IV Processor requests*) to the value in the column *Rows affected* (under *DB activity*). If, by changing the buffering for a table, you were not able to increase this ratio, reanalyze the buffer and, if in doubt, undo the changes you made to buffering.

Example of How to Identify Buffered Tables That Should Not Be Buffered

Figures 7.5 (earlier in this chapter) and 7.6 (below) show screen shots of the Table Access Statistics Monitor for all tables in two real R/3 Systems. Both screens are sorted by the column *Rows affected* (under *DB activity*).

FIGURE 7.6: Another example of values in the Table Access Statistics Monitor (Transaction *ST10*)

All tables (bbafddi1_P11_00)

Tune Edit Goto Monitor System Hilfe

Choose   Generic buffer   Single record buffer   Not buffered   Overview <-> Detail   Sort

System : bbafddi1_P11_00   All tables
Date & time of snapshot: 11.02.1998 13:55:00   System Startup: 11.02.1998 03:52:18

TABLE	Buffer State	Buf key opt	Buffer size [bytes]	Total	ABAP/IV Processor requests Direct reads	Seq. reads	Changes	Open	DB activity Fetch	Rows affected
Total			6.095.721	3.914.298	2.899.491	992.701	22.186	123.252	159.805	3.735.563
KAPOL A005	displcd	gen	0	2.338	0	2.338	0	0	2.499	1.406.353
KAPOL A004	valid	gen	979.282	488	0	488	0	0	847	539.694
KAPOL A006	valid	gen	940.632	612	0	612	0	0	853	455.149
KAPOL A017	pending	gen	0	392	0	392	0	0	364	128.818
T179	valid	gen	65.054	111.380	238	111.142	0	20	64	76.773
ATAB TMC73	pending	ful	0	580	0	580	0	0	58	62.818
ATAB TFAWX	pending	gen	0	14.039	0	14.039	0	0	106	62.492
T179T	valid	gen	124.992	551	491	60	0	178	215	57.754
VAPMA			0	48.757	0	48.757	0	0	207	46.894
VBUK			0	45.020	44.610	400	10	44.800	44.800	44.812
ATAB T130F	valid	gen	39.240	115.160	22	115.146	0	1	107	41.857
ATAB T156S	pending	gen	0	297	297	0	0	48	90	33.512
TFAVL	valid	gen	530.334	5.544	0	5.544	0	0	293	33.100
ICONT	valid	ful	115.895	513	502	11	0	46	75	30.148
T023T	valid	gen	44.847	510	498	12	0	39	49	20.519
ATAB TFAV	valid	gen	68.772	884	0	884	0	0	66	20.002

P11 (3) (066) ▼   bbafddi1   INS 01.55PM

Looking at Figure 7.5, you should expect that tables with transaction data or a large volume of master data would be at the top of the list—for example, the tables VBRK, S508, and MDVM. Instead, the top-listed tables are the condition tables A004, A005, and A952. That these are buffered tables is indicated by the fact that the buffering status for all three tables is *valid*.

In Figure 7.5, divide the value in the column *Rows affected* (under *DB activity*) by the value in the column *Total* (under *ABAP/IV Processor requests*). The result reveals that an average of 1,000 rows are read from the database for each request. For the three tables, a total of 7.5 million rows were read. This is around 75% of all the rows read from all tables (9.7 million rows). The very high load on these three tables is likely to be caused by frequent buffer loading processes.

To verify whether there is frequent buffer loading for a particular table, analyze the buffered table size and the number of invalidations. To do this, double-click the row containing the table that you want to analyze. This takes you to a screen summarizing all the available information on this table.

In the present example, you would see that tables A004, A005, and A952 are frequently invalidated (as shown by the number of *Invalidations*). Calculating the ratio of invalidations to total requests (see the column *Requests* under *ABAP processor*) reveals that the invalidation rate is greater than 1%. In addition, the size of the tables in the buffer as indicated in the column *Buffer size* in Figure 7.5 is between 3MB and 10MB.

The guidelines from step 3 above indicate that it is OK to buffer tables between 1MB and 5MB if the invalidation rate is smaller than 0.1%. Since, here, the invalidation rate for the tables A004, A005, and A952 is greater than 1%, you should deactivate the buffering for these tables.

You may be surprised that the tables A004, A005, and A952 are being invalidated although there are no changes indicated in the column *Changes* in Figure 7.5. This is because the column *Changes* displays only the local changes that are performed on the selected R/3 instance, which is the instance selected when calling the Table Access Statistics Monitor (here, *appserv5_DEN_00*). It does not display changes that are as follows:

- Performed on other R/3 instances

- Transported into the R/3 System after being performed to the Customizing table in another R/3 System, such as the development system

These changes from other R/3 Systems, however, do cause an invalidation of buffer entries on the selected instance, and therefore start a local buffer reloading process. All invalidations decrease the buffer hit ratio and increase the system load due to buffer reloads. Therefore, the statistic *Invalidations* rather than *Changes* is used for the analysis.

A similar analysis as that just performed for Figure 7.5 can also be performed for Figure 7.6, which is also sorted by *Rows affected* and also shows a number of buffered tables at the top of the list. The entry *displcd* in the column *Buffer State* shows that the table A005 was not invalidated by a change, but was displaced. In this example, two problems coincide:

- Tables are buffered that are possibly too large and too frequently changed to be buffered.

- The table buffer is too small and causes displacements.

If displacements are occurring in the table buffer, the column *Swap* in the Memory Configuration Monitor (Transaction *ST02*) will show a value corresponding to the table buffer that is greater than zero.

Since the example in Figure 7.6 reveals two problems, the corresponding solution strategy is more complex:

1. Increase the size of the table buffers.

2. Look at the sizes and the number of invalidations in the tables A005, A004, A006, and A017, and, based on the guidelines in step 3 above, decide whether to deactivate the buffering of these tables. For example, if table A005 is larger than 1MB and the number of invalidations is larger than 0.1%, you should deactivate the buffering on this table.

3. Verify the positive effects of your deactivation of buffering by checking whether it noticeably reduced the number of database accesses to buffered tables. If not, analyze the table access statistics further to determine whether you need to enlarge the table buffer size or deactivate the buffering for other tables.

NOTE   For computers with a large main memory, it is not unusual for the generic key table buffer to be configured with as much as 100MB and the single record table buffer to be configured with as much as 40MB.

Identifying Nonbuffered Tables That Should Be Buffered

This section provides an analysis that helps you to decide whether it is a good idea to activate buffering for particular tables that have not yet been buffered.

To perform the analysis, use the Table Access Statistics Monitor. To start this monitor, use Transaction code *ST10*, or, from the R/3 initial screen, choose *Tools* ➢ *Administration* ➢ *Monitor* ➢ *Performance* ➢ *Setup/Buffers* ➢ *Calls*.

In the dialog box that appears, select *All tables*, *Since startup*, and *This server*.

Step A: Analyzing Database Accesses

To identify the tables that are currently not buffered and may potentially benefit from being buffered, sort the Table Access Statistics Monitor by the column *Total* (under *ABAP/IV Processor requests*).

At the top of the sorted list, you will normally find the tables DDNTF and DDNTT. These are ABAP Dictionary tables that are stored in two of the *Nametab* (NTAB) buffers—that is, in the *field description* buffer and the *table definition* buffer.

The next tables in the list will be as follows:

- Tables that cannot be buffered, namely:
    - Transaction data tables or large master data tables. These include the logistics-related tables MARA, MARC, VBAK, and MKPF.
    - The SAP update tables VBHDR, VBMOD, and VBDATA.
- Buffered tables containing Customizing data

If there are nonbuffered Customizing tables at the top of the list sorted by requests, these are the tables for which you should consider activating buffering. These may include customer-created tables, such as:

- Tables explicitly created by the customer in the ABAP Dictionary (whose names usually begin with Y or Z)

- Condition tables generated during Customizing (for example, table A<nnn>, where *nnn* ≥ 500)

The result of step A is a list of nonbuffered Customizing tables that you might potentially want to buffer because they receive a high number of requests.

Step B: Technical Analysis

The tables potentially calling for buffering from step A must now be measured against further criteria, starting with technical criteria based on the invalidation rate and the size of the table.

As explained above, a table can be buffered if the change rate is sufficiently low or, if it is not low, if the table size is within the guidelines in step 3 of the previous section. The change rate is the ratio of the figure in the column *Changes* to the figure in the column *Total* (under *ABAP/IV Processor requests*).

You will find information about how to obtain the size of a table in the section "Detailed Table Analysis," below.

Step C: Logical Analysis

The tables potentially calling for buffering from step A, and which passed the criteria in step B, must now satisfy the responsible developer's evaluation of the logical requirements for buffering, which are related to:

- The function of the table

- The type of accesses made to the table

- The size of the table

- How frequently the table is changed

To perform the logical analysis of bufferability, proceed as follows:

- For customer-created tables:

  - Changes to table buffering should be made only after careful, joint consideration by the responsible developer and the system administrator.

  - After clarifying the purpose of the table, the criteria explained in the section "Buffering Guidelines" (earlier in this chapter) enables you to determine whether the table should be buffered. For example, condition tables are usually good tables to buffer. Bear in mind that single record buffering and generic buffering are useful only if the key fields are specified in the WHERE clause of the access requests. Finally, the developer sets the type of table buffering.

- For SAP-created tables:

    - The buffer status of SAP tables has a default setting when the R/3 System is delivered. Most of the tables that can be buffered are buffered. If you find an SAP table for which buffering is not activated and you think it should be buffered, check for related R/3 Notes in SAP's Online Service System (OSS). Never activate buffering for a table where buffering is set to *Buffering not allowed* without first obtaining explicit instructions from SAP.

WARNING Activating table buffering can lead to data inconsistencies between the database and the buffers on servers other than the server from which the database table change originated. This is because the buffer synchronization process for these servers is not completed until some time after the database table is changed. As these brief inconsistencies may make a difference to some business processes, you should not activate table buffering if you are unsure about the function of a table or the type of accesses made to the table. Activating table buffering can also cause performance problems if the table is too large or is changed too often.

Detailed Table Analysis (Transaction *DB05*)

The detailed table analysis using Transaction *DB05* enables you to find out the size of a table, the number of table entries, and the distribution of the generic regions in a table. To perform this analysis, proceed as follows:

1. Use Transaction code *DB05*.

    -   Alternatively, select a table in the Table Access Statistics Monitor (Transaction *ST10*) and choose *Analyze table*.

    -   For earlier R/3 Releases, you can start the report RSTUNE59.

2. If necessary, enter a table name and select *Analysis for primary key*. If immediate processing is required, deselect *Submit analysis in background*. Start the analysis. Be warned that processing the analysis can take a considerable time for large tables. The results of the analysis are then listed.

3. Use this list to determine the size of the table. The upper part of the screen indicates the number of table entries and the space that the table would occupy during full buffering. This space may be smaller or larger than the space required by the table in the database. For example, database fragmentation can cause the table to consume unnecessary space on the database. In addition, unlike some databases, the table buffer does not compress empty fields to minimize the need for storage space.

4. The table in the lower part of the screen shows the distribution of the generic regions in the table, and looks similar to Table 7.3.

TABLE 7.3: Distribution of the Generic Regions in Table TCURR as Revealed in Transaction *DB05*

Rows per Generic Key	Distinct Values	1 to 10	11 to 100	101 to 1,000	1,001 to 10,000	10,001 to 100,000	> 100,000
MANDT	1	0	0	0	0	0	1
KURST	41	10	14	11	0	6	
FCURR	1,311	877	209	175	50		
TCURR	5,188	1,921	2,920	347			
GDATU	169,795	169,795					

Example of Using the Generic Regions Distribution in Transaction *DB05*

Table 7.3 (in the previous section) shows an example of the information displayed in Transaction *DB05* concerning the distribution of generic regions in the table TCURR on production client 100. (Table TCURR was discussed earlier in the chapter in the section "Example of When Not to Buffer a Customizing Data Table.")

You can interpret the information in Transaction *DB05* (Table 7.3) as follows:

- Row *KURST:*
    - This second row in Table 7.3 is the one that would be relevant to generic 2 buffering. This row summarizes the distribution of generic regions for the key KURST. The key KURST indicates the course type. The number of different course types (41) is indicated under *Distinct values*. Of these 41 course types, Table 7.3 indicates that 10 course types have between 1 and 10 entries in the table. There are 14 course types with between 11 and 100 entries. There are 6 course types with between 10,001 and 100,000 entries. There are no course types with more than 100,000 entries.

- Row *FCURR:*

  - This row is the one that would be relevant for generic 3 buffering, as it summarizes the distribution of table entries for all combinations of the key FKUR and the previous key KURST in Table 7.3.

  - FCURR is the key for source currency in the table TCURR. The column *Distinct values* for this row indicates that there are 1,311 different combinations of the first two keys of table TCURR. Scanning across this row in Table 7.3, you see, for example, that no combination has more than 10,000 entries.

- Row *GDATU:*

  - This row is the one that would be relevant for generic 5 buffering, as it summarizes the distribution of table entries for all combinations of the first five keys in the table TCURR.

  - Table 7.3 indicates that there are 169,795 different entries with the key combination MANDT, KURST, FCURR, TCURR, and GDATU. This is also the total number of entries in client 100, because MANDT, KURST, FCURR, TCURR, and GDATU form the complete primary key for table TCURR.

The information shown in the generic regions distribution in Transaction *DB05* helps you decide how to set the buffering for table TCURR as follows:

- If the table is given full or generic 1 buffering, a change operation always invalidates the entire table. Therefore, 169,795 records must subsequently be reloaded into the buffer. In other words, the resource-intensive buffer loading process is justified only if users need to access a large part of these 169,795 data entries. The invalidation rate for this table must be extremely low to ensure that buffering the table does not cause too great a reduction in performance.

- If, for example, you were to set generic 3 buffering for table TCURR, a maximum of 1,311 generic regions would be buffered, as you can see in the column *Distinct values* for row *FCURR*. Since the 50 largest buffered regions in table TCURR then contain between 1,001 and 10,000 records, if a record is changed, a maximum of 10,000 records would be invalidated and reloaded.

- If you used generic 4 buffering, 5,188 generic regions would have to be buffered.

From this analysis, it is apparent that full buffering for table TCURR is out of the question. Depending on the invalidation rate, this table should be set to either generic 3 buffering or no buffering.

NOTE   The larger the table, the more you should favor either limited generic buffering or no buffering.

In the initial selection screen for the detailed table analysis with Transaction *DB05*, you can select *Analysis for specified fields*. This enables you to start analyses for any combination of table fields that you specify beside *Field 1*, *Field 2*, and so on. By specifying the fields of a particular secondary index, you can determine the selectivity of that index. (See Chapter 9, "Optimizing SQL Statements through Secondary Indexes.")

Monitoring Buffer Synchronization (DDLOG Entries)

The monitor for buffer synchronization displays the contents of the table DDLOG. This table records the buffered tables that were changed at the database level and therefore require invalidation in the various R/3 instance buffers. This monitor is found in the

Detail analysis menu of the Memory Configuration Monitor (Transaction *ST02*).

1. To start this monitor, use Transaction code *ST02* and choose *Detail analysis menu* ➢ *Buffer Synchron.*

    • Alternatively, from the R/3 initial screen, choose *Tools* ➢ *Administration* ➢ *Monitor* ➢ *Performance* ➢ *Setup/Buffers* ➢ *Buffers* ➢ *Detail analysis menu* ➢ *Buffer Synchron.*

2. The initial screen of this monitor is a selection screen in which you can specify the appropriate buffer under the header *selection classes*, as well as the host name, and so on. In the present analysis, choose *Select all*. Finally, choose *Read DDLOG*. The main screen of the monitor appears (see Figure 7.7).

    The columns in this monitor are explained in Table 7.4.

FIGURE 7.7: Monitor for buffer synchronization (within the Memory Configuration Monitor, Transaction *ST02*)

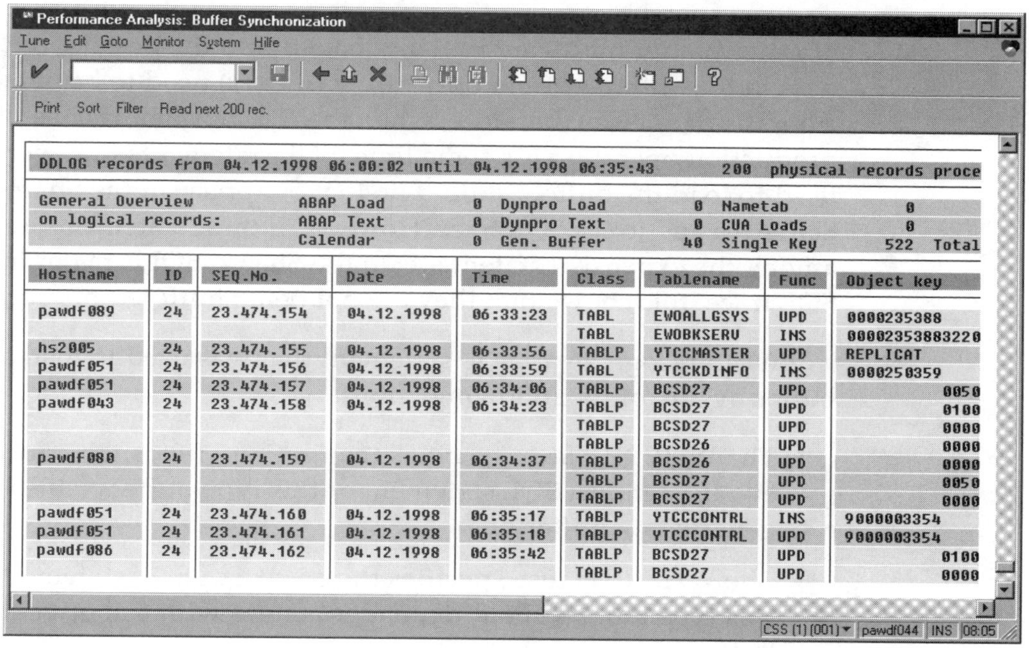

TABLE 7.4: Explanation of Columns in the Monitor for Buffer Synchronization (within the Memory Configuration Monitor, Transaction *STO2*)

Column	Explanation
Hostname	Name of the application server that refers a table for invalidation. If the referral originates from an import, this column shows the entry *tp* or *R3trans*.
ID and SEQ. No.	Unique identification (to assist developers).
Date and Time	Time stamp.
Class	Name of the buffer—for example, NTAB, ABAP, TABLP, or TABL.
Tablename	Name of the table to be invalidated.
Func	Database operation—for example, INS, DEL, or UPD.
Object key	Relevant key, if the invalidated area is a generic region.

Shared SQL Area and SQL Trace

Normally, after tables are initially loaded into the buffers, the data in the buffers should only rarely (if ever) need to be obtained from the database. Therefore, when the R/3 System has been in production operation for some time, SQL statements that were used to load the buffers should no longer appear in the Shared SQL Area and in the SQL trace. However, if these statements appear among the expensive statements in the Shared SQL Area or in the SQL trace, this shows that they are not being buffered properly.

You can recognize an SQL statement that was used to load a buffer by any of the following criteria:

- The WHERE clause specifies the first <n> fields with an equals sign. An SQL statement of this type buffers tables with generic <n> buffering.

- The WHERE clause specifies the client. An SQL statement of this type buffers client-dependent tables with full or generic 1 buffering.

- The SQL statement contains an *Order By* condition, which contains all the fields of the table key.

NOTE   An example of an SQL statement that buffers the generic 1 buffered table TMODU is the following: SELECT * FROM 'TMODU' WHERE 'FAUNA' = :AO ORDER BY 'FAUNA', 'MODIF', 'TABNM', 'FELDN', 'KOART', 'UMSKS'.

If the table to be buffered is a pooled table, the FROM clause contains the name of the table pool in which the table resides.

NOTE   An example of an SQL statement that buffers the pooled table A002, which is set to full buffering and resides in the table pool KAPOL, is the following: SELECT 'TABNAME', 'VARKEY', 'DATALN', 'VAR-DATA' FROM 'KAPOL' WHERE 'TABNAME' = :AO ORDER BY 'TABNAME', 'VARKEY'.

Important table pools include ATAB and KAPOL. The table ATAB contains many buffered tables of the R/3 Basis, such as tables with the form T<nnn>. The table KAPOL contains numerous condition tables, such as tables with the form A<nnn>.

Summary

Correctly buffering tables in the main memory of the R/3 application servers reduces the number of database accesses and thus is an important instrument for performance optimization. However, table buffering is effective only if the following conditions are met:

- The table is relatively small.

- The table is accessed relatively often.

- The invalidation rate for the table is low.

- The short-term inconsistency between the application servers that is caused by asynchronous buffer synchronization has no negative effect on business processes.

- The table is accessed using some or all fields of the primary key.

The synchronization and loading processes of incorrectly buffered tables can cause a reduction in performance that far outweighs the gain in performance provided by buffering. Users will often notice long response times in a transaction that normally runs quickly.

R/3's Table Access Statistics Monitor (Transaction code *ST10*) is the central monitor for R/3 table buffering, and enables you to decide whether the buffering of a particular table is effective. The main statistics to look at are as follows:

- The total number of ABAP requests (indicated in the column *Total* under the column *ABAP/IV Processor requests*)

- The size of the table (indicated in the column *Buffer size*)

- The number of invalidations (indicated in the column *Invalidations*)

- The number of rows affected by database activity (indicated in the column *Rows affected* under the column *DB activity*)

Figure 7.8 shows the corresponding procedure roadmap for analyzing table buffering.

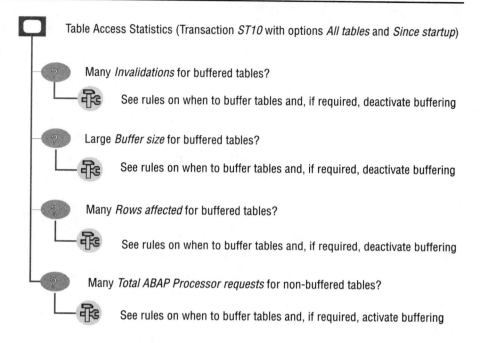

FIGURE 7.8:

Procedure roadmap for analyzing the efficiency of table buffering

Table Access Statistics (Transaction *ST10* with options *All tables* and *Since startup*)

Many *Invalidations* for buffered tables?

See rules on when to buffer tables and, if required, deactivate buffering

Large *Buffer size* for buffered tables?

See rules on when to buffer tables and, if required, deactivate buffering

Many *Rows affected* for buffered tables?

See rules on when to buffer tables and, if required, deactivate buffering

Many *Total ABAP Processor requests* for non-buffered tables?

See rules on when to buffer tables and, if required, activate buffering

Important Concepts in This Chapter

After reading this chapter, you should be familiar with the following concepts:

- Generic regions of a table
- Single record buffering and generic buffering
- Buffer synchronization
- Invalidation and displacement

Review Questions

1. Which of the following factors are reasons for not activating full buffering on a table?

   A. The table is very large.

   B. The SQL statement that is used most frequently to access the table contains the first two of five key fields in an EQUALS condition.

   C. The table is changed often.

2. Which of the following statements are correct in regard to buffer synchronization?

   A. During buffer synchronization, the application server where the change occurred sends a message through the message server to implement the change in the respective buffered table on the other application servers.

   B. After a transaction changes a buffered table, the transaction must first be completed with a database commit before the table can be reloaded into the buffer.

   C. In a central R/3 System, the R/3 profile parameter *rdisp/bufrefmode* must be set to *sendoff, exeoff*.

   D. In a central R/3 System, the entries in the table buffer are never invalidated, because the table buffer is changed synchronously after a database change operation.

Locks and Enqueues

In an R/3 System, many users can simultaneously cause *reads* of the same data in a database table. However, *changes* to database data must be restricted so that only one user can change a particular table row at one time. This is done by locking some or all of the table during each change operation.

Within R/3 itself, *enqueues* play a similar role to that of *locks* in the database. The first section of this chapter introduces you to the locking concepts of locks and enqueues.

If either R/3 enqueues or database locks remain in place for a long time, system performance may be reduced. Therefore, subsections within the first section of this chapter explain how to optimize performance by monitoring and tuning both locks and enqueues.

Special buffering techniques minimize lock time and thus maximize performance for:

- Number ranges used to generate unique numbers for business documents
- Availability checking with Available-to-Promise (ATP) logic

These buffering techniques are discussed in sections two and three of the present chapter.

When Should You Read This Chapter?

You should read this chapter when you want to:

- Find out more about database locks and R/3 enqueues.
- Analyze system problems that are caused by database locks or enqueues.

For help on issues relating to locks in the programming of R/3 transactions, see the ABAP handbooks or relevant R/3 Notes in the R/3 Online Service System (OSS).

Database Locks and R/3 Enqueues

To understand the role played by locks (database locks or R/3 enqueues) in a common business process, consider a travel booking. The different components of the booking, such as flights, hotels, and bus or boat transfers, are all interdependent. The person making your booking uses the *all or nothing* principle: If you can't take the flight, you won't need the hotel room, and so on.

Since the availability of the different components is usually checked chronologically, you want to be certain that no other user makes a change to items in the sequence before the entire booking is completed. This is enabled by locks, which thus preserve data consistency.

Both database locks and R/3 enqueues have the same ultimate purpose of preserving data consistency, but they are based on different technologies and used in different situations.

Database Lock Concept

Database locks are administered by the lock handler of a database instance. The locked entity is typically a row in a database table, but may also be an entire table or part of a table. Database locks are set by all *modifying* SQL statements—for example, statements that use UPDATE, INSERT, DELETE, or SELECT FOR UPDATE.

The SQL statement COMMIT, which executes a database commit, finalizes all changes and then removes the corresponding database locks. Instead of causing a database commit, a program can undo the effects of all modifying SQL statements by executing a database rollback with the SQL statement ROLLBACK. This also removes all database locks.

The time interval between two commits is called a *database transaction*. Each database transaction covers the entire time interval starting from the previous database commit, and includes the time when no database processing occurred.

A program using database locks to make travel bookings, for example, would use the SQL statement SELECT FOR UPDATE to read a particular item of travel data and concurrently lock it. When each relevant data item has been read and the booking is ready to be made, the program changes the data in the respective table rows with the command UPDATE. The command COMMIT subsequently finalizes the changes and releases all locks.

Once a lock has been set, other users can still read the affected data (for example, through a SELECT), but they cannot lock it. Therefore, they cannot effect an UPDATE or a SELECT FOR UPDATE. The original lock is then *exclusive*.

NOTE   After a transaction step is completed, the R/3 work process automatically triggers a database commit (or, alternatively, a database rollback), thereby removing all database locks. This means a *database* lock does not last through successive transaction steps or R/3 input screens. Locks that hold through different transaction steps are provided by *R/3 enqueues*.

Enqueue Concept

R/3's enqueue administration concept enables locks to remain in place through several steps of an R/3 transaction. An R/3 enqueue work process administers enqueues in the enqueue table, which is buffered in main memory. To retain these enqueues even when an R/3 instance is shut down, they are also saved in a local file on the enqueue server.

An enqueue locks a logical object, such as a business document. Thus, an enqueue can lock rows from several different database tables if these rows form the basis of a single business document.

An enqueue can also lock one or more complete tables. Enqueue objects are defined and modified in the ABAP Dictionary (see below, under "Locked Objects"). They are closely related to R/3 transactions and SAP logical units of work (LUWs), both of which are described extensively in the ABAP literature for dialog programming. Therefore, the present chapter focuses mainly on aspects of enqueues that are relevant to performance optimization.

Enqueues are locks that act only within R/3. If a row in a database table is locked by an R/3 enqueue, it can still be changed by an SQL statement triggered from the database, or by a customer-developed ABAP program that does not conform to R/3 enqueue conventions. Database locks, in contrast, resist all change attempts, and lock a table row not only against changes by database users, but also against changes by users outside the R/3 System.

For each object that can be held by an enqueue, there are two function modules: an *enqueue* module and a *dequeue* module. To set an enqueue, an ABAP program must explicitly call the enqueue module. Since the enqueue is not removed until the same program explicitly calls the dequeue module, the enqueue can remain in place through multiple transaction steps. At the completion of an R/3 transaction, however, all enqueues are automatically removed.

Consider how enqueues would be used by an R/3 application for making travel bookings. The planned trip has several different components, such as flights, hotels, and bus transfers, which are processed on several input screens and locked through enqueues until the entire booking is finalized. After determining the availability of each component, the trip is ready to be booked, and saving the booking concludes the dialog part of the transaction. Under the protection of the enqueues, an update work process then transfers the changes to the database tables. Once the update has been completed, the SAP LUW is finished, and the enqueues are unlocked.

An SAP LUW may also contain program modules that require an *update2* update. Since this type of update does not use enqueues, such modules should not be used to process data that requires the protection of enqueues.

Table 8.1 contrasts the main features of database locks and enqueues.

TABLE 8.1:   Features of Database Locks and Enqueues

Feature	Database Locks	Enqueues
Locked object	Individual row of a database table	Logical object such as a document defined in the ABAP Dictionary
How object is locked	Implicitly/automatically using modifying SQL statements such as UPDATE or SELECT FOR UPDATE	Explicitly/manually by the ABAP program calling an enqueue module
How lock is removed	Implicitly/automatically with the SQL statement COMMIT or ROLLBACK; usually at the end of a transaction step	Explicitly/manually by accessing a dequeue module; usually at the end of an R/3 transaction
Maximum duration	One transaction step	Several transaction steps
Result of lock conflicts	Wait known as an *exclusive lock wait*	Program-specific—for example, the error message *Material X is locked*
How to monitor	Database Lock Monitor (Transaction code *DB01*)	Enqueue Monitor (Transaction code *SM12*)

Enqueue administration uses the enqueue table, which is stored in the global main memory of the enqueue server. Enqueue work processes directly access the enqueue table, and set enqueues for the work processes of other application servers, communicating with them through the message service.

In Figure 8.1, which outlines this communication process, DIA indicates dialog work processes, ENQ is an enqueue work process, and MSG is the message service.

FIGURE 8.1:

Communication between different work processes to set and release enqueues

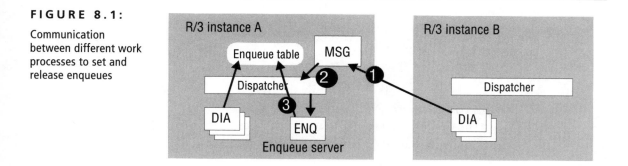

Setting and releasing an enqueue takes a work process on the enqueue server less than 1 millisecond, and takes a work process on another application server less than 100 milliseconds.

Monitoring Database Locks

The different items to monitor in relation to database locks include exclusive lock waits, lock programming, deadlocks, and table locks.

Exclusive Lock Waits

When a work process tries to lock a database object that already has a lock on it, the work process simply waits until the lock is removed. This wait is called an *exclusive lock wait*.

Most databases do not place a time limit on a lock. If a program fails to remove a lock, the lock wait will continue indefinitely. This could become a major problem if the program fails to release a lock on critical R/3 System data, such as the number range table

NRIV, and eventually creates a wait for all work processes. If all the work processes are waiting, no work process is available to allow you to intervene from within the R/3 System itself. If the program holding the problem lock can be identified, it can be terminated through the operating system.

To monitor current lock waits, call the Database Lock Monitor (Transaction *DB01*) and choose *Detail analysis menu ➤ Exclusive lockwaits*.

Alternatively, call the Systemwide Work Process Overview (Transaction *SM66*) and choose *Goto ➤ Database locks*. Troubleshooting using this monitor is explained in Chapter 2, under "Additional R/3 Monitors for the Database."

Lock waits increase the database time, which is indicated as *Av. DB request time* in the Workload Monitor (Transaction *ST03*).

Some database systems explicitly monitor lock wait times, and these lock wait times can be viewed in R/3 in the Database Performance Monitor (Transaction *ST04*). To find out where to look within this monitor, which varies according to your database, see the relevant R/3 Online Documentation.

Lock Programming

To avoid performance problems due to locks not being quickly released, programs should be programmed to request locks as late as possible. It is preferable for a program to read and process data *before* setting locks or making changes in the database.

Figure 8.2 illustrates the results of two methods of transaction programming that differ as to when the transaction triggers database locks. The top part of Figure 8.2 shows the method that is *not* recommended: programming the transaction so that it triggers a lock after each change. The lower part of Figure 8.2 shows the recommended method: programming the transaction so that it collects the changes in an internal table and then transfers these changes to the database as a group at the end of the transaction. This reduces the lock time in the database.

FIGURE 8.2:

Contrasting ways in which transactions can be programmed to trigger database locks

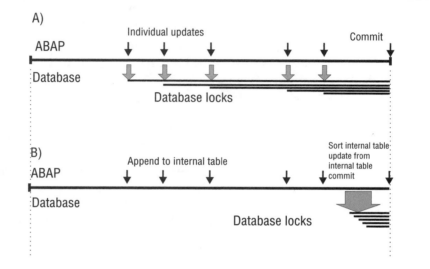

Performance problems due to delays in releasing locks frequently occur when customers modify the programming of update modules.

The separation of update modules from dialog modules in R/3 aims to reduce the number of locks needed in the dialog part of a transaction, since changes to the database and the associated locks are mainly the task of the update modules. This helps prevent users from waiting because of locks while working in the R/3 System.

However, when the update module is modified—for example, to supply a customer-developed interface with data—the modification may create performance problems by preventing locks from being released. For example, if the modification generates expensive SQL statements, and the update module has already set locks when these statements are activated, the locks cannot be released until the SQL statements are fully processed. Lengthy lock waits may result.

Performance problems due to locks not being quickly released also frequently occur when background programs set a lock and then continue running for several hours without initiating a database commit. If dialog transactions need to process the locked objects, they will be forced to wait until the background program finishes or initiates a database commit. To solve this problem, ensure that the background program does either of the following:

- Initiates a database commit at regular intervals (without sacrificing data consistency)

- Runs only when it will not interfere with dialog processing

Similar problems may occur when background jobs are run in parallel—that is, when a program is started more than once at the same time. In addition, parallel processing is recommended only when the selection conditions of the respective programs do not lock the same data.

While you are working in the ABAP debugger, databank commits are generally not initiated, and all locks stay in place until you are finished. Therefore, avoid using the debugger in a production R/3 System.

Deadlocks

To understand deadlocks, consider two work processes: WP1 and WP2, both of which want to lock materials in the same materials list. First, WP1 locks Material A, while WP2 locks Material B. Then, WP1 tries to lock Material B, and WP2 tries to lock Material A. Neither work process is successful, because the materials already have locks on them. Each process blocks the other, and this is known as a *deadlock*. The database instance recognizes the deadlock, and sends an error message to one of the work processes (which one is predetermined by the database system). This terminates the corresponding ABAP program. The error is logged in the R/3 Syslog.

Deadlocks can be avoided by correct programming. In the present example, the program should be changed so that its internal material list is sorted before any locks are set. Then, the lock on Material A will always be set before the lock on Material B, and thus programs requiring the same materials are serialized and not deadlocked.

Deadlocks should occur very rarely. Frequent deadlocks indicate incorrect programming or incorrect configuration of the database instance.

Table Locks

In database systems such as DB2 and ADABAS D, if a work process places single-row locks on more than, for example, 10% of the single rows in a table, the locks are automatically replaced by a table lock. Thus, the database decides that it is more efficient to lock the entire table for a work process than to maintain several locks on individual rows. However, this should occur only rarely.

Table locking has consequences for parallel processing in background jobs, where each program is intended to update a different part of the same table at the same time. If the database decides to lock the entire table for one of the jobs, the other jobs will have to wait, and parallel processing will become serial processing. One program that is particularly affected by this is the *period closing program* in materials management.

NOTE   There are database parameters you can use to specify when the database should convert single-row locks to a table lock.

WARNING Sometimes the database locks entire tables for administrative reasons. This happens when indexes are created or when particular tables and indexes are analyzed (for example, during the Oracle analysis VALI-DATE STRUCTURE). Therefore, index creation or analysis should not be performed during production operation, as substantial performance problems may result.

Monitoring Enqueues

To monitor currently active enqueues in your system, call the Enqueue Monitor by using Transaction code *SM12*, or, from the R/3 initial screen, choose *Tools* ➤ *Administration* ➤ *Monitor* ➤ *Lock entries.*

The screen *Select Lock Entries* is displayed. To check for errors related to enqueues, there are two test programs you can run from this screen by choosing *Extras* ➤ *Diagnosis* and *Extras* ➤ *Diagnosis in update.*

If the test programs identify errors, look for relevant R/3 Notes in the Online Service System (OSS) or contact SAP.

To view statistics on the activity of the enqueue server, from the initial screen of the Enqueue Monitor, choose *Extras* ➤ *Statistics.*

The first three figures in the list are as follows:

- The number of *enqueue requests*

- The number of *rejects* (enqueue requests that were rejected due to data already being locked by an enqueue)

- The number of *errors* that occurred during the processing of enqueue requests (normally none)

The proportion of rejected requests (indicated as *rejects*) should not exceed 1% of the total number of enqueue requests.

A rejected enqueue request causes a message to be returned to the program that requested the enqueue. The application developer will have predefined what happens next by suitable programming. For programs in dialog mode, the message is generally forwarded to the user—for example, the message *Material X is locked by User Y*. Background programs usually make another attempt to set the enqueue at a later time. After a certain number of unsuccessful requests, an error message is written to the background program log.

Rejected enqueue requests can cause performance problems, particularly when users must restart processes that unsuccessfully request enqueues. The problem is especially noticeable in transactions that set many enqueues. For example, after successfully setting 99 enqueues, a program may try to set the 100th enqueue and receive the error message *Material 100 is locked* if Material 100 is already being held by an enqueue. The program's previous changes to the other 99 materials are lost, and the user must subsequently retrigger the enqueueing process from the beginning. Thus, rejected enqueue requests can increase system load and render transactions inefficient.

Number Range Buffering

Number range buffering optimizes the assignment of new document numbers during business processing. This increases document throughput, provided number range buffering is implemented to avoid lock problems as described below.

How Number Ranges Work

To use or change the data of many business objects in R/3, you need to be able to access individual database records. To enable accesses that are so specific, each new record must receive a unique key as it is created.

The main part of this key is a serial number assigned using the system of *number ranges*. Examples of these serial numbers include order numbers or material master numbers. R/3 number range management is based on the database table NRIV and ensures that previously assigned numbers are not issued a second time.

A *number range object* is any business object in R/3 with a unique key based on a number range. A number range consists of one or more *number range intervals* defined in terms of a set of permitted alphanumerical characters and limited by the fields *from-number* and *to-number* in the table NRIV.

The *current number level* of a number range is the number that is to be assigned to the next new document. Table NRIV stores the current number level, as well as the name of each number range—for example, *MATBELEG*.

How a Program Obtains a Number Range for a New Document

If a program needs a number for a new document—for example, from the number range MATBELEG—it proceeds as follows:

1. The program locks the number range MATBELEG and reads the current number level from table NRIV. To set the lock, the SQL statement SELECT FOR UPDATE is applied to the line of table NRIV corresponding to the number range MATBELEG.

2. The program increases the number range level by one, by updating table NRIV accordingly.

3. The number range in the database remains locked until the program completes its database logical unit of work (LUW) by performing a commit or a database rollback. If an error occurs before the lock is released, the document cannot be

created, and the change in table NRIV is rolled back—that is, the previous number level is returned. This ensures that numbers are assigned chronologically and without gaps.

Avoiding Bottlenecks by Buffering Number Ranges

Bottlenecks can occur when many numbers are requested from a particular number range in a short period of time. Since the number range is locked in the database from the time of the initial reading of the current number level to the time of the database commit, all business processes competing for number assignment must wait their turn, and this limits transaction throughput.

A solution to this lock problem is provided by buffering the corresponding number range. R/3 offers two forms of buffering for number ranges:

- Buffering in main memory
- Buffering through an additional database table (NRIV_LOKAL) for each R/3 instance

Buffering Number Ranges in Main Memory

Buffering number ranges in the main memory helps avoid causing frequent database accesses to the number range administration table NRIV when assigning new document numbers.

Buffering causes a set of new document numbers generated from table NRIV to be stored in the buffer of each R/3 instance. The numbers remain in the buffer until assigned to new documents. When the numbers have been used up, a new set of numbers is obtained from the database. The number range level in database table NRIV is increased by the range of numbers transferred to the buffer. Therefore, when a number is taken from the buffer and assigned to a document, the number range level in the database remains unchanged.

Entering a set of new numbers in a buffer has several steps. If, when attempting to assign a number, a program discovers that the number range buffer of its R/3 instance is empty, it proceeds as follows:

1. The program, which is running in its own R/3 work process, starts an asynchronous RFC call to obtain a set of new numbers for the buffer.

2. This RFC call is processed in a second dialog work process, which reads and locks table NRIV, loads a new set of numbers into the number range buffer, updates table NRIV, and finalizes the database changes with a database commit.

3. Meanwhile, the work process in which the original program is running is paused. In the Work Process Overview (Transaction *SM50* or *SM66*), the column *Status* shows Stopped, and the column *Reason* shows NUM for this work process. After the number range buffer has received a new set of numbers, the original program can resume its work.

During this process, the program that checked the buffer for a number and the program that refills the number range buffer must run in separate database LUWs. This is the only way to ensure that the commit of the second program can finalize the changes in table NRIV and release the lock without performing a commit for the database LUW of the first program. To achieve this goal, the two programs are run in separate work processes.

To guarantee that work processes are available for refilling the buffer with new numbers, the work process dispatcher program gives preferential treatment to requests for new number sets.

Main memory buffering of number ranges has the following consequences:

- When an R/3 instance is shut down, the remaining numbers in the buffer—that is, the numbers that have yet to be assigned—are lost. This causes a gap in number assignment.

- As a result of the separate buffering of numbers in the various R/3 instances, the sequence in which numbers are assigned across the entire R/3 System is not the numerical sequence of the numbers themselves. In other words, a document with a higher number may have been created before a document with a lower number.

WARNING If you prefer to prevent gaps in the assignment of numbers to a particular document type or number range object, or if you are required to do so by business law, you should not use number range buffering for this document type.

Buffering Number Ranges Using Table NRIV_LOKAL

As an alternative to buffering number ranges in the main memory of each R/3 instance, you can buffer number ranges using the database table NRIV_LOKAL.

Instead of managing the number range for a particular type of document centrally in a single row of table NRIV, number intervals are selected for each R/3 instance and managed in NRIV_LOKAL, in which the name of the R/3 instance is part of the primary key. Database locks associated with number assignments for new documents will then appear only in those areas of table NRIV_LOKAL that correspond to a particular R/3 instance.

When using this type of buffering, keep in mind that:

- Buffering in NRIV_LOKAL is useful only when the same types of documents are being created on several R/3 instances.

- Numbers are not assigned to documents in numerical order, so that a document with a higher number may have been created before a document with a lower number.

- Some of the numbers in a particular interval may not be assigned—for example, at the end of a financial year or during the renaming of an instance.

To enter a new set of document numbers in table NRIV_LOKAL, a new interval is synchronously read from table NRIV, and the affected row of table NRIV remains locked until the commit occurs.

If the interval of numbers read from NRIV is too small, frequent accesses to NRIV to obtain new numbers during mass processing may cause lock waits, thus reducing document throughput. Therefore, when large quantities of similar documents are being created across a number of instances, ensure that the interval selected is sufficiently large. Guidelines for appropriate values can be found in R/3 Notes (e.g., in those mentioned in Appendix H).

Activating Number Range Buffering

To activate or deactivate number range buffering, call R/3's Number Range Object Maintenance screen. To do this, use Transaction code *SNRO*, or, from the R/3 initial screen, choose *Tools* ➢ *ABAP/4 Workbench* ➢ *Development* ➢ *Other Tools* ➢ *Number ranges.*

Enter the object name and choose *Change*. A dialog box may appear to ask you to identify or create a change request for the subsequent transport of your changes.

The screen *No. Range Object: Change* appears. From here, you can perform three tasks for the selected number range buffering object:

- Activate main memory buffering.
- Activate buffering in table NRIV_LOKAL.
- Deactivate all number range buffering.

Activating Main Memory Buffering

To activate main memory buffering, from the screen *No. Range Object: Change*, choose *Edit* ➤ *Set-up buffering* ➤ *Main memory*.

In the field *No. of numbers in buffer*, enter the quantity of numbers to be held in the buffer. To set this buffering method, choose *Save*.

Activating Buffering in Table NRIV_LOKAL

To activate buffering in table NRIV_LOKAL, from the screen *No. Range Object: Change*, choose *Edit* ➤ *Set-up buffering* ➤ *Local file*.

Deactivating Number Range Buffering

To deactivate buffering, from the screen *No. Range Object: Change*, choose *Edit* ➤ *Set-up buffering* ➤ *No buffering*.

NOTE   Number range buffering settings will be overwritten if the respective number range object is replaced—for example, during an R/3 Release update. After the update, check whether number range buffering has been affected.

Finding Out the Current Number Level

Different techniques enable you to find out the current number level in the database and in the buffer respectively.

To find out the current number level in the database table NRIV, use Transaction code *SNRO*, enter an object, and choose *Change*. Then choose *Number ranges* ➤ *Intervals*. The current number level is indicated in the field *Current number*.

For buffered number range objects, the level indicated here is the next available number that has not yet been transferred to the buffer.

To check the current level in the number range buffer of a particular R/3 instance, call the Number Range Buffer Monitor (Transaction *SM56*) and choose *Goto* ➤ *Items*. Enter the client, the object, and, if required, the relevant sub-object. The current number level in the buffer is indicated.

Monitoring Number Range Buffering

To identify performance problems related to number assignment, call the Database Lock Monitor (Transaction *DB01*) and examine the lock waits for table NRIV.

At peak processing times, lock waits of several minutes for table NRIV are too long. From the initial screen of the Database Lock Monitor, proceed as follows:

1. Identify the number range involved.

   • If you are using an Oracle database, double-click the row showing the lock on table NRIV. This brings you to a screen with detailed information. The name of the number range is indicated in the column *Object*.

- For other databases, start an SQL trace for a user who is waiting for the database lock to be removed. In the trace results, the number range affected by the lock is indicated in the SQL statement.

2. Find out whether any type of buffering is activated for the number range. This is indicated under *Customizing specifications* in Transaction *SNRO*.

   - If buffering is not activated, determine whether the corresponding object can be buffered.

   - If the number range is already buffered, check whether the quantity of numbers in the buffer can be increased. Table NRIV will then be accessed less frequently.

WARNING   Only experienced R/3 developers or consultants should change the buffering mode for number ranges. Activating buffering may cause gaps in number assignment that could be a problem if gap-free number assignment is desired or even mandatory under business law. A number range that is too small can cause performance problems by requiring the buffer to be refilled too often. A range that is too large has the disadvantage of losing too many numbers if the R/3 instance is shut down. Never change SAP's default buffering mode for the number range of an object without first looking for relevant R/3 Notes in the Online Service System (OSS).

R/3 Notes in the Online Service System (OSS) document the buffering modes and advise you as to how many numbers should be loaded into the number range buffer. Some relevant R/3 Notes are listed in Appendix H of this book.

The ATP Server

A materials *availability check* is used in the R/3 logistics modules to check the availability of materials required—for example, in sales orders, supply and distribution, or production. The particular availability check being discussed in this chapter is based on ATP (*Available-to-Promise* logic).

System performance during an availability check may be significantly reduced by either of the following:

- Locks: The material whose availability is being checked must be locked by an enqueue. When the lock is in place, it may block other users who need to deal with the material, especially if the lock remains for a long time or the material is required frequently.

- Read accesses for table RESB and table VBBE: An availability check is used to ensure that a material will be available at a specific time in the future. As part of the check, inward movements planned before that specific time are added to the current stock, while planned outward movements are subtracted. Table RESB is required for totaling the material reservations and secondary requirements for production orders, while table VBBE is required for totaling customer requirements for sales orders. Since both of these tables are very large, reading and computing these reservations and requirements can cause a high runtime for the availability check.

NOTE   Table RESB may become as large as 1GB or even larger. Depending upon how much data you specify as relevant to the availability check during Customizing, all RESB data for a specific material—from the current date to the date the material will be needed—may have to be read for every availability check.

As of R/3 Release 4.0, the availability check may be conducted using a dedicated R/3 instance, the ATP server. Thus, the ATP server is not external to R/3—it is an R/3 service running on an R/3 instance. It stores availability check data in a buffer in shared memory to dramatically reduce the number of accesses to the database tables RESB and VBBE.

How the ATP Server Works

Figure 8.3 shows how an ATP server performs its work in the system landscape.

FIGURE 8.3:

The role of the ATP server in the system landscape

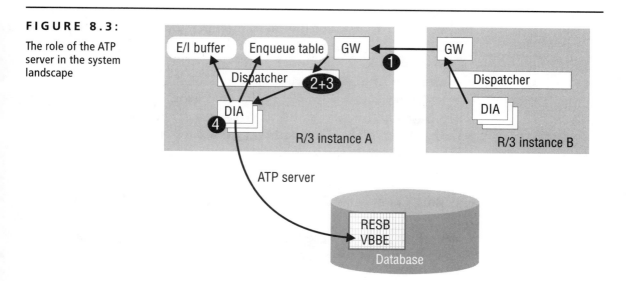

When an R/3 work process needs to check the availability of a material, it uses a *Remote Function Call* (RFC) to communicate its request through the network to the server where the ATP server resides. The RFC communicates between the gateway services of the respective R/3 instances. In Figure 8.3, the work process in

R/3 instance B then sends its request to the ATP server in instance A. The communication between the two gateway services is indicated as step 1.

The gateway service of R/3 instance A sends the request to the dispatcher program in step 2. The dispatcher sends the request to an available dialog work process in step 3. This work process then runs the program that performs the availability check in step 4.

In Figure 8.3, DIA is a dialog work process, GW is a gateway service, and the E/I buffer is the export/import buffer.

In the R/3 instance running the ATP server, a work process calculating the availability of a material uses the daily subtotals from previous availability calculations, which are stored in the export/import buffer of the main memory. These subtotals consist of a calculation for each day's material reservations (from table RESB) or sales requirements (from table VBBE) for every possible combination of material, plant, storage location, and batch. The export/import buffer thus contains two groups of entries: one for RESB data and one for VBBE data, whose size depends on the number of days for which subtotals exist for each combination of material, location, and so on.

Performance is kept at a high level because the work process checking material availability reads the RESB and VBBE data from the export/import buffer rather than from the database. Consistency between the buffer and the database is maintained by a synchronization process.

The work process checking availability also sets and removes enqueues, which are necessary to guarantee data consistency. To set and release enqueues with only a minimum of performance loss, the ATP server and the enqueue server should be run on the same R/3 instance.

Locking with Quantities

During an availability check with an ATP server, a special R/3 technique called *locking with quantities* is used. Instead of relying on *exclusive* enqueues, which allow only one user to lock a material, this technique uses *shared* enqueues—enqueues that can be concurrently set by several users on the same object. This allows several users to check the availability of a material at the same time.

NOTE   *Locking with quantities* during availability checks has been available since R/3 Release 3.0—that is, prior to the ATP server. When using *locking with quantities* for R/3 Release 3.0, the availability check is carried out centrally on the enqueue server, but without buffering the daily subtotals in the export/import buffer. See also related R/3 Notes in the Online Service System (OSS).

Configuring the ATP Server

Correctly configuring the ATP server enables it to avoid the performance problems that it was designed to overcome, such as frequent database accesses to tables RESB and VBBE during the availability check. To correctly configure the ATP server, you need to optimize the technical settings as explained under the following subheadings.

In addition to optimizing the technical settings, you need to optimize application-related aspects of the availability check during Customizing. For example:

- Set sensible reorder times and planning horizons for materials.

- Deactivate checking common materials in great demand— things that are often ordered in bulk, such as nails or screws.

- Regularly archive reservations.

An in-depth, results-oriented look at the numerous application-related measures for optimizing availability checks is provided in the SAP Empowering Workshop EWC10, *Technical Optimization of the Availability Check.*

NOTE   If an SQL trace indicates that accesses to tables RESB and VBBE during an availability check take a long time, you should consider using the ATP server. The SQL trace, however, does not show accesses to tables RESB and VBBE, but, rather, accesses to the corresponding database views. In R/3 Release 4.0, the relevant views in the SQL trace are ATP_RESB and ATP_VBBE. In R/3 Release 3.1, the SQL trace will show that table RESB is accessed through the view MDRS.

Activating the ATP Server

To activate the ATP server, set the R/3 profile parameter *rdisp/atp_server* to the name of the R/3 instance that provides the ATP server—for example, *enqhost_PRD_00.*

The value of this parameter must be identical for all R/3 instances and should therefore be set in the *default.pfl* profile.

The ATP server and enqueue server should be run on the same R/3 instance.

Sizing the Export/Import Buffer

To configure the size and maximum number of entries in the export/import buffer, use the R/3 profile parameters *rsdb/obj/buffersize* and *rsdb/obj/max_objects* respectively.

Each entry in the buffer consists of a string of available subtotals for each combination of material, location, and so on. The size of an entry depends on the number of days for which subtotals are available. For each added day, the size of the entry increases by around 50 bytes.

> **NOTE**
>
> If *reservations* were calculated for a single combination of material, plant, storage location, and batch for 20 individual days, the size of the entry would be about 1KB. Therefore, if in your company you expect a maximum of 10,000 combinations, and for each combination there are an average of 20 days of daily reservation subtotals, you would set the size of the export/import buffer to 20,000KB using the parameter *rsdb/obj/buffersize* and set the maximum number of entries at 20,000 using the parameter *rsdb/obj/max_objects*.

Activating *Locking with Quantities*

When using the ATP server to perform material availability checks, activate *locking with quantities* for each material to be checked. This is done using the *checking group* of each material. To activate *locking with quantities* for a checking group, proceed as follows:

1. Access R/3 Customizing by choosing *Tools* ➤ *Business Engineer* ➤ *Customizing*. A dialog box appears. Choose *Enter*. The *Customizing* screen appears.

2. From the *Customizing* screen, choose *Implement projects* ➤ *SAP Reference IMG*. The screen *Display structure: SAP Reference IMG* appears.

3. Drill down in the IMG tree structure as follows: *Sales and distribution* ➤ *Basic functions* ➤ *Availability check and transfer of requirements* ➤ *Availability check* ➤ *Availability check with ATP Logic or Against Planning*. Click the icon immediately to the left of *Define checking groups*. The screen *Change View "availability check control": Overview* appears.

4. To set *locking with quantities* for a particular checking group, mark the check box in column *Block QtRq*.

Other Configuration Settings for Availability Checks

When using *locking with quantities* on large R/3 installations, a large number of availability checks are made concurrently. Therefore, on the enqueue/ATP server, several parameters that may effectively reduce the number of RFC connections must be set to values that are sufficiently large. Table 8.2 lists these parameters.

TABLE 8.2: Minimum Parameter Settings for the Enqueue/ATP Server When Using *Locking with Quantities*

Parameter	Description	Minimum Value
rdisp/tm_maximum_no	Number of maximum possible terminal connections (or size of table TM_ADM)	500
rdisp/max_comm_ entries	Number of maximum possible CPIC/RFC connections (or size of table COMM_ADM)	500
gw/maximum_conn	Number of maximum possible gateway connections (or size of table CONN_TBL)	500
rdisp/work process_no_dia	Number of dialog work processes	5
em/initial_size_MB	Size of extended memory	250
rdisp/ROLL_SHM	Size of roll buffers in 8KB blocks	4,000 (=32MB)

To ensure that there are sufficient dialog work processes available for the availability check, you require at least five dialog work processes on the enqueue/ATP server—even if there are no users working on this server.

The enqueue/ATP server also requires sufficient extended memory. Monitor its use of extended memory at regular intervals.

NOTE   For the most recent information on sizing the export/import buffer, see R/3 Note 24762 and R/3 Note 99999. *Locking with quantities* is available as of R/3 Release 3.0—that is, prior to the ATP server. However, the parameter recommendations made above still apply.

Monitoring the ATP Server

The R/3 transactions you can use to monitor functions associated with the ATP server include Transaction *ACBD*, Transaction *ST02*, and Transaction *SM12*.

Transaction *ACBD*

Transaction *ACBD* offers several monitoring and administering functions such as:

- Deleting the export/import buffer (with regard to ATP data) completely or partially

- Adjusting the export/import buffer to the database

This transaction allows data from the database to be preloaded into the export/import buffer. Otherwise, data loading does not occur until the first availability check is made for each respective combination of material, plant, and table (RESB or VBBE).

Memory Configuration Monitor (Transaction *ST02*)

To monitor the contents of the export/import buffer, call the Memory Configuration Monitor (Transaction *ST02*) and choose *Detail analysis menu* ➤ *Export/import* (under *Other buffers*) ➤ *Buffered objects*.

The screen *Tune: contents of export/import buffer <R/3 instance name>* appears, showing a tabular display in which each row provides data about a single entry in the export/import buffer—that is, about a string of daily availability subtotals for a single combination of material, location, and so on, for a certain number of days. The main columns on this screen are as follows:

- *Table name*: For example, *ATPSB* is the table for ATP server objects.

- *Object name:* This column indicates the client, the plant, and the material number, and also indicates whether the row concerns an RESB entry (indicated as *RE*) or a VBBE entry (indicated as *VB*).

- *Size:* This column indicates the size of the entry in the buffer.

- *Used:* This column indicates the number of accesses to this entry in the buffer.

Enqueue Monitor (Transaction *SM12*)

The Enqueue Monitor (Transaction *SM12*) enables you to monitor the *shared enqueues* used for the function *locking with quantities*. These enqueues can be recognized in the list of enqueues since they have *ATPENQ* in the column *Table* (or *EV03V* in R/3 Release 3.1), and are marked with a cross in the column *Shared*. To calculate how long the enqueues have been held, subtract the time in the column *Time* from the time at which you called the monitor.

NOTE   Monitoring enqueues is one of the system administrator's regular duties. Enqueues that last several hours usually indicate incorrect programming or the incorrect use of a program.

Summary

The database and the R/3 System each have their own type of lock concept, realized through database locks and R/3 enqueues. A lock of either type, if it lasts too long, may cause performance problems or even bring the system to a standstill. You can monitor the database lock wait situations with the Database Lock Monitor (Transaction *DB01*) and the start times of current enqueues in the Enqueue Monitor (Transaction *SM12*).

Special attention should be given to the locks associated with both number ranges (used to generate, for example, order numbers or document numbers) and availability checks.

Important Concepts in This Chapter

After reading this chapter, you should be familiar with the following concepts:

- Database locks and enqueues
- Locking with quantities
- ATP server
- Number range buffer

Review Questions

1. Which of the following statements are correct with regard to locks and R/3 enqueues?

   A. An R/3 enqueue locks one or more tables in the database.

   B. After an R/3 enqueue has been placed, the corresponding database table can still be changed by an update request coming from programs such as customer-developed ABAP reports.

   C. A database lock is usually released at the end of a transaction step, while an R/3 enqueue is usually released at the end of an R/3 transaction.

   D. A database lock that lasts too long can cause an R/3 System standstill.

2. Which of the following statements are correct with regard to the ATP server?

   A. The ATP server should always be configured on the database server.

   B. The ATP server is an independent R/3 installation with its own database on a separate computer.

   C. The ATP server reduces the number of accesses to tables RESB and VBBE.

3. When buffering number range objects in main memory, which of the following considerations should you keep in mind?

   A. Since buffering occurs in all R/3 instances, buffer synchronization may cause some numbers to be assigned twice.

   B. Gaps occur in the number assignment when using buffered number ranges. You must check whether these gaps are permitted by business law and are acceptable from a business viewpoint.

C. If the quantity of numbers in the buffer is too small, performance problems will result, particularly during mass data entry using Batch Input or Fast Input.

D. Sufficient physical memory must be available, because number range buffering consumes much memory.

CHAPTER
NINE

9

Optimizing SQL Statements

Optimizing applications that are run in conjunction with a database begins with optimizing database design, and proceeds with the subject of the present chapter—optimizing the programming of SQL statements within those applications. Some references to documentation on database design are given in Appendix G.

During application programming, SQL statements are often written without sufficient regard to their subsequent performance. Expensive (long-running) SQL statements slow performance during production operation, resulting in large response times for individual programs and placing an excessive load on the database server. Frequently, you will find that 50% of the database load can be traced to a few individual SQL statements.

As the database and the number of users grow, so do the number of requests to the database and the search effort required for each database request. This is why expensive or inefficient SQL statements constitute one of the most significant causes of performance problems in large installations. The more a system grows, the more important it becomes to optimize the SQL statements.

When Should You Read This Chapter?

You should read this chapter if you have identified expensive SQL statements in your R/3 System and wish to analyze and optimize them. The first and second sections of this chapter can be read without previous knowledge of ABAP programming; the third section assumes a basic familiarity with ABAP programming.

This chapter is not an introduction to developing SQL applications. For this, refer to the ABAP textbooks referred to in Appendix G, SQL textbooks, or R/3 Online Documentation.

Identifying and Analyzing Expensive SQL Statements

There are two levels of analysis for identifying and analyzing expensive SQL statements: a preliminary and a more detailed analysis.

Preliminary Analysis

The preliminary step in identifying and analyzing expensive SQL statements is to identify those SQL statements for which optimization would be genuinely worthwhile.

> **NOTE** The preliminary analysis prevents you from wasting time with SQL statement optimizations that cannot produce more than trivial gains in performance.

For the preliminary analysis, there are two main techniques: using an SQL trace or using the shared SQL area.

An SQL trace is useful if the program containing the expensive SQL statement has already been identified—for example, through:

- Workload Monitor (Transaction *ST03*)
- Work Process Overview (Transaction *SM50* or *SM66*)
- Users' observations

In contrast, using the shared SQL area enables you to order statements according to the systemwide load they are generating.

The flowchart in Figure 9.1 shows the techniques for identifying expensive SQL statements that are worth optimizing. The following shapes are used in the diagram:

- A round-cornered rectangle indicates where you start a specific R/3 performance monitor.

- A diamond shape indicates a decision point.

- The parallelogram indicates the point at which you have successfully identified expensive SQL statements that are worth optimizing.

FIGURE 9.1:

Techniques for identifying expensive SQL statements that are worth optimizing

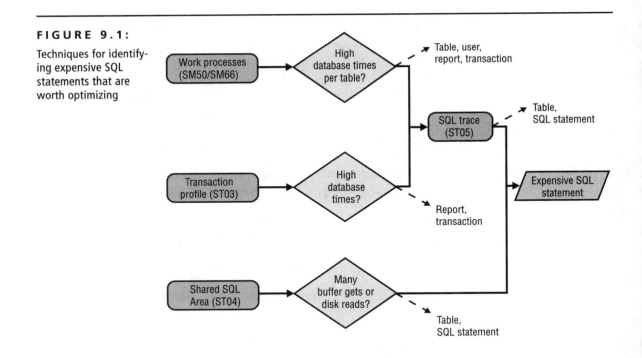

Preliminary Analysis Using the SQL Trace

Create an SQL trace using Transaction *ST05* as described in Chapter 4. Display the SQL trace results in one user session by choosing *List trace*. The *Basic SQL Trace List* screen appears.

Call Transaction *ST05* in another user session and display the compressed summary of the results by choosing *List trace* ➤ *Goto* ➤ *Summary* ➤ *Compress*.

If you sort the data in the compressed summary according to the elapsed database time, you can find out the tables that were accessed for the longest time. Use these tables in the *Basic SQL Trace List* screen to look up the corresponding SQL statements. Only these statements should be considered for optimization.

In a third user session, from the *Basic SQL Trace List* screen, access a list of all identical accesses by choosing *Goto* ➤ *Identical selects*.

Compare these identical selects with the user session showing the SQL trace results. Note which SQL statements receive identical selects, then, in the *Basic SQL Trace List* screen, examine the processing time for these SQL statements in the column *Duration*. By adding these durations, you can estimate roughly how much database time could be saved by avoiding multiple database accesses. Unless this time saving is sufficiently large, there is no need for you to perform optimization.

As a result of this preliminary analysis, you will have made a note of any statements you wish to optimize.

Preliminary Analysis Using the Shared SQL Area Monitor

To monitor the shared SQL area in R/3, from the main screen in the Database Performance Monitor (Transaction *ST04*), choose

Detail analysis menu and look under the header *Resource consumption by*. Then:

- For Oracle, choose *SQL request*.
- For Informix, choose *SQL Statement*.

In the dialog box that appears, choose *Enter*. The screen *Database performance: Shared SQL* appears. For an explanation of the screen, see Chapter 2.

Expensive SQL statements are characterized by a large number of logical or physical database accesses. To create a prioritized list of statements, where the top-listed statements are potentially worth optimizing, sort the shared SQL area according to logical accesses (indicated, for example, as *buffer gets*) or physical accesses (indicated, for example, as *disk reads*).

Further Preliminary Analysis

Regardless of whether you begin your analysis from an SQL trace or the shared SQL area, before you proceed to a detailed analysis, perform the following checks:

- Create several SQL traces for different times and computers to verify the database times noted in the initial SQL trace. Determine whether there is a network problem or a temporary database overload.
- If the expensive SQL statement is accessing a buffered table, use the criteria presented in Chapter 8 to determine whether table buffering should be deactivated—that is, whether the respective buffer is too small or contains tables that should not be buffered because they are too large or too frequently changed.
- Check whether there are any applicable R/3 Notes in the Online Service System (OSS) by using combinations of search terms, such as *performance* and the name of the respective table.

Detailed Analysis

After listing the SQL statements that are worth optimizing, perform a detailed analysis to decide the optimization strategy.

Whether to Optimize the Code or the Index

Optimization can take one of two forms:

- Optimizing the ABAP program code related to an SQL statement

- Optimizing the database—for example, by creating indexes

SQL statements that seek to operate on a great number of data records in the database can be optimized only by changes to the ABAP programming. The left-hand part of Figure 9.2 shows the activities of a statement requiring this kind of optimization. Data is depicted by the stacked, horizontal black bars. If you look at the amount of data records depicted both in the database process and in the application server, this shows that the statement has transferred much data to the application server. Therefore, a large number of data blocks (the pale rectangles containing the data bars) were read from the database buffer or the hard disk. For a statement like this, the relevant developer should check whether all this data is actually needed by the program, or whether a significant amount of the data is unnecessary.

The amount of data that constitutes a significant amount varies. For a dialog transaction, where you expect a response time of around 1 second, 500 records that are transferred by an SQL statement are a significant number. For a reporting transaction, 10,000 records would normally be considered a significant number. For programs running background jobs (for example, in the R/3 application module CO), the number of records that must be considered a significant number may be considerably larger yet again.

FIGURE 9.2:

Expensive SQL statements (Left: The statement transfers much data. Right: The statement unnecessarily reads too many data blocks.)

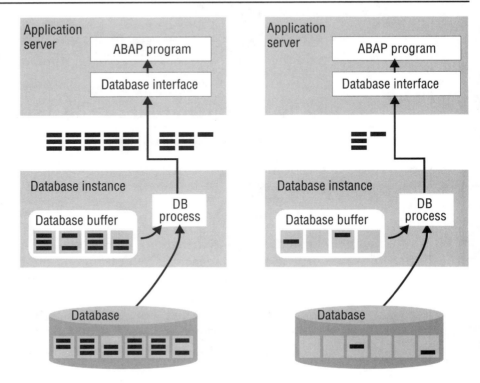

In contrast, an expensive SQL statement of the type requiring database optimization is shown in the right-hand part of Figure 9.2. Although you can see that only a few data records (represented by the horizontal black bars) were transferred to the application server by the SQL statement, the selection criteria has forced the database process to read many data blocks (the pale rectangles, some of which contain the data bars). As you can see, many of these data blocks do not contain any sought-after data; therefore, the search strategy is clearly inefficient. To simplify the search and optimize the runtime, it may help to create a new secondary index. Alternatively, a suitable index already may exist, but is not being used.

Detailed Analysis Using an SQL Trace

For each line in the results of an SQL trace (Transaction *ST05*), looking at the corresponding database times enables you to determine whether a statement can be optimized through database techniques such as creating new indexes.

Divide the figure in the column *Duration* by that in the column *Rec* (records). If the result is an average response time of less than 5,000 microseconds for each record, this can be considered optimal. Each FETCH should require less than around 100,000 microseconds. For an expensive SQL statement where a FETCH requires more than 250,000 microseconds, but targets only a few records, a new index may improve the runtime.

If the average response time is optimal, but the runtime for the SQL statement is still high due to the large volume of data being transferred, only the ABAP program itself can be optimized. To do this, from the screen *Basic SQL Trace List,* choose *ABAP display* to go to the ABAP code of the traced transaction and continue your analysis as described below.

Detailed Analysis Using the Shared SQL Area Monitor

Returning to the Shared SQL Area Monitor in Transaction *ST04*, you should now analyze the statistics more closely. The decisive data for evaluating an SQL statement's optimization potential is as follows:

- The number of logical read accesses for each execution (indicated as *Gets/Execution* for Oracle and *Buf.Read/Execution* for Informix)

- The number of logical read accesses for each transferred record (indicated as *Bufgets/record* for Oracle)

Statements that read on average less than 10 blocks or pages for each execution and appear at the top of the sorted shared SQL area list due to a high execution frequency cannot be optimized by using database techniques such as new indexes. Instead, consider improving the ABAP program code or using the program in a different way to reduce the execution frequency.

Good examples of SQL statements that can be optimized by database techniques such as creating or modifying new indexes include SQL statements that require many logical read accesses to transfer a few records. These are SQL statements for which the Shared SQL Area Monitor shows a statistic of 10 or higher for *Bufgets/record*.

For SQL statements where you need to change the ABAP code, you need to identify the various programs that use the SQL statement and improve the coding in each program. You can do this in ABAP Dictionary Maintenance. To access this Transaction, use Transaction code *SE11*, or, from the R/3 initial screen, choose *Tools ≻ ABAP Workbench ≻ Dictionary*. Proceed as follows:

1. Enter the name of the table accessed by the SQL statement you wish to optimize and choose *Where-used list*.

2. In the dialog box that appears, select *Programs*.

3. A list appears showing all programs in which the table is used. Check these programs to see if they use the expensive SQL statement that you want to modify.

NOTE The disadvantage of this search is that you may need to check a large number of programs. In addition, there may be a difference between the ABAP version of the SQL statement and the version created by the database interface. These factors mean that you may require considerable experience in using the ABAP programming language to identify the code causing the performance problem.

Further Detailed Analysis

After determining whether the SQL statement can be optimized through a new index or through changes to the program code, you require more detailed information about the relevant ABAP program. This information will be required when optimizing the SQL statements:

- The purpose of the program
- The tables that are involved and their contents—for example, transaction data, master data, or Customizing data
- The size of the tables and whether the current size matches the size originally expected for the table
- The users of the program; the developer responsible for a customer-developed program

After finding out this information, you can begin with the tuning as described in the following sections.

Optimizing SQL Statements through Secondary Indexes

To optimize SQL statements using database techniques such as creating new indexes, you require a basic understanding of how data is organized in a relational database.

Fundamentals of Database Organization

The fundamentals of relational database organization can be explained using a simplified analogy based on a database table corresponding to a Yellow Pages telephone book.

When you are looking up businesses in a Yellow Pages telephone book, you would probably never consider reading the entire telephone book from cover to cover. You are more likely to open the book somewhere in the middle and zone in on the required business by flipping back and forth a few times, using the fact that the names are sorted alphabetically.

If a relational database, however, were to try reading the same kind of Yellow Pages data in a database table, it would find that the data is generally not sorted, but is instead stored in a type of linked list. New data is either added—unsorted—to the end of the table or entered in empty spaces where records were deleted from the table. This unsorted Yellow Pages telephone book in the form of a database table is depicted in Table 9.1.

TABLE 9.1: Example of an Unsorted Database Table

Page	Column	Position	Business Type	Business Name	City	Street	Telephone No.
...	...	...	...	...	...	...	...
15	2	54	Video rentals	Video Depot	Boston	Commonwealth Ave.	(617) 367-0788
...	...	...	...	...	...	...	...
46	1	23	Florist	Boston Blossoms	Boston	Cambridge Street	(617) 445-0044
46	1	24	Video rentals	Beacon Hill Video	Boston	Cambridge Street	(617) 536-8600
...	...	...	...	...	...	...	...
98	3	12	Pizzeria	Blue Hill House of Pizza	Roxbury	Charles Street	(617) 350-6232

One way for the database to deal with an unsorted table is by using a time-consuming sequential read, record for record. To save the database from having to perform a sequential read for every SQL statement query, each database table has a corresponding primary index. In this example, the primary index might be a list that is sorted alphabetically by business type, business name, and the location of each entry in the telephone book (see Table 9.2).

TABLE 9.2: Primary Index Corresponding to the Sample Table (Excerpt)

Business Type	Business Name	Page	Column	Position
...	...	...	...	...
Florist	Boston Blossoms	46	1	23
Pizzeria	Blue Hill House of Pizza	98	3	12
...	...	...	...	...
Video rentals	Beacon Hill Video	46	1	24
Video rentals	Video Depot	15	2	54
...	...	...	...	...

Because this list is sorted, you (or the database) do not need to read the entire list sequentially. Instead, you can expedite your search by first searching this index for the business type and name (for example, *video rentals* and *Video Depot*), and then using the corresponding page, column, and position to locate the entry in the Yellow Pages telephone book (or corresponding database table). In a database, the position data consists of the file number, block number, position in the block, and so on. This type of data about the position in a database is called the *Row ID*. The *Business Type* and *Business Name* columns in the phone book correspond to the primary index fields.

A primary index is always unique—that is, for each combination of index fields, there is only one table entry. If the present example were an actual database index, there could be no two businesses of the same type with the same name. This cannot necessarily be said of a phone book, which may, for example, list two outlets of a florist in the same area with the same name.

Secondary Indexes

In the present example, the primary index helps you only if you already know the type and name of the business you are looking for. However, if you had only a telephone number and wanted to look up the business that corresponds to it, the primary index is not useful to you because it does not contain the field *Telephone No.* Consequently, you would have to sequentially read the entire telephone book. To simplify search queries of this kind, you could define a secondary index containing the field *Telephone No.* and the corresponding Row IDs or the primary key.

Similarly, to look up all the businesses on a street of a particular city, you could create a sorted secondary index with the fields *City* and *Street* and the corresponding Row IDs or the primary key.

In contrast to the primary index, secondary indexes are as a rule not unique—that is, there can be multiple similar entries in the secondary index. For example, "Boston, Cambridge Street" will occur several times in the index if there are several businesses on that street. The secondary index based on telephone numbers, however, would be unique, because telephone numbers happen to be unique.

Optimizer and Execution Plan

If you are looking up all video rental stores in Boston, the corresponding SQL statement would be as follows:

```
SELECT * FROM telephone book WHERE business type = 'Video rentals'
AND city = 'Boston'.
```

In this case, the database has three possible search strategies:

- To search the entire table

- To use the primary index for the search

- To use a secondary index based on the field *City*

The decision as to which strategy to use is made by the database optimizer program, which considers each access path and formulates an *execution plan* for the SQL statement. The optimizer is a part of the database program. To create the execution plan, the optimizer *parses* the SQL statement. If you want to look at the execution plan (also called the *explain plan*) in the R/3 System, you can use one of the following:

- SQL trace (Transaction *ST05*)

- Database Process Monitor (accessed from the *Detail analysis menu* of Transaction *ST04*)

- *Explain* function in the shared SQL area (also accessed from the *Detail analysis menu* of Transaction *ST04*)

NOTE   The examples presented here are limited to SQL statements that access a table and do not require joins through multiple tables. In addition, the examples are presented using the Oracle access types, which include *index unique scan*, *index range scan*, and *full table scan*. The corresponding access types of the other database systems are explained in Appendix B.

Index Unique Scan

An index unique scan is performed when the SQL statement's WHERE clause specifies all primary index fields through an EQUALS condition. For example:

```
SELECT * FROM telephone book WHERE business type= 'video rentals' AND
business name = 'Beacon Hill Video'
```

The database responds to an index unique scan by locating a maximum of one record, hence the name *unique*. The execution plan is as follows:

```
TABLE ACCESS BY ROWID telephone book
 INDEX UNIQUE SCAN telephone book___0
```

The database begins by reading the row in the execution plan that is indented the furthest to the right (here, INDEX UNIQUE SCAN telephone book____0). This row indicates that the search will use the primary index *telephone book____0*.

After finding an appropriate entry in the primary index, the database then uses the Row ID indicated in the primary index to access the table *telephone book*. The index unique scan is the most efficient type of table access—that is, the access type that reads the fewest data blocks in the database.

Full Table Scan

For the following SQL statement, a full table scan is performed if there is no index based on street names:

```
SELECT * FROM telephone book WHERE street = 'Cambridge Street'
```

In this case, the execution plan contains the row:

```
TABLE ACCESS FULL telephone
```

Especially for tables greater than around 1MB, the full table scan is a very expensive search strategy, causing a high database load.

Index Range Scan

An index range scan is performed if there is an index for the search, but the results of searching the index are not unique—that is, multiple rows of the index satisfy the search criteria. An index range scan using the primary index is performed when the WHERE clause does not specify all the fields of the primary index. For example:

```
SELECT * FROM telephone book WHERE business type= 'Florist'
```

This SQL statement automatically results in a search using the primary index. Since the WHERE clause does not specify a single record, but rather an area of the primary index, the table area for business type *Florist* is read record by record. Therefore, this search strategy is called an *index range scan*. The results of the search are not unique, and zero to <n> records may be found.

An index range scan is also performed through a secondary index that is not unique, even if all the fields in the secondary index are specified. Such a search would result from the following SQL statement, which mentions both index fields of the secondary index considered above:

```
SELECT * FROM telephone book WHERE city = 'Boston' AND street=
'Cambridge Street'
```

The execution plan is as follows:

```
TABLE ACCESS BY ROWID telephone book
 INDEX RANGE SCAN telephone book___B
```

The database first accesses the secondary index *telephone book___B*. Using the records found in the index, the database then directly accesses each relevant record in the table.

Without further information, it is difficult to determine whether an index range scan is effective. The following SQL statement also requires an index range scan:

```
SELECT * FROM telephone book WHERE business type LIKE 'V%'
```

This access is very expensive since only the first byte of data in the index key field is used for the search.

Analyzing an SQL Statement—Example Using Table MARA

Consider the following SQL statement:

```
SQL Statement
 SELECT * FROM mara WHERE mandt = :A0
   AND bismt = :A1
```

and the corresponding execution plan:

```
Execution plan
TABLE ACCESS BY ROWID mara
 INDEX RANGE SCAN mara___0
```

The primary index *MARA___0* contains the fields MANDT and MATNR. Because MATNR is not mentioned in the WHERE clause, MANDT is the only field available to help the database limit its search in the index. MANDT is the field for the client.

If there is only one production client in this particular R/3 System, the WHERE clause with `mandt = :A0` will cause the entire table to be searched. In this case, a full table scan would be more effective than a search using the index: A full table scan reads only the whole table, but an index search reads both the index and the table. You can therefore determine which of the strategies is more cost-effective only if you have additional information, such as selectivity (see below). In this example, you need the information that there is only one client in the R/3 System. (For more discussion of this example, see the end of the next section.)

Database Optimizers

Exactly how an optimizer program functions is a well-guarded secret among database manufacturers. However, broadly speaking, there are two types of optimizers: the *rule-based optimizer* (RBO) and the *cost-based optimizer* (CBO).

All database systems used in conjunction with the R/3 System use a cost-based optimizer—except for the Oracle database, which has both a CBO and an RBO. For Oracle, the database profile parameter *OPTIMIZER_MODE* lets you change the default optimizer to a cost-based optimizer. If you are unsure which optimizer is being used, in the Database Performance Monitor (Transaction *ST04*), choose *Detail analysis menu* ➤ *Parameter changes* ➤ *Active parameters*. This screen alphabetically lists current parameter settings. If the parameter *OPTIMIZER_MODE* is set to CHOOSE, the cost-based optimizer is activated. If the parameter is set to RULE, the rule-based optimizer is activated. For R/3 Release 3.*x*, this database parameter is set by default to the rule-based optimizer. For R/3 Release 4.*x*, this parameter is set by default to the cost-based optimizer.

WARNING   Do not change the default setting of the R/3 parameter *OPTI-MIZER_MODE* without explicit instruction from SAP.

Rule-Based Optimizer (RBO)

An RBO bases its execution plan for a given SQL statement on the WHERE clause and the available indexes. The most important criteria in the WHERE clause are the fields that are specified with an EQUALS condition and that appear in an index:

```
SELECT * FROM telephone book WHERE business type= 'Pizzeria' AND
business name = 'Blue Hill House of Pizza' AND city = 'Roxbury'
```

In this example, the optimizer decides on the primary index rather than the secondary index, because two primary index fields are specified (*business type* and *business name*), while only one secondary index field is specified (*city*).

One limitation on index use is that a field can be used for an index search only if all the fields to the left of that field in the index are also specified in the WHERE clause with an equals condition. Consider two sample SQL statements:

```
SELECT * FROM telephone book
 WHERE business type like 'P%' AND business name = 'Blue Hill House
 of Pizza'
```

and

```
SELECT * FROM telephone book WHERE business name = 'Blue Hill House
of Pizza'
```

For either of these statements, the condition *business name = 'Blue Hill House of Pizza'* is of no use to an index search. For the first of the two examples, all business types beginning with "P" in the index will be read. For the second example, all entries in the index are read since the *business type* field is missing from the WHERE clause.

While an index search is thus greatly influenced by the position of a field in the index (in relation to the left-most field), the order in which fields are mentioned in the WHERE clause is arbitrary.

Cost-Based Optimizer (CBO)

To create the execution plan for an SQL statement, the CBO considers the same criteria as described for the RBO above, plus the following criteria:

- Table size: For small tables, the CBO decides to avoid indexes in favor of a more efficient full table scan. Large tables are more likely to be accessed through the index.

- Selectivity of the index fields: The selectivity of a given index field is the average size of the portion of a table that is read when an SQL statement searches for a particular distinct value in that field. For example, if there are 200 business types and 10,000 actual businesses listed in the telephone book, then the selectivity of the field *business type* is 10,000 divided by 200, which is 50 (or 2% of 10,000). The larger the number of distinct values in a field, the higher the selectivity and the more likely the optimizer will use the index based on that field.

  - Tests with various database systems have shown that an index is used only if the CBO estimates that on average less than 5% to 10% of the entire table has to be read. Otherwise, the optimizer will decide on the full table scan.

- Amount of disk memory that needs to be read to read the index: The optimizer considers how many index data blocks or pages must be read physically on the hard disk. The more physical memory that needs to be read, the less likely that an index is used. The amount of physical memory that needs to be read may be increased by database fragmentation (that is, a low fill level in the individual index blocks).

- Distribution of field values: Most database systems also consider the distribution of field values within a table column—that is, whether each distinct value is represented in an equivalent number of data records, or whether some values dominate. The optimizer's decision is based on the evaluation of statistics on the data—for example, it uses a histogram or spot checks to determine the distribution of values across a column.

- Spot checks at time of execution: Some database systems—for example, ADABAS D and SQL Server—decide which access strategy is used at the time of execution and not during parsing. At the time of parsing, the values that will satisfy the WHERE clause are still unknown to the database. At the time of execution, however, an uneven distribution of values in a particular field can be taken into account by a spot check.

NOTE
To determine the number of distinct values per field in a database table, use the following SQL statement: `SELECT COUNT (DISTINCT dbfield) FROM dbtable`. To find out the number of distinct values from inside R/3 for each field of a database table, use Transaction *DB02* and (for Oracle) choose *Detailed analysis*. In the resulting dialog box, in the field *Object,* enter the name of the table and choose *OK*. Then choose *Table columns*. The resulting screen lists each field of the selected table (under *Database column*). The corresponding number of distinct values is indicated under *Distinct values*. The corresponding menu path for other database systems is explained in R/3 Online Documentation.

Table Access Statistics for the CBO

To make the right decision on the optimal access, the CBO requires statistics on the sizes of tables and indexes. These statistics must be periodically generated to make them up to date. To ensure that this occurs, schedule the relevant generating program using the DBA Planning Calendar (Transaction *DB13*).

If the table access statistics are missing or obsolete, the optimizer may suggest inefficient access paths, which can cause significant performance problems.

RBO or CBO? (Advantages and Disadvantages)

An advantage of using the RBO is that you do not need to generate table access statistics. Generating these statistics requires administrative work and places a load on the system. The program that generates the statistics must run several times a week at periods of low system load.

The advantage of the CBO is its greater flexibility because it considers the selectivity of specified fields. Recall the analysis example with table MARA that was considered above. The SQL statement was as follows:

```
SELECT * FROM mara WHERE mandt = :A0 AND bismt = :A1
```

Here, the CBO, which knows that MANDT contains only one distinct value, would decide on a full table scan, whereas the RBO, automatically preferring an index, would choose the less effective index range scan.

Sometimes you can help the RBO to choose the correct index by appropriately rewriting the indexes.

NOTE   Rewriting indexes for the RBO is not covered in the present book. For Oracle, see the article "Improving SQL Statements by Secondary Indexes" posted on SAP's TechNet site on the Internet.

Including *Hints* in SQL Statements

Some database systems allow you to influence the execution plan for various purposes by including what are called *hints* in an SQL statement. For example, in conjunction with an Oracle database, you can force the use of a full table scan with the following SQL statement:

```
SELECT /*+ FULL likp */ * FROM likp WHERE …
```

Up to R/3 Release 4.0B, the *ABAP Open SQL* interface does not support including *hints*. If a *hint* must be used, you can implement it using *ABAP Native SQL*.

WARNING   After an R/3 upgrade or a database upgrade, or even after a database patch, *hints* may become superfluous or, even worse, may cause ineffective accesses. Therefore, following an upgrade, all *hints* must be tested. To make system administration easier, use *hints* very rarely.

Analyzing an SQL Statement—Returning to the Example Using Table MARA

To see how indexes can improve performance for the execution of SQL statements, reconsider the above example of an SQL statement affecting table MARA:

```
SELECT * FROM mara WHERE mandt = :A0 AND bismt = :A1
```

In the R/3 System, the table MARA contains material master records. The primary index *MARA___0* contains the following fields: MANDT (which identifies the client system) and MATNR (the material number).

Another field in the table MARA is BISMT, which indicates the old material number. This field is used when new material numbers are introduced because of internal company reorganization, but the old, familiar material numbers are required to remain available to make searches easier for users. The above SQL statement is searching for a material using an old material number.

If there is no secondary index with the field BISMT, the database optimizer has two possible access paths: the full table scan or the index range scan through the primary index *MARA___0*.

If there are no table access statistics, the optimizer cannot recognize that the field MANDT is very unselective. After locating the field MANDT in both the WHERE clause and the index, the optimizer therefore decides on an index range scan through the primary index *MARA___0*.

If statistics on the table MARA are available, the optimizer decides on a full table scan.

Table 9.3 compares the runtimes of accessing table MARA in various situations, using a MARA with 50,000 entries. The full table scan has a runtime of 500,000 microseconds. This is clearly more effective than the index range scan through the unfavorable primary index *MARA___0* (using fields MANDT and MATNR), which requires 3,500,000 microseconds. The runtime decreases dramatically to 3,000 microseconds after the creation of a secondary index based on the field BISMT. Using this secondary index thus represents a thousand-fold improvement over using the primary index.

TABLE 9.3: Comparison of Runtimes for an SQL Statement Affecting Table MARA Using Different Search Strategies

Initial Conditions	Access Path	With Index Based on Fields...	Runtime in Microseconds
• Without table access statistics	Index range scan	MANDT, MATNR	3,500,000
• Without secondary index based on the field BISMT	Index range scan	MANDT, MATNR	3,500,000

Continued on next page

TABLE 9.3: Comparison of Runtimes for an SQL Statement Affecting Table MARA Using Different Search Strategies *(Continued)*

Initial Conditions	Access Path	With Index Based on Fields...	Runtime in Microseconds
• With table access statistics	Full table scan	—	500,000
• Without secondary index based on the field BISMT	Full table scan	—	500,000
• With table access statistics	Index range scan	BISMT	3,000
• With secondary index based on the field BISMT	Index range scan	BISMT	3,000

This example shows that it is important to create the right secondary indexes for frequently used SQL statements. In addition, up-to-date table statistics are required for the database optimizer to determine the best access path.

Administration for Indexes and Table Access Statistics

Administering primary and secondary indexes consists of creating indexes in R/3 and activating them on the database. Indexes that have gone missing in the database should be identified and re-created. Schedule table access statistics to be generated periodically and monitor the generation strategy and the statistics themselves.

Creating and Maintaining Indexes

Indexes are created and maintained in ABAP Dictionary Maintenance, which you can access by using Transaction *SE11*, or, from the R/3 initial screen, by choosing *Tools* ➤ *ABAP Workbench* ➤ *Dictionary*.

To see the table fields of an existing index, after entering a table name, choose *Display*. The screen *Dictionary: Table/Structure: Display fields* appears. The primary index fields of a table are marked in the column *Key*. To see the associated secondary indexes, choose *Indexes*. The primary index is not included in the resulting list of indexes, since it is shown on the preceding screen.

1. To create a new secondary index for a table, choose *Create* and enter an index name. Choose *Enter*.

2. In the resulting screen, enter a short description, name the index fields, and choose *Save*. The index now exists in the ABAP Dictionary, but has not yet been activated in the database.

3. To activate the index in the database, choose *Index ➤ Activate*. After the index has been activated in the database, the screen displays the message *Index MARA~T exists in database system Oracle*.

WARNING The process of activating an index for a large table in the database is especially time-consuming. During this process, INSERT, UPDATE, and DELETE operations affecting the corresponding table are blocked. Therefore, avoid creating new indexes for large tables during company business hours. To activate indexes by an appropriate background job, use Utilities for ABAP Dictionary Tables (Transaction *SE14*).

NOTE After activating a new index, you may need to generate new table access statistics so the optimizer can consider the new index when calculating the execution plan.

As of R/3 Release 4.0, the R/3 System includes database-dependent indexes that are activated as required. In ABAP Dictionary Maintenance (Transaction *SE11*), an index of this type is indicated by the field *for selected database systems* being marked.

Although an index may be defined as a database index in R/3, it may be (or become) missing in the database—for example, due to not being activated or due to being deleted and not re-created during database reorganization. This type of index is called a *missing index*. To determine whether a database index is missing, use Transaction *DB02* and choose *Missing indexes*. Alternatively, from the R/3 initial screen, choose *Tools* ➤ *Administration* ➤ *Monitor* ➤ *Performance* ➤ *Database* ➤ *Tables/Indexes* ➤ *Missing indexes*.

In the resulting display, missing primary and secondary indexes are listed separately.

WARNING Missing primary indexes require the urgent attention of the database administrator. If a primary index is missing, duplicate keys may be written, and therefore the consistency of the data is no longer guaranteed. Additionally, the lack of a primary index leads to inefficient database accesses, causing performance problems for large tables.

Re-creating a Missing Primary Index in the Database

To solve the problem of a missing primary index, which is known to the ABAP Dictionary, but does not yet exist (or no longer exists) on the database, re-create that index in ABAP Dictionary Maintenance:

1. Use Transaction *SE11*, or, from the R/3 initial screen, choose *Tools* ➤ *ABAP Workbench* ➤ *Dictionary*.

2. Enter the table name and choose *Display* ➤ *Utilities* ➤ *Database Utility* ➤ *Indexes* ➤ *Primary index* ➤ *Create database index*.

If no errors occur, the index has now been created on the database. If errors occur—for example, due to duplicate keys—contact SAP.

Missing Secondary Indexes

Missing secondary indexes can cause performance problems if the index belongs to a table that is larger than around 1MB.

To create the index that was missing:

1. Use Transaction *SE11*, or, from the R/3 initial screen, choose *Tools ➤ ABAP Workbench ➤ Dictionary*.

2. Enter the table name and choose *Display ➤ Indexes*.

3. Select the missing index and choose *Activate*.

Generating Table Access Statistics

You can schedule the program that generates table access statistics to run as a periodic background job using the DBA Planning calendar. To do this, use Transaction code *DB13*, or, from the R/3 initial screen, choose *Tools ➤ CCMS ➤ DB administration ➤ DB scheduling*.

The statistics generation programs are indicated in the calendar—for example, as *AnalyzeTab* for Oracle, *Update sta0* for Informix, and *Update Statistics* for SQL Server.

NOTE   To find out which programs need to be scheduled to run periodically and how to schedule them for a specific brand of database, see the R/3 Notes in Appendix H and the R/3 Online Documentation.

Updating or creating new table access statistics is a resource-intensive process with runtimes of several hours for an entire database. Most database systems use a two-step process:

- Requirement analysis: This first step finds out the tables for which statistics should be created.

- Statistics generation: This second step generates the statistics.

Statistics generation is controlled by the table DBSTATC. To view the contents of this table, use Transaction code *DB21*, or, from the R/3 initial screen, choose *Tools* ➤ *CCMS* ➤ *DB administration* ➤ *Cost based optimizer* ➤ *Control statistics*.

The resulting screen lists the R/3 tables whose cost-based optimizer statistics are to be checked and updated, and provides several columns of relevant information, such as:

- Column *Active:* Specifies how the table statistics are edited during an update. For example, an *A* indicates statistics should be generated. An *N* or *R* excludes the table from the analysis.

- Column *Todo:* In this column, the control table DBSTATC sets an *X* if statistics for a given table are to be generated when the generation program runs next.

Monitoring Statistics Generation Logs

For each run of the statistics generation program, you can monitor the logs created. To monitor these logs after a run of the statistics generation program *SAPDBA* for an Oracle database, choose *Tools* ➤ *CCMS* ➤ *DB administration* ➤ *DBA Logs* ➤ *DB Optimizer*.

The resulting screen might show, for example, the information in Table 9.4.

TABLE 9.4: Sample Log

Beginning of Action	End of Action	Fct	Object	RC
24.04.1998 17:10:12	24.04.1998 17:35:01	opt	PSAP%	0000
24.04.1998 17:36:30	24.04.1998 18:26:25	aly	DBSTATCO	0000

In the first row, the value *opt* in the column *Fct* indicates that a requirement analysis was performed. The value *PSAP%* in the column *Object* indicates that the requirement analysis was performed for all tables in the database. Comparing the beginning and ending times in the first row, you can see that the requirement analysis took 25 minutes.

In the second row, the value *aly* in the column *Fct* indicates that a table analysis run was performed. The value *DBSTATCO* in the column *Object* indicates that the table analysis was performed for all relevant tables. (These are all tables listed in the control table DBSTATC—usually only a small percentage of all database tables.) Comparing the beginning and ending times in the second row, you can see that the table analysis took almost an hour.

The operations in both rows ended successfully, as indicated by the value *0000* in the column *RC*.

Monitoring the Statistics Generated

The R/3 tools for generating table access statistics are specifically adapted to the requirements of the R/3 System. Certain tables are excluded from the creation of statistics because generating statistics for those tables would be superfluous or would reduce performance.

WARNING   Ensure that the table access statistics are generated only by the generation program released specifically for R/3.

When R/3 is used in conjunction with Oracle databases, no statistics are created for pooled and clustered tables such as the update tables VBMOD, VBHDR, and VBDATA. For these tables, the field *Active* in Transaction *DB21* displays the entry *R*.

To check whether statistics were generated for a particular table, use Transaction code *DB02*, or, from the R/3 initial screen, choose *Tools* ➢ *Administration* ➢ *Monitor* ➢ *Performance* ➢ *Database* ➢ *Tables/Indexes*.

Next, proceed as follows:

- For Oracle, choose *Detailed analysis*, enter a table, and choose *Enter*. Then choose *Table columns*.

- For Informix, choose *Checks* ➢ *Update statistics*. Enter a table and choose *Enter*.

- For MS SQL Server, choose *Detail analysis*. Enter a table and choose *Enter*. Choose *Show statistics*.

Depending on the database system, the resulting screen indicates, for example, the following information:

- The date of the last analysis

- The accuracy of the analysis

- The number of occupied database blocks or pages

- The number of table rows

- The number of different entries per column (distinct values)

There are similar monitor programs in Transaction *DB02* for database systems other than those listed above.

Rules for Creating or Changing Secondary Indexes

Creating or changing a secondary index changes the R/3 System and can improve or worsen the performance of SQL statements. Therefore, changes to indexes should be performed only by experienced developers or consultants.

Preliminary Checks

Before creating or changing an index, check whether the SQL statement for which you want to create a new index originates from a standard R/3 program or a customer-developed program.

If the SQL statement originates from a standard R/3 program, check the relevant R/3 Notes in the Online Service System (OSS) that describe ways of optimizing performance for the SQL statement. If there are no relevant R/3 Notes, enter your proposal concerning the creation of an appropriate index in a problem message in the Online Service System (OSS).

If the SQL statement originates from a customer-developed program, rather than create a new index, you may be able to do either of the following:

- Rewrite the ABAP program in such a way that an available index can be used.

- Adapt an available index in such a way that it can be used.

When optimizing customer-developed SQL statements, try to avoid creating secondary indexes on SAP transaction data tables. As a rule, transaction data tables grow linearly over time and cause a corresponding growth in the size of the related secondary indexes. Therefore, over time, searching in a secondary index will result in an SQL statement that runs more and more slowly. For transaction data, therefore, SAP uses special search techniques such as matchcode tables and R/3 business index tables such as the *delivery due index*.

Never create a secondary index on R/3 Basis tables without explicit recommendation from SAP. Examples of these tables include table NAST and tables beginning with D010, D020, and DD.

Rules for Creating Secondary Indexes

The following rules are the basic rules of secondary index design. For primary indexes, in addition to these rules, there are other considerations related to the principles of table construction.

Rule 1: Include Only Selective Fields in the Index

An index is useful only if each corresponding SQL statement selects only a small part of a table.

If the SQL statement that searches by means of a particular index field would cause more than 5% to 10% of the entire index to be read, the cost-based optimizer does not consider the index useful, and instead chooses the full table scan as the most effective access method.

Examples of selective fields normally include document numbers, material numbers, and customer numbers. Examples of nonselective fields usually include R/3 client IDs, company codes or plant IDs, and account status.

Rule 2: Include Few Fields in the Index

As a rule, an index should contain no more than four fields. If too many fields are used in the index, this has the following effects:

- Change operations to tables take longer because the index must also be changed accordingly.

- More storage space is used in the database.

- The large volume of data in the index reduces the chance that the optimizer will regard it as economical to use the index.

- The parsing time for an SQL statement increases significantly, especially if the statement accesses multiple tables with numerous indexes and the tables must be linked with a join operation.

Rule 3: Position Selective Fields to the Left in an Index

To speed up accesses through an index based on several fields, the most selective fields should be positioned furthest toward the left in the index.

Rule 4: Exceptions to Rules 1 to 3

To avoid the optimizer not using an index, it is sometimes necessary to use nonselective fields in the index in a way that contradicts rules 1 to 3.

Examples of such fields typically include the fields for client ID (field MANDT) and company code (field BUKRS).

Rule 5: Indexes Should Be Disjunct

Avoid creating nondisjunct indexes—that is, two or more indexes with largely the same fields.

Rule 6: Create Few Indexes per Table

Despite the fact that the ABAP Dictionary defines a maximum limit of 16 indexes for each table, as a rule, you should not create more than 5 indexes. One exception is for a table that is used mainly for reading, such as a table containing master data.

Having too many indexes causes similar problems to those that occur if an index has too many fields. There is also an increased risk that the optimizer will choose the wrong index.

Flexibility in Applying the Rules

Keep in mind that every rule has exceptions. Sometimes the optimal index combination can be found only by trial and error.

Generally, experimenting with indexes is considered safe, as long as you keep the following points in mind:

- Never change indexes for tables larger than 10MB during company business hours. Creating or changing an index can take from several minutes to several hours and blocks the entire table. This causes serious performance problems during production operation.

- After creating or changing an index, always check whether the optimizer program uses this index in the manner you intended. Ensure that the new index does not result in poor optimizer choices for other SQL statements. To do this, use the shared SQL area as described in the following section.

Monitoring Indexes in the Shared SQL Area

Before and after creating or changing an index, monitor the effect of the index in the shared SQL area:

1. To monitor the shared SQL area in R/3, from the main screen in the Database Performance Monitor (Transaction *ST04*), choose *Detail analysis menu* and under the header *Resource consumption by:*

    - For ORACLE, choose *SQL request.*

    - For Informix, choose *SQL Statement.*

    In the dialog box that appears, change the automatically suggested selection values to zero and choose *OK*.

2. Choose *Select table.*

    - Specify the table for which you want to create or change the index and choose *Enter*.

    - The resulting screen displays the SQL statements that correspond to this table.

3. Save this screen together with the execution plan for all SQL statements in a file.

4. Two days after creating or changing the index, repeat steps 1 to 3, and compare the results with those obtained earlier to ensure that no SQL statement has a loss in performance due to poor optimizer decisions. In particular:

   - Compare the number of logical or physical accesses per execution (these are indicated, for example, in the column *Reads/execution*).

   - Check the execution plans to ensure that the new index is used only where appropriate.

> **WARNING** To check the index design using the Shared SQL Area Monitor in a development system or test system, ensure that the business data in the system is representative, since the data determines the table sizes and field selectivity considered by the cost-based optimizer. Before testing, update the table access statistics so they reflect the current data.

What to Do If the Optimizer Ignores the Index

If you find that the cost-based optimizer program refuses to include a particular secondary index in its execution plan despite the fact that this index would simplify data access, the most likely reason is that the table access statistics are missing or not up to date.

Check the analysis strategy and determine why the table has not yet been analyzed (see R/3 Online Documentation on database administration). You can use Transaction *DB20* to manually create up-to-date statistics, and then check whether the optimizer then makes the correct decision.

More rarely, the optimizer ignores an appropriate index despite up-to-date table access statistics. Possible solutions include:

- If the WHERE clause is too complex and the optimizer cannot interpret it correctly, you may have to consider changing the programming. Examples are provided in the next section.

- Sometimes deleting the table access statistics or even appropriately modifying the statistics will cause the optimizer to use a particular index. (For this reason, the generation program released specifically for R/3 chooses not to generate statistics for some tables. Therefore, ensure that you create the table access statistics with the tools provided by SAP.)

In either of these cases, the solution requires extensive knowledge of SQL optimization. If the problem originates from the standard R/3 software, consult SAP or your database partner.

Rules for Efficient SQL Programming

This section explains the five basic rules for efficient SQL programming. It does not replace an ABAP tuning manual and is limited to a few important cases. Related programming techniques are explained with examples at the end of this section and in the following sections.

NOTE   For a quick guide to efficient SQL programming, call ABAP Runtime Analysis (Transaction *SE30*) and choose *Tips and Tricks*. The resulting screen lets you display numerous examples of good and bad programming.

Rule 1: Transfer Few Records

SQL statements must have a WHERE clause that transfers only a minimal amount of data from the database to application server or vice versa. This is especially important for SQL statements affecting tables of more than 1MB.

For all programs that transfer data to or from the database:

- If the program contains CHECK statements for table fields in SELECT… ENDSELECT loops, replace the CHECK statement with a suitable WHERE clause.

- SQL statements without WHERE clauses must not access tables that are constantly growing—for example, transaction data tables such as BSEG, MKPF, and VBAK. If you find such SQL statements, rewrite the program.

- Avoid identical accesses—that is, the same data being read repeatedly. To identify SQL statements that cause identical accesses, trace the program with an SQL trace (Transaction *ST05*), view the results, and choose *Goto* ➤ *Identical selects*. Note the identical selects and return to the trace results screen to see how much time these selects required. This tells you how much time you would save if the identical selects could be avoided.

Rule 2: Keep the Volume of Transferred Data Small

To ensure that the volume of transferred data is as small as possible, examine your programs as described in the following points:

- SQL statements with the clause *SELECT* * transfer all the columns of a table. If all this data is not really needed, you may be able to convert the *SELECT* * clause to a SELECT LIST (SELECT column 1 column 2) or use a projection view.

- There is an economical and an expensive way of calculating sums, maximums, or mean values in relation to an individual table column:

  - First, you can perform these calculations on the database using the SQL aggregate functions (SUM, MAX, AVG, etc.) and then transfer only the results, which is a small data volume.

  - Second, you can initially transfer all the data in the column from the database into the ABAP program and perform the calculations on the application server. This transfers a lot more data than the first method and creates more database load.

- A WHERE clause searching for a single record often looks as follows:

```
CLEAR found.
  SELECT * FROM dbtable WHERE field1 = x1.
   found = 'X'. EXIT.
  ENDSELECT.
```

The disadvantage in this code is that it triggers a FETCH on the database. For example, after 100 records are read into the input/output buffer of the work processes, the ABAP program reads the first record in the buffer, and the loop processing is interrupted. Therefore, 99 records were transferred for no benefit. The following code is more efficient:

```
CLEAR found.
  SELECT * FROM dbtable UP TO 1 ROWS WHERE field1 = x1.
  ENDSELECT.
  IF sy subrc = 0. found = 'X'. ENDIF.
```

This code informs the database that only one record should be returned.

Rule 3: Use Array Select Instead of Single Select

The number of fetches must remain small. Using array select instead of single select creates fewer, more lengthy database accesses instead of many short accesses. Many short accesses cause administrative overhead and network traffic in comparison to fewer, more lengthy database accesses. Therefore, avoid the following types of code:

- ```
  LOOP AT itab.
    SELECT FROM dbtable WHERE field1 = itab field1.
    <further processing>
  ENDLOOP
  ```
- ```
  SELECT * FROM dbtable1 WHERE field1 = x1.
    SELECT * FROM dbtable2 WHERE field2 = dbtable1 field2.
    <further processing>
    ENDSELECT
  ENDSELECT
  ```

Both examples make many short accesses that read only a few records. As of R/3 Release 3.0, you can group many short accesses to make a few longer accesses by using either the FOR ALL ENTRIES clause or a database view.

Rule 4: Keep the WHERE Clauses Simple

The WHERE clauses must be simple; otherwise the optimizer may decide on the wrong index or not use an index at all. A WHERE clause is simple if it specifies each field of the index using AND and an equals condition.

Virtually all optimizers have problems when confronted with a large number of OR conditions. Therefore, you should use the disjunct normal form (DNF) whenever possible, as described in the example below on avoiding OR clauses.

Try to avoid using NOT conditions in the WHERE clause. These cannot be processed through an index. You can often replace a NOT condition by a positive IN or OR condition, which can be processed using an index.

Rule 5: Avoid Unnecessary Database Load

Some operations such as sorting tables can be performed by the database instance as well as the R/3 instance. In general, you should try to transfer any tasks that create system load to the application servers, which can be configured with more R/3 instances if the system load increases. The capacity of the database instance cannot be increased so easily.

The following measures help to avoid database load:

- R/3 buffering: This is the most efficient tool for reducing load on the database instance caused by accesses to database data. (See Chapter 7.)

- Sorting on the application server rather than in the database: If a program requires sorted data, either the database or the R/3 instance must sort the data. The database should perform the sort only if the same index can be used for sorting as for satisfying the WHERE clause, since this type of sort is inexpensive. (See below, under "Sorting Techniques.")

Ways to Avoid OR Clauses

Instead of the following code:

```
SELECT * FROM sflight WHERE (carrid = 'LH' or carrid = 'UA')
 AND (connid = '0012' OR connid = '0013')
```

it is better to use:

```
SELECT * FROM SFLIGHT
 WHERE ( CARRID = 'LH' AND CONNID = '0012')
 OR ( CARRID = 'LH' AND CONNID = '0013')
 OR ( CARRID = 'UH' AND CONNID = '0012')
 OR ( CARRID = 'UH' AND CONNID = '0013')
```

The other way of avoiding problems with OR clauses is to divide complex SQL statements into simple SQL statements and cause the selected data to be stored in an internal table. To divide complex SQL statements, you can use the FOR ALL ENTRIES clause (see below, under "More about FOR ALL ENTRIES Clauses").

Sometimes you can use an *IN* instead of an *OR*. For example, instead of:

```
field1 = x1 AND (field2 = y1 OR field2 = y2 OR field2 = y3)
```

use

```
field1 = x1 and field2 IN (y1, y2, y3)
```

Sorting Techniques

Consider the table DBTABLE with the fields FIELD1, FIELD2, FIELD3, and FIELD4. The key fields are FIELD1, FIELD2, and FIELD3, and these compose the primary index *TABLE__0*.

To cause the data to be sorted by the database, you can use the following statement:

```
SELECT * FROM dbtable INTO TABLE itab
   WHERE field1 = x1 and field2 = x2
   ORDER BY field1 field2 field3.
```

Here, a database sort is appropriate, since the primary index *TABLE__0* can be used both to satisfy the WHERE clause and to sort the data.

A sort by the fields FIELD2 and FIELD4 cannot be performed using the primary index *TABLE__0* since the ORDER_BY clause does not contain the first primary index field. Therefore, to reduce the database load, this sort should be performed not by the database, but by the ABAP program. You can use ABAP statements such as:

```
SELECT * FROM dbtable INTO itab WHERE field1 = x1 and field2 = x2.
SORT itab BY field2 field4.
```

Similar considerations to those used in the case of sorting apply when using the GROUP BY clause or aggregate functions. If the database instance performs the GROUP BY, this increases the consumption of database instance resources. However, this must be weighed against the gain in performance due to the fact that the GROUP BY calculation transfers fewer results to the application server. (For more information on aggregate functions, see rule 2 above.)

Example of Optimizing an SQL Statement in an ABAP Program

This section uses an example to demonstrate each step in optimizing an SQL statement.

Preliminary Analysis

In this example, a customer-developed ABAP program is having performance problems. As an initial response, run an SQL trace (Transaction *ST05*) on a second run of the program, when the database buffer has been loaded. The results of the trace show the information in Table 9.5.

TABLE 9.5: Excerpt from an SQL Trace for the ABAP Program Listed Below

Duration in Microseconds	Object	Oper	Rec	RC	Statement
1,692	MSEG	PREPARE		0	SELECT WHERE MANDT...
182	MSEG	OPEN		0	
86,502	MSEG	FETCH	32	0	
326	MKPF	PREPARE		0	SELECT WHERE MANDT...
60	MKPF	OPEN		0	
12,540	MKPF	FETCH	1	1403	
59	MKPF	REOPEN		0	SELECT WHERE MANDT...
2,208	MKPF	FETCH	1	1403	
60	MKPF	REOPEN		0	SELECT WHERE MANDT...
2,234	MKPF	FETCH	1	1403	
61	MKPF	REOPEN		0	SELECT WHERE MANDT...
2,340	MKPF	FETCH	1	1403	
...28 more indiv. FETCHES					
43,790	MSEG	FETCH	32	0	
61	MKPF	REOPEN		0	SELECT WHERE MANDT...
2,346	MKPF	FETCH	1	1403	
60	MKPF	REOPEN		0	SELECT WHERE MANDT...
2,455	MKPF	FETCH	1	1403	

The trace begins with a FETCH operation on table MSEG, which reads 32 records, as indicated by the 32 in the column *Rec*. Next, 32 separate FETCH operations are performed on table MKPF, each returning one record as indicated by the 1 in the column *Rec*. This process is repeated with another FETCH operation that reads

32 records from table MSEG and 32 further single-record FETCH operations on the table MKPF, and so on, until all records are found.

Now view the compressed summary. To do this from the SQL trace results screen, choose *Goto* ➤ *Summary* ➤ *Compress*. The results are indicated in Table 9.6.

TABLE 9.6: Compressed Summary of an SQL Trace

TCode/ Program	Table	SQL Op	Accesses	Records	Time in Microseconds	Percent
SE38	MKPF	SEL	112	112	319,040	61.7
SE38	MSEG	SEL	1	112	197,638	38.3
Total					516,678	100.0

The compressed summary shows that almost two-thirds (61.7%) of the database time is used for the individual FETCH operations on the table MKPF, and more than one-third (38.3%) is used for the FETCH operations on the table MSEG.

Detailed Analysis

The detailed analysis is the step prior to tuning. In this step, you find out the tables, fields, and processes that are important for tuning the SQL statements you identified in the preliminary analysis.

To increase the performance of specific SQL statements, you can either improve the performance of the database instance or reduce the volume of data transferred from the database to the application server.

In Table 9.6, the SQL trace results show that the response times per record are approximately 3,000 microseconds for the accesses to table MKPF, and approximately 1,800 microseconds for accesses to table MSEG. Since these response times are good, you can conclude that the performance of the database instance is good. The only remaining way of increasing the performance of SQL statements in the ABAP program is to reduce the amount of data transferred.

View the identical selects: From the SQL trace (Transaction *ST05*) results screen, choose *Goto* ➤ *Identical selects*. In the present example, the resulting list shows 72 identical SQL statements on the table MKPF. This is around 60% of the total of 112 accesses to the table MKPF, as indicated in the compressed summary. Therefore, eliminating the identical accesses would result in about 60% fewer accesses and correspondingly less access time.

To access the code from the SQL trace results screen, position the cursor on the appropriate program in the column *Object* and choose *ABAP display*. In this example, accessing the code reveals that the following ABAP statements caused the database accesses analyzed in the SQL trace:

```
SELECT * FROM mseg INTO CORRESPONDING FIELDS OF imatdocs WHERE matnr
LIKE s_matnr.
   SELECT * FROM mkpf WHERE mblnr = imatdocs-mblnr AND mjahr =
   imatdocs-mjahr.
      imatdocs-budat = mkpf-budat.
      APPEND imatdocs.
   ENDSELECT.
ENDSELECT.
```

You now need to know from which tables the data is being selected. This is indicated in ABAP Dictionary Maintenance (Transaction *SE11*). In this example, the two affected tables, MKPF and MSEG, store materials documents for goods issue and receipt. MKPF contains the document heads for the materials documents, and MSEG contains the respective line items. The program reads the materials documents for specific materials from the database and transfers them to the internal table IMATDOCS. The materials are listed in the internal table S_MATNR.

The fields of these tables that you need to know in this example are as follows:

- Table MKPF:
    - MANDT: client (primary key)
    - MBLNR: number of the material document (primary key)
    - MJAHR: material document year (primary key)
    - BUDAT: posting date in the document
- Table MSEG:
    - MANDT: client (primary key)
    - MBLNR: number of the material document (primary key)
    - MJAHR: material document year (primary key)
    - ZEILE: position in the material document (primary key)
    - MATNR: material number
    - WERKS: plant

The above program excerpt selects the materials documents corresponding to the materials in the internal table S_MATNR and transfers the document-related fields MANDT, MBLNR, MJAHR, ZEILE, MATNR, WERKS, and BUDAT to the ABAP program.

In the above SQL statement, S_MATNR limits the data volume to be transferred to the ABAP program from table MSEG. Because the field MATNR is in the table MSEG, the data selection begins in table MSEG rather than in MKPF. For each of the records selected in MSEG, the data for the field BUDAT is read from table MKPF and transferred to internal table IMATDOCS.

The program in this example resolves these tasks with a nested SELECT loop. As you can see in the excerpt, the external loop executes a FETCH operation that returns 32 records. Then each record is processed individually in the ABAP program, and a relevant record from table MKPF is requested 32 times. After this, the program resumes the external loop, collecting another 32 records from the database, then returns to the internal loop, and so on, until all requested documents are processed.

Once you have identified the SQL statements that have to be optimized (in the preliminary analysis)—and the related tables, fields, and processes (in the detailed analysis)—you can start to tune these statements as follows.

Tuning the SQL Code

Comparing the excerpted programming with the rules for efficient SQL programming reveals three areas where these rules are contradicted in the present example:

- Contradiction to rule 1: Identical information is read multiple times from the database.

- Contradiction to rule 2: *SELECT* * statements are used, which read all the columns in the table. These statements are, however, few in number.

- Contradiction to rule 3: Instead of a small number of FETCH operations that read many records from table MKPF, the program uses many FETCH operations that read only one record. This creates an unnecessary administrative burden in terms of REOPEN operations and network traffic.

Two tuning solutions for this example of poor data accessing are provided in the following subsections.

Solution 1

This solution aims to avoid identical SQL statements, avoid *SELECT* * statements, and bundle FETCH operations.

Avoiding Identical SQL Statements

The identical database accesses occur because of the nested SQL statements.

In the example, the first SQL statement accesses the table MSEG to obtain the following data: MANDT=100, MBLNR=00005001, MJAHR=1998, and the field ZEILE specifies the 10 rows from 0000 to 0010. The second SQL statement searches the table MKPF based on the keys MANDT=100, MBLNR=00005001, and MJAHR=1998, and reads identical heading data 10 times.

Using nested SQL statements always poses the risk of identical accesses because the program does not recognize which data has already been read. To avoid identical accesses, read all the data from the table MSEG, and then read the heading data from the table MKPF only once, as indicated in the rewritten version of the program below.

Avoiding *Select* * Statements

To reduce the amount of data transferred for each table record, convert the *SELECT* * clause to a SELECT LIST.

Bundling Fetch Operations

To convert the numerous single record accesses to the table MKPF into larger FETCH operations, you can use the FOR ALL ENTRIES clause.

Rewriting the Program Accordingly

The program optimized in the above ways now looks as follows:

```
SELECT mblnr mjahr zeile matnr werks FROM mseg
   INTO TABLE imatdocs
   WHERE matnr LIKE s_matnr.
```

```
If sy subrc = 0.
    SORT imatdocs BY mblnr-mjahr.
    imatdocs_help1[] = imatdocs[]
    DELETE ADJACENT DUPLICATES FROM imatdocs_help1 COMPARING
    mblnr-mjahr.
    SELECT mblnr mjahr budat FROM mkpf
    INTO TABLE imatdocs_help2
    FOR ALL ENTRIES IN imatdocs_help1
    WHERE mblnr = imatdocs_help1-mblnr
    AND mjahr = imatdocs_help1-mjahr.
    SORT imatdocs_help2 BY mblnr-mjahr.
    LOOP AT imatdocs.
READ TABLE imatdocs_help2
WITH KEY mblnr = imatdocs-mblnr
    mjahr = imatdocs-mjahr BINARY SEARCH.
    imatdocs budat = imatdocs_help2 budat.
    MODIFY imatdocs.
    ENDLOOP.
ENDIF.
```

Here are some comments on the optimized program:

1. The required data is read from the table MSEG. The *SELECT* *
    clause has been replaced with a SELECT LIST, and the
    SELECT ... ENDSELECT construction has been replaced with
    a SELECT ... INTO TABLE ....

2. The statement IF sy subrc = 0 checks whether records
    have been read from the database. In the following steps, the
    internal table IMATDOCS_HELP1 is filled. To avoid double
    accesses to the table MKPF, the table IMATDOCS is sorted by
    the command SORT imatdocs, and the duplicate entries in
    MBLNR and MJAHR are deleted by the command DELETE
    ADJACENT DUPLICATES.

3. Finally, the data that was read from the table MSEG and is now
    stored in the table IMATDOCS, and the data that was read
    from table MKPF and is now stored in the table IMATDOCS_
    HELP2, are combined and transferred to the ABAP program. To
    optimize the search in the internal table IMATDOCS_HELP2,

it is important to sort the table and to include a BINARY SEARCH in the READ TABLE statement.

Verifying the Effectiveness of the Changes

After performing these changes, repeat the SQL trace to verify an improvement in performance. Now, the SQL trace results look as shown in Table 9.7.

TABLE 9.7: Excerpt from an SQL Trace for the ABAP Program Listed Above

Duration in Microseconds	Object	Oper	Rec	RC
1,417	MSEG	PREPARE		0
65	MSEG	OPEN		0
57,628	MSEG	FETCH	112	1403
6,871	MKPF	PREPARE		0
693	MKPF	OPEN		0
177,983	MKPF	FETCH	40	1403

You can observe the following access improvements as compared with the previous version of the program:

- Using SELECT LIST to access the table MSEG now allows all 112 records to be transferred in a single FETCH operation. Using *SELECT* * enabled only 32 records per FETCH operation. The time for the MSEG access is reduced from 197,638 microseconds to 57,628 microseconds.

- By avoiding identical accesses to table MKPF and using the SELECT LIST and the FOR ALL ENTRIES clauses, you have reduced the MKPF access from 319,040 microseconds to 177,983 microseconds.

In summary, the database access time is reduced by half.

More about FOR ALL ENTRIES Clauses

The FOR ALL ENTRIES clause is used to convert many short SQL statements into a few longer SQL statements, especially for LOOP … ENDLOOP constructions or, as in the above example, for nested SELECT loops.

NOTE   The table in the FOR ALL ENTRIES clause is known as a *driver table*. The corresponding programming code is, for example, FOR ALL ENTRIES IN imatdocs_help1. Here the driver table is IMAT-DOCS_HELP1.

When the FOR ALL ENTRIES clause is used, the database interface creates, for example, a WHERE clause that translates the entries of the internal driver table (in this example, IMATDOCS_HELP1) into separate conditions, which are then combined with each other through a disjunct normal OR. In this example, the database interface creates the following SQL statement:

```
SELECT
    "MBLNR", "MJAHR", "BUDAT"
FROM
    "MKPF"
WHERE
    ( "MANDT" = :A0 AND "MBLNR" = :A1 AND "MJAHR" = :A2 )
    OR ( "MANDT" = :A3 AND "MBLNR" = :A4 AND "MJAHR" = :A5 )
    OR ( "MANDT" = :A6 AND "MBLNR" = :A7 AND "MJAHR" = :A8 )
    <n times>
    OR ( "MANDT" = :A117 AND "MBLNR" = :A118 AND "MJAHR" = :A119)
```

To calculate <n>, the R/3 work process takes the smaller of the following numbers:

- The number of entries in the internal driver table (here, IMATDOCS_HELP1)
- The R/3 profile parameter *rsdb/max_blocking_factor*

If the number of entries in the internal driver table is larger than *rsdb/max_blocking_factor*, the work process executes several similar SQL statements on the database to limit the length of the WHERE clause. The R/3 work process joins the partial results excluding duplications.

The execution plan for the above statement is as follows:

```
Execution Plan
SELECT STATEMENT
 CONCATENATION
   TABLE ACCESS BY INDEX ROWID MKPF
   INDEX UNIQUE SCAN MKPF_____0
   TABLE ACCESS BY INDEX ROWID MKPF
   INDEX UNIQUE SCAN MKPF_____0
   <n times>
   TABLE ACCESS BY INDEX ROWID MKPF
   INDEX UNIQUE SCAN MKPF_____0
```

When using the FOR ALL ENTRIES clause, observe the following prerequisites:

- The driver table (here, IMATDOCS) must not be empty: If the driver table is empty of data, the FOR ALL ENTRIES clause reads the entire database table. In the present example, the driver table contains the header information for the materials documents. If it is empty, line item data is not required, and the second, expensive SQL statement need not be executed. To avoid executing the second statement, cause the program to check that the driver table is empty by using the ABAP statement IF sy subrc = 0. This ensures that the SQL statement with the FOR ALL ENTRIES clause is processed only if the table IMATDOCS was previously filled.

- The driver table (here, IMATDOCS) must contain no duplicate entries: If the driver table contains duplicate entries, the corresponding data is obtained twice from the database. Therefore, there should be no duplicate entries in the driver table.

In the above code example, duplicate entries are avoided by sorting the driver table and then deleting the duplicates.

NOTE   Depending on the database system, the database interface translates a FOR ALL ENTRIES clause into various SQL statements. In the present example, the database interface uses the FOR ALL ENTRIES clause to generate equivalent conditions based on OR. Alternatively, the database interface can also translate the clause into SQL statements using an IN or a UNION operator. This is controlled through R/3 profile parameters whose settings should not be changed without explicit instruction from SAP.

Solution 2

The second way of optimizing the program requires you to create a database view on the tables MSEG and MKPF. In this example, this would be the view Z_MSEG_MKPF with the following properties:

- Tables: MKPF and MSEG
- Join conditions:
    - MSEG MANDT = MKPF MANDT
    - MSEG MBLNR = MKPF MBLNR
    - MSEG MJAHR = MKPF MJAHR
- View fields:
    - MSEG MANDT
    - MSEG MBLNR
    - MSEG MJAHR
    - MSEG ZEILE
    - MSEG WERKS
    - MKPF BUDAT
    - MSEG MATNR

NOTE
To create a database view, use ABAP Dictionary Maintenance (Transaction *SE11*).

With this view, the ABAP program can be formulated as follows:

```
SELECT mblnr mjahr zeile matnr werks budat FROM z_mseg_mkpf
   INTO TABLE imatdocs
   WHERE matnr LIKE s_matnr.
```

The SQL trace then displays the information shown in Table 9.8.

TABLE 9.8: Excerpt from an SQL Trace for the ABAP Program Listed Above

Duration in Microseconds	Object	Oper	Rec	RC
1,176	Z_MSEG_MKP	REOPEN		0
149,707	Z_MSEG_MKP	FETCH	112	1403

In comparison with the optimized version in Solution 1 above, the database time has again been reduced by half!

The execution plan is as follows:

```
Execution Plan
SELECT STATEMENT
 NESTED LOOP
   TABLE ACCESS BY INDEX ROWID MSEG
     INDEX RANGE SCAN MSEG~M
   TABLE ACCESS BY INDEX ROWID MKPF
     INDEX UNIQUE SCAN MKPF~0
```

Checking for identical accesses and joining data in the ABAP program is no longer necessary.

The comparison of the two solutions—the first with the FOR ALL ENTRIES clause and the second with the database view—presents a clear argument in favor of converting nested SELECT loops into database views. However, using a database view means that, in addition to selecting the right indexes, the database optimizer must make correct choices on the following issues:

- The sequence of accessing the tables: In the present example, the optimizer should decide to read first the table MSEG and then table MKPF.

- The type of table join: In the present example, the optimizer should decide on a nested loop join to join the data from both tables. The available join methods vary according to the database system (see the manufacturer's documentation).

You should monitor the performance associated with using a view. During the corresponding join operation, partial sort operations occur on the database, during which performance problems may occur. If the database has problems choosing the appropriate execution plan for the SQL statement that accesses the view, it may be wiser to explicitly program the table accessing sequence and the joining of the data in the ABAP program.

Summary and Related Tuning Measures

The options available for optimizing execution performance for SQL statements include creating or changing indexes, creating table access statistics, and optimizing ABAP code. Figure 9.3 shows a procedure roadmap covering these optimization techniques.

In addition to these techniques, it can be helpful to investigate the users' ways of using programs associated with expensive SQL statements. Users may not be aware that they are contributing to the long runtime of an SQL statement by not using appropriate

FIGURE 9.3: Procedure roadmap for optimizing expensive SQL statements

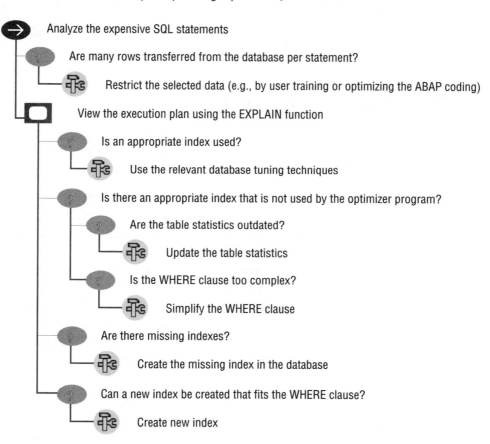

limiting conditions when searching the database. For example, users should:

- Limit the kind of selection data they enter in R/3 screens so that few records must be read.

- Use matchcodes when searching for business data.

- Use SAP's information systems (EIS, VIS, LIS, and so on) instead of writing one-off programs to obtain ad hoc reports.

The following sections explain additional tuning measures that you can use when you cannot further reduce the volume of data records transferred by an SQL statement and are sure that the optimal index is being used.

Reorganizing Indexes

If an SQL statement is expensive even when there is an appropriate index and the ABAP code is optimal, check whether the cause of the database time is index fragmentation.

To understand fragmentation, consider the example of an index containing a million records. If 99% of these records is deleted in the corresponding table and therefore in the index, in some databases, the blocks or pages that were occupied by the deleted records are not released, nor are the remaining valid entries automatically grouped together. Not only is the major part of the index now not serving any purpose, but the valid data is distributed across a large number of blocks. Therefore, an index range scan must read a large number of index blocks to return comparatively few data records. This condition is called *fragmentation*.

To defragment the index, reorganize the index by deleting and re-creating it. An example of an index that typically may need reorganizing is the index *RESB__M* (see R/3 Note 70513). The related table, RESB, contains the material reservations in production planning, and therefore undergoes extremely frequent changes.

| NOTE | Index fragmentation does not occur in all database systems. To find out if fragmentation affects your database system, consult the manufacturer's documentation. |

Bitmap Indexes

The indexes normally set up by the R/3 System are B* tree indexes. Some database systems also offer other types of indexes—for example, bitmap indexes. These other types of indexes were previously little used in the R/3 environment, but also provide a database-specific way of optimizing SQL statements. They are particularly significant in data warehouse applications like SAP's Business Information Warehouse.

Incorrect Buffer Settings

Expensive SQL statements may also be due to incorrect settings for R/3 buffering. The settings are incorrect if, for example, they make the buffer too small or perform buffering for tables that should not be buffered because they are too large or too often changed.

Examine the tables accessed by the expensive SQL statements in the Shared SQL Area Monitor (within Transaction *ST04*) or in the SQL trace (Transaction *ST05*).

If the tables accessed are the kinds of tables in Table 9.9, an incorrect buffer setting may be indicated. SQL statements that access these tables do not originate directly from an ABAP program, but are triggered on behalf of an ABAP program by the R/3 Basis to obtain background information—for example, load ABAP programs, ABAP Dictionary objects, or buffered tables.

For more information on buffering settings, see Chapter 2 and Chapter 7.

TABLE 9.9: R/3 Buffers and Related R/3 Basis Tables

R/3 Buffer	Related R/3 Basis Table
Table definitions (TTAB)	DDNTT
Field definitions (FTAB)	DDNTF
Program (PXA)	D010*
Screen	D020*
Table buffer	ATAB, KAPOL

The following SQL statement is an example of an SQL statement from the R/3 Basis that reads the table D010S to load an ABAP program into the program buffer:

```
SELECT
    "BLOCKLG", "BLOCK"
    FROM to second E in select
    "D010S"
    WHERE to second E in select
 "PROG" = :A0 AND "R3STATE" = :A1 AND "R3MODE" = :A2 AND "R3VERSION"
 = :A3 AND "BLOCKNR" = 1
```

DB Administration Tools

The Shared SQL Area Monitor (within Transaction *ST04*) may indicate expensive SQL statements (with many buffer gets) that do not originate from an R/3 application transaction, but from database monitoring programs such as:

- The analysis program RSORATDB
- The auxiliary program SAPDBA (for example, with the SAPDBA options -next, -check, -analyze)
- Non-SAP database monitoring tools

To avoid disrupting production operation, these programs should be run only during times of low workload. For example, the default setting for running RSORATDB causes it to run at 7 A.M. and 7 P.M. as a part of the background job SAP_COLLECTOR_FOR_PERFORMANCE.

You can identify SQL statements that are used for monitoring the database through table names such as DBA_SEGMENTS, DBA_INDEXES, and USER_INDEXES (for Oracle); or SYSTABLES and SYSFRAGMENTS (for Informix).

To find out if an SQL statement belongs to the R/3 System or to one of these database administration and monitoring tools, check whether the corresponding table exists in the ABAP Dictionary using Transaction *SE11*. If the table is not listed, the SQL statement is from a database administration and monitoring tool.

The following is an example of an SQL statement that is executed by SAP's administration and monitoring tool SAPDBA for Oracle:

```
SELECT OWNER,SEGMENT_NAME, SEGMENT_TYPE, NEXT_EXTENT/:b1,
PCT_INCREASE
FROM SYS.DBA_SEGMENTS
WHERE TABLESPACE_NAME=:b2 AND SEGMENT_TYPE = 'TABLE' OR SEGMENT_TYPE
= 'INDEX' OR SEGMENT_TYPE = 'CLUSTER') AND NEXT_EXTENT/:b1 * DECODE
(PCT_INCREASE,0,:b4, ((POWER(1+PCT_INCREASE/100, :b4), 1) /
(PCT_INCREASE/100))) > :b6
```

If administration programs like this cause expensive statements in a production system as indicated in the Shared SQL Area Monitor (within Transaction *ST04*) and are executed during times of high workload, they should be run infrequently.

Important Concepts in This Chapter

After reading this chapter, you should be familiar with the following concepts:

- Logical and physical read accesses (buffer gets, disk reads)
- Primary and secondary indexes
- Selectivity
- Database optimizer and execution plan
- Table access statistics

Review Questions

1. Which of the following statements are correct with regard to expensive SQL statements?

   A. They can lead to hardware bottlenecks (a CPU or I/O bottleneck) and negatively affect the runtime of other SQL statements.

   B. They can occupy a lot of space in the data buffer of the database, displace objects that are needed by other SQL statements, and negatively affect the runtime of other SQL statements.

   C. They can occupy a lot of space in the R/3 table buffer and displace objects, which causes unnecessary reload operations.

   D. If they are performed after database locks were set by the same program, this can cause exclusive lock wait situations in the database, which can cause a brief system standstill.

    E. Expensive SQL statements in programs for reporting or in background programs are not normally a problem for the database.

2. In the results of an SQL trace, you find an SQL statement that has a runtime of 1 second and selects only 10 records. Which of the following could be the reason for the long runtime?

    A. There is a hardware bottleneck (a CPU or I/O bottleneck) on the database server.

    B. There is a network problem between the application server and the database server.

    C. The database optimizer has created an inefficient execution plan—for example, by choosing an inefficient index.

    D. There is no appropriate index for the SQL statement.

    E. There are exclusive lock waits in the database.

3. In the Shared SQL Area Monitor, you find an SQL statement with 10,000 logical read accesses per execution (indicated as *Gets/Execution*). Which of the following could be the reason for this high number of read accesses?

    A. There is a hardware bottleneck (a CPU or I/O bottleneck) on the database server.

    B. There is a network problem between the application server and the database server.

    C. The database optimizer has decided in favor of an inefficient index, or there is no appropriate index for the SQL statement.

    D. There are exclusive lock waits in the database.

    E. A large number of records is being transferred from the database to the ABAP program.

APPENDIX

A

Performance Analysis Roadmaps and Checklists

Appendix A contains the most important procedure roadmaps and checklists for performance analysis. The prerequisites for performing an analysis are as follows:

- That the R/3 System starts without error
- That there are still sufficient work processes available to run the performance analysis, or, alternatively, that you can call the SAP auxiliary program *dpmon*

The program *dpmon* is called on the operating-system level and enables you to access basically the same information as that found in the Work Process Overview.

Roadmaps

The procedure roadmaps in this section explain how to proceed in the most important performance monitors.

You can access the six monitors mentioned in the roadmaps as follows:

1. To access the Workload Monitor, use Transaction *ST03*, or, from the R/3 initial screen, choose *Tools* ➣ *Administration* ➣ *Monitor* ➣ *Performance* ➣ *Workload* ➣ *Analysis.* Then choose one of the following:

   - *This application server* ➣ *Last minute load.* Select *15 min* and choose *Enter.*

   - *Performance database.* Select *Total* and choose *Enter.* In the following dialog boxes, select the desired time frame.

   - *Single statistics records* ➣ *This application server.* In the following dialog box, you can limit the statistics using the criteria offered.

2. To access the Work Process Overview, call either:

- *Local Work Process Overview*, using Transaction *SM50*, or, from the R/3 initial screen, choose *Tools* ➤ *Administration* ➤ *Monitor* ➤ *System monitoring* ➤ *Process overview*.

- *Systemwide Work Process Overview*, using Transaction *SM66*, or, from the R/3 initial screen, choose *Tools* ➤ *Administration* ➤ *Monitor* ➤ *Performance* ➤ *Exceptions/Users* ➤ *Active users* ➤ *All processes*.

Repeatedly update the display in either Work Process Overview using the *Refresh* button.

3. To access the Operating System Monitor (for example, to check hardware), use Transaction *ST06*, or, from the R/3 initial screen, choose *Tools* ➤ *Administration* ➤ *Monitor* ➤ *Performance* ➤ *Operating system* ➤ *Local* ➤ *Activity*. Then choose one of the following:

- *Detail analysis menu* ➤ *CPU* (under the header *Previous hours*)

- *Detail analysis menu* ➤ *Memory* (under the header *Previous hours*)

- *Detail analysis menu* ➤ *Top CPU processes*

4. To access the Memory Configuration Monitor, use Transaction *ST02*, or, from the R/3 initial screen, choose *Tools* ➤ *Administration* ➤ *Monitor* ➤ *Performance* ➤ *Setup/Buffers* ➤ *Buffers*. To access the mode list, next choose *Detail analysis menu* ➤ *SAP memory* ➤ *Mode list*. Alternatively, for an overview of allocated memory, choose *Detail analysis menu* ➤ *Storage*.

5. To access R/3 Table Access Statistics, use Transaction *ST10*, or, from the R/3 initial screen, choose *Tools* ➤ *Administration* ➤ *Monitor* ➤ *Performance* ➤ *Setup/Buffers* ➤ *Calls*. Make the appropriate selections and choose *Enter*.

6. To start, stop, or display an SQL trace, use Transaction *ST05*, or, from the R/3 initial screen, choose *System* ➤ *Utilities* ➤ *SQL Trace*.

NOTE   Appendix B, "Database Monitors, Buffers, and SQL Execution Plans," contains a list of the menu paths for the performance monitors in the different database systems.

The following key explains the icons that appear in the procedure roadmaps (see Figures A.1 through A.9):

- Rectangular monitor icon: This tells you to start a particular performance monitor.

- Question mark icon: This indicates that you are at a decision point. If you can answer the question beside this icon with *Yes*, you may proceed as described in the following line of the roadmap.

- Exclamation mark icon: This indicates the intermediate status of the analysis. Proceed to the next point on the roadmap.

- Horizontal arrow icon: This indicates another procedure roadmap. Continue the analysis in the roadmap indicated.

- Tools icon: This indicates possible solutions for performance problems. (See also the checklists for performance analysis in the next section.)

FIGURE A.1: Workload analysis I: General performance problems

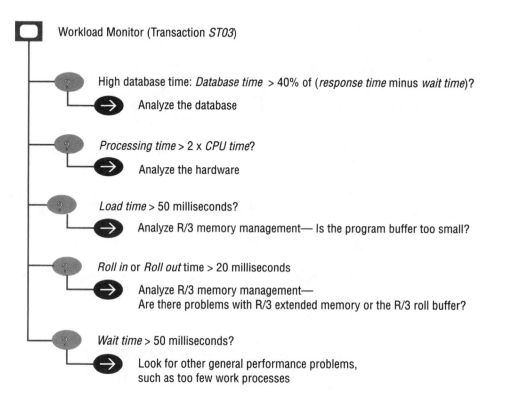

Workload Monitor (Transaction *ST03*)

High database time: *Database time* > 40% of (*response time* minus *wait time*)?
→ Analyze the database

Processing time > 2 x *CPU time*?
→ Analyze the hardware

Load time > 50 milliseconds?
→ Analyze R/3 memory management— Is the program buffer too small?

Roll in or *Roll out* time > 20 milliseconds
→ Analyze R/3 memory management—
Are there problems with R/3 extended memory or the R/3 roll buffer?

Wait time > 50 milliseconds?
→ Look for other general performance problems,
such as too few work processes

FIGURE A.2: Workload analysis II: Specific performance problems

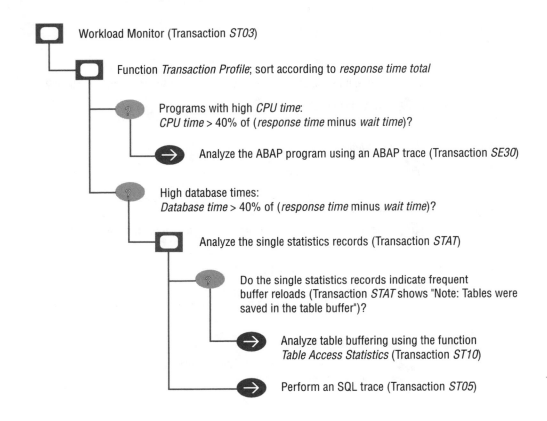

Workload Monitor (Transaction *ST03*)

Function *Transaction Profile*; sort according to *response time total*

Programs with high *CPU time*:
CPU time > 40% of (*response time* minus *wait time*)?

Analyze the ABAP program using an ABAP trace (Transaction *SE30*)

High database times:
Database time > 40% of (*response time* minus *wait time*)?

Analyze the single statistics records (Transaction *STAT*)

Do the single statistics records indicate frequent buffer reloads (Transaction *STAT* shows "Note: Tables were saved in the table buffer")?

Analyze table buffering using the function *Table Access Statistics* (Transaction *ST10*)

Perform an SQL trace (Transaction *ST05*)

FIGURE A.3: Detailed analysis of R/3 work processes I: Database problems

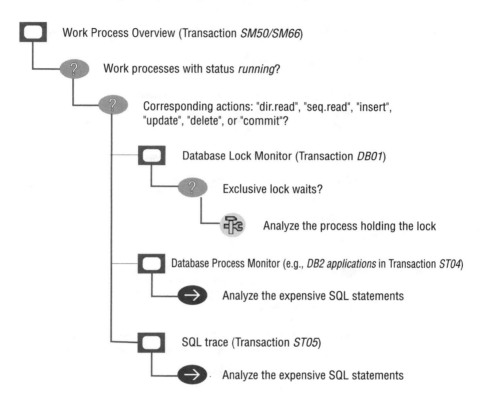

FIGURE A.4: Detailed analysis of R/3 work processes II: Problems on the application servers

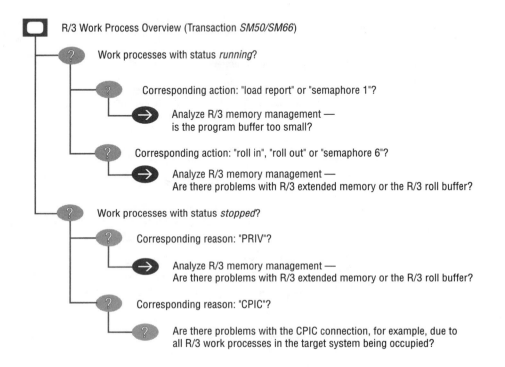

R/3 Work Process Overview (Transaction *SM50/SM66*)

Work processes with status *running*?

Corresponding action: "load report" or "semaphore 1"?

Analyze R/3 memory management — is the program buffer too small?

Corresponding action: "roll in", "roll out" or "semaphore 6"?

Analyze R/3 memory management — Are there problems with R/3 extended memory or the R/3 roll buffer?

Work processes with status *stopped*?

Corresponding reason: "PRIV"?

Analyze R/3 memory management — Are there problems with R/3 extended memory or the R/3 roll buffer?

Corresponding reason: "CPIC"?

Are there problems with the CPIC connection, for example, due to all R/3 work processes in the target system being occupied?

FIGURE A.5: Detailed analysis of a hardware bottleneck I: CPU

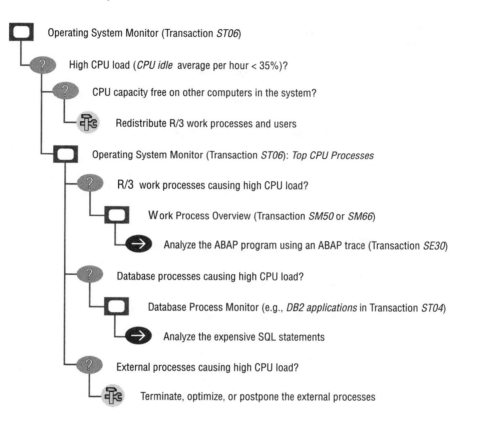

FIGURE A.6: Detailed analysis of a hardware bottleneck II: Main memory

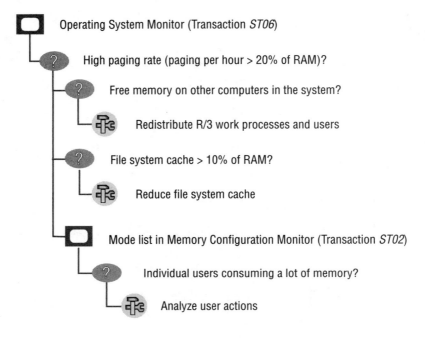

Operating System Monitor (Transaction *ST06*)

High paging rate (paging per hour > 20% of RAM)?

Free memory on other computers in the system?

Redistribute R/3 work processes and users

File system cache > 10% of RAM?

Reduce file system cache

Mode list in Memory Configuration Monitor (Transaction *ST02*)

Individual users consuming a lot of memory?

Analyze user actions

FIGURE A.7: Detailed analysis of R/3 memory configuration

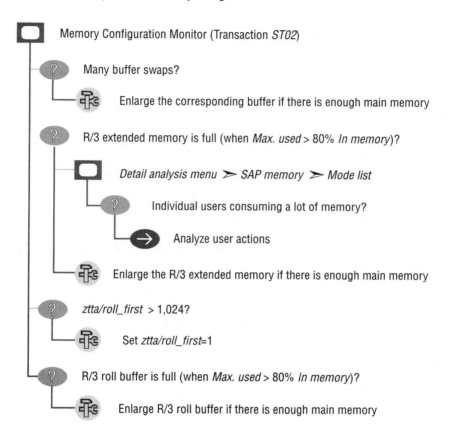

Memory Configuration Monitor (Transaction *ST02*)

? Many buffer swaps?

  Enlarge the corresponding buffer if there is enough main memory

? R/3 extended memory is full (when *Max. used* > 80% *In memory*)?

  Detail analysis menu ➤ *SAP memory* ➤ *Mode list*

   ? Individual users consuming a lot of memory?

   → Analyze user actions

  Enlarge the R/3 extended memory if there is enough main memory

? *ztta/roll_first* > 1,024?

  Set *ztta/roll_first*=1

? R/3 roll buffer is full (when *Max. used* > 80% *In memory*)?

  Enlarge R/3 roll buffer if there is enough main memory

FIGURE A.8: Optimization of table buffering

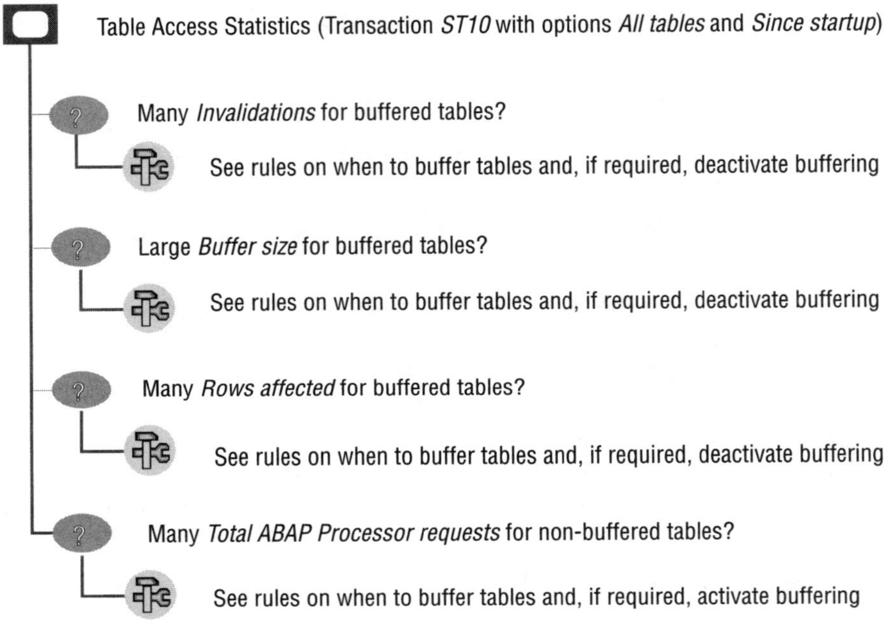

Table Access Statistics (Transaction *ST10* with options *All tables* and *Since startup*)

Many *Invalidations* for buffered tables?

See rules on when to buffer tables and, if required, deactivate buffering

Large *Buffer size* for buffered tables?

See rules on when to buffer tables and, if required, deactivate buffering

Many *Rows affected* for buffered tables?

See rules on when to buffer tables and, if required, deactivate buffering

Many *Total ABAP Processor requests* for non-buffered tables?

See rules on when to buffer tables and, if required, activate buffering

FIGURE A.9: Optimization of expensive SQL statements

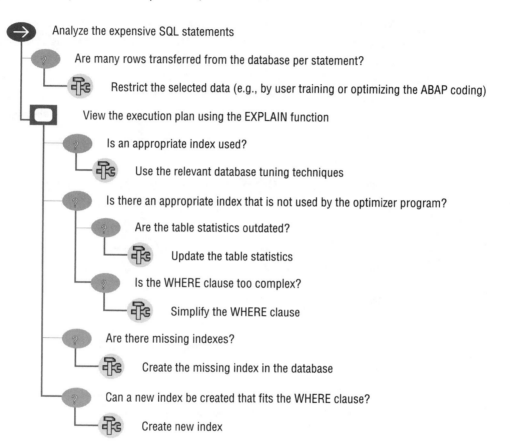

Analyze the expensive SQL statements

Are many rows transferred from the database per statement?

Restrict the selected data (e.g., by user training or optimizing the ABAP coding)

View the execution plan using the EXPLAIN function

Is an appropriate index used?

Use the relevant database tuning techniques

Is there an appropriate index that is not used by the optimizer program?

Are the table statistics outdated?

Update the table statistics

Is the WHERE clause too complex?

Simplify the WHERE clause

Are there missing indexes?

Create the missing index in the database

Can a new index be created that fits the WHERE clause?

Create new index

Checklists

This section contains problem checklists—that is, short summaries for individual problems that are frequently identified in performance analysis. Each checklist provides:

- The priority of solving the problem
- Indications and procedures for finding and analyzing the problem
- Applicable solutions
- A reference to the parts of this book that are relevant to the problem and essential reading prior to attempting to solve the problem

---

WARNING   When using the checklists, do not perform any changes in your system without referring to the detailed information and warnings in the indicated sections of this book.

The following priorities are suggested in the checklists:

- *Very high priority* is reserved for when there is a danger that performance will soon cause system standstill and there are no longer sufficient free work processes available to analyze or solve the problem.

- *High priority* is for problems that are likely to drastically reduce systemwide performance.

- *Medium priority* is for problems that are likely to drastically reduce the performance of individual programs or application servers. Do not underestimate the impact of these problems on critical business processes or the possibility of the problem escalating.

- *Low priority* performance problems are not listed in the checklists.

Detailed Analysis of Hardware Resources

This section contains the problem checklists for the following problems: CPU bottlenecks and main memory bottlenecks.

Problem: CPU Bottleneck

Priority	Medium to high: This problem can cause high response times on specific computers.
Indications and procedures	A computer has less than 20% CPU capacity available. Check this using the *Top CPU processes* function in the Operating System Monitor. To access this function, use Transaction *ST06* and choose *Detail analysis menu* ➤ *Top CPU processes*. The screen that appears shows individual processes that occupy considerable CPU over long periods of time.
Solution	• If there is still free CPU capacity on other computers, redistribute the R/3 work processes and, if necessary, configure new settings for R/3 memory, R/3 buffers, and user distribution.
	• If there are individual R/3 work processes with high CPU load:
	– Use the Work Process Overview (Transaction *SM50* or *SM66*) to identify the R/3 work process, the program, and the user.
	– Optimize the program or reschedule it.
	• If there are individual database processes causing a high CPU load:
	– Identify the database processes in the Database Process Monitor (*ST04* ➤ *Detailed analysis menu* ➤ *Oracle Session* [for example]).
	– Optimize the corresponding SQL statement.
	• For external processes with high CPU utilization: Optimize or terminate them.
	• If tuning options are exhausted, increase the CPU capacity.
See	• Chapter 2, under "Monitoring Hardware."
	• Chapter 6.

Problem: Main Memory Bottleneck

Priority	Medium to high: This problem can lead to high response times on specific computers.
Indications and procedures	• A computer displays high paging rates.
	• Calculate the main memory allocated by R/3 instances and the database, and compare it with the physically available main memory on the individual computers. If the allocated memory exceeds the physically available main memory by more than 50%, and there are high paging rates, you have a main memory bottleneck.
	• Call the Memory Configuration Monitor (Transaction *ST02*) and choose *Detail analysis menu* ➢ *SAP memory* ➢ *Mode list*. This displays the mode list, which tells you which users have the highest memory consumption.
Solution	• If there is still free main memory capacity on other computers, redistribute the R/3 work processes and, if necessary, configure new settings for R/3 memory, R/3 buffers, and user distribution.
	• If there are individual users with high memory consumption, identify the user's program and either optimize this program or reschedule it.
	• If tuning options are exhausted, increase the CPU capacity.
See	Chapter 2, under "Monitoring Hardware."

Detailed Analysis of R/3 Work Processes

This section contains the problem checklists for the following problems:

- Terminated work processes
- Work processes apparently stuck in private mode or in roll in or roll out
- A deactivated update service
- High database response times or long runtimes for individual programs

- Nonoptimal load distribution
- Insufficient work processes

Problem: Terminated Work Processes

Priority	High to very high.
Indications and procedures	In the Local Work Process Overview (Transaction *SM50*), if you detect numerous terminated work processes (indicated as *complete* in the column *Status*) and find that you cannot restart them, it is likely that there is a problem with the R/3 kernel or with logging on to the database.
Solution	Check whether the R/3 Kernel version is up to date by calling Transaction *SM51* and choosing *Release Info*. If necessary, install a current R/3 Kernel version. Refer to the Online Service System (OSS) for relevant R/3 Notes or contact SAP Support.
See	Chapter 2, under "Monitoring R/3 Work Processes."

Problem: Work Processes Stuck in Private Mode or in Roll In or Roll Out

Priority	Medium to high: This problem can lead to high response times on specific computers.
Indications and procedures	More than 20% of the work processes are indicated in the Work Process Overview (Transaction *SM50* or *SM66*) as being in mode PRIV or in roll in or roll out. The problem is in R/3 memory management.
Solution	Correctly set the parameters of R/3 memory management—for example, *em/initial_size_MB*, *rdisp/ROLL_SHM*, and *ztta/roll_extension*.
See	Chapter 2, under "Monitoring R/3 Work Processes" and "Monitoring R/3 Memory Management." See also the checklist for *R/3 Extended Memory is Too Small*.

Problem: Deactivated Update Service

Priority	Very high: This problem can lead to standstill in the R/3 System.
Indications and procedures	All update work processes (indicated as UPD in the Work Process Overview) are occupied. Transaction *SM13* indicates that the update has been deactivated.
Solution	Call R/3's system log (Transaction *SM21*) and check whether the update service has been deactivated. The system log contains an entry for the time, the user, and the reason for the deactivation. Resolve the reported problem— for example, a database error. Then reactivate the update service with Transaction *SM13*.
See	Chapter 2, under "Monitoring R/3 Work Processes" and "Monitoring the Database."

Problem: High Database Response Times

Priority	Medium to very high.
Indications and procedures	The column *Action* in the Work Process Overview (Transaction *SM50* or *SM66*) indicates *Sequential read*, *Direct read*, *Waiting for DB lock*, or other database activities for numerous work processes.
Solution	The problem is related to the database. Therefore, rather than increasing the number of R/3 work processes, examine the database more closely. (See below, under "Detailed Analysis of the Database.")
See	Chapter 2, under "Monitoring R/3 Work Processes" and "Monitoring the Database."

Problem: Long Runtimes for Individual Programs

Priority	Medium.
Indications and procedures	Work processes are blocked by programs with long runtimes. This is indicated in the Work Process Overview (Transaction *SM50* or *SM66*).
Solution	Determine whether the related R/3 program is still running properly. Analyze the affected programs and optimize or terminate them as appropriate.
See	• Chapter 2, under "Monitoring R/3 Work Processes." • Chapter 4.

Problem: Nonoptimal Load Distribution

Priority	Medium: This problem can lead to high response times on specific computers.
Indications and procedures	In a distributed system with multiple computers, you detect a work process bottleneck on at least one computer while other computers still have free work processes.
Solution	Call Transaction *SMLG* and check whether all the servers are available for load distribution with logon groups, or whether logon errors have been reported. Use Transaction *SMLG* to optimize the logon groups.
See	• Chapter 2, under "Monitoring R/3 Work Processes." • Chapter 6.

Problem: Insufficient Work Processes

Priority	Medium: This problem can lead to high response times on specific computers.
Indications and procedures	None of the previously listed problems apply, but there is still a problem with work processes.
Solution	If the computer has sufficient reserves of CPU and main memory, increase the number of R/3 work processes.
See	• Chapter 2, under "Monitoring R/3 Work Processes."
	• Chapter 6.

Detailed Analysis of the Database

This section contains the problem checklists for problems related to the database.

Problem: Long Database Locks

Priority	Medium to very high: This problem can lead to a standstill in the R/3 System.
Indications and procedures	• Call the Database Lock Monitor with Transaction *DB01*. Refresh this monitor several times within a short time frame and check whether long-lasting wait situations occur because of database locks.
	• In the Work Process Overview (Transaction *SM50* or *SM66*), use the fields *Client host* and *Client PID* to determine the programs and users holding the locks. Check whether the programs are still running properly.
Solution	Terminate a program or a process manually if required, after consulting the affected users.
See	• Chapter 2, under "Monitoring the Database."
	• Chapter 8.

Problem: CPU Bottleneck on the Database Server

Priority	High: This problem can lead to high database response times.
Indications and procedures	Call the Operating System Monitor (Transaction *ST06*) on the database server and see whether it shows a CPU bottleneck.
Solution	Check whether the CPU bottleneck originates from expensive SQL statements, incorrectly set database buffers, or an I/O bottleneck. You may need to reduce the load on the database server or increase its CPU capacity.
See	• Chapter 2, under "Monitoring the Database" and "Monitoring Hardware." • Chapter 6.

Problem: Number of Logical Processors for the Database Instance

Priority	High: This problem can lead to high database response times.
Indications and procedures	There is usually a profile parameter that specifies the maximum number of processors that are physically available to the database instance. Such parameters include MAXCPU (for ADABAS D) and NUMCPUVPS (for Informix). Check whether this parameter is optimally configured.
Solution	If necessary, adjust this parameter.
See	• Chapter 2, under "Monitoring the Database." • Chapter 6.

Problem: Database Buffer Too Small

Priority	Medium to high: This problem can lead to high database response times.
Indications and procedures	Call the Database Performance Monitor (Transaction *ST04*) and check whether the buffer quality and other key figures match the recommended values.
Solution	Increase the size of the respective buffer once by 25% and check whether the quality improves.
See	Chapter 2, under "Monitoring the Database."

Problem: Expensive SQL Statements

Priority	Medium to high: This problem can lead to high database response times.
Indications and procedures	In the Database Process Monitor, check whether there are any expensive SQL statements—that is, statements with either:

- *Disk reads* that amount to more than 5% of the total *physical reads*.

- *Buffer gets* that amount to more than 5% of the total *reads*.

To access the Database Process Monitor, call the Database Performance Monitor (Transaction *ST04*). Then:

- For Oracle, choose *Detail analysis menu* ➢ *SQL request*.

- For Informix, choose *Detail analysis menu* ➢ *SQL statement*.

See	- Chapter 2, under "Monitoring the Database."

- Chapter 9.

- For other database examples, see Appendix B.

Problem: Database I/O Bottleneck

Priority	Medium to high: This problem can lead to high database response times.
Indications and procedures	- Call the Database Performance Monitor (Transaction *ST04*). Then:

- For Oracle, choose *Detail analysis menu* ➢ *File system requests*.

- For Informix, choose *Detail analysis menu* ➢ *Chunk I/O Activity*.

- Call the Operating System Monitor for the database server (Transaction *ST06*). Choose *Detail analysis menu* ➢ *Disk* (under the header *Snapshot analysis*). If the value in the column *Util* is greater than 50%, this indicates an I/O bottleneck. Check whether data files that are heavily written to reside on these disks.

Solution	Resolve the read/write (I/O) bottleneck by improving table distribution in the file system. Ensure that heavily accessed files do not reside on the same disk. These include the files for the swap space, the redo log, and the transaction log.
See	Chapter 2, under "Monitoring the Database" and "Monitoring Hardware."

Problem: Statistics for the Database Optimizer Are Obsolete or Not Available

Priority	Medium to high: This problem can lead to high database response times.
Indications and procedures	To check whether optimizer statistics are created regularly, call the DBA Planning Calendar. To do this, from the R/3 initial screen, choose *Tools* ➤ *CCMS* ➤ *DB administration* ➤ *DB scheduling*.
Solution	Schedule the program for updating statistics.
See	• Chapter 2, under "Monitoring the Database."
	• Chapter 8.
	• R/3 Online Documentation for topics in Database Administration.

Problem: Missing Database Indexes

Priority	• Very high, if a primary index is missing: This can cause data inconsistencies.
	• Medium, if a secondary index is missing: This can cause high response times for individual programs.
Indications and procedures	Check whether there are any missing database indexes by calling the monitor for analyzing tables and indexes (Transaction *DB02*) and choosing *Detail analysis menu* ➤ *State on disk: Missing indices*.
Solution	Re-create the missing indexes.
See	• Chapter 2, under "Monitoring the Database."
	• Chapter 8.

Problem: Large Differences in Database Times Caused by Buffer Load Process

Priority	Medium: This problem can lead to high response times for specific programs.
Indications and procedures	To view occasional, long database accesses to buffered tables, use one of the following: • The Local Work Process Overview (Transaction *SM50*). • An SQL trace (Transaction *ST05*). • The single statistics records (Transaction *STAT*).
Solution	Call table access statistics and verify the efficiency of table buffering.
See	Chapter 7.

Problem: Network Problems

Priority	Medium to high: This problem can cause high response times on specific computers.
Indications and procedures	Determine whether there is a network problem between the database server and the application server by comparing SQL trace results on these two servers.
Solution	Resolve the network problem between the two servers. A detailed analysis of network problems is not possible from within the R/3 System, so use network-specific tools.
See	• Chapter 2, under "Monitoring the Database." • Chapter 4, under "SQL Trace."

Detailed Analysis of R/3 Memory Management and the R/3 Buffers

This section contains the problem checklists for the following problems: R/3 extended memory that is too small and displacements in the R/3 buffers.

Problem: R/3 Extended Memory Is Too Small

Priority	High.
Indications and procedures	To determine whether either the R/3 extended memory or the R/3 roll buffer is too small, use the R/3 Memory Configuration Monitor (Transaction *ST02*). See also the checklist entitled *Work Processes Stuck in Private Mode or in Roll In or Roll Out*.
Solution	Correct R/3 memory configuration parameters such as *em/initial_size_MB*, *rdisp/ROLL_SHM*, and *ztta/roll_extension*. If you have sufficient main memory on the server, you can increase the memory size by 20% to 50%. Check whether this improves the situation.
See	• Chapter 2, under "Analyzing R/3 Memory Configuration." • Chapter 5.

Problem: Displacements in R/3 Buffers

Priority	Medium.
Indications and procedures	Look for displacements in the R/3 buffers in the column *Swaps* in the R/3 Memory Configuration Monitor (Transaction *ST02*). Displacements mean that the buffers are configured too small.
Solution	Increase the maximum number of buffer entries or increase the size of the respective buffer provided that the computer still has sufficient main memory reserves.
See	Chapter 2, under "Analyzing R/3 Memory Configuration."

Database Monitors, Buffers, and SQL Execution Plans

Currently, the R/3 System can be implemented with seven different relational database management systems, each with its own architecture. However, the R/3 System has database monitors that cover basic database functioning irrespective of the database system.

Database Process Monitor

The Database Process Monitor (see Table B.1) displays the currently active database processes, which are called *agents*, *shadow processes*, or *threads*, depending on the database system. The monitor displays the SQL statements that are being processed, and can indicate the R/3 work process to which a database process is allocated.

NOTE   Use the Database Process Monitor to identify currently running, expensive SQL statements. With the process ID (in the column *Clnt proc.*), you can find the corresponding R/3 work process, R/3 user, and ABAP program indicated in the Work Process Overview (Transaction *SM50*).

TABLE B.1: Menu Paths for Accessing the Database Process Monitor According to Database System

Database System	From the R/3 Initial Screen, Choose...
ADABAS D	*Tools* ➤ *Administration* ➤ *Monitor* ➤ *Performance* ➤ *Database* ➤ *Activity* ➤ *Detail analysis menu* ➤ *DB processes*
DB2/OS390	*Tools* ➤ *Administration* ➤ *Monitor* ➤ *Performance* ➤ *Database* ➤ *Activity* ➤ *Detail analysis menu* ➤ *Thread Activity*
DB2/Universal Database	*Tools* ➤ *Administration* ➤ *Monitor* ➤ *Performance* ➤ *Database* ➤ *Activity* ➤ *Detail analysis menu* ➤ *DB2 applications*

Continued on next page

TABLE B.1: Menu Paths for Accessing the Database Process Monitor According to Database System *(Continued)*

Database System	From the R/3 Initial Screen, Choose...
Informix	*Tools ➤ Administration ➤ Monitor ➤ Performance ➤ Database ➤ Activity ➤ Detail analysis menu ➤ Informix session*
Oracle	*Tools ➤ Administration ➤ Monitor ➤ Performance ➤ Database ➤ Activity ➤ Detail analysis menu ➤ Oracle session*
MS SQL Server	*Tools ➤ Administration ➤ Monitor ➤ Performance ➤ Database ➤ Activity ➤ Detail analysis menu ➤ SQL processes*

Shared SQL Area Monitor

For almost all database systems, you can monitor statistics for the previously executed SQL statements (see Table B.2). Monitoring these statistics is also known as monitoring the shared SQL area (which in some database systems is called the *Shared Cursor Cache* or *Shared SQL Cache*).

These statistics on the shared SQL area help you to analyze expensive SQL statements. They cover, for example, the number of executions of an SQL statement, the number of logical and physical read accesses per statement, the number of rows that were read, and the response times.

In some database systems, the system starts collecting these statistics when the database is started. For other database systems, statistics collection has to be activated explicitly.

NOTE Monitor the shared SQL area to identify and analyze expensive SQL statements that were executed previously.

TABLE B.2: Menu Paths for Accessing the R/3 Monitor for the Shared SQL Area According to Database System

Database System	From the R/3 Initial Screen, Choose...
ADABAS D	*Tools ➤ Administration ➤ Monitor ➤ Performance ➤ Database ➤ Activity ➤ Detail analysis menu ➤ Diagnoses monitor*
DB2/AS400	*Tools ➤ Administration ➤ Monitor ➤ Performance ➤ Database ➤ Activity ➤ Detail analysis menu ➤ SQL request*
	Tools ➤ Administration ➤ Monitor ➤ Performance ➤ Database ➤ Activity ➤ Detail analysis menu ➤ 50 slowest queries
DB2/OS390	*Tools ➤ Administration ➤ Monitor ➤ Performance ➤ Database ➤ Activity ➤ Detail analysis menu ➤ Stmt cache Statistics*
Informix	*Tools ➤ Administration ➤ Monitor ➤ Performance ➤ Database ➤ Activity ➤ Detail analysis menu ➤ SQL statement*
Oracle	*Tools ➤ Administration ➤ Monitor ➤ Performance ➤ Database ➤ Activity ➤ Detail analysis menu ➤ SQL request*
MS SQL Server	*Tools ➤ Administration ➤ Monitor ➤ Performance ➤ Database ➤ Activity ➤ Detail analysis menu ➤ Stored proc. stats*

Hard Disk Monitor

To ensure optimal database performance, the load on the hard disks should be spread as evenly or symmetrically as possible—that is, all disks should show roughly equal numbers of read and write accesses.

NOTE   When analyzing the distribution of I/O on the hard disk, use the Hard Disk Monitor (see Table B.3). This lets you identify files that are accessed especially frequently. These areas are sometimes called *hot spots*.

TABLE B.3: Menu Paths for Accessing the Hard Disk Monitor According to Database System

Database System	From the R/3 Initial Screen, Choose...
ADABAS D	*Tools* ➤ *Administration* ➤ *Monitor* ➤ *Performance* ➤ *Database* ➤ *Activity* ➤ *Detail analysis menu* ➤ *Runtime environment*
DB2/AS400	*Tools* ➤ *Administration* ➤ *Monitor* ➤ *Performance* ➤ *Database* ➤ *Activity* ➤ *Detail analysis menu* ➤ *File activity*
DB2/Universal Database	*Tools* ➤ *Administration* ➤ *Monitor* ➤ *Performance* ➤ *Database* ➤ *Activity* ➤ *Detail Analysis Menu* ➤ *Table activity*
	Tools ➤ *Administration* ➤ *Monitor* ➤ *Performance* ➤ *Database* ➤ *Activity* ➤ *Detail analysis menu* ➤ *Tablespaces*
Informix	*Tools* ➤ *Administration* ➤ *Monitor* ➤ *Performance* ➤ *Database* ➤ *Activity* ➤ *Detail analysis menu* ➤ *Chunk I/O Activity*
Oracle	*Tools* ➤ *Administration* ➤ *Monitor* ➤ *Performance* ➤ *Database* ➤ *Activity* ➤ *Detail analysis menu* ➤ *Filesystem request*

Database Lock Monitor

The R/3 System provides the Database Lock Monitor to help you identify exclusive lock wait situations on the database.

Use Transaction *DB01* to call this monitor for all database systems (except for DB2/AS400 and DB2/390), or, from the R/3 initial screen, choose:

> *Tools* ➤ *Administration* ➤ *Monitor* ➤ *Performance* ➤ *Database* ➤ *Activity* ➤ *Detail analysis menu* ➤ *Exclusive lockwaits*

or

> *Tools* ➤ *Administration* ➤ *Monitor* ➤ *Performance* ➤ *Database* ➤ *Exclusive lockwaits*

For DB2/AS400, choose *Tools* ➤ *Administration* ➤ *Monitor* ➤ *Performance* ➤ *Database* ➤ *Wait situations.*

NOTE   Use the Database Lock Monitor to identify exclusive lock waits on the database.

Monitoring Database Buffers

Every database has different buffers in main memory to reduce the number of accesses to the hard disks. The buffers contain user data in tables and administrative information for the database. Accessing objects in main memory through these buffers is 10 to 100 times faster than accessing the hard disks.

The main monitor for database buffers is the Database Performance Monitor. To call this monitor for any database system, use Transaction *ST04*, or, from the R/3 initial screen, choose *Tools* ➤ *Administration* ➤ *Monitor* ➤ *Performance* ➤ *Database* ➤ *Activity.*

The screen *Database Performance Analysis: <Database type> Database Overview* is displayed, showing information on different buffers depending on the type of database you are using. These buffers are explained for each respective database in the following sections.

WARNING   The guideline values provided below for each database system are simply rules of thumb for good performance. A database instance may still be able to run well even if the buffer quality is poor. Thus, to avoid unnecessarily investing time and energy in optimizing the buffer quality, check the database response times. See Chapter 2, under "Analyzing the Database Buffer."

ADABAS D Database

The ADABAS D database allocates the following buffers in the main memory of the database server:

- *Converter cache*, which stores the logical numbering assigned to physical page numbers for database administration.

- *Data cache*, which buffers table pages and index pages.

- *Catalog cache*, which stores the SQL statement context, including its table-accessing strategy or execution plan.

- *Rollback buffer* (*rollback cache*), which is used to speed up rollbacks that may be required for incomplete transactions. In a normal R/3 environment, this cache is not often used.

The buffer quality of the converter cache and the data cache is particularly important for the performance of an ADABAS D database. The converter cache and data cache reside in the shared memory of the database server.

ADABAS D Converter Cache

To speed up accesses to database data, pages from the converter area on the hard disk are held in the *converter cache* as a part of main memory. The *converter area* on the hard disk of an ADABAS D database is used to assign physical page numbers to logical numbers for database administration. The size of a data page in an ADABAS D database is 4KB.

The ideal size for the converter cache depends on the data volume in the ADABAS D database. As a guideline value, the size of the converter cache should be equivalent to approximately 0.6% of the occupied pages in the database. The hit ratio for this cache should be around 98%. Extreme deviations from these guideline values can cause delays, especially when performing database backups.

The size and hit ratio of the converter cache are displayed beside *Converter* in the Database Performance Monitor (Transaction *ST04*).

NOTE   As an example of defining the optimal size of the ADABAS D converter cache, consider the following. If the ADABAS D database requires 50GB of space on the hard disk, you can assume that converter pages require roughly 300MB (0.6% of 50GB). The optimal size of the converter cache is therefore 300MB.

ADABAS D Data Cache

To find out the size of the ADABAS D data cache in the Database Performance Monitor (Transaction *ST04*), look in the screen area *Cache Activity* in the column *Size Kb* for the row *Data*.

A hit ratio (indicated as the *Hitrate*) of at least 99% is optimal. The size of the data cache should be at least 160MB, but may vary depending on the size of the database and the R/3 application modules being used.

ADABAS D Catalog Cache

For each active ADABAS D database user, a catalog cache is created in the virtual memory of the database server. Note that a database user is not the same as an R/3 user. Each R/3 work process opens a connection to the database, so the number of database users is related to the number of configured R/3 work processes. The catalog cache is used to buffer the context of the SQL statement, including the table-accessing strategy or execution plan of the statement. The catalog cache enables multiple executions of the same SQL statement to refer back to an execution plan that is already recorded in the catalog cache. Hit ratios of approximately 90% are desirable. The size and the hit ratio of the catalog cache are indicated in the Database Performance Monitor (Transaction *ST04*) in the row *Catalog*.

Sizing for the virtual memory areas of ADABAS D database instances to be allocated at instance startup is performed using the ADABAS D administration tool, XControl.

Poor hit ratios are not always due to insufficient sizing, so investigate the causes of poor buffer quality before changing the size of the buffers.

See Table B.4 for a summary of guideline values for evaluating ADABAS D database buffers.

TABLE B.4: Guideline Values for Evaluating the Performance of ADABAS D Database Buffers

Name of Buffer	Hit Ratio Guideline Value	Sizing Parameter
Converter cache	≥ 98%	*CONVERTER_CACHE*
Data cache	≥ 99%	*DATA_CACHE*
Catalog cache	≥ 90%	*CAT_CACHE_SUPPLY*
Rollback cache	≥ 90%	*ROLLBACK_CACHE*

DB2 Universal Database (DB2 UDB)

The memory allocated by a DB2 UDB database instance consists of two parts:

- *Database global memory*, which is allocated in the shared memory of the database server

- *Agent private memory*, which is memory for the individual database processes

For DB2 UDB, database processes are called *agents*. Since for each R/3 work process at least one agent is started, the total memory consumption is calculated as follows:

Total memory = database global memory + (agent private memory × number of R/3 work processes)

The main parts of the database global memory are as follows:

- *Buffer pool*, for buffering table pages and index pages
- *Database heap*, for internal control structures
- *Lock list*, for administering database locks
- *Package cache*, for buffering the executions plans for executed SQL statements
- *Catalog cache*, for buffering the database's Data Dictionary information

Agent private memory consists of the *application support layer* and the *sort heap*, which is the memory area for sorting the quantities yielded by SQL statements.

Note that most of these memory areas are truly allocated only after they are actually used. Exceptions to this are the buffer pool, the lock list, and the application support layer, which are all permanently allocated at database instance startup.

DB2 UDB Buffer Pool

The size of the DB2 UDB buffer pool is defined by the parameter *buffpage* (in 4KB blocks).

The Database Performance Monitor (Transaction *ST04*) shows the number of logical read accesses to the buffer pool according to table pages (indicated as *Data Logical Reads*) and index pages (indicated as *Index Logical Reads*). Similarly, the number of physical read accesses are indicated as *Data Physical Reads* and *Index Physical Reads*.

See Table B.5 for a summary of guideline values for evaluating DB2 UDB database buffers.

TABLE B.5: Guideline Values for Evaluating the Performance of DB2 UDB Database Buffers

Name of Buffer	Guideline Value	Sizing Parameter
Buffer pool	Overall buffer quality should be at least 95%.	*buffpage, dbheap*
Package cache	Package cache quality should be at least 95%.	*pckcachesz*
Catalog cache	• Catalog cache quality ≥ 90% • Catalog cache overflows ≈ 0 • Catalog cache heap full ≈ 0	*catalogcache_sz*
Lock list	Lock escalations ≈ 0	*locklist*

Oracle Database

At database instance startup, an Oracle database allocates memory in three areas:

- *Data buffer*, allocated as shared memory and indicated in Transaction *ST04* as *Data buffer*.

- *Shared pool*, allocated as shared memory and indicated in Transaction *ST04* as *Shared pool*. The data buffer and the shared pool form the *system global area* (SGA).

- *Program global area* (PGA), allocated as variable local memory by Oracle database processes. As a guideline, for each database process, you can allocate from 2.5MB to 5MB. To find out the number of Oracle database processes, use Transaction *ST04* and choose *Detail analysis menu* ➤ *ORACLE session*.

The total size of the allocated memory in an Oracle database equals the sum of the sizes of these three areas.

Oracle Data Buffer

The size of the Oracle data buffer is defined by the parameter *DB_ BLOCK_BUFFERS* (in 8KB blocks) in the file `init_<SID>.ora`.

Under the header *Data buffer* in the initial screen of the Database Performance Monitor (Transaction *ST04*), the number of logical read accesses to the data buffer is indicated as *Reads*. The number of physical read accesses is indicated as *Physical reads*.

If the database is using a rule-based optimizer, the quality of the data buffer (indicated as *Quality* %) is optimal if it is at least 97%. If a cost-based optimizer is being used, the quality of the data buffer is optimal if it is at least 95%.

Oracle Shared Pool

Oracle uses the shared pool to store administrative information. The shared pool consists of the *row cache* and the *shared SQL area:*

- The row cache contains, for example, the names and the characteristics of tables, indexes, extents, fields, and users.

- The shared SQL area stores the execution plans for SQL statements, so that these do not have to be continuously recalculated.

Under the header *Shared Pool* in the initial screen of the Database Performance Monitor (Transaction *ST04*), the field *Size* indicates the allocated size of the shared pool in KB. The size of the shared pool is defined in bytes by the parameter *SHARED_ POOL_SIZE* in the file `init_<SID>.ora`.

There are two indicators for the buffer quality of the shared pool. One is the buffer quality of the shared SQL area, indicated in *ST04* under the header *Shared pool* as *pinratio*. This value should be at least 98%. The other indicator is the quality of the row cache, indicated as the ratio of *user calls* to *recursive calls* (in *ST04* under the header *Calls*). *User calls* is the number of queries sent by the R/3 System to the database. To respond to each query, the database requires administrative information from the row cache. If the database cannot obtain this information from the row cache, it performs a *recursive call* to import the information from the hard disk. Therefore, the ratio of *user calls* to *recursive calls* should be as large as possible and should not be less than 2:1.

A typical size for the shared pool in a production R/3 System is between 100MB and 300MB.

See Table B.6 for a summary of guideline values for evaluating Oracle database buffers.

TABLE B.6: Guideline Values for Evaluating the Performance of Oracle Database Buffers

Name of Buffer	Guideline Value	Sizing Parameter
Data buffer	Data buffer quality should be at least: • 97% for the rule-based optimizer • 95% for the cost-based optimizer	DB_BLOCK_BUFFERS
Shared pool	The ratio of *user calls* to *recursive calls* should be at least 2:1.	SHARED_POOL_SIZE
	The *pinratio* should be at least 98%.	SHARED_POOL_SIZE

SQL Server Database

With regard to the total memory allocation, SQL Server database version 7.0 offers you a choice between two different strategies: Either you assign the database a fixed memory size, or you leave it up to SQL Server to allocate memory within certain limits.

NOTE   The following information on the SQL Server database is valid for SQL Server Version 7.0. The guideline values were derived through SAP's First Customer Shipment (FCS) program and First Productive Customer (FPC) program.

In the Database Performance Monitor (Transaction *ST04*), the current total memory allocated by SQL Server to the database is indicated as *Dynamic memory KB*. The limits within which SQL Server can decide how much memory to allocate are indicated as *Maximum memory KB* and *Minimum memory KB*. If the Database Performance Monitor shows that *auto growth* is activated, the database memory can vary dynamically between 0GB and 2GB.

The parameters for defining memory limits are *MIN SERVER MEMORY* and *MAX SERVER MEMORY*.

If an R/3 instance is located on the database server, it is currently recommended that you assign a fixed memory size for the SQL Server database, rather than allow the size of the allocated memory to vary dynamically.

SQL Server allocates memory in three areas:

- *Data cache*, for buffering table pages and index pages.

- *Procedure cache*, for buffering recently used stored procedures and the associated execution plans at runtime. *Stored procedures* are what the R/3 database interface transforms SQL statements into in order to optimize performance for an SQL Server database instance. The procedure cache is thus equivalent to the Oracle shared SQL area.

- A *fixed portion* of memory totaling from 20MB to 100MB, depending on the size of the system, is allocated—for example, for:

  - Connections between the R/3 work processes and the database (around 400KB of memory for each work process)

  - Database locks (around 60 bytes of memory for each lock)

  - Open objects (around 240 bytes of memory for each open object)

SQL Server Data Cache

The Database Performance Monitor (Transaction *ST04*) indicates the size of the SQL Server data cache as *Data cache KB*. The performance of the data cache is reflected in the buffer quality, indicated as *cache hit ratio*. In production operation, *cache hit ratio* should be higher than 95%.

SQL Server Procedure Cache

In the Database Performance Monitor (Transaction *ST04*), the size and utilization of the procedure cache are indicated as *Procedure cache KB* and *Procedure cache in use*.

See Table B.7 for a summary of guideline values for evaluating SQL Server database buffers.

TABLE B.7: Guideline Values for Evaluating the Performance of SQL Server Database Buffers

Name of Buffer	Hit Ratio Guideline Value	Sizing Parameters
Data buffer	≥ 95%	*MIN SERVER MEMORY, MAX SERVER MEMORY*

NOTE At runtime, SQL Server dynamically defines the sizes of the *procedure cache* and the *fixed portion* of database memory. The remaining memory is used for the *data cache*. Therefore, the size of the data cache is determined by the total memory allocated to the SQL Server database and does not require separate adjustment by the database administrator. Note that this memory total is the memory available to the database server, not to one database instance alone as in other database systems. If there is more than one database on a database server, SQL Server distributes the configured buffers to the various databases. You cannot influence this distribution. Therefore, it is best not to run additional databases, such as test systems or training systems, on the same computer as the database of the production R/3 System.

Execution Plans for SQL Statements

SQL statements perform read/write/delete operations on tables in the database. When an SQL statement is executed, there are often several possible strategies for locating the relevant fields in the database tables, and some of these strategies may involve indexes. The search strategy adopted for using available indexes and scanning the tables is called the *execution plan* and is determined by the database optimizer program.

This appendix provides examples of execution plans for various database systems that are used in conjunction with R/3. These examples illustrate accesses to a single database table, without taking into consideration database views and joins. The execution plans have been abbreviated in some places.

The examples aim to teach you to recognize whether an index is being used for a search, and to identify not only the index, but also the index fields being used.

All the examples involve searches on the table MONI. The table MONI has the key fields RELID, SRTFD, and SRTF2. These form the primary index MONI ~ 0. In the R/3 Systems on which the sample execution plans were created, the table MONI consists of approximately 2,000 to 2,500 rows.

For each database, the following four different types of accesses to the table MONI are illustrated:

- Sequential read using a full table scan: In this type of access, no WHERE clause is specified:

```
SELECT * FROM "MONI"
```

  Because the SQL statement contains no information about how to limit the search, the database table is read sequentially with a full table scan. A full table scan is also executed if the limiting information provided does not match the available indexes.

- Direct read: In this type of access, all three of the key fields in MONI's primary index are specified with an EQUALS condition. This is known as a fully qualified access or a direct read:

```
SELECT * FROM "MONI" WHERE "RELID" = :A0 AND   "SRTFD" = :A1 AND
"SRTF2" = :A2
```

The SQL statement contains all the information required to directly access data through the primary index.

- Sequential read using the first primary key field: In this type of access, the first key field of the primary index is specified with an EQUALS condition:

```
SELECT * FROM "MONI" WHERE "RELID" = :A0
```

- Sequential read using the second primary key field: In this type of access, the second key field of the primary index is specified with an EQUALS condition:

```
SELECT * FROM "MONI" WHERE "SRTFD" = :A0
```

This type of access does not result in a binary search.

NOTE To show what is meant by a binary search and a sequential search, consider a telephone book, which is sorted by surname (*first primary key field*) and then by first name (*second primary key field*). If you are searching for the surname, you begin by entering the list at a more or less random point and try to get closer to the correct name in jumps, doing as little name-by-name scanning as possible. For a computer, this is known as a binary search, because a computer's jumps decrease by a factor of two each time. However, if you are searching by first name only, you must sequentially search the entire telephone book. A sequential search is equivalent to a full table scan.

Instead of using a binary search, a sequential read using the second primary key field uses one of two database access strategies:

- Indexes are not used at all, or the first field in an index may be missing: Here, an access must use a full table scan.

- Indexes are read sequentially to subsequently access the appropriate table row through a direct read: This strategy is advantageous if the index in the database occupies far fewer blocks or pages than the table and only a small number of table fields are being sought.

Oracle

Chapter 9 explains the Oracle execution plans, but they are included here to enable you to compare them with the execution plans of the other database systems more easily.

Sequential Read Using a Full Table Scan

Execution plan:

```
SELECT STATEMENT
    TABLE ACCESS FULL MONI
```

As this is a full table scan, no index is used.

Direct Read

Execution plan:

```
SELECT STATEMENT
    TABLE ACCESS BY INDEX ROWID MONI
        INDEX UNIQUE SCAN MONI~0
```

The row INDEX UNIQUE SCAN MONI~0 indicates that the index MONI~0 is used. The use of the search strategy *Index Unique Scan* means that all the key fields are specified. Therefore, the search uses the primary index.

Sequential Read Using the First Key Field

Execution plan:

```
SELECT STATEMENT
   TABLE ACCESS BY INDEX ROWID MONI
      INDEX RANGE SCAN MONI~0
```

The row INDEX RANGE SCAN MONI~0 indicates that the index MONI~0 is used. The index fields that are actually used for the index search are not indicated.

Sequential Read Using the Second Key Field

Execution plan:

```
SELECT STATEMENT
   TABLE ACCESS FULL MONI
```

Here the optimizer program has decided that the specified field is of no help when limiting the blocks to read, since no index exists for a second primary key field. The optimizer thus decides to perform a full table scan.

ADABAS

This section shows execution plans for an ADABAS D database.

Sequential Read Using a Full Table Scan

Execution plan:

OWNER	TABLENAME	COLUMN OR INDEX	STRATEGY
SAPR3	MONI		TABLE SCAN

As this is a full table scan, no index is used.

Direct Read

Execution plan:

```
OWNER TABLENAME COLUMN OR INDEX   STRATEGY
SAPR3 MONI                        EQUAL CONDITION FOR KEY COLUMN
              RELID               (USED KEY COLUMN)
              SRTFD               (USED KEY COLUMN)
              SRTF2               (USED KEY COLUMN)
```

The search strategy identifies the fields RELID, SRTFD, and SRTF2 as relevant for the search. The strategy EQUAL CONDITION FOR KEY COLUMN shows that all the fields of the primary index are specified. This enables a direct read of the table.

Sequential Read Using the First Key Field

Execution plan:

```
OWNER TABLENAME COLUMN OR INDEX   STRATEGY
SAPR3 MONI                        RANGE CONDITION FOR KEY COLUMN
              RELID               (USED KEY COLUMN)
```

ADABAS stores tables sorted by key fields, so that a table and its primary index constitute one database object. Here, with the field RELID as the first key field, the table is accessed without an index using the strategy RANGE CONDITION FOR KEY COLUMN.

Sequential Read Using the Second Key Field

Execution plan:

```
OWNER    TABLENAME    COLUMN OR INDEX    STRATEGY
SAPR3    MONI                            TABLE SCAN
```

Since only the field SRTFD is specified, ADABAS also performs a full table scan.

> **NOTE**
>
> In contrast to many other database systems, ADABAS differentiates between accesses through the primary index and the secondary index. For primary index accesses, it uses the access strategy RANGE CONDITION FOR KEY COLUMN. For accesses through a secondary index, it uses the access strategy RANGE CONDITION FOR INDEX.

DB2/AS400

This section shows execution plans for a DB2/AS400 D database.

Sequential Read Using a Full Table Scan

Execution plan:

```
Arrival sequence was used for file R3B4ADATA / MONI
Arrival Sequence used to perform record selection.
Reason Code: T1: No indexes exist.
Physical File Accessed: R3B4ADATA/MONI
```

As this is a full table scan, no index is used.

Direct Read

Execution plan:

```
Access path of file "MONI+0" was used by query for file MONI
Index R3TM4DATA/"MONI+0" was used to access records from file
Reason Code: I1: record selection RELID SRTFD SRTF2
Key row positioning using 3 key field(s).
```

The search strategy *Key row positioning using 3 key field(s)* identifies all three fields of the index MONI+0 as relevant for the search and therefore performs a direct read.

Sequential Read Using the First Key Field

Execution plan:

```
Access path of file "MONI+0" was used by query for file MONI
Index R3TM4DATA/"MONI+0" was used to access records from file
Reason Code: I1: record selection RELID SRTFD SRTF2
Key row positioning using 1 key field(s).
```

The database optimizer chooses the index MONI+0. That the first field in this index is used for the search is indicated by the 1 in the line *Key row positioning using 1 key field(s).*

Sequential Read Using the Second Key Field

Execution plan:

```
Arrival sequence was used for file R3TM4DATA / MONI
Arrival Squence used to perform record selection.
Reason Code: T3 Query optimizer chose table scan over available indexes.
Physical File Accessed: R3TM4DATA/MONI
```

The database optimizer chooses a full table scan because this is more efficient than an access through an index. This is indicated in the statement *Query optimizer chose table scan over available indexes.*

DB2/390

This section shows execution plans for a DB2/390 database.

Sequential Read Using a Full Table Scan

Execution plan:

```
Explanation of query block number: 1    step: 1
Performance is bad. No Index is used. Sequential Tablespace Scan
```

```
Method: access new table.
        new Table:  SAPR3.MONI
        Accesstype: sequential tablespace scan.
```

As this is a full table scan, no index is used.

Direct Read

Execution plan:

```
Explanation of query block number: 1    step: 1
Performance is optimal. Index is used. Index Scan by matching Index.
Method:   access new table.
          new Table:  SAPR3.MONI
  Accesstype: by index.
    Index: SAPR3.MONI~0 (matching Index)
      Index columns (ordered): RELID SRTFD SRTF2
      with 3 matching columns of 3 Index-Columns.
```

The search strategy *with 3 matching columns of 3 Index-Columns* indicates that all three fields of the index MONI~0 will be used for the search.

Sequential Read Using the First Key Field

Execution plan:

```
Explanation of query block number: 1    step: 1
Performance is good. Index is used. Index Scan by matching Index.
Method:   access new table.
          new Table:  SAPR3.MONI
  Accesstype: by index.
    Index: SAPR3.MONI~0 (matching Index)
    Index columns (ordered): RELID SRTFD SRTF2
    with 1 matching columns of 3 Index-Columns.
```

The database optimizer chooses the index MONI~0. The search strategy *with 1 matching columns of 3 Index-Columns* indicates that the first field of the index MONI~0 will be used for the search.

Sequential Read Using the Second Key Field

Execution plan:

```
Explanation of query block number: 1    step: 1
Performance is good. Index is used. Index Scan by nonmatching Index.
Method:    access new table.
           new Table:  SAPR3.MONI
           Accesstype: by index.
                    Index: SAPR3.MONI~0 (non-matching Index)
                        Index columns (ordered): RELID SRTFD SRTF2
 DB2 can at least use the index to pick out those
 pages from the table space, that contain data of
 the table: MONI
```

The database optimizer chooses to use the index MONI~0 for the search. Since the field SRTFD specified in the SQL statement is the second field, and the first field RELID is missing from the WHERE clause, the index must be read sequentially. This is indicated by the access strategy *Index Scan by nonmatching Index*.

The comments on performance that are visible in the DB2/390 execution plans are automatically displayed depending on the access type. However, they should not be understood as a valid description of the current performance situation. For a *sequential tablespace scan* (a full table scan), the automatic text is *performance is bad*; for an *index range scan*, the text is *performance is good*; and for an *index unique scan*, the text is *performance is optimal*. However, a full table scan on a small table does not cause a performance problem, while an index range scan on a large table with selection conditions that do not strictly limit the data volume can considerably reduce performance.

DB2 Universal Database (DB2 UDB)

This section shows execution plans for a DB2 Universal Database.

Sequential Read Using a Full Table Scan

Execution plan:

```
Execution Plan ( Opt Level = 5 )
   SELECT STATEMENT
      TBSCAN MONI
```

As this is a full table scan, no index is used.

Direct Read

Execution plan:

```
Execution Plan ( Opt Level = 5 )
   SELECT STATEMENT
      FETCH MONI
         RIDSCN
            SORT
               IXSCAN MONI~0 #key columns:   3
```

The search strategy *IXSCAN MONI~0 #key columns: 3* indicates that all three fields of the index MONI~0 will be used for the search.

Sequential Read Using the First Key Field

Execution plan:

```
Execution Plan ( Opt Level = 5 )
   SELECT STATEMENT
      FETCH MONI
         RIDSCN
            SORT
               IXSCAN MONI~0 #key columns:   1
```

The line *IXSCAN MONI~0* shows that the table is accessed through the index MONI~0. The expression *#key columns: 1* indicates that the first field of the index will be used for the search.

Sequential Read Using the Second Key Field

Execution plan:

```
Execution Plan ( Opt Level = 5 )
   SELECT STATEMENT
      FETCH MONI
         IXSCAN MONI~0 #key columns: 0
```

The database optimizer chooses a sequential *index scan* of the index MONI~0.

Like the DB2/390 database, DB2 UDB thus decides to read the index MONI~0 despite the fact that this index is not useful for the search since the WHERE condition specifies only the second field in the index. The irrelevance of the index is indicated by the number of used *key columns* being zero.

Informix

This section shows execution plans for an Informix database.

Sequential Read Using a Full Table Scan

Execution plan:

```
Execution plan of a select statement (Online optimizer)
1) sapr3.moni: SEQUENTIAL SCAN
```

As this is a full table scan, no index is used.

Direct Read

Execution plan:

```
Execution plan of a select statement (Online optimizer)
1) sapr3.moni: INDEX PATH
   (1) Index Keys: relid srtfd srtf2
```

```
Lower Index Filter: (relid = ... AND (srtfd = ... AND srtf2 =
...))
```

The line *sapr3.moni: INDEX PATH* indicates that Informix accesses the table through an index. The next line lists the fields in the index: RELID, SRTFD, and SRTF2. To determine the name of the index used from the listed fields, check the fields as listed in the ABAP Dictionary (Transaction *SE11*).

The line *Lower Index Filter* indicates which fields of the index will be used for the search. Here they are RELID, SRTFD, and SRTF2.

Sequential Read Using the First Key Field

Execution plan:

```
Execution plan of a select statement (Online optimizer)
1) sapr3.moni: INDEX PATH
    (1) Index Keys: relid srtfd srtf2
        Lower Index Filter: sapr3.moni.relid = 'DB'
```

The line *sapr3.moni: INDEX PATH* signifies that Informix accesses the tables through the index. The line *Index Keys: relid srtfd srtf2* indicates which index keys are in the index. The line *Lower Index Filter: sapr3.moni.relid = 'DB'* indicates which index field will be used for the search. In this execution plan, it is the field RELID.

Sequential Read Using the Second Key Field

Execution plan:

```
Execution plan of a select statement (Online optimizer)
1) sapr3.moni: SEQUENTIAL SCAN
```

Here Informix decides to perform a *sequential scan*—in other words, a full table scan.

SQL Server

This section shows execution plans for an SQL Server database.

Sequential Read Using a Full Table Scan

Execution plan:

```
Clustered Index Scan(EW4..MONI.MONI~0)
```

The SQL Server database stores tables sorted by their key field. The primary index is a *clustered index*. Therefore, even when reading the entire table, SQL Server accesses the table through the clustered index MONI~0.

Direct Read

Execution plan:

```
Clustered Index Seek(EW4..MONI.MONI~0, SEEK:(MONI.RELID=@1 AND
MONI.SRTFD=@2 AND MONI.SRTF2=@3) ORDERED)
```

The search strategy is indicated in the parentheses after *SEEK:* and shows that the fields RELID, SRTFD, and SRTF2 will be used for the search.

Sequential Read Using the First Key Field

Execution plan:

```
Clustered Index Seek(EW4..MONI.MONI~0, SEEK:(MONI.RELID=@1) ORDERED)
```

The search strategy *Clustered Index Seek* indicates that the index MONI~0 and the field RELID will be used for the search.

Sequential Read Using the Second Key Field

Execution plan:

```
Clustered Index Seek(EW4..MONI.MONI~0, WHERE:(MONI.SRTFD=@1))
```

Here SQL Server also chooses the clustered index. This is indicated by the use of the search function *WHERE*. (In the previous SQL Server examples, the search function was *SEEK*.) However, since the WHERE condition specifies the field SRTFD, which is the second field in the index, and the first field, RELID, is not specified, the index is of little use for the search.

NOTE   In contrast to many other database systems, SQL Server differentiates between accesses through the primary index and the secondary index. The access strategy using the primary index is called *Clustered Index Seek*. The access strategy using the secondary index is called *Index Seek*.

R/3 Performance Parameters

This appendix lists the R/3 profile parameters that are relevant to performance. Guideline values for setting these parameters are not included, since the optimal values vary considerably from one R/3 System to another.

To display the list of current parameter settings for a given R/3 instance, call the R/3 Memory Configuration Monitor (Transaction *ST02*). Then choose *Current parameters*.

WARNING There may be operating-system limits affecting memory management for your R/3 Release. Ensure that the operating system can administer the memory size you wish to configure. For information on operating-system limits, see Chapter 5.

When changing memory management parameters, always keep a backup of the old instance profiles. This backup will enable you to revert to the former parameter values if required. Before restarting the instance, test the new instance profiles using the auxiliary program *sappfpar* on the operating-system level. After instance restart, verify that the instance is running without error. To obtain a description of the program *sappfpar*, execute the operating-system command `sappfpar` `?`. Ensure that you are using the most current version of *sappfpar*.

WARNING When you are seeking to change particular parameters, warnings may appear indicating that changes should not be made without express instructions from SAP. You must heed these warnings. Instructions from SAP on changing the parameters can be provided by SAP employees, by hardware or database partners who have analyzed your system, or through an R/3 Note. R/3 Notes can be found in the Online Service System (OSS) or on SAP's Internet site, SAPNet. Ensure that the R/3 Note applies to your R/3 System, database, operating system, and the respective versions of these systems.

For help on R/3 profile parameters, use Transaction *RZ11*. Enter the R/3 profile parameter for which you require more information and choose *Documentation*. For help on changing R/3 profile parameters using Transaction *RZ10*, see *SAP R/3 System Administration* (also part of the "Official SAP Guide" book series).

R/3 Buffer Parameters

Table Group C.1 contains a table for each R/3 buffer describing the buffer and the related R/3 profile parameters.

TABLE GROUP C.1: Parameters for R/3 Buffers

Buffer Name: Table Definition (TTAB)

The TTAB buffer is the buffer for R/3 table definitions.

Parameter	Description
rsdb/ntab/entrycount	This parameter specifies the maximum number of entries in the TTAB buffer.
	The size of the TTAB buffer is approximately equivalent to the maximum number of entries multiplied by 100 bytes.

Buffer Name: Field Description (FTAB)

The FTAB buffer is the buffer for R/3 field definitions.

Parameter	Description
rsdb/ntab/ftabsize	Buffer size allocated at instance startup in KB.
rsdb/ntab/entrycount	The maximum number of buffer entries in the FTAB buffer equals double the value of this parameter.

Continued on next page

TABLE GROUP C.1: Parameters for R/3 Buffers *(Continued)*

Buffer Name: Initial Record (IRBD)

The IRBD buffer is the buffer for the data originally in R/3 tables at the time of initial access.

Parameter	Description
rsdb/ntab/irbdsize	Buffer size allocated at instance startup in KB.
rsdb/ntab/entrycount	The maximum number of buffer entries in the IRBD buffer equals double the value of this parameter.

Buffer Name: Short Nametab (SNTAB)

The Short NTAB buffer is the buffer for the short descriptions of R/3 tables and fields.

Parameter	Description
rsdb/ntab/sntabsize	Buffer size allocated at instance startup in KB.
rsdb/ntab/entrycount	The maximum number of buffer entries in the SNTAB buffer equals double the value of this parameter.

Buffer Name: Program (PXA)

The PXA buffer is the buffer for ABAP programs.

Parameter	Description
abap/buffersize	Buffer size allocated at instance startup in KB.

Continued on next page

TABLE GROUP C.1: Parameters for R/3 Buffers *(Continued)*

Buffer Name: CUA

The CUA buffer is the buffer for menu bars.

Parameter	Description
rsdb/cua/buffersize	Buffer size allocated at instance startup in KB.
	The maximum number of buffer entries in the CUA buffer equals half the value of the parameter *rsdb/cua/buffersize*.

Buffer Name: Screen

The screen buffer is the buffer for R/3 screens.

Parameter	Description
zcsa/presentation_buffer_area	The buffer size allocated at instance startup (in bytes) equals half the value of this parameter.
sap/bufdir_entries	Maximum number of buffer entries.

Buffer Name: Export/Import

This buffer is the buffer for the ABAP commands *export to database* and *import from database*.

Parameter	Description
rsdb/obj/buffersize	Buffer size allocated at instance startup in KB.
rsdb/obj/max_objects	Maximum number of buffer entries.
rsdb/obj/large_object_size	Typical size of the largest objects in bytes.

Continued on next page

TABLE GROUP C.1: Parameters for R/3 Buffers *(Continued)*

Buffer Name: Calendar

This is the buffer for applicable work days and public holidays.

Parameter	Description
zcsa/calendar_area	Buffer size allocated at instance startup in KB.
zcsa/calendar_ids	Maximum number of buffer entries.

Buffer Name: Generic Key Table

This is the table buffer for generic buffering.

Parameter	Description
zcsa/ table_buffer_ area	Buffer size allocated at instance startup in KB.
zcsa/database_max_buftab	Maximum number of buffer entries.

Buffer Name: Single Record Table

This is the table buffer for single record buffering.

Parameter	Description
rtbb/buffer_length	Buffer size allocated at instance startup in KB.
rtbb/maximum_tables	Maximum number of buffer entries.

R/3 Memory Management Parameters

Table C.2 lists the R/3 profile parameters for R/3 Memory Management.

With Zero Administration Memory Management, the parameters in Table C.2 are automatically set at instance startup. These automatic settings are overwritten if there are differing values for these parameters in the instance profile. If Zero Administration Memory Management is used in your system, SAP recommends deleting the parameters listed in Table C.2 from the instance profile and configuring only the parameter *PHYS_MEMSIZE*. See also Chapter 5 and R/3 Note 88416.

NOTE   Zero Administration Memory Management is available for particular combinations of operating system and R/3 Release. For example, it is available for Windows NT with an R/3 Release of 4.0 or higher.

The following classifications are shown in the column *Type* in Table C.2:

- *P* denotes parameters that directly affect the performance of the R/3 System.

- *S* denotes parameters that ensure the secure operation of the R/3 System under high load.

TABLE C.2: Parameters for R/3 Memory Management (These Should Be Deleted from the R/3 Profile under Zero Administration Memory Management.)

Parameter	Description	Unit	Type
ztta/roll_area	Total local R/3 roll area for all work processes.	Bytes	P, S
ztta/roll_first	Portion of the local R/3 roll area allocated to a dialog work process before R/3 extended memory is allocated.	Bytes	P
rdisp/ROLL_SHM	Size of the R/3 roll buffer in shared memory.	8KB blocks	P
rdisp/PG_SHM	Size of the R/3 paging buffer in shared memory (as of R/3 Release 4.0, this has little effect on performance).	8KB blocks	P
rdisp/ROLL_MAXFS	Size of the global R/3 roll area, which comprises the R/3 roll buffer plus the R/3 roll file.	8KB blocks	S
rdisp/PG_MAXFS	Size of the R/3 paging area, which is comprised of the R/3 paging buffer plus the R/3 paging file.	8KB blocks	S
em/initial_size_MB	Initial size of the R/3 extended memory.	MB	P, S
em/max_size_MB	Maximum size of the R/3 extended memory. Some operating-system limits keep the size of R/3 extended memory smaller than this value.	MB	P, S
em/blocksize_KB	Size of a block in R/3 extended memory. The default value of 1,024KB should not be changed without explicit instructions from SAP.	KB	P
em/address_space _MB	The address space reserved for the R/3 extended memory (currently applies only under Windows NT).	MB	P, S
ztta/roll_extension	Maximum amount of R/3 extended memory that can be allocated for each user context.	Bytes	P, S
abap/heap_area _dia	Maximum R/3 heap memory for each dialog work process.	Bytes	S
abap/heap_area _nondia	Maximum R/3 heap memory for each nondialog work process.	Bytes	S
abap/heap_area _total	Maximum R/3 heap memory for all work processes.	Bytes	S

Continued on next page

TABLE C.2: Parameters for R/3 Memory Management (These Should Be Deleted from the R/3 Profile under Zero Administration Memory Management.) *(Continued)*

Parameter	Description	Unit	Type
abap/heaplimit	A limit in the R/3 heap memory that flags work processes so they are restarted after the end of the current transaction and can thus release the heap memory.	Bytes	S
abap/use_paging	If set to 1, conventional R/3 paging is used; if set to 0, conventional R/3 paging is not used. This parameter is no longer used as of R/3 Release 4.0.	—	—

Additional Parameters

This section lists additional R/3 profile parameters (see Tables C.3 through C.6).

TABLE C.3: R/3 Profile Parameters for the Database Instance

Parameter	Description
rsdb/max_blocking_factor	Split factor for dividing the results of ALL ENTRIES queries in SQL statements into smaller blocks. See Chapter 9 under "Example: Optimizing an ABAP Program." Warning: This parameter should not be changed without explicit instructions from SAP.
dbs/io_buf_size	Size of the data area in an R/3 work process, through which data is transferred to or copied from the database by an SQL statement (in bytes).

TABLE C.4:   R/3 Profile Parameters for Buffer Synchronization

Parameter	Description
rdisp/bufrefmode	Defines the type of buffer synchronization. Possible settings: sendon or exeauto (for a distributed system) and sendoff or exeauto (for a central system).
rdisp/bufreftime	Time interval between two buffer synchronizations (in seconds). Warning: This parameter should not be changed without explicit instructions from SAP.

TABLE C.5:   R/3 Profile Parameters for Load Distribution

Parameter	Description
rdisp/mshost	Name of the computer where the message server is running.
rdisp/msserv	Name of the message service.
rdisp/enqname	Name of the R/3 instance where the enqueue server is running.
rdisp/atp_server	Name of the R/3 instance where the ATP server is running.
rdisp/vbstart	This parameter controls the behavior of the update service at R/3 System startup. At startup, the update service checks its queue to see whether there are any update requests that have not yet been processed. Such requests are specially marked and then processed. If the parameter is set to 1 (this is the default setting), the update service processes update requests that have not yet been processed. If the parameter is set to 0, waiting update requests are not automatically processed.
rdisp/vb_dispatching	Activates or deactivates update dispatching. If the parameter is set to 1 (this is the default setting), update dispatching is activated. If the parameter is set to 0, update dispatching is not activated.
rdisp/wp_no_btc	Number of background work processes.
rdisp/wp_no_dia	Number of dialog work processes.
rdisp/wp_no_enq	Number of enqueue work processes.
rdisp/wp_no_spo	Number of spool work processes.

Continued on next page

T A B L E   C . 5 :   R/3 Profile Parameters for Load Distribution *(Continued)*

Parameter	Description
rdisp/wp_no_vb	Number of update work processes.
rdisp/wp_no_vb2	Number of work processes for update2 updates.
rdisp/max_wprun_time	This parameter limits the maximum runtime of a transaction step in a dialog work process (in seconds). When this time has expired, the user request is terminated with the error message *TIME_OUT*. The default setting for this parameter is 300 seconds. Warning: If a COMMIT WORK command is executed in a program, this runtime starts again. While an SQL statement is being processed on the database, the program is not terminated even when this runtime expires.
rdisp/tm_max_no	Maximum number of front-end connections in table *tm_adm*.
rdisp/max_comm_ entries	Maximum number of CPIC/RFC connections that can be administered in the communication table *comm_adm*.
gw/max_conn	Maximum number of CPIC/RFC connections that can be administered by the gateway service in table *conn_tbl*.

T A B L E   C . 6 :   R/3 Profile Parameters for Configuring Monitoring Tools

Parameter	Description
rstr/file	Name of the SQL trace file.
rstr/max_diskspace	Size of the SQL trace file in bytes.
abap/atrapath	Path name for the ABAP trace files.
abap/atrasizequota	Size of the ABAP trace files.
rdisp/wpdbug_max_no	Maximum number of work processes that can be run simultaneously in debugging mode.

APPENDIX

D

Selected Transaction Codes

Table D.1 lists the most important R/3 Transaction codes for performance optimization in the R/3 System. You can enter R/3 Transaction codes in the command field of an R/3 screen in the following ways:

- /n<Transaction code>
  - Entering the Transaction code in this way exits the current R/3 screen and displays the initial screen of the Transaction.
- /o<Transaction code>
  - Entering the Transaction code in this way sends the current user session to the background and creates a new user session to display the initial screen of the Transaction.

TABLE D.1 Transaction Codes for Performance Analysis

Code	Description
AL08	Global user overview
AL11	Display SAP directories
AL12	Display table buffer (buffer synchronization)
BALE	ALE administration and monitoring
DB02	Analyze tables and indexes (missing database objects and space requirements)
DB05	Table analysis
DB12	Overview of backup logs (DBA protocols)
DB13	DBA Planning Calendar
DB20	Generate tables statistics
OSS1	Log on to Online Service System (OSS)
RZ01	Job Scheduling Monitor
RZ02	Network graphics for R/3 instances

Continued on next page

TABLE D.1 Transaction Codes for Performance Analysis *(Continued)*

Code	Description
RZ03	Control Panel for operation modes and server status
RZ04	Maintain R/3 instances
RZ10	Maintain profile parameters (by profile)
RZ11	Maintain profile parameters (by parameter)
SE11	Maintain ABAP Dictionary
SE12	Display ABAP Dictionary
SE14	Utilities for ABAP Dictionary tables
SE15	ABAP Repository information system
SE16	Data Browser for displaying table contents
SE38	ABAP Editor
SEU	R/3 Repository Browser
SM01	Lock Transactions
SM02	System messages
SM04	User Overview
SM12	Display and delete R/3 enqueues
SM13	Display update requests and resolve errors
SM21	System log
SM37	Background Job Overview
SM39	Job analysis
SM49	Execute external operating-system commands
SM50	Local Work Process Overview
SM51	List of servers
SM56	Reset or check the number range buffer
SM58	Asynchronous RFC error log

Continued on next page

TABLE D.1 Transaction Codes for Performance Analysis *(Continued)*

Code	Description
SM59	Display or maintain RFC destinations
SM63	Display or maintain operating modes
SM65	Execute tests to analyze background processing
SM66	Systemwide Work Process Overview
SM69	Maintain external operating-system commands
SMLG	Maintain logon groups
SNRO	Maintain number range objects
ST01	R/3 System trace
ST02	R/3 Memory Configuration Monitor (also known as the function *Setups/Tune Buffers*)
ST03	Workload Monitor
ST04	Database Performance Monitor
ST05	Start, stop, or view SQL trace, enqueue trace, or RFC trace
ST06	Operating System Monitor
ST07	Application Monitor
ST08	Network Monitor
ST09	Network Alert Monitor
ST10	Display statistics on table accesses (table call statistics)
ST11	Display developer traces
ST14	Application analysis—statistics relating to business document volume
ST22	ABAP runtime error analysis
STAT	Single statistics records on the application server
STMS	Transport Management System
STUN	R/3 Performance Menu
TU02	Parameter changes—display active parameters and a history of changes

Review Questions and Answers

Chapter 2

1. Which of the following can cause a CPU bottleneck on the database server?

    A. External processes that do not belong to the database or an R/3 instance are running on the database server.

    B. The R/3 extended memory is configured too small.

    C. Work processes that belong to an R/3 instance running on the database (for example, background or update work processes) require CPU capacity.

    D. There are expensive SQL statements—for example, those that contribute 5% or more of the entire database load in the Shared SQL Area.

    E. The database buffers are set too small, so that data must be continuously reloaded from the hard disks.

    Answer: A, C, D, E

2. Which of the following are necessary to achieve optimal database performance?

    A. Table analyses (through a program such as Update Statistics) must be regularly scheduled.

    B. The number of R/3 work processes must be sufficiently large, so that there are enough database processes to process the database load.

    C. The database buffers must be sufficiently large.

    D. You should regularly check whether expensive SQL statements are unnecessarily occupying CPU and main memory resources.

    E. The database instance should be run only on a separate computer without R/3 instances.

    Answer: A, C, D

3. Which points should you take into consideration when monitoring R/3 memory management?

   A. The total memory allocated by the R/3 and database instances should not be larger than the physical main memory of the computer.

   B. The extended memory must be sufficiently large.

   C. If possible, no displacements should occur in the R/3 buffers.

   Answer: B, C

4. In the Local Work Process Overview, the information displayed for a particular work process over a considerable time period is as follows: Running, Sequential Read, and a specific table name. What does this tell you?

   A. There may be an expensive SQL statement that accesses the table that can be analyzed more closely in the Database Process Monitor.

   B. There may be a wait situation in the dispatcher, preventing a connection to the database. The dispatcher queue should be analyzed more closely.

   C. There may be an exclusive lock wait that you can detect in the monitor for exclusive lock waits.

   D. There may be a network problem between the application server and the database server.

   Answer: A, C, D

Chapter 3

1. Which of the following statements are correct?

   A. The CPU time is measured by the operating system of the application server.

   B. The database time is measured by the database system.

   C. High network times for data transfers between the presentation server and the application server are reflected in an increased response time in the Workload Monitor.

   D. High network times for data transfers between the application server and the database server are reflected in an increased response time in the Workload Monitor.

   E. The roll out time is not part of the response time because the roll out of a user occurs only after the answer has been sent to the presentation server. Nevertheless, it is important for the performance of the R/3 System to keep the roll out time to a minimum, as during the roll outs, the R/3 work process remains occupied.

   Answer: A, D, E

2. How is the term *load* defined in the R/3 environment?

   A. The *load* generated by a particular process is defined as the percentage of time that that process occupies the CPU of a computer, and can be monitored in the Operating System Monitor as *CPU utilization*.

   B. *Load* is the sum of response times. Thus, *total load* refers to the total response time, *CPU load* refers to the total CPU time, and *database load* refers to the total database time.

   C. *Load* means the number of transaction steps for each unit of time.

   Answer: B

3. The Workload Monitor displays increased wait times for the dispatcher, such that *Av. wait time* is much greater than 50ms. What does this tell you?

    A. There is a communication problem between the presentation servers and the dispatcher of the application server—for example, a network problem.

    B. There is a general performance problem—for example, a database problem, a hardware bottleneck, or insufficient R/3 extended memory; or there are too few R/3 work processes. This statement does not provide enough information to pinpoint the exact problem.

    C. An increased dispatcher wait time is normal for an R/3 System. It protects the operating system from being overloaded, and can be ignored.

Answer: B

Chapter 4

1. What do you have to consider when you perform an SQL trace?

    A. There is only one trace file in each R/3 System. Therefore, only one SQL trace can be performed at a time.

    B. The user whose actions are being traced should not run multiple programs concurrently.

    C. You should perform the SQL trace on a second execution of a program because the relevant buffers are then already loaded.

    D. SQL traces are useful on the database server, but not on application servers, which yield inexact results due to network times.

Answer: B, C

2. When should you perform an ABAP trace?

    A. If a problem occurs with the table buffer

    B. For programs with high CPU requirements

    C. For I/O problems with hard disks

Answer: B

Chapter 5

1. Which R/3 profile parameters define the amounts of extended memory and heap memory that should be kept in the physical main memory or in the paging file?

    A. R/3 extended memory is always kept completely in the physical memory, and R/3 heap memory is created in the operating-system paging file.

    B. None. The memory areas in the physical main memory and the paging file (that is, the page-out or page-in process) are automatically distributed by the operating system. An application program (such as R/3 or a database program) cannot influence the distribution.

    C. The R/3 profile parameter *ztta/roll_extension* defines the amount of R/3 extended memory in the physical memory. The parameters *abap/heap_area_ dia* and *abap/heap_area_nondia* define the amount of R/3 heap memory.

Answer: B

2. Which of the following can cause an R/3 instance to not start, or to start with an error message, after you change R/3 parameters for memory management?

   A. The program buffer size specified in the parameter *abap/buffer_size* exceeds the limit that exists due to address space restrictions.

   B. There is not enough physical memory to allow the new settings.

   C. The paging file is not large enough to allow the new settings.

   D. The amount of R/3 extended memory specified in the parameter *em/initial_size_MB* exceeds the limit that exists due to address space restrictions.

   Answer: A, C, D

Chapter 6

1. Where should background work processes be configured?

   A. Background work processes should always be located on the database server. Otherwise, the runtime of background programs will be negatively affected by network problems between the database server and the application server.

   B. If background work processes are not located on the database server, they must all be set up on a dedicated application server known as the background server.

   C. Background work processes can be distributed evenly over all the application servers.

   Answer: C

2. How should you configure and monitor the dynamic user distribution?

    A. By setting the appropriate R/3 profile parameter—for example, *rdisp/wp_no_dia*

    B. By using Transaction *SM04*, User Overview

    C. By using Transaction *SMLG*, Maintain Logon Groups

    Answer: C

Chapter 7

1. Which of the following factors are reasons for not activating full buffering on a table?

    A. The table is very large.

    B. The SQL statement that is used most frequently to access the table contains the first two of five key fields in an EQUALS condition.

    C. The table is changed often.

    Answer: A, C

2. Which of the following statements are correct in regard to buffer synchronization?

    A. During buffer synchronization, the application server where the change occurred sends a message through the message server to implement the change in the respective buffered table on the other application servers.

    B. After a transaction changes a buffered table, the transaction must first be completed with a database commit before the table can be reloaded into the buffer.

    C. In a central R/3 System, the R/3 profile parameter *rdisp/bufrefmode* must be set to *sendoff, exeoff.*

    D. In a central R/3 System, the entries in the table buffer are never invalidated, because the table buffer is changed synchronously after a database change operation.

Answer: B

Chapter 8

1. Which of the following statements are correct with regard to locks and R/3 enqueues?

    A. An R/3 enqueue locks one or more tables in the database.

    B. After an R/3 enqueue has been placed, the corresponding database table can still be changed by an update request coming from programs such as customer-developed ABAP reports.

    C. A database lock is usually released at the end of a transaction step, while an R/3 enqueue is usually released at the end of an R/3 transaction.

    D. A database lock that lasts too long can cause an R/3 System standstill.

Answer: B, C, D

2. Which of the following statements are correct with regard to the ATP server?

    A. The ATP server should always be configured on the database server.

    B. The ATP server is an independent R/3 installation with its own database on a separate computer.

    C. The ATP server reduces the number of accesses to tables RESB and VBBE.

Answer: C

3. When buffering number range objects in main memory, which of the following considerations should you keep in mind?

   A. Since buffering occurs in all R/3 instances, buffer synchronization may cause some numbers to be assigned twice.

   B. Gaps occur in the number assignment when using buffered number ranges. You must check whether these gaps are permitted by business law and are acceptable from a business viewpoint.

   C. If the quantity of numbers in the buffer is too small, performance problems will result, particularly during mass data entry using Batch Input or Fast Input.

   D. Sufficient physical memory must be available, because number range buffering consumes much memory.

   Answer: B, C

Chapter 9

1. Which of the following statements are correct with regard to expensive SQL statements?

   A. They can lead to hardware bottlenecks (a CPU or I/O bottleneck) and negatively affect the runtime of other SQL statements.

   B. They can occupy a lot of space in the data buffer of the database, displace objects that are needed by other SQL statements, and negatively affect the runtime of other SQL statements.

C. They can occupy a lot of space in the R/3 table buffer and displace objects, which causes unnecessary reload operations.

D. If they are performed after database locks were set by the same program, this can cause exclusive lock wait situations in the database, which can cause a brief system standstill.

E. Expensive SQL statements in programs for reporting or in background programs are not normally a problem for the database.

Answer: A, B, D

2. In the results of an SQL trace, you find an SQL statement that has a runtime of 1 second and selects only 10 records. Which of the following could be the reason for the long runtime?

A. There is a hardware bottleneck (a CPU or I/O bottleneck) on the database server.

B. There is a network problem between the application server and the database server.

C. The database optimizer has created an inefficient execution plan—for example, by choosing an inefficient index.

D. There is no appropriate index for the SQL statement.

E. There are exclusive lock waits in the database.

Answer: A, B, C, D, E

3. In the Shared SQL Area Monitor, you find an SQL statement with 10,000 logical read accesses per execution (indicated as *Gets/Execution*). Which of the following could be the reason for this high number of read accesses?

A. There is a hardware bottleneck (a CPU or I/O bottleneck) on the database server.

B. There is a network problem between the application server and the database server.

C. The database optimizer has decided in favor of an inefficient index, or there is no appropriate index for the SQL statement.

D. There are exclusive lock waits in the database.

E. A large number of records is being transferred from the database to the ABAP program.

Answer: C, E

Glossary

NOTE A term in italics indicates that there is an entry for this term in the glossary.

ABAP

Advanced Business Application Programming. Programming language of the R/3 System.

ABAP Dictionary

Central storage facility containing metadata (data about data) for all objects in the R/3 System.

address space of a process

Virtual storage that can be addressed by a process. The size of the addressable storage in 32-bit architecture ranges from 1.8 to 3.8GB ($\leq 2^{32}$=4GB), depending on the operating system.

ALE

Application Link Enabling. ALE is a technology for building and operating distributed applications. The basic purpose of ALE is to ensure a distributed—but integrated—R/3 installation. It comprises a controlled business message exchange with consistent data storage in nonpermanently connected SAP applications.

Applications are integrated not through a central database, but through synchronous and asynchronous communication. ALE consists of three layers: application services, distribution services, and communication services.

Alert Monitor

Graphical monitor for analyzing system states and events.

ANSI

American National Standards Institute.

application server

A computer on which at least one R/3 instance runs.

ArchiveLink

Integrated into the Basis component of the R/3 System, a communications interface between the R/3 applications and external components. ArchiveLink has the following interfaces: user interface; interface to the R/3 applications; and interface to external components (archive systems, viewer systems, and scan systems).

archiving object

A logical object comprising related business data in the database that is read from the database using an archiving program. After it has been successfully archived, a logical object can be deleted by a specially generated deleting program.

ASAP

AcceleratedSAP. Standardized procedural model to implement R/3.

background processing

Processing that does not take place on the screen. Data is processed in the background, while other functions can be executed in parallel on the screen. Although the background processes are not visible for a user and run without user intervention (there is no dialog), they have the same priority as online processes.

BAPI

Business Application Programming Interface. Standardized programming interface that provides external access to business processes and data in the R/3 System.

Batch Input

Method and tools for rapid import of data from sequential files into the R/3 database.

button

Element of the graphical user interface. Click a button to execute the button's function. You can select buttons using the keyboard as well as the mouse. Place the button cursor on the button and select Enter or click the Enter button. Buttons can contain text or graphical symbols.

CATT

Computer Aided Test Tool. You can use this tool to generate test data and to automate and test business processes.

CCMS

Computing Center Management System. Tools for monitoring, controlling, and configuring the R/3 System. The CCMS supports 24-hour system administration functions from within the R/3 System. You can use it to analyze the system load and monitor the distributed resource usage of the system components.

client

From a commercial, legal, organizational, and technical viewpoint, a closed unit within an R/3 System with separate master records within a table.

CO

Customizing Organizer. Tool to administer change and transport requests of all types in an R/3 System.

context switch on the operating-system level

On the operating-system level, there are generally more processes (R/3 work processes, database processes, etc.) than available processors. To distribute the CPU capacity among all processes, the processors serve them in time frames. A context switch is when a processor switches from one process to another.

context switch on the R/3 level

In the R/3 System, there are generally more users logged on than available R/3 work processes. The *user contexts* are therefore attached only to the R/3 work process when the R/3 work process processes a user request. A context switch on the R/3 level is when an R/3 work process switches from one user to another. Switching between user contexts consists of a roll out and a roll in of user context data.

Control Panel

Central tool for monitoring the R/3 System and its instances.

CPI-C

Common Programming Interface-Communication. Programming interface—the basis for synchronous, system-to-system, program-to-program communication.

CTO

Change and Transport Organizer. Set of tools used to manage changes and development in the R/3 System, as well as to transport these changes to other R/3 Systems.

Customizing

Adjusting the R/3 System to specific customer requirements by selecting variants, parameter settings, etc.

data archiving

Removing data that is no longer needed from the R/3 database and storing it in archives. (See also *archiving object*.)

database

Set of data (organized, for example, in files) for permanent storage on the hard disk. Each R/3 System has only one database.

database instance

An administrative unit that allows access to a database. A database instance consists of database processes with a common set of database buffers in *shared memory*. There is normally only one database instance for each database. DB2/390 and Oracle Parallel Server are database systems for which a database can be made up of multiple database instances. In an R/3 System, a database instance can either be alone on a single computer or together with one or possibly more R/3 instances.

database locks

Like *enqueues* on the R/3 level, database locks help to ensure data consistency. Database locks are set by all data-changing SQL statements (UPDATE, INSERT, DELETE) and by the statement SELECT FOR UPDATE. Database locks are released by the SQL statements COMMIT (used for database commit) and ROLLBACK (used for database rollback).

database optimizer

Part of the database program that decides how tables are accessed for an SQL statement (for example, whether an index is used).

database server

A computer with at least one database instance.

DBA

Database administrator.

DCL

Data Control Language. SQL statements to control user transactions.

DDL

Data Definition Language. SQL statements to define relationships.

deadlock

Mutual blocking of multiple transactions that are waiting for each other to release locked objects.

DIAG protocol

Communication protocol between SAPGUI and dialog work processes on the R/3 instance.

dialog work process

R/3 work process used to process requests from users working online.

dispatcher

The process that coordinates the R/3 work processes of an R/3 instance.

DML

Data Manipulation Language. Language commands to query and change data.

dynpro

The DYNamic PROgram that consists of a screen and the underlying process logic.

EDI

Electronic Data Interchange. Electronic interchange of structured data (for example, business documents) between business partners in the home country and abroad who may be using different hardware, software, and communication services.

enqueues on the R/3 level

Like *database locks*, R/3 enqueues help to ensure data consistency. An R/3 enqueue is set explicitly within an ABAP program by an enqueue function module and explicitly released by a dequeue function module. R/3 enqueues can continue to be in effect over several steps within an R/3 transaction. Remaining R/3 enqueues are released at the end of the R/3 transaction.

Enterprise IMG

Company-specific Implementation Guide.

entity

Uniquely identifiable object—may be real or imaginary. The connections between entities are described by relationships.

execution plan

A strategy created for an SQL statement by the database optimizer tool to define the optimal way of accessing database tables.

extended memory

Storage area for storing *user contexts* in the *shared memory* of the application server.

FDDI

Fiber Distributed Data Interchange.

firewall

Software to protect a local network from unauthorized access from outside.

GUI

Graphical User Interface. The medium through which a user can exchange information with the computer. You use the GUI to select commands, start programs, display files, and perform other operations by selecting function keys or buttons, menu options, and icons with the mouse.

heap memory on the operating-system level

The local memory of an operating-system process. The operating-system heap of an R/3 work process includes the permanently allocated local memory of the R/3 work process and the variable local memory of the R/3 work process (*heap memory on the R/3 level*).

heap memory on the R/3 level

Variable local memory of an R/3 work process for storing *user contexts*. R/3 heap memory is temporarily allocated by the R/3 work process and released when no longer required.

high availability

Property of a service or a system that remains in production operation for most of the time. High availability for an R/3 System means that unplanned and planned downtimes are reduced to a minimum. Good system administration is decisive here. You can reduce unplanned downtime by using preventive hardware and software solutions that are designed to reduce single points of failure in the services that support the R/3 System. You can reduce the planned downtime by optimizing the scheduling of necessary maintenance activities.

Hot Package

Delivered by SAP, software corrections or enhancements for a specific R/3 Release.

IDES

International Demo and Education System. IDES contains multiple model companies, which map the relevant business processes of the R/3 System. Using simple user guidelines and different master and transaction data, scenarios with large data volumes can be tested. IDES is therefore well suited as a training tool to assist in instructing project teams.

IDoc

Internal Document. An *IDoc type* filled with real data.

IDoc type

Internal Document type. SAP format, into which the data of a business process is transferred. An IDoc is a real business process formatted in the IDoc type. An IDoc type is described by the following components:

- A control record. Its format is identical for all IDoc types.

- One or more records. A record consists of a fixed administration segment and the data segment. The number and format of the segments differ for different IDoc types.

- Status records. These records describe stages of processing that an IDoc can go through. The status records have the same format for all IDoc types.

IMG

Implementation Guide. A tool for making customer-specific adjustments to the R/3 System. For each application component, the Implementation Guide contains:

- All steps to implement the R/3 System
- All default settings and all activities to configure the R/3 System
- A hierarchical structure that maps the structure of the R/3 application components
- Lists of all the documentation relevant to the implementation of the R/3 System

instance

R/3 instance. Administrative unit that groups together components of an R/3 System that offer one or more services. An R/3 instance can provide the following services:

- D: Dialog
- V: Update
- E: R/3 enqueue management
- B: Background processing
- S: Printing (spool)
- G: R/3 gateway

An R/3 instance consists of a dispatcher and one or more R/3 work processes for each of the services, as well as a common set of R/3 buffers in the shared memory.

The dispatcher manages the processing requests. Work processes execute the requests. Each instance provides at least one dialog service and a gateway. An instance can provide further services. Only one instance can be available that provides the service R/3 enqueue management. In accordance with this definition, there can be two (or more) R/3 instances on an application server. This means that with two or more instances on one server, there are two or more dispatchers and R/3 buffers. (See also *database instance*.)

IPC

Inter Process Communication.

ITS

Internet Transaction Server. The gateway between the R/3 System and the World Wide Web.

LAN

Local Area Network.

local memory of a process

Virtual memory that is allocated to only one operating-system process. Only this process can write to or read from this area of memory. (See also *shared memory*.)

locks

See *database locks* and *enqueues on the R/3 level*.

LUW

Logical Unit of Work. From the viewpoint of R/3, an indivisible sequence of database operations that conform to the ACID maxims. From the viewpoint of a database system, this sequence represents a unit that plays a decisive role in securing data integrity. (See also *transaction*.)

NSAPI

Netscape Server API (Application Programming Interface).

OLAP

Online Analytical Processing.

OLE

Object Linking and Embedding.

OLTP

Online Transaction Processing.

operation mode

Defined numbers and types of R/3 work processes for one or more instances in a particular time period. Operation modes can be automatically changed.

optimizer

See *database optimizer*.

OS

Operating system.

OSS

Online Service System.

paging on the operating-system level

See *swap space*.

paging on the R/3 level

Memory area used by particular ABAP statements, consisting of a local paging area for each R/3 work process, an R/3 paging buffer in *shared memory*, and possibly an R/3 paging file on the hard disk of the application server.

PAI

Process After Input. Technical program processes after data is entered in a screen in R/3.

PBO

Process Before Output. Technical program processes before a screen is output in R/3.

performance

Measurement of the efficiency of an IT system.

pop-up window

A window that is called from a primary window and displayed in front of that window.

Q-API

Queue Application Programming Interface. The interface to buffered, asynchronous data transfer between decentralized applications and R/2 and R/3 Systems, based on CPI-C.

R/3

Runtime System 3.

R/3 System service

Logical function required to support the R/3 System, such as the database service and the application services, which may include the services Dialog, Update, Enqueue, Batch, Message, Gateway, and Spool.

RAID

Redundant Array of Independent Disks. Hardware-based technology that supports disk redundancy through disk mirroring and related methods.

RDBMS

Relational Database Management System.

RFC

Remote Function Call. RFC is an SAP interface protocol, based on CPI-C. It allows the programming of communication processes between systems to be simplified considerably. Using RFCs, predefined functions can be called and executed in a remote system or within the same system. RFCs are used for communication control, parameter passing, and error handling.

roll in

See *context switch on the R/3 level*.

roll memory

Memory area used to store the initial part of *user contexts*. It consists of a local roll area for each R/3 work process, a roll buffer in *shared memory,* and possibly a roll file on the hard disk of the application server.

roll out

See *context switch on the R/3 level*.

SAPGUI

SAP Graphical User Interface. See *GUI*.

SAProuter

A software module that functions as part of a firewall system.

server

The term *server* has multiple meanings in the SAP environment. It should therefore be used only if it is clear whether it means a logical unit, such as an R/3 instance, or a physical unit, such as a computer.

session

A user session in a SAPGUI window.

Session Manager

The tool used for central control of R/3 applications. The Session Manager is a graphical navigation interface used to manage sessions and start application transactions. It can generate both company-specific and user-specific menus. The Session Manager is available from R/3 Release 3.0C under Windows 95 and Windows NT.

shared memory

Virtual memory that can be accessed by multiple operating-system processes. Where there are several R/3 instances or an R/3 instance and a database instance on the same computer, a semaphore management system ensures that the processes of each instance access only the shared memory of that instance, and not the global objects of other instances. The maximum size of the shared memory is limited on some operating systems. You can set the size of the shared memory using operating-system parameters. (See also *local memory*.)

SID

SAP System Identifier. Placeholder for the three-character name of an R/3 System.

SQL

Structured Query Language. A database language for accessing relational databases.

swap space

Storage area on a hard disk or other device used for storing objects that cannot currently be stored in the physical memory. Also called a paging file. The processes of storing objects outside the physical memory and retrieving them are respectively known as page out and page in.

system landscape

A real system constellation installed at a customer site. The system landscape describes the required systems and clients, their meanings, and the transport paths for implementation and maintenance. Of the methods used, client copy and the transport system are particularly important. For example, the system landscape could consist of a development system, a test system, a consolidation system, and a production system.

TCP/IP

Transmission Control Protocol/Internet Protocol.

TDC

Transport Domain Controller. Application server of an R/3 System in the transport domain, from which transport activities between the R/3 Systems in the transport domain are controlled.

TemSe

Temporary sequential objects. Data storage for output management.

TMS

Transport Management System. Tool for managing transport requests between R/3 Systems.

TO

Transport Organizer. Tool for managing all the change and transport requests with more extensive functionality than the CO and the WBO.

transaction

Database transaction: a database *LUW*. A unit of database operation that conforms to the ACID principles of atomicity, consistency, isolation, and durability.

R/3 transaction: an R/3 *LUW*. R/3 transactions conform to the ACID principles over multiple transaction steps. For example, creating a customer order is an R/3 transaction in which the ACID principles are adhered to in several successive screens up to completion of the R/3 transaction at order creation. An R/3 transaction may consist of several database transactions.

Reference to an ABAP program: for example, Transaction *VA01*. (See also *Transaction code*.)

Transaction code

Succession of alphanumeric characters used to name a transaction—that is, a particular ABAP program in the R/3 System. For example, Transaction *VA01* (*create customer order*).

transport

Term from software logistics in R/3: data export and import between R/3 Systems.

transport domain

Logical group of R/3 Systems between which data is transported in accordance with fixed rules. The Transport Domain Controller exercises control over the transport domain.

TRFC

Transactional RFC. Remote Function Control to which the ACID principles are applied.

URL

Uniform Resource Locator. Address in the World Wide Web (WWW).

user context

User-specific data, such as variables, internal tables, and screen lists. The user context is stored in the memory of the application server until the user logs off. A user context is connected with an R/3 work process only while the R/3 work process is working on the user request (*context switch on the R/3 level*). User contexts are stored in R/3 *roll memory*, R/3 *extended memory*, or R/3 *heap memory*.

virtual memory

In all operating systems, you can allocate more virtual memory than is physically available. Virtual memory is organized by the operating system either in the physical main memory or in *swap space*.

WAN

Wide Area Network.

WBO

Workbench Organizer. Tool for managing change and transport requests that are generated from the use of the ABAP Workbench.

WP

Work process. The application services of the R/3 System have special processes—for example, for dialog administration, updating change documents, background processing, spool processing, and enqueue management. Work processes are assigned to dedicated application servers.

APPENDIX
G

Literature

This section provides information on the R/3 online help, R/3 training courses and workshops, and Internet links, and includes a bibliography related to R/3 performance topics.

R/3 Online Help

To access R/3 Online Documentation as of R/3 Release 4.0, from the R/3 initial screen, choose *Help* ➤ *Extended help*.

Then, for help on R/3 performance monitors, choose *Basis* ➤ *Computer Center Management System* ➤ *R/3 System monitoring*.

R/3 Training Courses

SAP currently offers the following R/3 training courses for performance optimization:

- BC315 *Workload Analysis*
- BC411 *Advanced ABAP Programming*
- WT520 *ABAP Performance Analysis*

Empowering Workshops

SAP Empowering Workshops (see Table G.1) are available to SAP employees and partners to deepen their understanding of technical optimization and application optimization.

TABLE G.1: SAP Empowering Workshops

Workshop	Title
EWB10	Oracle Shared SQL Area Analysis
EWA17	ALE Processing
EWA10	Technical Optimization of Pricing
EWA11	Technical Optimization of Due List Processing and Scheduling
EWA12	Technical Optimization of Backflushing of Production Orders
EWA18	Profitability Analysis CO-PA
EWA20	Technical Optimization of MRP Run and Long Term Planning
EWC10	Technical Optimization of the Availability Check

SAP Performance Sites on the Internet

SAPNet is separate from SAP's public Internet site (`http://www.sap.com`). With appropriate authorization, customers, partners, SAP employees, and others can access SAPNet at `http://sapnet.sap.com`. To access the homepage of the Technical Core Competence (TCC) group, you can use the URL `http://sapnet.sap.com/tcc`.

SAP TechNet

SAP TechNet is a part of SAPNet and contains up-to-date articles explaining technical performance optimization and application performance optimization. To enter SAP TechNet, choose from the SAPNet table of contents *Services* ➤ *Education Services* ➤ *TechNet*.

Alternatively, in the Web browser address field, enter the address `http://sapnet.cap.com./technet`.

SAP Performance & Benchmark Group

To display the home page of the SAP performance experts known as the SAP Performance & Benchmark Group, use the Internet address `http://sapnet.sap.com/performance`.

Quick Sizer

The Quick Sizer is an Internet-based tool to make sizing your system easier and faster. This tool is the result of a joint effort between SAP and all platform partners. The aim of this tool is to help you estimate your hardware requirements and thus to support your initial budget planning. The results apply to the most current R/3 Release.

You can enter the number of users working in each R/3 module—the Quick Sizer calculates the processor speed, the main memory size, and the hard-disk capacity you will need. Although the number of users is useful for a rough estimate, the exact extent of your hardware requirements depends on many more factors. For example, it depends on the background processing load and the number of invoices or delivery notes that are changed or displayed by users each day. To take these aspects into consideration, the Quick Sizer can also calculate sizing based on a quantity structure, where you enter the most important figures for each module. These numbers can be determined only in consultation with the respective business departments. R/3 consultants or hardware partners may also be able to help you with these figures.

To use the Quick Sizer, enter SAPNet (`http://sapnet.sap .com/quicksizing`) and, in the *Quick Find* window, scroll down to *Quick Sizing*.

Select Bibliography

This bibliography lists books and manuals that are relevant to the topics covered in this book or that explore related issues in greater detail.

ABAP/4 Development Workbench Dokumentation. Produkt-nummer 50014371. Walldorf: SAP AG, 1996 (available only in German).

Aronoff, E., and Loney, K., and Sonawalla, N. *Oracle 8 Advanced Tuning & Administration.* Berkeley: Oracle Press, Osborne/McGraw-Hill, 1998.

Brand, Hartwig. *SAP R/3 Implementation with ASAP: The Official Guide.* San Francisco: Sybex, 1999.

Buck-Emden, Rüdiger, and Galimov, Jürgen. *SAP Systems R/3: A Client/Server Technology.* Bonn: Addison-Wesley, 1997.

Cassidy, Pete. *High Performance Oracle 8 SQL Programming & Tuning.* Scottsdale: Coriolis Group, 1998.

Corey, M.J., and Abbey, M., and Dechichio, D.J., and Abramson, I. *Oracle 8 Tuning.* Berkeley: Oracle Press, Osborne/McGraw-Hill, 1997.

Date, C.J., and Darwen, Hugh. *A Guide to the SQL Standard: A User's Guide to the Standard Relational Language (SQL).* Bonn: Addison-Wesley, 1997.

Gardinier, Kenton. *Windows NT Performance Tuning & Optimization (Windows NT Professional Library).* Berkeley: Osborne/McGraw-Hill, 1998.

Haugen, Signe, and Lyman, Catherine, and Ludloff, Mary, and Cortesi, David. *Informix Guide to SQL.* New Jersey: Prentice Hall, 1994.

Manual OSS—Online Service System. Walldorf: SAP AG, 1998.

Mortensen, Lance, and Sawtell, Rick, and Lee, Michael. *MCSE SQL Server 6.5 Administration Study Guide*. San Francisco: Sybex, 1997.

Patterson, David, and Gibson, Garth, and Katz, Randy. *A Case for Redundant Arrays of Inexpensive Disks (RAID)*. Berkeley: University of California, Berkeley Press, 1987.

Petkovic, Duπan. *SQL Server 7: A Beginner's Guide*. Berkeley: Osborne/McGraw-Hill, 1998.

R/3 Installation Guide. Walldorf: SAP AG, 1998.

R/3 System Manuals. Walldorf: SAP AG, 1998.

Sanders, Roger E. *The Developer's Handbook to DB2 for Common Servers (McGraw-Hill Series on Database Warehousing and Data Management)*. New York: McGraw-Hill, 1997.

Sawtell, Rick, and Mortensen, Lance. *MCSE Exam Notes: SQL Server 6.5 Administration*. San Francisco: Sybex, 1998.

Schneider, Robert D, and Garbus, Jeffrey R. *Optimizing SQL Server 7: Planning and Building a High-Performance Database (Prentice Hall Series on Microsoft Technologies)*. New Jersey: Prentice Hall, 1999.

Will, Liane. *SAP R/3 System Administration: The Official SAP Guide*. San Francisco: Sybex, 1999.

H

Selected R/3 Notes

The tables in this appendix contain selected R/3 Notes that are of central importance for performance optimization. Use these R/3 Notes and the further references they may contain to keep up to date with current developments and recommendations.

| NOTE | For help in using the R/3 Notes in SAP's Online Service System (OSS), see *SAP R/3 System Administration* (also part of the "Official SAP Guide" book series). |

TABLE H.1: R/3 Notes on System Configuration and Load Distribution

R/3 Note Number	Title
19466	Downloading a patch from SAPSERVx
39412	How many work processes to configure
21960	Two instances/systems on one UNIX computer
26317	Set up LOGON group for autom. load balancing
51789	Bad user distribution in logon distribution
26417	System request for frontend wk centers /SAPGUI
75248	Performance during direct input w. ALE Distribution

TABLE H.2: R/3 Notes on R/3 Memory Management According to Operating System

R/3 Note Number	Title
103747	Performance R/3 4.0: Parameter recommendations
33576	Memory Management in Release as of 3.0C, Unix and NT
38052	System Panic, terminations due to low swap space
68544	Memory Management under Windows NT
88416	Zero administration memory management from 40A/NT
78498	High paging rate on AIX 4.x database servers
98084	AIX: ABAP program buffer PXA is larger than 256MB
95260	Many shared memories possible as of AIX 4.2.1
95454	A lot of extended memory on AIX
43427	HP UX: Shared Memory limits
106819	More than 1.75GB Shrd Memr.f.32-bit R/3 vers. HP-UX
27269	Error message: TSV_TNEW_INDEX_NO_ROLL_MEMORY
30606	Entries in /etc/sysconfigtab under Digital UNIX
146528	Configuration of R/3 on hosts with much RAM
146289	TCC Recommendations for 64-Bit R/3 Kernel

TABLE H.3: R/3 Notes on R/3 Enqueues, Number Range Buffering, and ATP Server

R/3 Note Number	Title
5424	Questions and answers on enqueue/locking
97760	Enqueue: Performance and resource consumption
62077	Info: Internal Number assignment is not continuous
37844	Performance: Document number assignment RF_BELEG
23835	Buffering RV_BELEG/Number assignment in SD
40904	Performance during availability check
24762	Blocking with quantities and late exclus. block
99999	ATP-Server: Installation and Sizing

TABLE H.4: R/3 Notes on System Requirements

R/3 Note Number	Title
85524	R/3 Sizing (Quick Sizer)
89305	Resource requirements for Release 4.0A/4.0B

TABLE H.5: R/3 Notes on Database Systems

R/3 Note Number	Title
105012	Collective note: ADABAS for R/3 Version 6.2 (only)
123418	AS/400: Performance 4.0B on AS/400
38307	Reducing shared memory consumption (Informix)
41360	Database configuration via onconfig parameter (Informix)
12184	Improved performance with "UPDATE STATISTICS" (Informix)
109034	CBO: Anchor note on topic "Cost Based Optimizer" (Oracle)
93098	Changes to the upgrade to 4.0—CBO Oracle
62849	MS SQL Server: News for R/3

TABLE H.6: R/3 Notes on R/3 Performance Monitors

R/3 Note Number	Title
12103	Contents of table TCOLL
16083	Standard jobs, reorganization jobs
23984	Workload analysis: duration of data storage

INDEX

Note to the Reader: Page numbers in **bold** indicate the principal discussion of a topic or the definition of a term. Page numbers in *italic* indicate illustrations.

D

F

K

L

M

S

W

Testing Your R/3 Knowledge with the CD-ROM

The CD-ROM included with this book provides a test engine designed to familiarize you with the Certified Technical Consultant (CTC) exam format. The test questions are taken from the pages of the book and can help you gauge your preparedness for the real world of SAP R/3 Optimization and for the CTC test.

The test contains proprietary software components and information of SAP AG and AsseTGmbH Assessment and Training Technologies.

Testing Your R/3 Knowledge with the CD-ROM

The CD-ROM included with this book provides a test engine designed to familiarize you with the Certified Technical Consultant (CTC) exam format. The test questions are taken from the pages of the book and can help you gauge your preparedness for the real world of SAP R/3 Optimization and for the CTC test.

The test contains proprietary software components and information of SAP AG and AsseTGmbH Assessment and Training Technologies.